BATTERY ACTION!

BATTERY ACTION!

The Diary of a Gunner 1916–19

Paul Cobb

Reveille
PRESS

Reveille Press is an imprint of
Tommies Guides Military Booksellers & Publishers

Gemini House
136–140 Old Shoreham Road
Brighton
BN3 7BD

www.tommiesguides.co.uk

First published in Great Britain by
Reveille Press 2015

For more information please visit
www.reveillepress.com

© 2015 Paul Cobb

ISBN 978-1-908336-64-4

Cover design by Reveille Press
Typeset by Vivian@Bookscribe

Printed and bound in Great Britain

ABOUT THE AUTHOR

Paul Cobb has had a long-standing interest in the Great War 1914-18 strengthened at an early age by his first visit to the battlefields of France and Flanders in 1969. His grandfathers – Dorsetshire Regiment and The Queens (Royal West Surrey Regiment) – served in the conflict in Egypt, Italy, Ireland and on the Western Front; a great-grandfather was killed serving with the 55th Kite Balloon Section, Royal Flying Corps. Paul has been a member of The Western Front Association since 1984 (and a former Membership Secretary and later Vice Chairman of the WFA and is chairman of the Wiltshire branch of the association) and of the Gallipoli Association since 1988. He is a regular visitor to the battlefields and since the 1980s has had a particular interest in the Action at Fromelles in July 1916; he is the author of the acclaimed Fromelles 1916 (History Press) and a contributor to Stand To! and to various radio and television programmes.

CONTENTS

FOREWORD

BY MAJOR GENERAL SIR EVELYN WEBB-CARTER KCVO, OBE, DL

I had five uncles who fought in the Great War, two of whom perished on the Western Front and so I feel uncannily close to this momentous event we are about to commemorate. Reading a diary, particularly if it is well written is a sure way to gain an understanding of what it was like to live in this war to end all wars. None of my uncles kept such a diary so I will never get any closer to them than the grave on the Somme or the name on the Memorial to the Missing at Arras. However "Battery Action", a diary of a Gunner in a heavy battery from 1916 to the end of the war will transcend the reader to a battery line on the Western Front in all its many, both tragic and comical, dimensions. Over the next few years we will all have the desire to know what it was like to be a soldier in this conflict; this book is certainly well timed to do just that.

In 1914 Sydney Hall, who had been badly advised to forego full time education, found himself in a dull and unexciting job as a clerk. He joined the Royal Garrison Artillery as a volunteer in 1916 just before the days of conscription. He did so out of a sense of patriotism but perhaps more to avoid the boredom of the clerical work in an armaments factory in Sheffield. His story is told through the lines of his diary which he transcribed just after the war and is thus a vivid account untarnished by time or exaggeration.

Sydney whom I have got to know quite well by reading his diary is a complex character. Clearly intelligent and articulate, as you will soon learn, he had all the ability to gain promotion and reach commissioned rank but there was something in his character that clearly irked others, so much so that all his early ambitions were frustrated by the actions and views of his superiors. Neither did he always exist comfortably with his peers nor few real friends did he make. For example it is sad to learn at the end of the book that he made little effort, with one dramatic exception, to keep in touch with his former comrades. He was a loner and frequently kept his views to himself and his diary. It would seem that once he accepted that promotion was beyond reach bitterness made him all the more acute in his observations of life in his battery. Initially he was with a tractor borne unit and then with 81 Siege Battery a horse drawn battery with whom he remained till the end. His descriptions of individuals and events are sharply etched and he would appear to be a good judge of character. As a battery commander's assistant (BCA) he got to know all his various and contrasting battery commanders particularly well and these alone make a fine and entertaining study.

Of more historical interest are Sydney's dramatic descriptions of the March 1918 German offensive, his experience of the medical chain, the intricacies of the feeding system and the lapses of discipline at the depots and rest camps in rear areas. To every aspect of like in the battery his keen eye is drawn and an acerbic comment made. Sometimes he is hilarious but more often than not he is critical. He doesn't miss much so if you want to learn about some of the minutiae of life in a heavy battery this is the book for you.

Paul Cobb found these diaries by chance and soon realised what a gem he had found. He has helpfully edited the manuscript by placing each chapter in the context of the campaign which Sydney would have not known although I was surprised by how much of a grasp of the war Sydney did have. The footnotes are a useful cross reference particularly in regard to the fate of many personalities Sydney comes across in his service with the two batteries. Sadly all too many, and surprisingly for a battery deployed well to the rear, are in War Grave Commission cemeteries or on memorials to the missing.

This is an interesting and thought provoking personal account by an intelligent man who saw the best and worst in the people and events he witnessed. Anyone interested in the human aspect of war will find this diary, like I did, fascinating. One of my surviving uncles was a Gunner officer and I feel sure he would have recognised and enjoyed this story as I am equally sure you will.

Evelyn Webb–Carter
Fairford
20 August 2013

INTRODUCTION

Amid the torrent of ways chosen to commemorate the centenary of the Great War 1914-18 will be the publication of accounts that have been hidden for decades awaiting the attention of writers and historians keen to explore various aspects of that tumultuous conflict. Among those unseen manuscripts was the thick folder containing the account written by Sydney Hall.

Sydney Hall kept a diary during his service with the Royal Garrison Artillery and wrote his account more fully in 1926 while memories were still fresh; he then typed the manuscript in 1967 which enabled a clear, legible text to survive. It remained in the possession of the family until his grandson, Brian Hall, showed it to me one day in 2011 suggesting that I may be interested in his grandfather's experiences during the war.

The account stood aside from many I have seen over the years as it contained detailed descriptions of so many aspects of a soldier's life that seldom get mentioned in accounts of the war. I felt it deserved wider exposure and so set about securing publication as well as preparing a short presentation sharing among members of The Western Front Association 1914-18.

Hall's story could have reached a wider audience much earlier. The folder contained correspondence dating between 1967 and 1975 from his home (29 Churchill Ave, Southport) with Mr V. Rigby at the Imperial War Museum. Rigby wrote to Hall, when the museum and BBC were preparing the epic television series *The Great War*, noting that he had written to them saying he had a *"form of diary which I expanded into a rough narrative in 1926"*. Rigby said that the document would be of great interest to the museum. It seems that a copy was lodged at the IWM along with an annotated copy of the history of 81 Siege Battery, Royal Garrison Artillery. The manuscript was microfilmed by the IWM but does not appear in the museum's current catalogue.

Rigby's summary of *Battery Action!* provides a handy summary:

> *"...a gunner's experiences from his enlistment in July 1916 to his demobilisation in February 1919, most of this time being spent with 242 and 81 Siege Batteries. It is a narrative with a quality of its own. Because the units described are comparatively small in size, the picture drawn is of great detail, so that the reader gets to know the problems and the triumphs of a battery; and to know also the men that Sydney Hall observed with such discernment, appreciation, and (in a few cases) contempt. There is a note of frustration in parts of the book – characterised by the author's unsuccessful efforts to get a commission; the long months he spent, although a trained BCA, as a "spare man" doing fatigues; and his service with a commander who delighted in doing everything the hardest*

way − but then, frustration is an ingredient of military life. It is of course a picture seen from the ranks, and the sketches of officers are especially good….all aspects of battery life are described, lightened or darkened by the author's mood of that time.

The quality of this narrative does not come out well in extracts, for the effect is cumulative. The reader soldiers on from day to day, admiring this member of the gun team, changing his opinion of another, and sharing the glory of the BCA's achievement of 27th September 1918 when Sydney Hall controlled the fire for the whole four hour attack".

My approach in handling this manuscript has been to add a brief narrative to set the scene at the start of each chapter and to add footnotes to explain certain features and to confirm, where possible, people and events. It is regrettable that the National Archives does not have a copy of the war diary of 81 Siege Battery as this could have been of great benefit in verifying dates and places; fortunately, there is a concise, if not accurate, history of the battery drafted by Gnr Hall but not properly verified and corrected by the eventual author Major H.J.G Gale. My research, however, does confirm Hall's account including some very specific battery positions such as the one used at Vaulx Vraucourt on 21 March 1918.

I would also acknowledge the contribution from Paul O'Rourke who has a very specific and profound interest in 81 Siege Battery and who willingly shared material he had gathered on the battery. This contact exemplified the benefit and value of reliable contacts made via the excellent Great War Forum.

In addition, thanks go to David Syme-Grant for preparing the maps, Linda Henson (grand-daughter of Sydney Hall) for the loan of a series of trench maps belonging to Gnr Hall, Melanie Chalk for allowing use of a photograph of her grandfather (147623 Gnr W. Usher) − one of very few known photographs of 81 Siege Battery, and to Geoff Spring, a long-standing member of The Western Front Association 1914-18 with considerable knowledge in his specialist area − artillery.

Finally, my thanks go to Brian Hall for calling by one day with a large folder of typed foolscap sheets which proved to be not only a splendid account of the experience of one man in the Great War but also one that will help explain the role and activities of gunners and the heavy guns of the Royal Garrison Artillery.

CHAPTER 1
SETTING THE SCENE

W e are fortunate that the Great War was recorded extensively in film and photography but it is the veterans' accounts that provide the personal stories of their small part in the campaigns that brought about victory in 1918. Not all these texts can be considered reliable or of value to researchers though a significant proportion merit serious consideration. Memories and pencil written accounts in notebooks faded over the years and actual experiences might become merged with apocryphal stories. Sydney Hall's circumstances in the immediate post war period enabled him to devote time to typing his story using a diary he kept during the war. Both his diary and his fresh memories enabled a valuable account to be created of an artilleryman's service during those turbulent times.

Eighty five years later his son Dennis recalled the creation of this remarkable account:

> "I remember as a young schoolboy my father spending most of the evenings writing what he called his composition. It was the ultimate bedtime story. Once or twice a week I would lie in bed listening to Daddy reading the latest chapters of the 'composition'.
>
> After the war he sat the civil service exams by special dispensation, his war service overriding the age limit. He did incredibly well; I believe he was in the top ten in the country. He accepted an offer in the Ministry of Labour in London and then transferred to HM Customs and Excise in Southampton when I was about 6 years old. At this time he started to write 'Battery Action'".

Towards the end of the nineteen-twenties I conceived the idea of writing these memoirs. My wife and I with our small son were then living in the outskirts of London whence I had been transferred on my appointment to the Customs and Excise. We had very little money, no friends and no wireless and time was lying heavy on our hands. One day on looking through some old papers we came across certain diaries which I had kept during the war years of 1914/18 and my wife suggested that I might expand these to form a narrative. I agreed and over a period of years compiled the work, writing a few pages at a time, reading them over to my wife and son and then filing them where they have remained ever since. In 1967 the Director General of the Imperial War Museum expressed an interest in the work so I decided to revise it and have it typed.

On reflection I thought it best to leave the narrative exactly as it was first written omitting only a few passages of a purely personal nature.

In order to explain certain incidents in the narrative however, I have felt that I should give a synopsis of my life prior to enlistment. I was born in the steel town of Sheffield in 1896. My father was Chief Draughtsman to Messrs John Brown & Co Limited, a large firm specialising in armour plates and heavy forgings and in a sense I was born into armaments. In 1909 I qualified for the Central Secondary School with the object of completing a four year Sheffield trades' course when at the age of seventeen I should be able to obtain some unspecified position in the firm where my father had considerable influence. I made good progress at school particularly in chemistry.

The Hall family — Sydney second left

In 1911 a friend of my father enquiring about my future suggested that I might do well, in the firm's laboratory. There was one snag, the firm liked to engage such staff young and train them itself – they could not possibly wait until I was 17. The result was that with the full agreement of my parents I terminated my studies at 15½ after completing only two years of the course.

This was undoubtedly the greatest mistake of my life and I have suffered its effects ever since. Ironically enough the laboratory job somehow fizzled out and I found myself as an office boy at five shilling a week and detesting every minute of it. Then in August 1914 war broke out and I was made a works clerk in the Heavy Forgings Department a much more worthwhile job for here I was intimately concerned with the war effort, heavy guns, armour for battleships, machinery for destroyers etc.

I have often wondered what would have happened had I completed my full course at school. In 1913 jobs for seventeen year-olds were not too easy to come by but at that age I certainly should not have accepted the position of office boy. Perhaps the Civil Service would have afforded some opportunities. With the outbreak of war I would not have been so firmly entrenched in an armaments firm. Probably I should have joined an Officer Training Corps and I think I should have had a reasonable chance of a Commission.

However, here I was tied to Brown's. It is true that during the first weeks of the war enlistment in the forces was allowed if not actually encouraged but as soon as it was realised that munitions were as essential as men all further recruitment from such firms was stopped and a blanket extended which covered every member of the staff.

Early in 1915 a special certificate and a particularly ugly enamel badge was issued to all members of the staff. This was later replaced by an official brass badge 'On War Service' which I kept for many years but eventually lost and this served to keep recruiting agents and over-zealous females at bay.

As 1915 drew to a close the position of the munition worker became more suspect. Men attracted by the good pay had drifted to the works in large numbers and there is no doubt that many who turned a deaf ear to the Recruiting Sergeant more readily responded to the Works Employment Officer who was competing for his services.

At this stage public opinion was being roused and it was because of this that the Derby Scheme[1] was welcomed. Large employers such as John Brown's were dealt with en masse and on December 17 1915 a couple of magistrates attended the works and attested practically every man on the place. It was thought that after being sworn in, receiving a day's pay and being issued with a khaki arm band our position would be clarified. Henceforth we were soldiers at the disposal of the Crown for service either in the field or at the workshop as the military were pleased to direct.

Recruiting under the Derby Scheme proceeded more rapidly than was expected and I was in one of the first groups to be called up. Actually I received notice on the 6 January 1916 to report for service a week later. But the Company had already made preparation for dealing with such eventualities and instructions had been issued that any such calling-up notices should not be acted upon but referred to the Employment Officer who would arrange for their cancellation. Since every attestee was automatically called up the Employment Department had a busy time but in every case exemption was granted formal notice being sent to each man by the Recruiting Officer with the words *"You are informed that the calling upon you to report for Military Service is hereby cancelled"*. Such few men who tried to act upon the calling-up notice were promptly chased back by the recruiting officer with curt remarks about wasting his time. It appeared that, willy-nilly, I must perforce play the part of civilian during the Great War.

Sydney Hall on his grandfather's knee

But public opinion was still not satisfied the more so in Sheffield because the City Battalion (12 Yorks & Lancs)[2] after nearly two years of training had at last been sent overseas and on arrival had been practically annihilated[3] at the Battle of the Somme. Great indignation was shown on those who "stayed behind" and though I was not actually given the white feather there were plenty of comments that anybody who "really tried" could join the army.

Actually I had made my first formal application for release in February 1916 and again in May when although my immediate chief told me that I could go I was snapped up by another department.

By the end of July seeing that no satisfaction could be obtained I approached the Managing Director Mr Alan Grant who over-ruled the Secretary and ordered my release. It was now July 20. I was entitled to a week's leave and so due for enlistment on July 27.

In the few days that remained to me I made enquiries as to my new life. First I made a desperate effort to join the local Officer Training Corps only to be told that under the new regulations they were unable to accept candidates over the age of 18. My application was just three weeks too late.

Then I went to the local recruiting office at the Corn Exchange, Sheffield. I was technically a volunteer and so entitled to some choice of regiment but when I suggested the Royal Engineers I was told there are no vacancies except for tradesmen. Then Lieut Fowler looked me up and down and said that there were a few jobs going in the Royal Garrison Artillery *"a very decent crowd"* if my height and weight came up to their standard. I agreed and the following day attended for a very thorough medical examination at the end of which I was pronounced satisfactory. I was thereupon directed to report at 8am on July 27.

---

1   In spring 1915, enlistments averaged 100,000 men per month but this could not be maintained so in May 1915 the upper age limit was raised from 38 to 40 with a view to ensuring enough recruits were obtained. The National Registration Act (passed on 15 July 1915) required men between 15 and 65 who were not already in the forces to register. On 11 October 1915, Lord Derby was appointed Director-General of Recruiting and he devised the recruiting programme that became known as the Derby Scheme. Men who attested under the Derby Scheme were sent back to their jobs until they were called up. They wore a grey armband with a red crown as a sign that they had so volunteered.

2   12 (Service) Battalion (Sheffield) The Yorkshire and Lancashire Regiment was raised in Sheffield on 5 September 1914 by the Lord Mayor and City. By May 1915 it was at Penkridge, Cannock Chase in 94 Brigade, 31 Division. After further periods in Ripon and Salisbury Plain it went to Egypt in December 1915. In March 1916 it went to France where it was disbanded on 17 February 1918.

3   12 Yorks & Lancs (also known as the Sheffield City Battalion) served in the July 1916 offensive on the Somme and suffered severe casualties on 1 July in their attack on Serre losing 17 officers and 495 other ranks killed. A memorial to the battalion can be found there.

CHAPTER 2
THE NEW RECRUIT

Sydney Hall was drafted into the Royal Garrison Artillery (RGA). The RGA was an arm of the Royal Artillery that was originally tasked with manning the guns of forts and fortresses, including coastal artillery batteries (such as the Clyde defences where Hall trained), the heavy gun batteries attached to each infantry division, and the guns of the siege artillery. It came into being on 1 June 1899 as a separate formation under the provisions of a Royal Warrant when existing coastal defence, mountain, siege and heavy batteries of the Royal Artillery were merged into a new sub-branch.

His opening paragraphs demonstrate the typical experience of troops joining the army including being billeted in requisitioned hotels, the issue of uniform and other details of early days in His Majesty's forces.

My first day on duty with HM Forces was 27 July 1916. As directed I presented myself at the recruiting office, Sheffield. It appeared that I was the only man for the Royal Garrison Artillery so I was given a railway pass and some identity papers and told to find my own way to No. 4 Depot, Yarmouth Barracks the first stage of my journey being the 8.57am train to Lincoln. After several changes and various delays I got to Yarmouth and at 8pm presented myself at the barracks.

I was greeted in quite a friendly manner. My particulars were taken and I was assigned a number, 108527, which I carried right through my army career. Then the Sergeant fetched (yes, actually fetched) me a basin of soup with the words *"its grand stuff – have as much as you like"*. After I had eaten I was taken to my quarters by an NCO whom I afterwards learnt was Bombardier Butler.[1] He explained as we went *"it's not much of a place but you'll be all right in the morning when you get into billets"*. With that he left me.

I was in a large room which in peacetime had been the gymnasium but in which there were now some sixty trestle beds. Most were occupied by recruits, some already asleep but most sitting on their beds with their heads in their hands or writing letters. All seemed to be strangers and reluctant to enter into conversation with one another. I chose a vacant bed next to what appeared to be a respectable man and for some time we observed one another with mistrust. Then at last my companion opened the conversation with the words *"Isn't it a -----"*. I agreed and so my friendship with Gunner Malloy was formed.

When the Sergeant, a few minutes later, told us that we could all leave the barracks provided that we returned at 10 o'clock we adjourned to a nearby pub. Malloy, it appeared was a colliery deputy from Co. Durham, a decent enough chap 36 years of age and typical of the other recruits. They were mostly late Derby Scheme men whose call up had been deferred although I learned there was a sprinkling of conscripts among the company. I seemed to be by far the youngest of the intake.

Everyone returned to barracks in time and soon the gymnasium closed for the night. I remove my shoes but nothing else and passed a disturbed night among the unfamiliar surroundings.

Next morning we were all much happier. As of common accord we determined to make the best of things. We were no longer civilians, we were soldiers and, as we surveyed one another, not such bad chaps either. Malloy chatted merrily in his high pitched north-country accent; a deeper tone joined in and Hickton lately a foreman in a Nottingham tobacco factory introduced himself, then a fourth man joined the circle Turner a journeyman printer. By breakfast time Malloy and Hickton had paired off while Turner and myself had cemented a friendship that was to last for months.

The first day was very busy. Not having the necessary tackle few of us had shaved but after ablutions we were marched to a hall where breakfast of tea and sausages was served. Then off for medical inspection and after this to the tailor's store for uniform. As we marched before the Sergeant tailor we called our height and our size in hats and boots. The tailor's assistants threw out various garments which we caught in our arms. Then a kit-bag, content so far unknown, was issued and we bore our load off to the gymnasium. First we emptied the kit-bags, checked off the contents with the aid of the NCO in charge and replaced them according to instructions. Next we donned our new uniforms and paraded in front of the Sergeant tailor. He cast a practiced eye over us in turn noting imperfections in our attire. This man's great coat too long — try another; next man's tunic sleeves require shortening — the garment was duly chalked and was left at the stores to be called for in a few days. Particular care was taken to ensure a perfect fit in boots and cap. After parade we presented a most

incongruous appearance for most of us had left some part of our uniform for alteration. For my part it was the tunic and for some days I walked about Yarmouth in khaki trousers and civilian jacket.

After dinner we were marched down to billets for the barracks could not hold a tenth of the recruits. My party was halted outside Goode's Hotel[2] on the promenade. Then we followed the NCO along the corridors where he allocated four or five men to each room. We four friends were able to share the same room.

Goodes Hotel, Great Yarmouth

During our stay at Yarmouth we remained in the same billet keeping to the same bedrooms and dining in the ball-room. This presented an incongruous appearance. Down the sides were gilded chairs and settees, now rather dilapidated, on which soldiers were apt to recline and consume liquid refreshment but three lines of trestle tables filled the body of the hall while a smaller serving table stood at the entrance.

Cooking was done by a civilian staff provided by the management. We would file into the ball-room take a plate and pass before the two assistant cooks who served vegetables and the chef himself, a very fat man who carved the joint at a prodigious rate. After meat came desert when those who wished could order beer and the two girls who waited on us had a busy time replenishing the glasses.

The proprietor cooks and these girls constituted the total staff of this once busy hotel. There were, of course, no visitors to Yarmouth during the war years and but for the military the town was deserted. Along the front was a tangle of barbed wire while the hulks of three torpedoed ships presented a pitiful sight in the bay. Most of the largest hotels had been commandeered by the military and it was the practice to draft a day's recruits to each hotel in turn. We recruits of July 27 were all taken by Goode's. In this we were not considered particularly fortunate for at the Garibaldi[3] the troops slept in spring beds (as against our trestles). Be that as it may I have no complaint against Goode's.

Twice a day we were marched to the barracks for training. On the square the parades were taken by the Sergeant-Major and we were assembled in "Companies", eight companies of sixty to eighty men each drawn from different hotels in the town. A Sergeant was in charge of each company assisted by two Bombardiers. Goode's party was known as 'C' company and eventually became the nucleus of 221 Siege Battery.

At night the Sergeants remained in the barracks while the Bombardiers slept in their respective billets. Their job was no sinecure for air raids were frequent. One occurred during our first night. The Bombardier called us out of bed and took us down a bewildering mass of stairs and corridors to the comparative safety of the basement. Then he went back to look for stragglers. The raid was unpleasant while it lasted but did little damage and after a couple of hours we were allowed to return to our rooms.

The following morning (July 29) we had our first squad drill, the first of many pretty hard going while it lasted. Then after dinner, it being Saturday we were free so Turner and I feeling very self-conscious in our new uniforms or rather part-uniforms had a look round the town. Occasionally we passed officers whom we awkwardly tried to salute but we soon learned to avoid streets frequented by the commissioned ranks.

In the evening we called at the tailor's shop for the remainder of our uniforms and this fitting being passed to the Sergeant tailor's satisfaction was duly issued. Then bundled up our civilian clothes and handed them in for dispatch home. The final tie with our old life was severed.

Sunday (July 30) brought one parade only an important one known as "final approval". In complete uniform we marched slowly before the officer commanding the depot. One or two men were rejected as being physically unfit for the RGA and sent to other units.

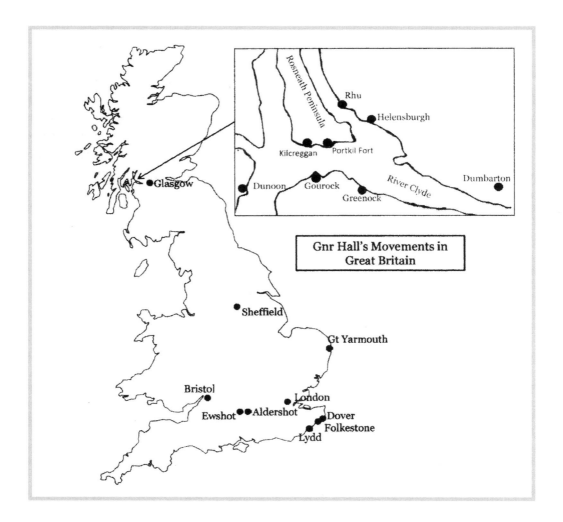

Gnr Hall's Movements in Great Britain

Gnr Hall's Movements in Great Britain

During the week our training continued, physical jerks, squad drill and light route marches in the surrounding country. We were in charge of an excellent Sergeant, firm but good hearted and from him we learnt the rudiments of a soldier's education, to *"jump to it"*, to keep steady on parade, to clean up our rooms in the morning, never to neglect shaving, to polish our buttons and to hold up our heads. Finally we were charged to forget that we had ever been civilians, to respect our regiment and to regard ourselves as the salt of the earth.

And we learnt our lessons well; the soldierly spirit entered into all that motley crew, conscript and volunteer alike and we realised that the army wasn't so bad after all.

On August 2 came vaccination. I took it rather badly and had a stiff arm for some days. Apart from this I can truthfully say that I enjoyed every minute of my stay in Yarmouth. But all good things come to an end. On Sunday August 6 we had another medical inspection and were directed to pack as far as possible in readiness for departure to another place.

On the Monday morning August 7 we lay resting on the sands with our kit bags besides us for we had finished with Goode's Hotel. At last it was time to go. The Sergeant called us up and his last words to us were *"Good bye, lads and good luck – you'll remember Great Yarmouth".* And so we marched back to barracks for our final meal after which we were given a bag of sandwiches to last us on our long journey. Then shouldering our loads we marched to the station where we entrained for an outlandish place on the west coast of Scotland.

---

1   Bdr Butler – no firm identification has been made but Gnr Hall met him at Great Yarmouth and later at Lydd.

2   Goode's Hotel, Marine Parade, Great Yarmouth is still there (2013) and recognisable despite a modern frontage at street level.

3   Garibaldi Hotel, 25, St Nicholas Road. This pub has now been demolished to make way for housing.

CHAPTER 3
THE FORMATION OF A SIEGE BATTERY

By 1917 the Allies on the Western Front were in a position to turn the tide and new units, including artillery batteries, were being formed to provide the resource to achieve this strategic objective. Hall was posted to Kilcreggan on the north shore of the Clyde opposite Gourock where one of the forts defending the Clyde was located. The area has changed little since 1916, the pier at Kilgreggan looks much as it did when Hall disembarked, the houses on the main street are readily recognisable and by taking a brisk twenty minute walk Portkil Fort can be visited. Much remains of this position and some parts have been amalgamated with domestic dwellings.

The journey north was long and tedious and it was not until early morning of August 8 that we stretched our limbs in Glasgow Central station. The NCO in charge of the party knew his job for he soon had marched us to one of the justly famous Lockhart's restaurants. Breakfast at seven o'clock in the morning for a hundred or so hungry men might have been an everyday occurrence for in a matter of minutes we were consuming with avidity the ham and eggs put before us. Then a wash and shave and a short march to Queen Street station where we entrained for Craigendoren Pier on the Clyde. The rest of the journey was by steamer and we disembarked at the small village of Kilcreggan.

The Clyde at this point is four miles wide and almost opposite our destination stood the large and rather squalid town of Greenock. Kilcreggan is located on the northern and wilder side of the river on what is known as the Roseneath Peninsular a narrow tongue of land bounded on the north by moorlands, on the east by the beautiful Gare Loch, on the west by the equally charming Loch Long and on the south by the river Clyde itself. Kilcreggan is the largest place on the peninsular which is not saying much for on investigation it proved to be a score or so houses on a steep hill leading inland. Even so it was large compared with Row[1] on Loch Long and Roseneath on the Gareloch.

It was eleven o'clock in the morning when we disembarked at the tiny pier and made our way up the steep little street to our new quarters. As we passed we were struck by the strange silence of the place and the preoccupation of the inhabitants. Not a woman paused at her work, not a child in its play deigned to cast a glance at the soldiers marching along the street. This strange indifference persisted the whole time of our stay in Kilcreggan. We might not have existed so far as the civilians were concerned.

Our guide had some difficulty in finding his way to the encampment for he marched us quite a long way round before he brought us up in front of a number of wooden huts above the village. Here then was Portkil Fort. Our guide handed over his charges and hurried away. The Commanding Officer, Capt Saunders, coldly looked us over and passed us on to his

Sergeant-Major. The latter marched us to a number of wooden huts, detailed fifteen men to each and left us to our own devices. When later some bolder spirits sallied forth in search of dinner they were told that the meal had been served and that we had missed it. Clearly we should have to look after ourselves in this inhospitable place.

Thus perforce we became acquainted with the geography of the fort. As I have said the ground sloped steeply to the Clyde. On the highest point overlooking the river emplacements for two 6 inch naval guns were cut in the solid rock.[2] About 100 yards from these and on a lower level stood two 4.7 inch guns. In rear of the latter were built underground quarters for the storage of ammunition and for the accommodation of the gun crews. One of these chambers had been turned into a dining hall. The wooden huts to which we had been introduced were war-time erections. Some of these were occupied by a siege battery the significance of which we did not understand at the time. They seemed to be a self-contained unit and took no part in the running of the fort. We recruits had the others.

Part of Portkil Fort August 2012

The original defenders of the fort were Territorials, Clyde RGA they called themselves. They were quartered near the 6 inch guns. Except that they prepared our food and that their NCO's sometimes took us at drill they had little to do with us perhaps just as well.

The object in sending us to the fort was twofold. First we were to continue our training and eventually formed into a siege battery for service overseas and secondly to man the fort in case of emergency. In this we were poaching on the preserves of the Territorials. These men argued, with some justification, that the terms of their enlistment covered Home Defence[3] only, in their case the manning of the Clyde forts, overseas service being restricted to regular soldiers and their supporters. In spite of this they were steadily being drafted into siege batteries until there were only about twenty of the original defenders left. (In due course we took half a dozen of these into 221 Battery.)

We soon learnt that we were not expected to be idle. Company orders were posted up and applied to us as well as the Territorials. Parades were at 6.30 and 9am and at 2pm. At first parade we appeared in trousers, shirt and canvas shoes for an hour's Swedish drill[4] before breakfast. The 9 o'clock parade was in full uniform when we were inspected to see that we were properly shaved and boots and buttons polished. An hour's squad drill followed by a ten minutes break. After this rifle drill using old German rifles captured in the Far East with long curly French bayonets dating from the war of 1870 – a rather strange combination.

Kilcreggan Pier from the ferry August 2012

Dinner, such as it was, followed and the afternoon was devoted to more interesting work such as the use and care of fixed guns, knotting and lashing, semaphore etc. On Saturdays we washed out the huts after which they were inspected by Capt Saunders while on Sundays Divine Service was held, that is if the clergyman could get over from the mainland for no steamers plied on the Sabbath and the Padre had to charter a rowing boat. When the sea was too rough for the passage no service was held.

Dining arrangements were appalling, the worst I encountered during the whole of my army career. Meals were served in one of the underground shelters in rear of the guns, the cookhouse being 200 yards away. Potatoes cooked in their jackets were dragged on the ground from the cookhouse in a big net and thrown on the table, net and all. A huge piece of meat burnt black on the outside but quite raw inside was similarly thrown on the bare boards. Meanwhile the troops were waiting on the steps before the locked doors of the mess room. These would suddenly be thrown open and we surged inside. The original defenders of the fort by long practice knew how to attack the joint and with knife and fork at the alert, cut off slices of the only edible portion and withdrew seizing a couple of potatoes en route. By the time we recruits had reached the joint it was quite raw and uneatable. Later some of the rougher elements found it possible to jostle a way to the meat but the bulk of us were prepared to leave the battle to the strong and console ourselves with two penny packets of biscuits purchased from the surly manager of the canteen.

Kilcreggan Pier looking east (August 2012). The fort is beyond the trees on the left

It was on August 9 the second day after our arrival that Turner and I observed a boy of eighteen weeping bitterly under a tree near one of the huts. We did our best to console him and at length he agreed to come for a walk with us. On the way we learnt some of his history. His name was Ernest McHugh[5]. This was the first time he had left home, a village in Northumberland. I don't know how he arrived at Portkil for he certainly had not travelled with us from Yarmouth. At any rate he was alone and friendless. He was a likeable lad and we took him under our care. We fixed up a bed for him next to mine and he soon settled down to army life. Later on we drifted away from Turner as I had already parted from Malloy but little Ernest and I remained the firmest of friends.

Routine was broken on August 15 and again on the 24 for inoculation against tetanus. Not very severe but it made us seedy for a bit and we were given a couple of days rest to recover.

On August 19 there was grouse shooting on the moors. The officers were invited and a dozen men selected to act as beaters being given a good meal and five shillings for their services. I was one of those taken; I didn't like the job but I knew too much to refuse. The game-keeper gave his orders in the broadest Scots accent which few of us could understand and we trudged across the moor doing I fancy more harm than good. I know I sent a lot of birds in the wrong direction to the old man's wrath and my own secret delight. When at the end of the shoot the game-keeper stated that the Black Watch who acted as beaters the previous year gave a much better account of themselves we were not disposed to dispute his assertion.

Then towards the end of the month there was great activity in the fort. The siege battery moved south leaving their huts vacant for a time. But not for long as we heard that another battery was to be formed to take their place.

The first step was the inevitable medical inspection held on August 23. This was a pretty serious affair and only those quite fit were passed quite a number being thrown out even for dental treatment. Those of us who were passed vacated our own huts and took over these recently occupied by the siege battery. Here our numbers were augmented by troops from other forts on the Clyde including some we had known from the Garibaldi Hotel in Yarmouth. Half a dozen of the original Clyde Territorials were drafted to us under protest. From such origins 221 Siege Battery, Royal Garrison Artillery came into existence on 23 August 1916.

We were much more comfortable now the battery was formed. There were eighteen of us to a hut. I was in hut 14 along with my three original friends and Ernest McHugh. The occupants of this hut became 'C' sub-section destined to serve No.3 Gun in due course. We were a mixed crowd aged between 18 and 42 averaging well over thirty, mostly late Derby Scheme men with a small sprinkling of conscripts.

Bob Hickton was appointed battery cook. Although completely inexperienced he made a much better job of it than the Scotsmen. Then we had our own mess. No longer would we be fed like wild beasts in a cage but would dine decently from tables in our own huts. There were no NCO's at first so each sub-section was directed to appoint one of its number to act as leader, being responsible for the messing and good order of the hut.

As far as 'C' sub-section was concerned we had no hesitation George Royle the oldest and most dignified looking man was unanimously elected. We had no reason to regret our choice. George ruled the mess wisely and well. Two of us in turn brought the food from the cookhouse and afterwards cleaned the dishes and tables. From now on we could truly say *"no complaints"* as far as meals were concerned.

As a self-contained unit we had to have a Commanding Officer. Captain Saunders commandant of the fort was appointed pro-tem but we saw little of him. Later he relinquished command of the fort to be with us full time. He accompanied us to England but we lost him after a few weeks.

View from Portkil Fort along the Clyde towards Dumbarton

Of more importance to the troops was our new Warrant Officer. Sgt-Major Netherway arrived with a single Bombardier a few days after the formation of the battery, a typical time serving Warrant Officer florid of complexion and with a voice of brass, nevertheless a highly efficient man and good at heart. He was posted from India and had a perfect horror of getting wet, an idiosyncrasy which stood us in good stead. We had plenty of rain on the Clyde and often on parade BSM Netherway could be seen scanning the clouds with an anxious look. Then at the first drop of rain he would bellow *"Battery, to No.3 hut, double"* and woe betide any laggard on such an occasion. Once safely indoors he would spin yarn after yarn about life in India or set us to work tying knots in bits of string. He was also a keen Signaller but weather often interfered with our instruction in semaphore and we had no facility for indoor signalling at that time.

The solitary NCO, Bombardier Whiting was a gaunt sad-faced man with a gold stripe[6] to testify to wounds received on active service. At first he got on well with the Sgt-Major but later the two men became estranged and Whiting never received the promotion he richly deserved.

We were now receiving our pay regularly every Friday, five shillings a week spending cash mostly on biscuits. On Saturday afternoons we were free to go by steamer to Greenock or Gourock. Greenock had few attractions but Gourock was quite a pleasant place. One had to be careful to catch the last boat home failure meaning stranding until Monday with unpleasant consequences. There were no steamers on Sundays but we could always fall back on a pleasant walk to Roseneath thence by ferry boat to Row and an exploration of the woods on the mainland. We planned a tour to Loch Lomond but had to abandon it on account of difficulties in transport.

Most evenings we would walk along the sea road to Cove sometimes backwards and forwards two or three times for there was no hospitality in the tiny hamlet. On one occasion H.M.S. *Repulse*[7] was in the river and a splendid spectacle she made at night as she swept her searchlights round picking out Greenock and the hills on both sides of the water.

Occasionally we tried bathing in the river but the Clyde though picturesque is dirty and some of us sustained nasty cuts from broken glass.

During the whole time we were at Portkil, Turner, McHugh and I kept together although we would sometimes join larger parties. We spent little time at the canteen which in any case was noisy and rather foul but preferred walking often in silence on the sea roads watching the sun setting on the water each of us absorbed in our own thoughts.

But at last we reached another stage in our training On September 18 we packed up our belongings, cleared the huts and paraded for the last time. It was evening when we marched down the hill to the little pier. A small boy was playing in the village street but on our approach he turned his back and went indoors. No-one else was visible. The steamer arrived at the pier; we embarked and so left Kilcreggan.

---

1   Row is Rhu on the Helensburgh shore of Gare Loch

2   The fort commands views eastwards to Dumbarton and south west towards Dunoon and Rothesay.

3   Home Defence – traditionally Territorials were for home defence but in the Great War when Territorial Force troops agreed to overseas service they signed the Imperial Service Obligation "to subject himself to liability to serve in any place outside the United Kingdom in the event of National emergency" (Army Form E.624). These Territorials were entitled to wear over their tunic right pocket the Imperial Service Brooch – this was a metal brooch formed of a bar with a cord-like border bearing the words Imperial Service with a King's crown above.

4   Swedish drill was pre-war innovation whereby ranks of soldiers (or school pupils etc) would undertake various stretching actions and movements without the need for any special facilities or equipment.

5   108541 Gnr Ernest McHugh. Served in France & Flanders 11 January 1917 to 8 June 1918. Later served as 319125 F/Cadet RAF.

6   A wound stripe was a cloth or brass stripe (Russian braid) two inches long worn on the lower left sleeve on the service dress jacket by all officers and soldiers who have been wounded in any of the campaigns since 4 August, 1914. The stripe was first authorised under Army Order 204 of 6 July 1916 supplemented by Army Council Instruction No. 1637 of 22 August 1916 and No. 2075 dated 3 November 1916.

7   HMS Repulse had been launched that year and Hall's sighting must have been one of the battlecruiser's first voyages as it was launched (at John Brown, Clydebank) on 8 January 1916 and commissioned on 18 August 1916. HMS Repulse was sunk by a Japanese air attack off Malaya on 10 December 1941.

CHAPTER 4
TRAINING THE BATTERY

Following his basic training in Scotland, Hall progressed to the next stage in the huge encampment in and around Aldershot, 'Home of the British Army'. Inevitably training at first was undertaken using obsolete guns and some of the personnel were soldiers who had already seen service overseas witnessed by their wound stripes. This chapter also introduces the reader to the complex science of dropping an artillery shell on a target and later we will see the culmination for Hall when he controlled a shoot in France on 27 September 1918 during the capture of the Canal du Nord.[1]

We entrained at Greenock for the long journey south. It was I remember at two o'clock in the morning that I looked out of the window and saw the empty station of my native Sheffield. And so we went southwards until in the afternoon we reached Fleet station on the main L&SW[2] line. Here we detrained, picked up our kit bags and were soon happily marching along tree-clad roads until we reached Ewshot Barracks[3] some four miles distant. Here tea awaited us. The meal over we went to our new quarters and were told that we were free until 9am next morning.

But Bob Hickton was still to be reckoned with. He and his satellites had taken possession of the cook-house and, having a day's rations in hand proceeded to cook dinner forthwith. With the camp tea at 4.30 and a full dinner two hours later we seemed to have arrived at a land of milk and honey. When supper was announced at 9 o'clock few partook of it.

September 20 saw us busy on camp fatigues and the following days we followed the camp routine with three parades 6.30am, 9am and 2pm.

Ewshot Barracks was then one of the showpieces of the country so far as accommodation was concerned. It was beautifully situated on the hillside with glorious views in every direction. It consisted of a large number of corrugated iron huts arranged in blocks each block accommodating a complete battery. The living huts were more like small bungalows than the usual type of army building and the usual offices adjoined, a great convenience to us. There was also a splendid riding school, gymnasium and canteens. In addition to the large parade ground there was a smaller area attached to each block so that the batteries could parade independently or en masse as desired. In practice the large parade ground was used only for church parade and similar ceremonial occasions when a dozen or so batteries were mustered. Otherwise we had but little contact with our neighbours.

At this point gun drill was introduced some strange pieces being used for this purpose. Obsolete 5 inch and 6 inch 30cwt howitzers and 15 and 18 inch guns were dragged from their sheds and run into the adjoining fields where we were put through the motions of loading, laying and firing independently and by sections. Meantime in a corner a squad of men would be driving iron shod pickets into the ground and then extracting them by means of levers and, if the youngsters were more nippy on the guns the older men could beat them every time when it came to maul and picket. Specialists now began to arise. One man would fancy himself on the dial sights a potential gun-layer was born, another happy with oil and cotton waste had the beginnings of a Limber Gunner while those who fancied their strength had plenty of scope as ammunition numbers. The enthusiasm of the troops in these early days was remarkable. Derby men and conscripts we might be but once the army spirit had entered into us we would not give place to those gallant men who had enlisted in the first flood of war.

Our first Commanding Officer, Capt Saunders, soon left us a man of no consequence he passed un-regretted out of sight.

He was followed by Capt Wyllie a somewhat blustering type of officer who soon made his presence felt. He seemed a good straight man however and a couple of wound stripes showed they had been through the mill. Meantime our numbers kept steadily increasing. A Quartermaster-Sergeant was posted to us, NCO's arrived in ones and twos and took charge of sections and it was noticed that this Corporal wore one wound stripe, that Bombardier two, while a certain Sergeant boasted of no less than three on his arm. No promotions had yet been made from the rank and file and it seemed that with this arrival of wounded NCO's none would be probable. Nevertheless we had every confidence in our leaders and felt that here were experienced men on whom we could rely.

Officers were slower to arrive. 2/Lt Guiton[4] was the first a young gentleman from Jersey and very self-conscious on his first parade. It was some time before he was joined by brother officers indeed complement of commissioned ranks was not complete until we were almost ready for overseas. Mr Guiton was freshly commissioned but most of the others were ex-overseas.

Up to now although I had done a little gun-laying I had shown no particular desire towards specialisation. On September 25 however it appeared on orders that a short course on map reading was to be opened at headquarters and volunteers were called for. I approached the Sergeant-Major and persuaded him to let me take the course. I had as companion from 221 Battery Gunner Potter a bookmaker's clerk. The course was interesting enough consisting of field work with map and compass together with indoor instruction. A test was held at the end of the course when I came top with maximum marks. It is only fair to add that some of my companions feared that unpleasant consequences might follow too close a knowledge of map-reading and probably failed deliberately. They may have been correct; all those who passed eventually became Observers.

On October 4 equipment was issued, bandolier, belt water-bottle and mess-tin. Much of this had been salvaged from the battlefield and carried ominous marks such as bullet holes in bandoliers. We felt that this was carrying economy a bit too far.[5]

On October 6 I had my first weekend leave from 6pm on Friday to 9am roll call on the Monday morning – a bit of a rush but worth it.

On October 17 the Signallers arrived. Twenty men in charge of a Corporal and Bombardier. All Londoners and mostly commercial travellers so much of a type that one felt that enlistment for them merely meant changing one uniform for another. An exceedingly jovial crowd NCO's and men alike addressing one another by their christian names they had about six months service and so were senior to the bulk of the battery. Originally they had enlisted at No. 1 Depot, Dover, where the procedure was somewhat different from Yarmouth recruits, it seemed, were kept under observation and those who showed any aptitude were put through a short course of signalling. A test eliminated the duds and the rest were sent forward to training schools. Here they received instruction in the Morse code and signalling by flag, heliograph and field telephone together with such practical work as the laying and maintenance of telephone lines. When they finally passed out and could send Morse at speed they received their crossed flags, a decoration they wore on their sleeves,[6] and were awarded sixpence a day proficiency pay. They were then posted to siege batteries in formation as 'first line' telephonists.

But more Signallers were required to complete the establishment and the Sgt-Major called for twenty volunteers for training as 'second line' telephonists or linesmen. These were quickly forthcoming and after morning parade the battery broke into three sections, the qualified Signallers who continued training under their Corporal, the signalling school to whom the Bombardier was imparting the rudiments of telephony and the rest of the battery who marched down to the guns.

The enrolment of second line Signallers did not go without comment. The Yarmouth contingent had been given no such opportunity as our Dover friends and it did not seem quite fair to expect us to pick up in a few weeks that which the newcomers had acquired in six months of specialised training. It was felt that the second line men would never attain the proficiency of the qualified Signaller and, when the time arrived, would be fitted only for the unpleasant and dangerous task of maintaining lines under shell fire. It was doubtful too, whether they would ever draw proficiency pay. It is only fair to say that our London friends never presumed on their superior qualifications. Turner and I were among those who enrolled. McHugh at that time had ambitions towards a layer's badge[7] and would not join us. It looked at that time that the partnership would break up.

I was not destined to become a Signaller, however. On October 20 three more men arrived at the battery, a Corporal, a Bombardier and a Gunner each bearing on his arm the mysterious letter O surrounded by a laurel wreath and there was much speculation as to their purpose.

The symbol was soon explained. The O signified Observer and the newcomers represented the nucleus of our observation staff. Their history was similar to that of the Signallers. At Dover a few men with an aptitude for figures were selected periodically and sent to an Observation School. At the end of a six months course an examination was held, the rank of Corporal being awarded for a first class pass, that of Bombardier for a second while those who merely qualified received the laurel wreath and proficiency pay. The three men Corporal

Tudhope,[8] Bombardier Shepherd and Gunner Moody represented the three stages of success at the academy. But three trained Observers was deemed insufficient for the battery staff and similar procedure to that taken for the Signallers was adopted that is a school for 'second line' Observers was started. Volunteers were called for and McHugh and I determined to try our luck. Ernest was accepted at once but I had a little difficulty as I was already committed for the signalling school. My recent success at map reading however was the deciding factor and on October 24 I was transferred, another, Gunner Earle, making up the third man. The class then settled down to work although it seemed strange having as many teachers as pupils.

Corporal Tudhope was a young Scots architect, a remarkably clever man and a particularly bad teacher. The theory and practice of Gunnery he knew from A to Z but quickly lost patience with those unable to follow him. Gunner Moody, who had trained with him and had just scraped through with a third class pass, was in particular an object of his contempt while his attempt to explain the elements of Euclid to Gunner Earle met with no success. Earle had never heard of Euclid and all his works and certainly did not want to learn now. In a few days he gave up the course in disgust and returned to the guns. During the lessons Bdr Shepherd would lounge about smoking a cigarette and occasionally interjecting a remark which would arouse the Corporal to fury and make him more incomprehensible than ever. Later it was thought that three teachers to two pupils was rather overdoing things so Shepherd and Moody often went out on the guns to try their hands at gun laying. This made things rather easier for McHugh and I and, by sticking at the Corporal, eventually made out what he was driving at. When at last we persuaded him to lend us his original notes we were able to make good progress.

In such a manner McHugh and I received our instruction in the theory and practice of gunnery. We also learnt that the title Observer was really a misnomer and that little or no practical observation work would fall to our lot. We were being trained to perform all the mathematical calculations necessary for training the guns on their targets and when qualified would be designated Battery Commander's Assistants, BCAs for short.

While it is common knowledge that in heavy artillery the Gunners rarely see their target few realise the amount of calculation indirect laying involves. The guns are laid on a prominent object in rear (the aiming point) by day and on a lamp stuck on a picket (the auxiliary aiming point) by night. All targets have to be transmitted to the gun layer with reference to these aiming points. As the guns will be some distance apart it is often necessary to concentrate their fire on the target, quite a calculation in itself. Further the force and direction of the wind has to be analysed and corrections applied to counterbalance its effect. As regards the range, in addition to the wind, we have the wear of the gun (loss of muzzle velocity) to be allowed for as well as corrections for temperature of the air, temperature of the charge, barometric reading, weight of the shell and the type of fuse. The range thus obtained in yards has to be converted into degrees and minutes for the Gun Captain to set on his clinometer.

The workings for a single gun, and there were four to each battery, might be set out as under:

RANGE

As measured on the map 7150 yards
For wear of gun (loss of MV) add 247 yards
For temperature of the air add 16 yards
For temperature of charge deduct 10 yards
For barometer add 20 yards
For excess weight of shell deduct 15 yards
For wind 30 ft per second @ 30 degrees against line of fire add 154 yards
Giving a corrected range of 7562 yards
Which converted to degrees = 21° 22' full charge

LINE

Gun's reading to aiming post (zero line) 157° 30' left
Target reading from zero line 20° 25' right
Concentration 25 yards @ 7000 yards range 15' right
Wind as above 12' right
Giving a line for the gun layer 136° 78' left

The Observer reports too had to be corrected before they could be applied to the guns. Thus an Observer watching from an angle forward of the battery position might see shells appearing to fall short whereas in fact the guns would be correctly ranged and the line be at fault. Factors comparing the Observer's position with that of the battery had first to be worked out and corrections applied to the reports before any attempt could be made to range the guns.

For field work we had a 'director' an instrument for measuring angles not unlike a theodolite, prismatic compasses, binoculars and slide rules. The work was hard but we were young and enthusiastic and entered into the spirit of the game, indeed McHugh and I discussed little else when we were off duty either wandering over the heath towards Aldershot, boating on the Basingstoke Canal or sitting beside Fleet Pond.

On the guns many of the men had presented themselves for training as Gun Layers and most of these had qualified. Then a goodly number become 'employed men' and did not parade. Some of these appointments such as battery clerk, cook etc were more or less permanent but there were other positions held on the strict understanding that the jobs would lapse on embarkation. There were no vacancies on active service for Sgt-Major's batman, Quartermaster's clerk and so forth.

Co-operation between the various branches was now planned. Field days were held when Gunners manned the guns, Signallers laid out lines of communication and BCAs calculated ranges all under the direction of the CO who professed himself well satisfied with the performance. We only wished we had been practising with real guns instead of the obsolete fifteen pounders.

Then at the end of October we saw modern guns for the first time. We were marched over the hill to Aldershot where at Ramillies Barracks a couple of the new 6 inch 26cwt howitzers were on show, the ordnance we should probably take overseas. It was a splendid piece modelled on a German 5.9 howitzer captured early in the war and such an improvement on the 6 inch 30cwt the standard British equipment at the time that orders were given that the older gun should be superseded as soon as possible. The changeover was completed I believe in time for the Battle of the Somme in late 1916. The weight 26cwt referred to the gun proper but the complete weight with carriage and mountings about 5 tons the whole so beautifully balanced that when a man sat on the muzzle the trail of the gun rose in the air and from this position the howitzer could be run all over the place. She fired a shell weighing 100lbs a distance of nearly 10,000 yards. We lifted a dummy shell and found it well within our capabilities. We were shown the knack of slamming the breech and the proper way of loading the gun. We were told that while ten men were allowed for fighting the gun five or six would suffice at a pinch, a statement that we fully believed and we returned to Ewshot with a light heart and in the full belief that we should have a really soft job overseas.

Besides the specialised training there was other work to be done. Every day there was physical training before breakfast the only exception being the battery cook. Then there were route marches and wonderful marches they were too in light order, that is no other equipment than belt and bandolier we set forth along the pleasant country lanes of Surrey and Hampshire. Once clear of the camp the order 'march easy' was given and we would swing along singing and talking as we marched through the villages, we northerners marvelling at the neat gardens and the thatched roofs of the cottages.

Everywhere we were welcomed. Women came to the cottage doors, children waved to us, there was never a labourer in field but would pause at his work and pass a cheery word to the troops. The contrast from the dour Scots was amazing. Then there were the hop fields the green grass, the honeysuckle and the blackberries that grew so abundantly in the hedgerows. Then when we returned to camp, healthily tired and full of the joys of life, we did full justice for the meal that Hickton had prepared for us.

One day we were set to work digging trenches and gun pits but the ground was of red sand and the task more like children digging on the sea shore than grown men training for war.

At night we had concerts in the hall and there was some rare talent in the camp. There was one man with a wonderful tenor voice and he always gave as his final encore the song 'A Perfect Day'. I felt at this time that the world had nothing better to offer indeed I count the short stay at Ewshot the happiest in my army career.

1   See Chapter 27 The Capture of the Canal du Nord

2   London & South Western – the mainline from Waterloo to Southampton, Weymouth and Exeter Central

3   Ewshot is about three miles north of Farnham in west Surrey and adjoins the Aldershot Garrison which expanded during the war utilising many acres of heath land for training. The barracks were located midway between Ewshot and Church Crookham.

4   2/Lt Guiton – most probably Philip Andrew Guiton, formerly 689 Gnr Honourable Artillery Company, later 2/ Lt and Lt. Served in Egypt from 21 April 1915. His medal index card shows his address as Natal University College, South Africa.

5   Divisions had salvage units which recovered material that could be reused so it is not at all surprising that recruits were issued with damaged items when training.

6   The Signaller appointment badge was one of many used by the British Army to indicate qualifications and can be useful when searching for clues in photographs of the period.

7   The Layer's badge was another appointment badge worn by RGA men on the right sleeve, upper.

8   Corporal Tudhope – possibly 109705 Cpl James N. Tudhope.

10   Officer Commanding

11   Ramillies Barracks were part of Marlborough Lines in Aldershot named after victories in the campaign of 1704-09. Although located at North Camp it was always regarded as part of Aldershot Camp even though it was north of the boundary line of the Borough and Farnborough UDC (which also ran through the Officers' Mess of St Omer Barracks).

CHAPTER 5
FIRING THE COURSE

Having passed through Aldershot Garrison Hall inevitably found himself transferred to a specialist artillery training area. He was posted to Lydd in Kent which was a well established gunnery school and where experiments had been conducted with explosives for 25 years; the explosive Lyddite was named after the town. Training was now on the guns that would be used overseas these being howitzers, that is, heavy guns (6 or 8 inch) rather than smaller field guns or rail mounted guns. Sydney Hall's description of the work of a gun team provides essential background for his experiences on a daily basis in France and Flanders and assist understanding of the operation of a gun. We also encounter the recurring theme of seeking a commission (as an officer) and the fateful decision described in the introduction to terminate "my studies at 15½ after completing only two years of the course. This was undoubtedly the greatest mistake of my life and I have suffered its effects ever since".

On November 2 we move to Lydd. We arrived at 8pm had a cold supper and turned in for the night. Training was resumed the following day. Lydd had been a School of Gunnery for many years and was ideally situated for the purpose. The town is in the south of Kent about four miles inland from the promontory of Dungeness. The sea has retreated considerably at this point and left a vast stretch of shingle between the town and Dungeness lighthouse. Here the ranges were situated. Lydd itself had little of interest except for a very large church dating from the time when the town was a busy port. The church tower the only conspicuous object in a dead flat country came in useful as an aiming point for the guns. At the time the camp consisted of three divisions known as Brick Town, Tin Town and Wood Town respectively. Headquarters Staff and the Officers' Mess were in Brick Town while the other camps were occupied by the batteries in residence. There were six batteries in the camp and the course lasted six weeks one battery thus passing out each week.

The whole of the period was devoted to technical training and lectures. The training staff consisted of a member of experts both military and civilian but mostly officers and Warrant Officers who were styled Instructors of Gunnery, I.G. for short. These took charge of the different sections of the battery and piloted us through the most difficult part of our training. When we arrived at Lydd we were almost up to strength and here our establishment was completed. Commanding the battery was Capt Wyllie, now promoted Major. He had a full Lieutenant as second in command and four subalterns in charge of sub-sections.

Except for 2/Lt Guiton I never got to know any of these officers. Then there was Battery Sgt-Major Netherway and Quartermaster Sergeant Fursden both time serving soldiers followed by four Sergeants six Corporals (one for each gun plus one Signaller and one BCA) six full and six Acting Bombardiers. The commanding officer and at least two of the other officers had seen active service as had four of the Corporals and four of the Bombardiers. Most were time serving men and had been wounded in action Sgt Henshaw no less than three times. The six acting ranks were chosen from the battery among them being Bob Hickton who as battery cook received a protection stripe, another was the ex-Bombardier Butler I had met at Yarmouth. (He forfeited his original stripe when posted to 221 battery.) No further promotions were made from the ranks before we left for overseas. With so many experienced leaders we felt a complete sense of security. They told us quietly that much we had learnt in training we should have to unlearn in the field, that reliefs would have to be provided. 24 hours on and 24 hours off duty was the general rule and this would involve the complete reorganisation of the gun crews as we knew them.

The guns provided for training at Lydd were the new 6 inch 26cwt howitzer. The 8 inch and 12 inch howitzer and the 6 inch Mark 7 guns were developments of the 6 inch howitzer and were also available but the 9.2 inch howitzer a British designed piece of pre-war origin was not being sent out at present. All these guns I was to meet later on in France.

At drill ten men were required to work the 6 inch howitzer. No. 1 the Gun Captain (usually the Sergeant) was responsible for working and in particular setting the range. His position was usually on the left of the gun. On the right were No's 2 and 4. No.2 was the Limber Gunner, opened and closed the breech and fired the gun with a short lanyard. He also operated the quick motion lever which depressed the gun for loading and raised her to the approximate elevation for firing (the final setting to the clinometers was done by No. 1 on the slow motion screw); No. 4 behind No. 2 was the Gun Layer. He used the dial sight and was responsible for the 'line' of the gun. The rest of the crew were concerned with the loading. No's 10 and 8 were away from the gun in charge of shells and cartridges respectively. The loading tray would normally be resting on the gun trail. No. 9 would carry a shell and place it on the tray. No's 5 and 7 one on each side of the gun would pick up the tray and its load and lift it onto the cradle where it rested. No.3 would now be following up with the rammer and with No.5 would ram the shell well home into the breach in two motions 'half way' and 'home'. No.3 would then withdraw with his rammer and No.7 would receive the charge from No.6 the cartridge runner and insert it behind the shell. No's 5 and 7 would now remove the loading tray No.2 slam the breech with his left hand and release the quick acting lever with his right. The gun now being in the firing position No.4 would lay for line and No.1 for elevation while No.2 would insert his friction tube for firing. The gun laid sights and clinometers removed No.2 would now attach his lanyard and await the order to fire. Firing over he would bring the gun down to the loading position and the business would start over again.

The new gun differed from the one it replaced by the provision of a 'spade' a piece of steel set at an angle beneath the foot of the trail the object being that after the first shot the spade would dig in and hold the gun firm for the rest of the shoot. After this she would require pulling out. No's 3 and 5 were provided with iron shod levers for this purpose and the rest of the team would pull on drag ropes inserted in an eye on the wheels of the gun. If these efforts proved insufficient more leverage could be obtained by fixing the ropes on a spoke and carrying them round over the rims of the wheels. So much for theory but the thorny problem as to whether the gun should be allowed to dig in kept cropping up and was never really settled by the end of the war.

The instructor confirmed that the gun could easily be fought by five or six men as against the ten provided for in drill. The two cartridge men were obviously sinecures, while if plenty of shells were fused in advance No.10 could be dispensed with while the loading could easily be done by two men instead of the four provided. With these economies it would be possible to provided reliefs. Twenty four hours on and twenty four off was the usual practice up the line. All this seemed very satisfactory as the matter was discussed in the canteen at night.

As for the specialists the CO tested us individually on November 8. The trained Signallers were passed as a body while many of the second line were found sufficiently proficient to leave the school and take their place with them. All the Gun Layers passed out. As regards the Observers Major Wyllie placed as Battery Commander's Assistants Corporal Tudhope, myself and Ernest McHugh (in that order). Tudhope, McHugh and I were thereupon appointed to the Battery Commander's Staff while Shepherd was directed to instruct half a dozen first line Signallers in the elements of gunnery so as to replace any casualties among us.

Early in November I became very friendly with 2/Lt Guiton. This young officer took his duties very seriously and would spend much of his time with the BCA's class; here he was obviously more at home than on the parade ground. Once he asked us very diffidently if we would mind going over to his quarters that evening after mess so that we could discuss the theory of gunnery together. We did so and several evenings were pleasantly spent together working out theoretical shoots and chalking lines on his walls and floor much to the disgust of his servant who had to clean them off the following day. The batman was further annoyed when asked to provide cups of cocoa for the officer and his BCA friends. Tudhope then went on leave so McHugh and I visited Mr Guiton's quarters together. It was when leaving the officer's quarters one evening and crossing the barrack square towards my own hut that I revived the idea of applying for a commission.

I was on leave from November 15 to the 20 and after discussion with my parents and friends became more favourably disposed to the idea. On my return I spoke quietly to Corporal Tudhope. He seemed rather evasive but said that he had thought about a commission himself and might apply *"later on"*. I left it at that.

On November 28 we started firing our course. The first shoot was on fifteen pounder guns. The teams were selected and those not actually fighting the guns were drawn up in rear to accustom us to the sound. A second shoot with fresh teams took place two days later.

Sydney Hall with his parents 1916

On December 4 our turn came for firing the six inch howitzers, a course that was to last several days. The first day I did not take any active part in the shoot but stood with the spectators behind the guns. Next day I accompanied Mr Guiton to the Observation Post while on December 6 we successfully engaged and partly demolished the target.

Then came musketry. On December 7 we all went to the butts. The Gunners fired twenty rounds at various ranges but when it came to the turn of the employed men five rounds were deemed sufficient. I was one of the last to fire and being handed a loaded rifle by the

Sgt-Major was told to do my best to hit the target. This was the only time that I fired a rifle during the war.

It is a great pity that I did not approach Major Wylie about a commission immediately on my return from leave. Had I done so I would have been spared a lot of misery during the months to come. It is probable that he would have advised me to defer my application until I had gone overseas and proved myself. Then with my BCA's experience coupled with the CO's support I might have overcome the formidable obstacle of my defective education and gained a commission on the field. Alternatively I could have consulted 2/Lt Guiton who was more like a friend than a superior officer and who would surely have paved the way for me. As it was I kept my own council until December 8 when I asked to see the CO.

But immediately after the shoot Major Wyllie had gone on leave. His place was taken by the Captain who as Lieutenant had joined the battery a few weeks earlier and who was quite unacquainted with me. When I stated my business he was quite non-committal but stated that if I made an application it would be sent forward. Next day I obtained a form from the Sgt-Major completed it as far as possible and sent it to my father to deal with the references.

There was another shoot on the 6 inch howitzers on December 11 when all the employed men and specialists took part. In my case I was one of the loading numbers. Still more shoots on the 13 and 14 this time on the fifteen pounders and our course was complete. A final medical inspection on December 15 and everyone was passed fit for active service.

Meanwhile at home my father was busy getting the necessary references on my application form. He ran into a snag with Mr Iliffe, Headmaster of the Central Secondary School, Sheffield, who, because I had left before completing the full year's term, felt unable to give the certificate of education as it stood. Eventually he was persuaded to give a modified certificate stating that I had attended the school but had left after the end of the second year. During my stay my conduct and progress had been "satisfactory". When I received the form I handed it to the Captain (Major Wylie still not being available) only to have it returned to me for some technicality. After amendment it was accepted without comment and sent forward on December 18.

We were now due for our overseas leave. In order to allow as many to be home for Christmas three quarters of the Battery were liberated on December 20. We were told that the battery would be moved during our absence and that we should report to Ashton Gate Barracks, Bristol, on December 26 without fail. The remainder of the battery would get New Year's leave from Bristol. The Sgt-Major appealed to us not to let him down and no-one did. I was thus able to be home for Christmas 1916 and to report that my application for a commission had gone forward.

CHAPTER 6
221 BATTERY GOES OVERSEAS

From 29 June to 15 August 1914 the White City had hosted the Bristol International Exhibition consisting of English buildings through the ages, plus the large white pavilion. It was held in what was then Ashton Meadows and is now Greville Smyth Park next to the River Avon. It was taken over as soon as the exhibition ended and Hall found himself there on the brink of embarkation for overseas service. His diary recorded the detail of preparations to taken men and guns to the Western Front as well as bringing the battery up to full strength using experienced troops returned to Britain from overseas postings which was to delay Hall's departure for the front.

It was on Boxing Day 1916 when at the end of my overseas leave I re-joined my unit. It was eight o'clock at night when I arrived at Temple Meads station, Bristol. It was bitterly cold and raining hard. I had some difficulty in finding Ashton Gate Barracks until some civilians identified it with the White City an old exhibition ground. Then I was put on a tram car which took me to the doors.

A more miserable place than the White City it was impossible to conceive. The drives were a sea of churned up mud, the plaster ornamentation had fallen from the exhibition buildings and no trace of grass remained on the lawns. I found my battery in the Palace of Industry which accommodated two other batteries besides ourselves. Here amid baulks of timber, coils of rope, drums of oil, lifting tackle and gun stores of every description I found my colleagues, some huddled round the coke stoves while others, although it was still early, had already turned in and were lying uneasily in their blankets. The wind howled through the broken windows, swaying the electric lamps and causing them to cast strange moving shadows while water dripped continuously from the rotting roof.

Throughout the day men had been returning from leave and they continued to arrive well into the night; the parties round the stoves broke and reformed again while we discussed what had happened in our absence and what the future had in store. It seemed that shortly after I had left Lydd to go on leave, a party of men were detailed to draw stores from Woolwich Arsenal while the remainder proceeded direct to Ashton Gate Barracks.

The Woolwich party had arrived at Bristol just before Christmas bringing with them the huge masses of stores round which we were grouped – twenty four loads in all. They also had drawn the guns. This was the main topic of conversation. They had been issued with, not the six inch howitzers we had expected but the larger eight inch howitzers which, even now, with their attendant tractors, stood outside in the mud on the so called parade ground. Like the rest of the new arrivals, I made my way to see the ordnance and there in the darkness of the December night saw for the first time the monstrous guns we were to serve.

With the guns were four of the most grotesque looking contrivances imported from America, the Holt Caterpillar Tractors.[1] These and twenty four lorries were henceforth attached to the battery as our ammunition column. With the vehicles were some sixty Army Service Corps men[2] under a Lieutenant. These and an Artificer Sergeant and Artificer Gunner completed our establishment. We were now a complete unit of 4 guns, 4 tractors, 24 lorries and some 170 all ranks. Of the guns nothing too bad could be said. *"Wait until you have tried to fight them" "bloody big things with traction engine wheels" "totally unworkable"* were a few of the remarks and Sergeants with experience in the field wondered how on earth the monsters would be manned. With such unpleasant thoughts we passed a restless night.

On the face of it the eight inch howitzer was merely a larger edition of the standard six inch of which we were by now well acquainted. It fired a 200lb shell a distance of 12,000 yards against the lighter guns 100lbs 9,500 yards. There was in the field a 9.2 inch howitzer which fired a 280lb shell but this was of a totally different design being completely immobile (it had to be erected for firing and dismantled for travelling). In addition it was loaded by means of a derrick. The 8 inch howitzer was an attempt to combine the firing capacity of the 9.2 with the mobility of the 6 inch.

In this the designers were largely successful but only at the expense of an enormous amount of human effort on the part of the gun crews but seem to have been completely ignored from their calculations.

In the first place there was the weight of the shells. A reasonably strong man could lift and stack 6 inch shells but 200 pounders were much too heavy to be lifted and had to be rolled into position and stood on their bases. In loading, since the shell could not be carried to the loading tray, the tray had to be brought to where the shells stood on end. It had then to be up-ended and a shell wriggled on to it. Shell-tray and its load then had to be carried by four men (instead of two) to the breech, where owing to the extra length of the projectile it could not be rested on the cradle but had to be supported during the ramming operations. Ramming home required three movements instead of two and here again four men were required. The greater width of the trail had two serious disadvantages, first back loading was impossible and side loading meant two of the loading numbers with their heavy burden walking over the trail, one step of eighteen inches upwards, two across the trail itself and a similar step down the other side, followed by a straight lift of a foot or more, a most laborious task. The second trouble affected the Gun Captain who was unable to operate the elevating wheel from his side of the gun and for each lay had actually to step inside the trail, a most dangerous job as if the gun were accidentally fired he would have been smashed to a pulp by the recoil. A further weakness was in the quick motion elevating gear, quite reliable in the case of the 6 inch howitzer it proved most uncertain with the larger gun and broke down even at drill in England. This fault threw upon the Gun Layer the arduous task of winding up the gun after every round. Even the cartridge men found their work far from being a sinecure as the charges instead of being packed twenty four to a box were supplied individually in long tin containers and in rapid action had all their work cut out in keeping up with the firing. Added to this was the heavier gear, the huge iron slatted wheels instead of the smooth wooden ones we had expected and the interminable heaving on drag ropes when the spade was well dug in for it was obvious from the first that there would be no case of throwing over the gun with the mere touch of a handspike.

Part of 221 Siege Battery in Bristol. Hall is top row first from left

With such a design much of the extra work was unavoidable but it could have been mitigated to some extent had extra staff been supplied. If at drill ten men were allocated to fight a six inch howitzer surely fifteen or sixteen would not have been unreasonable for a gun twice the size. Instead of this we were allowed one extra man per gun, four for the battery.

After reveille on December 27 we made our way to the ablutions shed, a most primitive arrangement, to find that of the fifty taps all but three were frozen solid. The severe winter of 1916–17 had set in. Then we examined the gun stores. Corporal Tudhope had been to Woolwich and had drawn the Observers' stores. There were a large number of boxes to be unpacked and the contents examined. There were four directors, the same number of prismatic compasses, a variety of telescopes, plane tables, measuring chains, drawing instruments, glass headed pins and various other items. Meantime the Gunners and Signallers were busy sorting out their respective stores and soon got them in some sort of order. In the afternoon the CO took us for a route march, probably the best thing to do to keep our minds off the wretched guns.

The next day was similarly occupied. In fact, route marches were the order of the day and the pleasantest part of our stay at Bristol. Always in light order we marched over the pleasant roads of Clifton round by the wonderful Avon Gorge and in some measure recaptured the spirit of Ewshot.

With New Year's Day came changing into active service kit. We exchanged our boots for those of a stouter kind, handed in our kit-bags, spare uniform and cleaning material and were issued with gas masks, steel helmets and field dressings.

But behind everything remained the problem of the guns and how they were to be manned. All sorts of rumours were flying about Major Wyllie seemed to be doing everything to keep our minds away from them but the fact was known to every officer and man – our work was to be doubled if not trebled.

Eventually some sort of gun drill was held but only in a half-hearted manner and this confirmed our worst suspicions. Men could not work continuously and twenty-four hour shifts were the recognised thing in the artillery. But how were such shifts to be maintained? Here was no case of ten men being allocated for the work of five; the full team of eleven men would be hard pressed to fight the eight inch howitzer. How then could the eighty eight men required for double manning be raised out of a total complement of just over a hundred making allowances for Signallers, BCA's, cooks, servants and the battery staff? The rank and file talked the matter over among themselves, in the Sergeants' mess the problem was discussed daily; it was known that Major Wyllie and his officers were deeply concerned with the problem. Then one thing emerged the CO determined that at all costs reliefs must be worked probably on the basis of eight men to a team. To do this all the staff would have to be pruned to the bone. The second line Signallers would have to go back to the guns as well as any officers, servants, clerks, cooks, assistants and odd job men that could possibly be spared.

I was now wondering how I personally should be affected. It had been taken for granted that the battery was to have three BCA's but could this number now be justified? Corporal Tudhope was, of course, certain and Bdr Shepherd had gone over to the guns weeks before. That left McHugh and myself, one of us might well be dropped but who?

Then there was another aspect. The large influx of ex-overseas NCO's had made the battery over strength and we were not allowed to carry any surplus overseas. (Similarly units were always brought up to strength before proceeding overseas.)

The order came on January 7. Six men were to be dropped. Four of these were very bad characters; the opportunity to get rid of them could not be missed. The other two were Gunner Mason, a very decent chap who applied for a commission in the Royal Army Veterinary Corps, and myself.

I was astonished at this order. Did this mean that my acceptance for a Commission was so imminent that it was not worthwhile taking me overseas? I might have asked the CO. Had I known what was in store for me I should have asked, nay begged that I should go overseas with him, in any capacity if necessary, and willingly withdrawing my application for a commission if that was an obstacle to this. As it was I handed in my overseas kit to the Quartermaster's Stores and was now merely attached to this battery and not part of it. We six continued to take part in the parades and that was all. The on January 14 1917 221 Siege Battery left for France. We six accompanied the battery to the station in case anyone fell out at the last moment when we would have taken the place of the absentee but alas no-one did. We said goodbye to McHugh, Turner, Corpl Tudhope, Malloy, Bob Hickton and to the other friends I had made during the past six months. Then the train moved out of the station and we six were left standing on the platform. That wonderful comradeship I had made for the first time in my life was severed forever.

1   In 1914 RGA batteries sent to France were horse drawn but supported by 3 ton Army Service Corps lorries to transport gun platforms and ammunition. In 1915 brigades formed of two batteries were sent to France with FWD tractors which replaced horses though larger guns were pulled by steam tractors. All batteries that landed in France after April 1915 were drawn by Holt Caterpillars imported from America – see Young, Michael *Army Service Corps 1902-1918* Leo Cooper, Barnsley (2000) p85.

2   The Imperial War Museum Sound Collection, piece 10646, contains interviews with Alfred Woodcock who served as a Holt Tractor driver with Mechanical Transport Section, Army Service Corps attached to siege batteries of Royal Artillery in GB and on Western Front, 1915-1918 including 81 Siege Battery, Gnr Hall's final unit.

CHAPTER 7
POSTED TO 242 SIEGE BATTERY

*S*ydney Hall's disappointment at not going overseas with 221 Siege Battery was clear but that was the nature of deployment of troops, they went where they were needed. On being sent to 242 Siege Battery he makes specific reference to conscripted men. Earlier we encountered the Derby scheme which was a step towards the controversial measure of conscription but it did not produce the number of volunteers needed by the War Office. In January 1917 the Military Service Act was introduced and thus all British males were now regarded as conscripted provided that, on 2 November 1915, they were aged between 18 and 41 and resided in Great Britain (excluding Ireland) and were unmarried or widowers. Conscripted men were no longer given a choice of which service, regiment or unit they joined (the exception being that if a man preferred the navy it got priority over other services); married men were encompassed by the Act on 25 May 1916.

There were difficulties even with this Act in force. 93,000[1] men did not report when called up, leading to many prosecutions. 748,587 men claimed some form of exemption and these would be heard by tribunals. In addition were the 1,433,827 already in a war occupation or those who were ill or who had already been discharged on these grounds.

We six men returned to Ashton Gate Barracks and, in accordance with instructions reported to the Camp Commandant's office where the Regimental Sergeant Major at once informed us that we had all been posted to 242 Siege Battery and were to report to the OC[2] of that unit forthwith. Mason and I looked at one another. We protested; surely there was some mistake, our applications for commissions were being considered and we presumed that was the reason for being dropped from 221 Battery. The RSM gave us a hearing. He replied that there was nowhere to put troops except in a Siege Battery. 242 was under strength and there we should have to go; still, he would consult the adjutant. He returned a few minutes later. The adjutant knew all about our applications which had gone forward in the ordinary way. There was no mistake about our allocation to 242 Siege Battery; we were to remain with that unit until we heard further. Were we to go overseas with them? Yes, unless otherwise directed. There was nothing to do except obey orders.

We made our way to the exhibition hall where 242 Siege Battery was housed, reluctantly for we knew that battery by repute. We reported to the Sergeant-Major and told him our history. We also mentioned that I was a trained BCA and Mason a qualified Gun Layer. The facts were duly noted and we were detailed, myself to No. 1 sub-section, Mason and another man to No. 3 and rest to 2 and 4, thus separated we joined our new colleagues.

The new battery was very different from the one we had left. In the first place the average age was a good deal younger. 242 Battery had been formed on the Isle of Grain on the

Medway only a month later than 221 but while my old battery was formed mainly by the tail end of Derby men, 242 was frankly all conscripts. It was commanded by Major Tomasson[3] whom I understand had formerly been a Staff Captain. A short podgy man with red puffy cheeks he spoke with a peculiar high pitched voice. His second in command Captain Sanderson[4] was unlike his superior officer in every way, tall and broad, with a voice like a bull, a swaggering gait and a blustering manner. The subaltern in charge of No. 1 gun, 2/Lt Tharpe was a pimply faced youth with ginger hair. No. 2 gun was controlled by 2/Lt Horner, a man with white hair and a stooping gait nearer fifty than forty I should say. The other two subs were the usual type of British officer, about 25 years of age and wore the short moustache affected at that time. None of the subalterns had been overseas.

Sgt–Major Cavalier[5] was a small man with a sharp grating voice and a sarcastic manner. He had a wonderful figure and his walk was almost suggestive of a ballet dancer. If he did not actually wear corsets he certainly looked as if he did. Formerly a Sergeant in 81 Siege Battery he had been promoted in the field to his present rank and sent home to form a siege battery.

As for the NCO's the battery had been formed on totally different lines from 221. I have referred to the constant drafting of ex-overseas NCO's which began at Portkil Fort and continued until Lydd (and incidentally was responsible for the eventual surplus which led to my being dropped). But in 242 Siege Battery there was one ex-overseas Sergeant and that was all. It appeared that within two weeks of enlistment the first Bombardiers had been promoted from the ranks, from these Acting Corporals were selected a fortnight later, six weeks from the date of joining up the chevrons. Sergeants Peake, Rees, Sturt and Rowbottom were all promoted in this way. The promotions were made before technical training had begun with the result that we carried a number of Bombardiers who had actually failed at gun-laying.

The inevitable result of such a policy was a complete lack of confidence in the NCO's and a general feeling of envy and mistrust. This became intensified once the CO's intentions on running the battery became known. Like 221 Siege Battery eight inch howitzers had been drawn but Major Tomasson had decided that reliefs were out of the question. There was to be no departure from the rule of eleven men to a gun and the teams were to be selected forthwith. When I arrived the scheme was in full operation. We fell into sub-sections on parade, then the selected teams doubled to their respective guns. No attempt had been made to reduce the number of employed men and these left for the prescribed duties. This left about two dozen men on parade who were known as 'spare men' and were available for various fatigues. Any feeling of comradeship that might have existed was effectively destroyed by such an arrangement. A superiority complex developed among the members of the gun teams who regarded the spare men with contempt. The call *"fall in all spare men"* which I grew so much to hate was heard even before the battery went overseas. In the eleven days between my transfer and embarkation no fewer than three piquets had fallen to my lot. This disagreeable job consisted in marching up and down Bristol streets, visiting public houses, seeing that all the troops were sober and generally maintaining order. I was very much depressed at this time; I had left all my friends and was to go overseas with a party of men I cordially disliked. Most of my previous training had been done in the company of officers and educated men; here I was forced to associate with the dregs of the battery and be at every man's beck and call with the certain knowledge that soon matters would be infinitely worse. To add to the irony of the situation I was receiving letters from home congratulating me on having achieved the first steps towards attaining a commission.

There was however one bright spot in those dark days. One day tramping alone on the Bristol streets and I discovered a YMCA. A notice invited soldiers to enter and a wonderful welcome I received. There were but few people about and often I had the place to myself. The resident secretary and his wife took me into the private part of the building and gave me tea. I had several meals with them; in fact I spent the whole of my fast dwindling time there. On my last day there was a small gathering. There was a young lady who played the piano divinely. All realised that this was no occasion for levity but when I asked for Chopin's *Marche Funebre* she broke down and was unable to finish. Then the secretary called for prayers that it should please Almighty God delivery me safe from the ordeal I was to undergo.

The following day we left for France.

---

1   Figures quoted from The Long, Long Trail website.

2   The CO 242 Siege Battery in July-August 1917 was Major John Noble MC, later Maj-Gen Sir John Noble GCMG, KCVO, KBE, CB, MC (1893-1970). Papers in the Liddle Hart Centre for Military Archives, King's College, London. Reference code: GB99 KCLMA Kennedy, J N.

3   Major James Frederick Hugh Tomasson, of Woodthorpe House, Nottingham, CO 242 Siege Battery RGA. His first theatre of war was France and Flanders from 30 March 1915. From 1898 to 1939 the Tomasson Family lived in Woodthorpe House, his father being Captain William Hugh Tomasson – later Sir William (1858-1922) who had previously been an army officer, and had fought in the Anglo-Zulu War in 1879. In 1881 he was a Police Superintendent in Mansfield and become Chief Constable of Nottinghamshire in 1892. When Sir William died suddenly in 1922, the house passed to his wife, Lady Eliza, and later to their son, Major J.F.H. Tomasson, who lived there throughout the 1930's with his wife and two daughters. Co-incidentally, in the Second World War Woodthorpe House was used as the Regimental HQ of 161 Mixed Heavy A.A. Regiment and the buildings were also used as a prisoner of war camp.

4   Captain Sanderson, second-in-command 242 Siege Battery RGA

5   9455 Sgt–Major A.J. Cavalier. His first theatre of war was France and Flanders from 5 March 1915.

CHAPTER 8
THE JOURNEY UP THE LINE

At last Sydney Hall was to go overseas. He describes the final preparations and in Major Tomasson we get one of Hall's many pen portraits of individuals with whom he served. Like thousands of troops he experienced the remarkable operation of crossing the channel via Folkestone under the protection of the Royal Navy in case German submarines were operating in those busy shipping lanes. Two more features of a soldier's life are mentioned – the overburdened transit camps around Boulogne and the tedium of guard duty – but getting the guns to the front takes a whole chapter as he describes what was an avoidable ordeal for the battery.

It was in keeping with 242 Siege Battery's reputation that our departure overseas should be marked with the maximum of ceremony, formality and red tape. A month previously my old battery had left Bristol for the Western Front via Folkestone. There was no secret about the matter – on the appointed day they packed up marched to Bristol station and so passed out of sight.

But such procedure would not do for Major Tomasson. The appointed day was announced in orders, the battery was confined to camp, there were parades and call-overs every few hours and when we were not checking and re-checking stores, the Major would have us lined up in the exhibition hall and lecture us for hours. How he loved to talk; I can see him now, standing on a pile of timber haranguing like a soap-box orator – the little podgy man with such an infinite belief in his own capabilities. We listened while he recounted the history of the war by land and sea and of the events that led up to it. Then he would tell us of the part that we were to play in the conflict, the care that would have to be taken to avoid observation, the work that was in store for us, of digging and heaving, of forced marches, the perils of the line, the need for implicit obedience to orders and, of course, the penalty for default. How I detested him then, he and his conscript Sergeants! His written orders were equally verbose. Foolscap sheets of closely written orders adorned the notice boards, how we were shortly to entrain for an *"unknown destination"*, the strictest marching order was to be maintained, the *"utmost circumspection"* to be exercised in writing home etc.

On January 24 an advance party left with the guns for an *"unknown destination"* which in their case turned out to be Southampton. From there they embarked for Havre thence to make their way by road to Boulogne to join up with the main force.

Our turn came the following night January 25. At 7pm we paraded and after much checking and re-checking solemnly marched to Temple Meads station in perfect silence and under strict instructions that no lights were to be shown or smoking allowed – this in the main streets of Bristol on a busy evening. If ever a man was utterly devoid of any sense of humour it was Major Tomasson! Once aboard the train the CO himself saw that all the windows were shut and blinds drawn. So at last we steamed out of the station. At midnight we came to a halt; we had reached our *"unknown destination"*.

Well, it didn't take us long to recognise Folkestone Harbour, bleak enough on the quay that winter night with the wind howling and the waves dashing against the pier. We were lined up for a considerable time while the officers took stock of the situation, then we were marched to a hotel on the promenade, bare and desolate, that had been requisitioned for the passing troops. *"Have a sleep,"* said the Sergeant-Major *"God knows when you will get the next."* But sleep was difficult on the bare boards in the cold and draughty rooms and we were pleased when morning came.

The hotel and the quay were separated from the town by a high fence of barbed wire. Here, like prisoners, we awaited the boat that was to take us to France. On the quay stood a YMCA hut where tea and biscuits were served and where the troops could write their last real letters home, for all future correspondence would be censored. Every hour or so a bell would sound and a religious service was held. During the few hours I was in Folkestone I participated in half a dozen or so and I suppose most of us did the same. It was a memorable sight, the hut packed with men mostly on their knees praying, the months of training and the preparations were over. The unknown lay in front of us – there was nothing left but to pray. For myself the strain was doubly felt for I felt so much alone. All my companies had left a month ago and I had made no friends in 242 Siege Battery. Although a new life was beginning I felt that this was the graveyard of all my ambitions for I realised even then that I should never hold a commission. I had no room for fear – my only emotion was a bitter, crushing disappointment.

At 2pm (January 26) the Sergeant-Majors had difficulty in keeping a check on their charges. At length we were lined up, the roll was called and in a few minutes we were marching up the gangway. As we embarked lifebelts were handed out and we followed our leader to a part of the deck where the whole battery seemed to occupy but little room in such a multitude. We cast off our equipment, donned the lifebelts and watched the shores of England recede from view.

There was nothing eventful about the voyage except that the sea was very rough and many were sick. So closely were we packed that the unfortunates were unable to reach the ships side and vomited where they stood. The state of the ship when we reached France can be imagined. Two destroyers escorted us and could be seen racing sometimes ahead, sometimes astern, now towering above our ship later to wallow in the trough of the sea. But no hostile craft was sighted and in due course we reached Boulogne where we discarded our lifebelts, took up our equipment and disembarked.

There was a good deal of confusion at first but eventually the various units were sorted out and went their different ways. For our part we marched through the main streets of Boulogne, then up a steep hill to a high plateau where a large number of dreary looking tents showed up against the thick white snow. Here we were addressed by a Staff Officer – our own officers were not much in evidence at this stage, presumably they had gone to their own quarters. This camp, which was known at St Martin's was to be our quarters for the present and must not be left without permission – we must remember that we were on active service – must not write home for three days – and so on. Then we were turned over to BSM Cavalier who detailed us to our tents, twenty men to each. A party went off to draw blankets and these were rolled out on the snow until distributed.

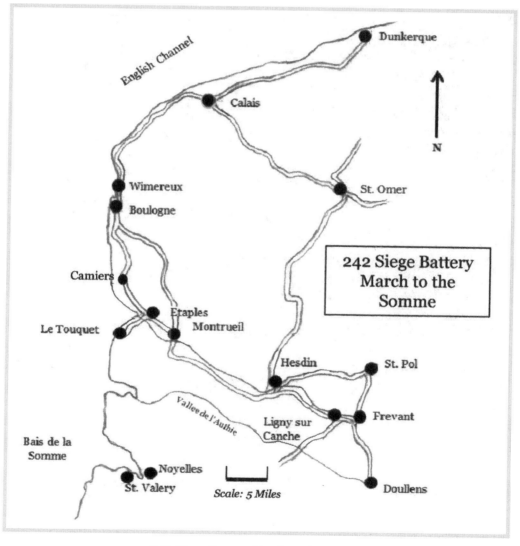

242 Siege Battery March to the Somme

Conditions at St Martin's Camp were deplorable. It was bitterly cold and there were no warm rations. There was a canteen of sorts but they had sold out of food and had no water to make tea. As a matter of fact it transpired that St Martin's Camp had been frozen up for some days. We passed an uneasy night.

In the morning (January 27) there was a little lukewarm tea made from melted snow and some bully beef and biscuits but no water was available for washing. We hung about the tents wondering what was to happen next.

Then we were told that the guns had arrived from Le Havre and were now standing in the Market Place. A guard was to be mounted at once, three men and a Bombardier. I was one of those selected.

At ten o'clock in the morning we four took up our equipment and marched down the hill to the Market Place where we found the four guns. A sentry was posted and the rest of us went to fix up a guard room. The Market Place was full of bales of flax, each about four feet square and these kept arriving in queer looking carts throughout the day. Mostly they were stacked three bales high but we found a spot where for some reason the two uppermost bales had been removed and this being the most sheltered place we clambered on top of the remaining bales and used it as our guard room.

Never before or since have I seen such a guard. We were dirty and unshaven when we were mounted and we remained on duty thirty six hours during which time we never removed our equipment. Whether by orders of the CO because the NCO in charge had the wind up I do not know but for the whole time everything we possessed was on our backs even to the extent of a couple of blankets worn bandolier fashion, i.e. like a horse collar round our necks. I suppose we received some cold rations of a kind but have no recollection. I only remember pacing to and fro trying to keep small boys away from the guns. Then as night drew on, the boys went home and the traffic ceased but still, the guard continued. It was, I remember, my turn off duty 10pm to 2am I had crawled on to the flax, doubled up for there was no room to lie down. My mess tin and steel helmet were digging in my back but out of sheer exhaustion I slept on. It seemed but minutes ere I was aroused and, rubbing my eyes saw the stars shining against the clear sky and felt the nip of the winter wind. Then I stamped my frozen feet and resumed my vigil on the guns.

At 10am January 28 our tour of duty should have come to an end but no relief arrived and so in the absence of orders the guard continues. In the afternoon Capt Sanderson arrived critical at first at our dishevelled appearance but more sympathetic when he learnt how long we had been on duty and left promising that we should be relieved as soon as possible. The new guard arrived 4pm with a spare man to guide us back to quarters. The men were in good fettle clean shaven and dressed in light order without vast amount of kit with which we were burdened. They quickly took over the guard and our long spell of duty came to an end.

We did not return to St Martin's Camp but were led to a converted down-town warehouse bearing the name of Vidors Rest Billets. Conditions had, it appeared, become so bad at St

Martin's that the whole camp had been evacuated and the troops accommodated in various centres in Boulogne itself.

Vidors was a cheerful place, warm and cosy. Stoves were burning brightly, a canteen at one end of the warehouse was doing a roaring trade in hot drinks and cigarettes, while in an annex was a place for ablutions and a latrine, luxuries denied us since we left Bristol. We threw off our equipment, sat down to a belated dinner, washed and shaved and finally turned in for a well-earned sleep.

Next day (January 29) we learned of the trouble with the guns. It seemed that on their way from Havre they had run into a lot of mud. On delivering the guns at Boulogne the drivers had taken the tractors to a parking place without attempting to clean them and had left them there for the night. A sharp frost had set in with the result that, in addition to the working parts being frozen up, the mud, hard as cement and over a foot thick. Our job was to thaw out the tractors and a formidable task it turned out to be. With pickaxe and crowbar, with hammer and cold chisel, we attacked the frozen mass while blow lamps were brought into action and gallons of petrol burnt in attempts to liquidify the mud. Not before several grease caps and minor working parts had been knocked off were the tractors free from their clinging mantel and it was not until later afternoon of the January 30 that the last Caterpillar, after much shaking and groaning, was able to move forward under her own power. That night fires were kept burning under the tractors to prevent any further freeze up.

The distance from Boulogne to the Somme front was a matter of seventy miles. It was the usual practice to convey siege batteries by train to railhead and I do not know why this method was not adopted. Rumour had it that Major Tomasson had volunteered to travel by road in order to test the mobility of the guns; certainly there was no question of urgency as the battery was not brought into action for some time after our arrival. Moreover the roads were known to be ice-bound and perilous.

Like all Major Tomasson's instructions, the Order of March was most meticulous. One sub-section was detailed to accompany the guns each day the rest of the battery was going by convoy. The convoy party were to march behind the lorries until well clear of the town when they were allowed to ride on top of the stores. They would make for the first halting place where billets would be chosen for the night and there would await the arrival of the slower moving gun party. The gun party would march all the way so many behind each ordnance. Next day another escort would be chosen and the battery would move forward in like manner and so on until the front was reached.

It was natural, if unfortunate for me, that 'A' sub-section should act as gun escort for the first stage. After he had read the orders Sgt Peake came bustling about full of his own importance, giving instructions and talking to his cronies. I well mark his words *"Now remember everything about these goons has to be doon at the dooble"*. I always loathed Peake with his pugnacious face and his foul Staffordshire accent but never more than at this moment.

On the early morning of January 31 the whole battery paraded outside Vidors Rest Billets.

Then the main party under Major Tomasson moved off at a smart pace, leaving Sgt Peake and some 30 men of 'A' sub-section to bring up the guns. First we made for the parking place where the tractors were preparing to start, then we accompanied them to the Market Place where we coupled up the four guns each to its own tractor. Then seven or eight men were detailed to follow each gun and at last we started off at an irregular pace, which seldom exceeded two miles an hour. Progress along the narrow streets of Boulogne was difficult but the greatest trouble arose when a bridge over a wide river outside the town had to be crossed. The piers were understood to be incapable of bearing the combined weight of gun and tractor so the only alternative was to uncouple the guns, send the tractors over first and draw the guns with long wire hawsers. In this way the weight of the two heavy objects never fell on the same pier. It was exhausting and dangerous work. The guns swung from one side to the other on the icy road, sometimes mounting the pavement and threatening to break over the parapet. Meantime the thirty of us were holding on like grim death forcing the piece to keep to its allotted path. Only one gun could be dealt with at a time and it was with a sigh of relief that the last gun was brought over the bridge, the sharp turn safely negotiated, the guns re-coupled and our long journey resumed. We were now clear of Boulogne but several hours had been lost on the bridge.

Now the trek began in earnest, we resumed our places behind our respective guns, an interval of 100 yards was maintained and the tractors coughed and spluttered as we slowly made our way along Route Nationale No. 1 on our way to the front.

An 8 inch gun and Holt Tractor of 61st Siege Battery RGA at Saintes, near Brussels, Belgium 1919. (Image ref AL/158.18 Courtesy of Firepower Museum, Woolwich)

The Holt track-laying tractor or Caterpillar as it was familiarly called, was a thing to be remembered. The size of a traction engine with a single wheel in front, it was driven forward by iron plates mounted on an endless chain, similar to the now familiar tank. The noise it made was deafening and the vibration so terrific that it always seems to be falling to pieces. When the load became too heavy, it would rear like a horse the single front wheel lifting a couple of feet in the air, only to fall again with a sickening thud. Its consumption of petrol was enormous and flames would belch out of it chimney. There was no seat for the drivers but they were partly protected from the elements by a piece of corrugated iron extending over the top of the whole contraption. At best the tractor was capable of three or even four miles an hour but with the terrible conditions prevailing at that time it rarely reached half that speed and it was its very slowness that made the first day's march an agony never to be forgotten.

As on guard four days previously, full kit was carried including a couple of blankets. Over our ordinary uniform we wore first a leather jerkin and then our great coat, the pockets bulging with as much underwear as could be crammed into them. Then from our right shoulder hung the haversack crammed to capacity attached to which was a muslin bag, holding a pound of biscuits and a tin of bully beef (our iron rations). From our left shoulder was suspended the water-bottle and a bandolier, the whole being kept in position by a leather belt which carries our mess tin at the back. Inside the mess tin was an enamel mug which rattled at every step. The greatest bugbear however was the huge roll which we wore across the bandolier. This consisted of a couple of blankets wrapped round with a waterproof sheet. Inside the blankets were a couple of shirts, vest and pants, spare socks and any personal belongings. This great horse collar as it was called forced us to keep our heads on one side while the other equipment prevented us from keeping our arms to our sides or swinging them while marching. In addition to these we carried a steel helmet over the left shoulder and a gas mask over all the other equipment.

And so we followed the guns, mile after mile, hour after hour, not at a smart pace that even with full marching order might have sent the blood coursing through our veins but at the soul destroying crawl of little more than a mile an hour, our heads held at a grotesque angle, arms stuck out from our bodies, unable to sing or talk owing to the deafening roar of the tractors. Not that we wished to sing; we were too dispirited.

No halt was called for meals. A few biscuits were passed round but the dreadful crawl continued. Night came upon us. We staggered against one another cursing when a lurch from a colleague dislodged our steel helmet or set our mess tins rattling. Our clothes were sticking to us yet our feet were numb with cold, while the pain in our necks seemed intolerable. Still on we went – we knew that we had fallen behind schedule yet the pace of the tractors could not be accelerated.

As night advanced, the tractors drew further apart. I was following the second gun and, in the darkness, it was impossible to tell how far we had fallen behind the leader, nor had we any knowledge as to how the rear guns were faring. We were conscious, however, of ascending a fairly steep hill when our tractor started misfiring, spluttered horribly and finally stopped dead. The driver cursed and tried in vain to restart the engine but the steep gradient and the slippery state of the road proved too much. Help must be sought.

A Gunner was sent forward to find the Army Service Corps officer who, with Capt Sanderson, was somewhere ahead with No. 1 gun. The first tractor, it appeared, had taken the hill comfortably and was preparing to make the descent on the other side when it was decided to uncouple and go to the assistance of the cripple. In the darkness, the leading tractor could be seen cautiously picking her way to our rescue. When the breakdown was reached the two tractors were coupled together with stout chains but their combined efforts were unable to move the gun.

Meantime the two rear guns had reached the foot of the hill and their drivers leaning of the breakdown stopped their tractors to await orders. No. 3 tractor was now called upon to help but even with three tractors coupled together it was impossible to shift our gun; moreover the grotesque objects straddled across the road completely blocking all communications. Capt Sanderson was now for abandoning No. 2 gun until morning and going forward with the others. He had in fact sent No. 1 tractor forward to pick up her gun but while this move was successful, it was found that No. 3 Caterpillar was unable to move in either direction. That settled the matter and even before the driver of No. 4 tractor had reported that his engine was misfiring badly, it was decided that no further progress was possible and that quarters must be found for the night.

A more desolate spot could not be imagined. There seemed to be no building in sight and we sat down moodily in the road wondering what would happen next and seizing the opportunity of removing the strangling horse collar and endeavouring to straighten our necks. After some time Capt Sanderson showed up flashing his electric torch and calling out *"follow me boys"*, he led the way down a narrow lane which we had missed in the darkness. At the end of the lane the Captain broke into an isolated farm building which proved to be nearly full of hay and farm implements – a truly wretched place, seemingly incapable of holding half a dozen men let alone the thirty of us. So bad it was that several Gunners declined to occupy the hut at all and started unrolling their blankets in preparation for sleeping outside. When Capt Sanderson saw what was happening he was furious and packed them inside the building by sheer force of muscle. *"If you stop outside you'll freeze to death,"* he exclaimed and this was probably no exaggeration.

During the march I had been next to Gnr Levinson, a young Jew and we two had been among the first to enter the miserable billet. He found a precarious perch on the hay very near the roof and very generously pulled me up to share his narrow pitch – one of the very kind actions I ever experienced at the hands of this wretched battery. Curled up my head touching my knees I slept – my lot, though bad, being preferable to that of the unfortunate four who had been selected for guard duty and were on sentry go on that steep and slippery hill.

There was no-one to rouse us in the morning (February 1) but we were all very cramped and hungry and left the hut to take stock of the situation. There at the crest of the hill stood No. 1 gun coupled to its tractor and ready to continue its journey. Two broken down tractors were hitched to No. 2 gun about half way up the hill, while the last Caterpillar and the remaining two guns remained at the foot where we had left them the night before. The vicinity however did not seem so desolate as on the previous night. A little beyond the point where the leading gun had halted, a by-road was seen leading to a small village, while, at the road junction stood an estaminet and a barn appeared a large advertisement for Chocolat Menier and a blue direction plaque bearing the words 'Lacres La Verte Vois – Route Nationale No. 1 – Boulogne 24km'.

So we had covered a matter of 15 miles on the first day, nothing very brilliant but under what conditions. Authority had so far not put in an appearance so we all trooped into the estaminet and regaled ourselves with coffee and cognac and later some homemade brown bread. Still further along the main road was a fairly large camp, where, had we but known it accommodation for the night was available. It was here at that moment that Capt Sanderson was seeking assistance.

Later the Transport Officer put in an appearance and was able to diagnose the trouble with his Caterpillars. Nos. 1 and 4 tractors had been left with their engines running all night and, with some adjustment, could be made ready to continue their journey. Even so they could not be trusted to pull the guns up the hill and about nine o'clock No. 4 Caterpillar could be seen making her way slowly and cautiously to the summit, hugging the grass verge all the way. The two middle tractors, helpless cripples, stone cold and frozen up, had to be abandoned to the Army Service Corps experts while the Transport Officer sent to St. Pol for replacements.

At ten o'clock Capt Sanderson had obtained his assistance and appeared at the head of a hundred or so men loaned by the nearby camp, complete with drag ropes and crowbars. We joined the throng and hooking up No. 2 gun had no difficulty in hauling her to the summit where No. 4 tractor took her in tow. The remaining guns were a bigger job as they had to be man-handled the whole of the way but, with so many helpers, the task was accomplished without undue strain.

Capt Sanderson's original intention as to remain at Lacres until the replacement tractors had been obtained and then to continue the journey with all four guns.

Accordingly the ordnance was neatly parked on the roadside and a fresh guard mounted. There was nothing for the rest of us to do but hang about Lacres and its estaminet.

For the night of February 1 new and better billets had been found in a barn and for once, we slept soundly. In the morning Sgt Peake showed himself in a very different light. The first man to rise, he was helping the cook to prepare breakfast. Not content with this he, actually served the meal to us while we were still in our blankets. A comic song of the period had it *"We never get up in the morning till the Sergeant brings our breakfast to bed"* and this was actually being done for us by Sgt Peake of all people. Some of his detachment had said *"you never know what Sgt Peake will do next"* and this proved to be the case. But Peake and I never liked one another and this was the only kindness I received at his hands.

There was some delay in securing the relief tractors from St. Pol and Capt Sanderson now decided to send the two leading guns forward, leaving the others to follow when transport could be obtained. At 10am (February 2) a couple of lorries arrived with 'B' sub-section who were taking over from us for the next stage of the journey. The men alighted, some to escort the leading guns while the others remained at Lacres awaiting the tractors. For ourselves our spell of duty was over so, gathering up our belongings we boarded the lorries and we soon speeding along the pleasant roads of France to Maresquel where the battery awaited our arrival.

Maresquel was a nondescript looking place with a large village green. The battery had taken possession of a barn, a very poor construction of wattle and daub that is laths covered with mud, very cold and draughty, particularly where the mud coating had fallen away. The scene was animated enough. French peasants bustled about and the sound of the animals was pleasant to the ear. On the village green a company of French soldiers had lighted fires and were warming up their tins of preserved rations. Our men were fraternizing and exchanging our tins of bully beef for their bottles of wine, both parties being satisfied with the deal.

Our cooks were having the worst time. Everything was frozen; the meat was being attacked with axes and flying off in chips, while potatoes were a crystalline mass. There was the inevitable shortage of water. Dinner was served at three and only half cooked but we realised that we were lucky in getting anything to eat at all.

Late that night two guns arrived from Lacres, the escort very tired and bad tempered. They had, however, been spared one torment – the terrible horse collar was no longer worn, nor was it resumed for the rest of the journey. By being first 'A' sub-section had the worst of the deal.

We remained at Maresquel a couple more days and Major Tomasson saw to it that we were well occupied the whole time. Gun drill, physical exercises and, in particular, route marches were the order of the day.

The remaining two guns were brought up from Lacres by two new tractors on the afternoon of February 5 and we were ordered to pack up in readiness for the resumption of the journey the following morning.

The next stage of the journey (February 6) was not particularly interesting nor fatiguing for 'C' sub-section, who formed the escort. The main body rode most of the way and we halted at a somewhat sinister looking village called Ligny-Sur-Canche. Here the presence of the line became apparent. As we advanced distant rumblings could be heard. This became louder until the reports of the heavier guns could be distinguished above the general hub-hub. It was evening when we arrived and we had our first sight of the firing line by night, a spectacle that had a peculiar fascination on all who witnessed it. The ever changing outline of gun flashes quivering as the field batteries carried on their night firing the sudden bright periods when the larger guns opened out and the streams of unparalleled brilliance when, on occasions, an ammunition dump caught fire.

Ligny-sur-Canche had that taut expectant atmosphere of a forward village. There were of course no lights, the villagers always seemed to talk in whispers, soldiers and civilians viewed each other with suspicion. There had been so many tales of spies floating around and what business had these civilians so near the line anyway? From the peasants' point of view we were foreigners and yet their safety depended upon the British. Could we be relied upon to protect them or would we withdraw as we had done before, leaving them to the mercy of the Boche.

There was, however, one touch of home life at Ligny. There was a chateau in the neighbourhood and we were invited by the proprietress to make ourselves at home. We did so and I have a shadow recollection of our crowding into a large and ornate drawing room, some of us sitting on the settee and the others writing letters on a carved table. There was a little old lady in black who spoke to some of us, though what she said I have forgotten, if I ever knew – it was all so strange.

That night we were billeted in a barn and the gun escort party arrived in the small hours of the morning. After breakfast on February 7 we again moved forward.

The last part of the journey to the front proved more trying. 'D' sub-section formed the gun escort and were soon left behind. Our blankets were carried but there was no transport available for the men, some lorries having been detailed to draw ammunition. Our course as first due east to the town of Frevent, after which we turned southwards following the valley of the River Authie until we reached Doullens, a pleasant town but one which has rather painful memories. Doullens was a headquarters of some sort and abounded in Staff Officers, every other building being marked with flags and symbols indicating the functions of the great men who lived there and conducted the war from the comparative safety of eighteen miles from the front line. We were pretty well fagged when we reached the town and had still a dozen miles to go. Nevertheless we had to march to attention through the town and give the *"eyes right"* on several occasions, which did not improve our tempers. A steep hill beyond the town did not make things any easier. Once clear of Doullens we turned east again, left the main road and finished the journey on country lanes badly cut up by heavy traffic and difficult going. In the evening we reached our destination, the village of Courcelles-au-Bois. We were now 'up the line' although not yet in the actual battery position. The lorries retired to some place of shelter and we were directed to some Nissen huts where we immediately went to sleep. As usual the gun party arrived much later and in an absolutely exhausted condition.

That virtually was the end of the journey. The battery position lay a mile or so ahead of the village but the guns could not be brought up until the following evening.

Major Tomasson evidently thought the occasion called for further speechmaking. It was the morning of February 8 when we formed a hollow square to hear the great man declaim.

First he referred to the trek from the Boulogne. He spoke of hardships and praised the way we had overcome them (a little less talk and more riding would have been better I thought). *"And now,"* he said *"we are going into action – the battery position lay in front of us – but, there was a great secret about it – no, he would not tell us what it was, that we must find out for ourselves – but, having discovered the secret, we must guard it, yes even with our lives if need be."* He finished as usual by exhorting us to still greater efforts, the future of civilisation depended upon us and so on with the usual clap-trap of which he seemed to have an inexhaustible supply.

Then he passed us over to the Sergeant-Major and he seemed to swell with pride as the latter recited his orders *"Orders of the Day by Major H.G. Tomasson, R.G.A. commanding 242 Siege Battery R.G.A."*. The guns would be brought into action that night. Throughout the operation the strictest discipline must be maintained – no smoking or talking would be permitted – every action to be at the double. The tractors would bring up the guns at fixed intervals to the edge of the road and then withdraw, leaving the guns to be manhandled into position; Capt Sanderson to take charge of operations. Once in position a guard to be mounted, in addition, two men from each detachment must sleep on the gun. Stores and ammunition would arrive later and must be dealt with at once. Three shells and no more were to be kept fused (it was this rule that was to give us so much trouble later on). Finally there was a strange sounding instruction to the Signallers that they were always to enter the Observation Post *"by back door"* and to *"close it on leaving"*. As the Observation Post had not been chosen at the time and when selected it turned out to be a shell-hole, strict compliance was difficult. Nevertheless the order was repeated daily for a week.

As soon as it was dark we left the huts and marched to the battery position there to await the arrival of the guns.

CHAPTER 9
THE CONCEALED POSITION

The artillery had a critical role in battle but were vulnerable to counter-battery fire. Locating the enemy's guns was a constant task for spotters and for the Royal Flying Corps. Hall describes a very effectively camouflaged position created by another battery illustrating the lengths that might be taken to conceal a position. As with other areas of warfare, camouflage techniques developed during the war and utilised the skills of artists and other imaginative and innovative people. As we will see in Hall's account of March 1918, once spotted, the effect of shelling on a battery position could be devastating. Mention is made of the front moving forward. At this time, the Battle of the Somme that had run from July to November 1916, had ended and the front was relatively quiet.

Major Tomasson may have been theatrical in his description of Courcelles but the battery position we were to occupy proved to be the most remarkable I have ever seen. Some way in front of the village was a hay-field. Dotted about were a dozen small round hay-stacks, while masses of ungathered hay lay about in untidy heaps. One might pass by without suspecting anything unusual but closer investigation revealed that while most of the stacks were genuine, four of them were dummies intended to conceal guns. The original occupiers of the position had erected four sets of framework and thatched them with straw so that they were indistinguishable from the genuine article. When in action the roof was made to fold back so that the guns could fire through the aperture, while in rear was a door to allow admission to the crew. So good was the deception that more than once I walked round a stack only to discover that this was a real one after all; the next stack was counterfeit. The untidy heaps of straw concealed dug outs, cartridge recesses, etc.

The position had it seemed been constructed by a six inch howitzer battery who had occupied it for a long time but with the Battle of the Somme the enemy had been driven back some distance which meant that they were forced to move forward and vacate their splendid position in favour of guns with a longer range.

As a matter of fact Courcelles was really too far back even for us. We could reach the enemy's lines at a range of 9,000 yards and we trained our guns on his sensitive points but we were never called upon to fire from the position. Perhaps it was just as well; the dummy stacks suitable for the smaller weapon proved a very tight squeeze for our larger guns and it was questionable whether the framework would have stood up to the shock of our gun-fire. The concealment had been so effective however that there was not a shell hole anywhere in the vicinity.

Our occupation of the position went according to plan. A tractor arrived at 10pm on February 9 with the first gun in tow. At the roadside it was unlimbered and withdrew leaving us to manhandle the gun into its emplacement. Capt Sanderson directed the work and was obviously in his element. Drag ropes were brought out and fifty men aside hauled the piece over the frozen ground right into the body of one of the dummy stacks, a party following in rear with spades and mauls obliterating the tell-tale tracks. The work was well timed and by eleven the first gun was safely housed and the second had made its appearance. The last gun was in position by 2am. Stores presented no difficulty but the shells weighing 200lbs each seemed heavier than we expected and for some little time we did not know how to handle them. The problem was solved by rolling them down planks from the tail boards of the lorries and then over the frozen ground to their places behind the guns. It is noteworthy that no attempt was made as yet to carry shells from the lorries. Dawn saw the work completed and we retired to our dugouts. Outwardly the hay field presented no change from the previous twelve hours but now, safely concealed and ready for action, were four heavy howitzers, while within that small compass a hundred men were sleeping after their exertions.

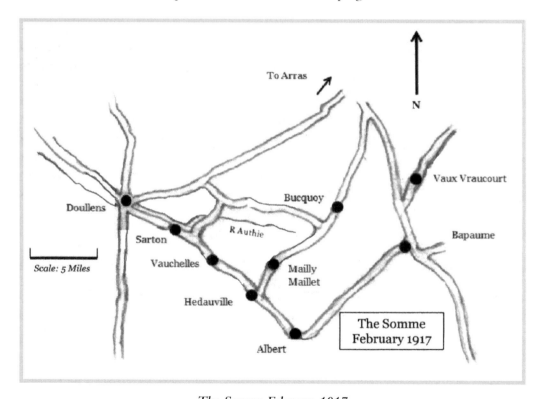

The Somme February 1917

We remained at Courcelles-au-Bois until the end of February, the ground being frozen the whole time. Water was scarce and could be allowed only for cooking. We washed and shaved in snow, quite easy when one got used to it. The dugouts proved very cold at night and we experienced agonies with cold feet. We slept in our clothes but were allowed to remove our boots at night. Incidentally these froze solid and had to be banged about before we could put them on in the morning. The men detailed for guard and those who, by Major Tomasson's orders, *"slept on the guns"* were colder still but in course of time this order was rescinded and never re-imposed.

But, considering all things, if this was active service, it seemed more monotonous and uncomfortable than perilous. Except for guard duty our nights were unbroken. We rose at six and breakfasted at seven, each man receiving a quarter of a loaf of bread, our rations for the day. Those who wished were allowed to dip one side of the bread in a pan of bacon fat, A rasher of bacon and a pint of tea completed the meal, which we ate in our dugouts. At eight we paraded in sub-sections, that is we crowded into what little room was left in the dummy stacks. Roll was called and the names of the sick taken, these being marched to the medical officer later in the day. Then the Orders of the Day were read out, all set out in meticulous detail and after this whole pages from the Manual of Military Law. 2/Lt Tharpe, who performed this duty dwelt on the gruesome portions prescribing death as the penalty for certain offences with evident sadistic enjoyment. After this it was gun drill and cleaning shells, gallons of perfectly good mineral oil being rubbed on the latter. Everyone shared in gun drills, spare men, Signallers and all but these did not share in the key posts and there was no attempt to train any more Gun Layers.

Gun drill continued until noon when an hour's break was allowed for dinner, a thin stew consisting of varying proportions of fresh and preserved meat and potatoes boiled in their jackets, after which the drill was resumed without intermission until five o'clock tea time. For this meal we had a pint of tea with cheese or butter and jam to be consumed with what was left of the morning bread. It was now dark but work was continued until 7pm by candle light after which we were dismissed. There was nothing to do now except lounge about in the dugouts until bedtime, for we were strictly confined to the battery position and were not allowed to go into the village or visit neighbouring batteries. It is little wonder that by 9 o'clock most of us had taken off our boots and were trying to settle for the night.

There was one exception to this rule when Sgt-Major Cavalier took a party of us to see what he called his *"old battery"*, which was in action in an orchard in the neighbourhood.[1] He was well received by his old colleagues who addressed him by his christian name. We watched the Gunners who seemed to be a happy enough crowd as they fought their six inch howitzers. Long afterwards I learnt this was 81 Siege Battery.[2]

I have often thought that we should have been happier if we had gone straight into action instead of the three weeks of interminable gun drill. We certainly learned to carry out the motions according to the book but except for the Sgt-Major and one of the Sergeants, none of the men had a scrap of battle experience. We had no confidence in the NCO's who, at every problem, would have to refer to their drill-books. Sgt-Major Cavalier was, of course, a practical man but completely under the thumb of the CO, while Capt Sanderson, left on his own, would probably have made a most efficient commander. He had already shown his skill at getting the guns into position but here again discipline forbade any interference with the Major's arrangements.

The interim allowed Major Tomasson to put his staffing arrangements into operation. He had already decided on four full gun teams and no reliefs. Leaving England about 120 strong our numbers had been reduced by the rigours of the march to under 100.[3] The twenty 'first line' Signallers were irreducible. It was now that the Major started creating extra posts. First he insisted on a double guard, a Bombardier and six men. Then there was the specialised staff, officers' servants, mess waiter, dispatch riders, battery cooks, cooks' mates, sanitary orderly and aeroplane spotter. There were four men in the BC Post, Sgt Rowbottom with a Bombardier and a Gunner to assist him in running the Battery Office, three men helping the Quartermaster, Bdr Boulton in charge of the ammunition and Bdr Maxton[4] always in a desperate hurry doing some special job for the CO, an expert on gas, on first aid, in fact on anything except the guns. There was also Bdr Pateman, the detested battery orderly whose job it was to assist the Sgt-Major with the parades and find men for the various jobs. It must not be supposed that these specialised jobs were sinecures; Major Tomasson saw that they were all kept busy but the point is that they did not help in the running of the guns.

Although the gun teams had been fixed in England long ago, there was still room for minor adjustments mainly in the loading numbers. For some time Sgt Peake had shown himself not too pleased with Gnr Levinson, though an excellent worker, had shown himself argumentative and quick tempered and the Sergeant had indicated that on a suitable opportunity he would be replaced by someone more tractable. The opportunity arrived on February 18 when we were told of an advanced position at Auchonvillers. All the Sergeants were to take their detachments forward to prepare gun emplacements leaving the spare men at Courcelles in case of emergencies and Peake decided to drop Levinson from the team and take me in his place.

Next day February 19 the selected teams with picks, shovels and earth rammers and, of course, with our personal equipment were taken in lorries to the new position.

---

1   As Sydney Hall's notes confirm, this was 81 Siege Battery which Hall was to join in December 1917 in the Ypres Salient.

2   The History of 81 Siege Battery (drafted by Hall in late 1918) confirms the presence of the battery in this position at this time.

3   All formations had theoretical strengths but seldom were they at full strength as men were killed, wounded, sick, on leave or away on training courses or other duties.

4   Bdr Maxton – possibly 174970 Bdr Maxton.

CHAPTER 10
IN ACTION ON THE SOMME

*A*s the Germans advanced westwards in 1914 the front line halted with the Germans holding key
*locations on the high ground north of the River Ancre. Their trenches ran south from Gommecourt,
in front of the fortified village of Serre, past Beaumont Hamel and nearby Hawthorn Ridge, along
to the site of the Newfoundland Memorial Park and then dropped to the river valley before rising
steeply to Thiepval Ridge now crowned by the Memorial to the Missing of the Somme. The hamlet
of Auchonvillers had been close to the front and shelled heavily and this is where Hall's battery was
now located. One casualty sustained here, Gnr Rees, cannot be identified though Hall's diary usually
recording names accurately. A search of variations similarly does not reveal him in Commonwealth
War Graves Commission records so either he is not recorded or, possibly, despite Hall's conclusion, he
may have survived his wounds. Sydney Hall also introduces the reader to the experience of treatment
of the wounded and the work of the medical services. He also qualified for a wound stripe despite
receiving what some may consider a minor wound. A further indication of the stage now reached on
the Western Front is reference to the Hindenburg Line. The Germans shortened their line by creating,
from late 1916, a new defensive position east of the Somme battlefield. Their Operation Alberich laid
waste to the ground they gave up – trees were cut down, roads damaged, water supplies polluted and
booby-traps laid for unsuspecting soldiers. From 14 March to 5 April their troops moved back and
occupied well constructed trenches with concrete blockhouses and immense barbed wire belts. Breaching
the Hindenburg Line would be a major challenge for the British army and later chapters describe Gnr
Hall's participation in this Herculean task.*

Auchonvillers lay some 2½ miles south east of Courcelles and was about 5,000 yards from
the enemy's lines. The village had been badly shelled and of the houses which lined its single
street, nothing was left but the cellars. The chateau to the east of the village was, however, of
more solid construction and its walls were intact up to the first floor, although the roof and
the walls above this point had completely disappeared. The chateau had extensive cellarage
and the fallen debris had rendered them practically shellproof. All the outbuildings had gone
with the solitary exception of a pigeon-cote in the courtyard, an isolated brick tower ten feet
square and about forty feet high. The roof and most of the windows of this were intact and
even the weather cock still functioned.

In the orchard adjoining the chateau a 4.5 inch howitzer battery was in action when we
arrived. The range was getting too long for them and they intended advancing in a few days'
time, handing the position over to us. They had made a very strong gun position although
their emplacements were far too small for us. Like most emplacements erected early in
the war, they had head cover and were proof against splinters and small shells. As the war

progressed, emplacements became more flimsy until at the end they disappeared altogether and one fired from the ground without any protection or disguise. The emplacements were quite waterproof and when the Field Gunners moved out our men lived in them until they were vacated. However, we were billeted in the cellars in the village, three or four men being allotted to each cellar. The one I occupied had partly fallen in. There was a great hole in the roof and tons of fallen debris had made half the cellar unusable. Vibration from passing lorries used to dislodge great lumps of chalk from the roof. As a matter of fact the whole cellar fell in a few weeks later.

Auchonvillers Military Cemetery

We were not left to speculate about our quarters but were told to dump our equipment and made for the orchard where Capt Sanderson and the Sgt-Major were marking out the gun emplacements. The position reserved for the No.1 gun was directly in front of one of the 4.5 inch howitzers and the Sgt-Major warned us not to get in front of the gun when it was firing. The ground was hard with frost and levelling proved a much bigger job than anticipated. Then the field battery called out *"we are going to fire"* and we had a not unwelcomed break while they blazed off a few rounds. There were several interruptions of this nature, welcomed to the rank and file but not to Sgt Peake, who was fuming at the loss of time. The Sergeant was undoubtedly being harassed by Capt Sanderson who was annoyed by the slow progress being made by No.1 team, while other teams more favourably situated were forging ahead with their emplacements. A slow shoot by the fields finally decided him. The field howitzers were now firing every two or three minutes and showed no signs of stopping. Work was proceeding steadily by the other three teams while his own men were sitting round smoking and munching sweets. The Captain would be round again soon and expected to see the work being done, not to hear explanations. *"Never mind the bloody guns,"* ordered Sgt Peake, *"get on with the -------work."*

I was working with a Gunner Rees who, that day, had received a parcel from his wife. He had given me a piece of butterscotch which I was sucking at the time. On hearing Sgt Peake's orders he took a pick and I a shovel and we moved over to continue our excavations, When the 4.5 inch howitzer fired, we heard its peculiar shrill bark and then Rees collapsed, carrying me down with him. The shell had exploded prematurely, why we never knew, the branch of a tree in front of the Line of Fire, a worn gun or more likely faulty ammunition. I picked myself up but Rees did not move. Blood was streaming from him. Four of us carried him to the Dressing Station which the RAMC had set up just across the road. He said nothing but only moaned slightly.

At the Dressing Station they examined him. An abdominal wound – they would have an ambulance down in a jiffy and get him to the Casualty Clearing Station straight away. But although the ambulance was quick, it was not in time to save Gunner Rees[1]. We four returned to the Battery position and then I realised that the whole affair had happened so quickly that I was still sucking his piece of butterscotch.

The accident happened at 2pm (February 19). We resumed work on the new emplacements but now paid more respect to the guns behind us. It was two hours later during a period of enforced idleness that I had a feeling of numbness in my right leg and observed a trickle of blood. I thought at first that I might have been struck by the pick that Rees was carrying when he fell against me but the troops gathering round found a small wound just above the knee. It was evident that I had been struck by a fragment of the shell that had killed my comrade. Sgt Peake ordered me to be taken to the Dressing Station. The medical officer in charge examined my injuries and cauterized and dressed the wound. He could not tell whether a fragment was still embedded in the flesh – if so it would probably show itself in a few days. Then he gave me an anti-tetanus injection, excused me from duty for the rest of the day and told me to report the following morning. So I retired to my cellar and made myself as comfortable as possible.

That night was our first rum issue, carried out as usual with the maximum of pomp and ceremony. We paraded in front of the pigeon-cote which had been appropriated by the cooks, and as we passed in front of the Major, he poured a measure into our mess-tins which we had to gulp down in his presence. Taken this way the raw spirit had an almost instantaneous effect on the troops, particularly on the younger men who approached the issuing point in a dejected though perfectly orderly manner and reeled away laughing and singing after the drink. For myself, I had considerable difficulty in locating my billets and getting down the steps when I arrived. I believe I trod on one of my companions, a fact which afforded me considerable amusement. Whatever the cause, I slept well that night.

In the morning I reported to the Dressing Station. The wound had swollen considerably and I was excused duty. The same thing happened the next two days.

The rest was not of a particularly comfortable nature. I would lie on my back in the cellar looking at the sky through the roof and speculating how long the ceiling would hold up. As it was, large pieces of stone kept falling from time to time. The thaw had now set in and we realised that the place was by no means watertight, for in addition to the slush that kept sliding down; water was constantly dripping on us. I also noticed that we were not the only occupants of the premises – large rats would appear even in the daylight and I realised that the things that fell on us at night were not only stones from the roof. It was thus that I formed the habit of covering my face with my blanket at night and have been thankful of its protection when I felt the patter of feet over my face. One Gunner who inadvertently exposed his feet at night found in the morning all the hard skin nibbled away, a fact which caused him much pain when he tried to walk. Every night my comrades would come in from working on the gun-pits, wet and tired and there is no doubt that my own lot was enviable to theirs. I learnt that the 4.5 inch howitzers had left, that the new emplacements were nearly ready and that the guns would be advanced from Courcelles any night.

The fourth day after my accident the medical officer thoroughly examined the wound. The swelling was as large as a small egg and the limb exceedingly stiff. He said that I had better go down the line. Let me fetch my kit from the battery and I could go down with the next ambulance. Needless to say I wanted no second telling and was soon back at the Dressing Station ready for my first experience of the army hospital service.

With a few other minor casualties I was taken in a Ford motor ambulance to the next village Mailly-Maillet. Here situated in a barn was the headquarters of the Field Ambulance and here most casualties received their first medical attention, for many came direct from the line by-passing the Advanced Dressing Stations. After dirty dressings had been replaced the cases were sorted out; serious cases being sent forward to the Casualty Clearing Stations while slight casualties were dispatched to a Rest Station, there to be kept under observation for a few days before being returned to their units. I arrived at Mailly-Maillet at 10am but a good number of serious cases were rushed through and some of us had to wait until an ambulance became available. It was noon when we left and the ambulance took us to the Divisional Rest Centre at Bertrancourt, some three miles in rear, returning for further loads as it had been decided that the Field Ambulance must be cleared that day. We dined at Bertrancourt after which we were segregated the troops for rest and observation being left behind while the others, including myself, were bundled into another motor ambulance for the Casualty Clearing Station.

The Casualty Clearing Station was situated between villages of Acheux and Varennes, some seven or eight miles behind the front line. In this place within easy range of the enemy guns and with no protection beyond that afforded by the Red Cross, the main work of the

Royal Army Medical Corps was carried out. Here were surgeons and nurses and scores of major operations were performed daily. It has been alleged that the enemy disregarded the Geneva cross, possibly so on isolated occasions but the fact remains that it was safer in a tent under the protection of the cross than in a concrete shelter without it.

Unlike other military installations the Casualty Clearing Station was designed to be conspicuous. The white marquees plainly marked with the red cross could be seen from miles away; the Geneva flag fluttered in the breeze and ambulance trains pulled into their railway sidings quite openly. The trains were painted white and their roofs marked with the Red Cross. One day in three the Casualty Clearing Station was open to receive casualties; this was Reception Day. The next was a kind of general examination and stocktaking while the third day was Evacuation Day, when as many cases as possible were discharged, the fit back to their units and the badly injured to the Base Hospitals or to England. To work this cycle, Casualty Clearing Stations worked in pairs so that when one was receiving the other was evacuating and vice versa.

They had had a heavy day with many serious cases and when we arrived at 6pm February 23 the medical officer merely looked at our cards, asked us if we were comfortable and adjusted bandages in the few cases where this was necessary. Our equipment was then taken from us and we were sent to the wards. The main wards were in large marquees with wooden floors. Down each side were stretchers resting on trestles, while in the centre were a line of coke stoves. The marquees were double, that is one tent inside another so that however foul the weather outside, the ward was always warm and cosy. Beds had been made up on stretchers, brown blankets outside and red ones to lay on, while there were white linen pillows for our heads. It seemed like heaven after the foul cellar at Auchonvillers. Before we were allowed into bed we had to have a bath, not as thorough as we would have wished for there was still little water available. Bowls here handed round and we performed our ablutions as best we could, assisting those few of our neighbours as were unable to look after themselves. Then we donned hospital pyjamas and got into bed. Hitherto we had encountered male orderlies only but now an angel appeared in the form of a nurse who tucked us in and asked if we were comfortable. Later the ceremony was repeated by the sister and again by the night nurse. We now had tea and later at night a wonderful luxury cocoa for supper. After such an eventful day I felt very tired and soon went to sleep.

We were roused early in the morning (February 24) and soon after breakfast the medical officer visited the ward and examined each case thoroughly. Some were marked for evacuation the following day. The excitement of those detailed for Base Hospital presented a marked contrast from the gloom displayed by others who were to re-join their units. The lump on my leg was well prodded; there was certainly something inside but the Doctor thought it would work out in a day or two.

The next few days passed peacefully enough. I got used to hospital routine and got on well with my colleagues. The battery seemed miles away. There were two extremely good fellows from the Honourable Artillery Company, a Corporal and a private. One evening outside the marquee, Twivey, for that was the private's name confided to me what an extraordinary fascination the ever changing lines of gun flashes had for him. *"I feel,"* he said *"that I want to be there amongst it all – I love it – there's something glorious in war after all."* Strange sentiments they seemed at the time but later I got to understand them.

In marked contrast to these two was an elderly man, the most optimistic chap I have ever met. On his way back from the trenches he got stuck in the mud and lost his gum boots with the result that he had to walk some miles in his stockinged feet. To make matters worse he had trodden on some barbed wire and his feet were in a shocking state. *"I always wear three pairs of socks under my gum boots,"* he explained. *"If I hadn't I might have lost the use of my feet."* Probably true. Another man had a nasty wound on his palm where it had been pierced by a pick during night operations and which could not heal. There were many cases of trench feet, a kind of frostbite caused by standing in icy water. These were all evacuated to the base hospitals as their treatment was prolonged. They looked grotesque enough with their feet swathed in cotton wool and bandages to the size of a football. Invariably cheerful at the thought of the long rest before them and a possible 'blighty'[2], these patients caused much work to the orderlies as they were quite unable to walk and had to be carried. It seemed highly amusing to see these small RAMC men staggering about under the weight of an infantryman twice the size of themselves. Then, at a later stage, I was pressed into carrying service the joke did not seem so funny.

February 26 was my twenty-first birthday and a particularly peaceful day. The lump had come to a head and the medical officer was able to extract the small piece of shell that had caused the trouble. The foreign matter, once removed, the swelling rapidly decreased and I was marked fit for return to my unit. The matron, however, asked if I would care to stop for a few days to help out the orderlies whose ranks had been depleted by sickness and I readily consented. I was told to assist the RAMC orderlies in 'Q' ward from 8am to 8pm, taking my meals with them but returning to my own ward to sleep.

My experiences for the next few days were unique and horrifying, for 'Q' ward was reserved for men whose injuries were so severe that it would be fatal to move them, even to those hospitals where better facilities were available. The ward was a wooden hut with an annex at each end. Twenty iron beds were arranged down each side and there was the usual coke stove in the centre. The seriously wounded, on being brought into the Casualty Clearing Station, were operated on as soon as possible. Such operations were not always the final ones but it must be remembered that casualties were received with pieces of shell, sometimes of considerable size, still lodged in their bodies and these had to be removed at once. Whenever possible the patient, after the operation, was removed to the main surgical wards and evacuated to base hospitals as soon as he was fit to travel. It was only in the most exceptional cases that 'Q' and its sister ward were used. Nevertheless most of the beds were occupied. My work was light; there was a sister and an orderly constantly on duty and I was detailed to help as far as I could in feeding the patients, writing letters for them, washing up and the like. *"And don't,"* said the RAMC man *"let the abdominal cases have any water."* It was indeed difficult to resist the entreaties of the badly wounded men but a drop of water might have had fatal consequences. One boy begged so hard that the orderly bluntly told him of the consequences. Perhaps the lad might have had his drink of water after all for he died the same night.

In such circumstances fatalities were dreadful and in the fortnight I was there nearly a hundred died in the ward. In one bed alone six patients died in succession during that time. Most of the deaths took place at night and when I reported for duty in the morning, there were invariably screens round several of the beds. When dressings were changed the scene was particularly harrowing for though some were stoic enough to bear the pain in silence, the screams of the others were terrible to hear. I caught glimpses of wounds so dreadful that it was a relief to see a cleanly amputated leg.

We had our star patient, an elderly man who had been in that ghastly place for over four months. Admitted with dreadful abdominal wounds, he had surprised the staff by surviving the first night. He had obeyed the surgeon's instructions to the letter. He neither moved nor spoke, although he must have been in fearful agony the whole time and his hair had turned snow white. The sister told me that it seemed impossible that anyone should suffer so much and make no sign and yet had he in all that time screamed or turned in his agony he would have died at once. He was fed through a tube in his side as were many of the abdominal cases. While I was there the fateful day had arrived; the doctors agreed that he was fit to be moved to base hospital. The last man to be taken to the ambulance train, lifted on to his stretcher like a most fragile piece of china and carried under the personal supervision of the doctor and the matron, he was borne away to the Base, silent to the last.

I assisted at one evacuation though not from 'Q' ward, whose patients were too delicate for my 'prentice hands. The ambulance train drew in to the siding; we lifted the casualties on to stretchers and ran them down to the train on a light railway. Then we loaded them into the carriages. Heavy work indeed.

There was a lighter side to the 'Q' ward. The dangerously wounded men were nevertheless entitled to a soldier's ration. There were dainties like chicken broth and jellies for those who could take them and for many who could not and, in addition, the regulation twelve ounces of meat per heard was issued daily. From my point of view the fortnight was a continual feast. Far more chicken broth was issued that could possibly be consumed so the orderlies and I did our best to avoid wastage but without avail. Maconochies[3] were there for the asking. I took a large number to my friends in the main ward and when I came to leave I was given as many as I could take away, together with tins of jam butter and the like.

I was in Varennes altogether three weeks when I saw more human suffering than I dreamed possible. At length the time came to leave; I drew my kit from the stores and with a bag full of rations on my shoulder set out to re-join my battery.

Tramping up the line in search of one's unit was an irksome job. I was too much of a raw hand to be conversant with the fine art of lorry jumping. Instead I wore my equipment in regulation style or as near as I could get it and set off across the country. Someone told me of an overland track that would cut off a big corner but the track was very muddy and the going hard. I passed a dead horse, a horrible sight it looked at the time. Later I became only too familiar with such things. Later my blankets became undone and my underwear fell out into the mud. I reached the battery at tea time.

But if I expected being greeted as the wounded hero returning home I was soon to be disillusioned. Bdr Pateman, the battery orderly, bluntly told me that the gun teams had been made up and that I must parade with the spare men. I went to my old cellar only to find it completely blocked; the roof had at last fallen in. I tried to find other accommodation only to be churlishly informed that they were full up. Bdr Pateman at length appealed to, promptly bundled me into another cellar much to the protests of the already overcrowded occupiers. At length resigning ourselves to the inevitable, confidences were exchanged. I learnt that the guns were now in action; the detachments had taken over the dugouts of the 4.5 inch battery and were living off the fat of the land. The spare men were still in the filthy cellars and were having no rest day or night having to turn out for any job about the battery. I took this to be the grumblings of the disgruntled men for I remembered that I had been on the advance party from Courcelles and expected to take my place on the gun crew before long. In any case there was the matter of my commissioning in the offing.

I was soon to learn that my colleagues had not exaggerated the situation. In the mornings the whole battery would parade in the courtyard, now a quagmire, in front of the pigeon-cote. The roll called, Major Tomasson would deliver his daily oration. He would explain the conduct of the war, praise our shooting and urge is to even greater efforts. How I detested this pinchbeck Napoleon and his everlasting lectures! Then the unemployed men would fall out for their respective duties after which the gun detachments would move to one side under their respective Sergeants and on the word of command double to their guns – that was the last we should see of them. Tasks had now to be found for the remainder, the spare men. Eight for water fatigue, two for finding and chopping wood for the cook's fire, others cleaning shells and shifting cartridges. In addition the spare men always had to provide the guard.

Water fatigue was a vile and filthy job. We had a couple of springless carts, trench carts they were called, among the battery stores. They were originally designed for drawing by a mule. On one of these crafts was lashed a galvanised iron tank. With two men in the shaft and three on each side pulling on drag ropes, we proceeded to drag the whole contraption to the water tanks at Mailly-Maillet, some three miles away. Going was bad enough for the road was in vile condition, broken by traffic and with plenty of shell-holes full of liquid mud. We kept having to draw to one side to let other traffic pass and were well splattered with dirt. On our arrival at the tanks we had to take our turn with motor lorries and water carts of all descriptions. When the queues moved, we would haul the trench cart forward a few yards in the mud and water. The stand pipe reached at length we filled our tank, often getting drenched in the process and then we proceeded back to the battery position.

But if the way to the watering station was unpleasant, the return journey was a nightmare. When one of the team would stumble in a shell hole which was pretty often for they were all concealed by mud, the cart would lurch and almost overturn and the water would spill, drenching us all. Sometimes we had to man-handle the wheels over a difficult part. When at length we arrived at the cook-house, a good deal of the water had been lost and we were cursed for bringing short measure. We were late for dinner and had to content ourselves with any half warm dregs that were left. In the afternoon we had to make another journey and yet another after tea, often to the gibes and ribald laughter of the troops on the road who had never seen a water-cart pulled by men before. As a matter of fact I never saw or heard of such a contraption myself. Our Army Service Corps column would willingly have supplied us with all the water we needed. They did so at Courcelles and again at later positions. I am convinced that water fatigue was a device of Major Tomasson to keep us employed.

At night our ammunition would arrive in lorries and all hands had to turn out for unloading. A serious difference of opinion soon developed between the men who wished to roll the shells and those who preferred to carry them from the tail of the lorry. As stated, the shells weighed 200lbs each, a load much heavier than the average man is called upon to handle. At first there were no two ways about things. Planks were laid from the tail of the lorry to the stacking area. Men were placed at intervals and guided the shells along the planks; a method which I am still convinced is the best for dealing with such objects. The exponents of the carrying school had as their chief advocates Gunners Sibley and Waddington, both of No.1 team. These men had been meat porters in civilian life and were of immensely powerful physique. On one occasion Sibley, without waiting for the plank to be fixed in position, walked up to the lorry and told the driver to lower a shell on his shoulder, then promptly walked off with it and on reaching the gun emplacement easily and gracefully pitched it off. Not to be outdone, Waddington promptly followed suit. Sgt Peake now tested the new method and find that he himself could manage a shell, called on the rest of us to follow suit. Thus started the trouble that was to continue for many months. Some of the smaller and weaker men made no attempt to carry shell and devoted themselves to the lighter cartridges and fuses (60 and 40lbs respectively). Others carried their shells with more or less comfort. A third class found themselves, however willing, physically incapable of bearing this load. I found myself in this unhappy group. Standing with my back to the lorry, the heavy shell was laid on my shoulder. I tried to walk away with it but the weight bore me down, my knees gave way and the shell fell to the ground. I had to get down my hands and knees in the mud to roll it away amid howls of derision. Many others failed in like manner.

This weakness exposed me to a good deal of contempt for in appearance I was taller than many of those who carried their shell with ease. I tried repeatedly and as often failed and it was not until the end of June that I found that I could at last essay this difficult task. I did not realise it at the time but it is possible that the injury to my leg had something to do with the difficulty. But whatever the cause, it was equally certain that Sgt Peake and the strong men of the battery regarded me as a malingerer. There were others in the same condition and as soon as the ammunition lorries arrived, we would try to fix up the planks and start rolling them down the shells but we were usually frustrated by the strong men who would pour scorn on our efforts and take the planks away.

The aversion between Sgt Peake and myself developed, in my case, at any rate into virtual detestation. It is possible that the Sergeant had been severely criticised about his part in the premature explosion when Gnr Rees lost his life and I was wounded and my return from hospital must have added coals to the fire, particularly when I put up a wound stripe. He had the ear of the Sgt-Major and the fact of my application for a commission was well known to him. He took care to spread the information round and let it be known that the would-be officer was not good enough to be taken into his gun team.

It was not that the gun detachments were having a particularly easy time. They were kept well at it, fighting the guns and keeping the emplacements clean and in good order and it must be admitted that many of the spare men were shysters, who would volunteer for nothing and try to *"dodge the column"* whenever possible. Nevertheless, the gun-crews developed a sense of superiority to an alarming extent. Had we been criminals or men of a different colour we could not have been worse treated and this was only a prelude to what we were to experience later on.

Meanwhile developments were taking place on the front. With the end of the frost the Battle of the Somme was resumed. Serre[4] had fallen on February 24 and Tilloy on the 28. As these and other villages were taken, the range of the guns was lengthened. Then came the greatest surprise of the war. On March 14 came the news that the enemy was withdrawing to what extent no-one knew. On March 17 the Australians marched into Bapaume without a shot being fired and all the heavy artillery on the sector were stranded like fish out of water, completely out of range and unable to come into action again until it was established where the Germans had come to rest. On March 18 the patrolling infantry were pulled up sharply. Contact with the enemy had at last been made; the Germans had established themselves in their impregnable position the Hindenburg Line.

Now our next move was known. We were to advance to a position some 9 miles eastward to cover the Hindenburg Line at Quéant. Nine miles as the crow flies but between Auchonvillers and the new position lay the River Ancre, so churned up as to be known the Sea of Mud. The trenches both the British and those lately in enemy occupation lay in the way and the narrow country lanes had long since been obliterated. It would have been a difficult job in peace time getting the heavy artillery across the river and up the other bank towards Quéant. With the ground so churned up it was clearly impossible. The only alternative was to travel due south along a secondary road to Albert, 8 miles distant from Auchonvillers, then 12 miles northeast along the Route Nationale which ran straight as an arrow between Albert and

Bapaume and finally 6 miles north along bye roads to Ervillers, the selected position; a two or even three days journey.

Major Tomasson decided to divide the battery. He himself would take a working party to the new position via Beaumont Hamel, the Sea of Mud and the old no-man's-land; a distance on paper of 12 miles. They would carry picks and shovels and prepare a position at Ervillers in readiness for the guns. Meantime Capt Sanderson would take the guns to Albert and stop there the night, moving up the following day to occupy the position which then would be ready. I was with the Captain's party and later on I was to thank my lucky stars that I had been so chosen. We saw the working party move off and set to work to get the guns on the road. It was hard work and involved a lot of digging and heaving but at last we hitched on to the tractors and moved off.

On the line of the march Capt Sanderson showed himself considerate enough. Our equipment was carried on the lorries and we marched light. We reached Albert wet, for it had been raining hard but without particular discomfort. The Captain found us particularly comfortable billets.

Parts of the town had not greatly suffered from shellfire and we were lodged in some pretty solid working class houses. He then called us out saying that he would give us something to *"keep out the cold"* and forthwith issued an enormous tot of rum, almost a mug full to each man. A merry party went to sleep that night and none more jovial that Capt Sanderson himself.

Contrary to expectations we did not move forward the following day. Major Tomasson's party had fared far worse than they imagined. Roads shown on the map had no existence in reality, they were hours in finding a crossing over the River Ancre, they fell into shell-holes, got lost in a maze of trenches and had difficulty in getting through the barbed wire. When at last they reached Ervillers it was midnight, the place was in ruins and there was no shelter to be found. I have often wondered precisely what Major Tomasson expected to find at Ervillers. Surely he could not have expected the Germans to have left ready-made billets for the accommodation of his troops. In any case the men were so exhausted they would gladly have laid in the open until morning. Be that as it may he did the worst thing possible in the circumstances – he decided to return to Auchonvillers. So as the great Napoleon led the retreat from Moscow he, Major Tomasson, led the retreat from Ervillers. But there is a limit to human endurance and if I am rightly informed, it was a frightened man who led his exhausted troops to their cold billets at Auchonvillers, secured rations for them and promised that come what may they should not more forward again until they were thoroughly rested and then they should ride.

So the Captain's party got an extra days rest in Albert and on us devolved the duty of preparing the new gun emplacements.

Captain Sanderson rose considerably in our esteem. He seemed to be a good natured giant, a bit of a bully perhaps but he knew his work well and above all how to handle men. How different it would have been if only he had been CO instead of only second in command. The following day we paraded at the very reasonable hour of 9am His words were short and to the point. Today we were free; he didn't believe in keeping men at work when there was no need for it (we detected a dig at Major Tomasson in this); let everybody rest as much as possible today for there was a hard day tomorrow when we were to move forward again. If there were billets at Bapaume we should stay there but that was very doubtful and we must expect to have to go forward to the new position. We strolled round the town, found a canteen and were duly impressed by the hanging virgin[5] above the cathedral. Jovial as ever, Capt Sanderson again produced the medicine that evening.

The Route Nationale between Albert and Bapaume was 12 miles long and cut straight across the old front line. It had now been repaired and was in fair condition for the lorries and guns. Albert lays in the valley and as we mounted the hill, all signs of civilisation were left behind. On either side were trenches and shell holes; trees were shattered stumps. A heap of stones alongside and we knew we were marching through Pozieres.[6] When the macadam changed to pave we knew we were passing through Le Sars. Destruction was now at its peak but soon, in the distance we could discern houses, ruined it is true but at least their form could be seen and the trees alongside the road had not been shattered by gun fire but had deliberately been sawn down. We had now reached the evacuated area and then Bapaume came in sight, the town from which so much had been expected. A town torn from the hand of the enemy, a refuge for troops, a railhead, a distributing centre for the advancing army. A fair town is seemed from the distance but, when we drew nearer we knew that what we had seen from the high road was a mirage. The whole town was but a mockery and a sham, smoke was still rising from the ruins and even as we passed through, houses were collapsing like cards. We halted outside the remains of a sugar factory. The machinery was a tangled mass of steel and great holes had been knocked in the tanks and boilers. Clearly there was no rest in this inhospitable town. So after a while we continued our trek to the new position.

Our road now lay due north. We were now feeling the journey and were allowed to take turns riding on the lorries. It was evening when we passed through the twin villages of Behagnies and Sapignies, sinister they seemed in the dim light. Who dared venture into these deserted barns? What dreadful secrets were contained in the cellars? Was the road safe? Was that crossing mined? The great fear of the evacuated land descended upon us. And so in those days batteries were making their way slowly and painfully across the unknown land, fearful of mines and booby traps; cross roads could blow up, houses would collapse without warning, all the trees had been felled to allow the enemy full observation, all manner of filth had been deposited in the wells, dead horses were poisoning the atmosphere, nothing that could have been the slightest use to use had been left behind. Even tins had holes punched in them. And all the while he was watching us like some great spider from his impregnable position on the top of the hill, the Hindenburg Line, that great system of trenches that he had been constructing for months without our knowledge. We had been so completely fooled that some batteries were having to advance with shells still in the bore of their guns. So rapid had been the withdrawal that they dared not empty guns for fear of firing on reconnoitring troops.

We reached Ervillers on the evening of March 22. At the time it seemed to be a reasonable place for a battery but, like so many of those villages, it fell to pieces before our eyes until at length the engineers erected a signpost bearing the somewhat theatrical inscription: *"This village was Ervillers"*.

Capt Sanderson selected a battery position within the village itself where the rafters would mask the guns and where once the ground had been cleared, some accommodation for the men might be built. On our arrival he told us about his system of reliefs. We were all pretty well exhausted when we arrived; nevertheless the emplacements would have to be built and there was no time to be lost. First he gave us all a good tot of rum and then he divided us into two parties, the first to sleep as best they could for four hours. The second party started unloading the lorries and levelling the ground. Then as if the relief system had not gone far enough, once the real hard work of excavation was on its way, we were further sub–divided one squad *"digging like hell"* as he termed it for five minutes by his watch while the others were having a breather. He himself threw off his tunic and threw out great shovelfuls of soil. At the end of the four hours the sleepers were aroused, another issue of rum given all round and those of us who had finished our spell sank down to rest unashamedly drunk and deliriously happy. Work preceded apace, chalk blocks were obtained from ruined houses and used for foundations, while those too drunk to stand unaided could still do useful work on the rammers. And so, working spells about, the drunken battery finished four splendid gun emplacements in record time and sat down to await the arrival of the guns.

But disappointment awaited us. We were not to occupy the position after all. When Major Tomasson and his party arrived it was decided that we must go forward to Mory. The guns were pulled on to the platforms and left there while the new position was being prepared. The ground at Ervillers was retained however and was eventually used as the Quartermaster's Stores.

---

1   The CWGC records and Soldiers Died in the Great War 1914-1919 do not list any casualty matching Gnr Rees on or around this date.

2   'Blighty' was the troops' nickname for Britain. To get a 'Blighty' wound often was cherished as it took troops away from the front.

3   Maconochies – a vegetable and meat stew in a tin

4   Serre was a fortified village on the Somme front and had been an objective for the troops on 1 July 1916 and it was here that the Sheffield City Battalion – 12th (Service) Battalion (Sheffield) The Yorkshire and Lancashire Regiment – had suffered huge numbers of casualties.

5   The basilica in Albert had a gilded statue of the Virgin Mary on top of the spire. Inevitably this became a target for enemy gunners and there was a saying that whoever brought it down would lose the war or when it fell, the war would end.

6   Pozieres was a hamlet on the high ground above Albert and had been the scene of ferocious fighting in the summer of 1916.

CHAPTER 11
AFTER THE EVACUATION

Hall was a keen observer of those around him and Major Tomasson's characteristics feature extensively in his notes particularly his aptitude for not necessarily utilising the best way to achieve a task with the resources at his disposal. The fate of his reputation in Battery Action must have been sealed by the incident in this chapter concerning an interview for a commission though in Hall's account of the capture of Messines he recognises Tomasson's deep concern when a gunner is killed in what was supposed to be a safe area. Moving any formation around the Western Front was an arduous task and Hall provides further insight to the establishment of a battery position, an essential task before the enemy can be engaged. At this stage of the war the battery was in support of the Easter 1917 offensive at Arras which consisted of a number of phases the most notable of which was the capture of Vimy Ridge by British and Canadian forces. Other features of a soldier's existence noted by Hall include the rum ration and lice but it is Gnr Hall's loathing for others in the battery that shines through topped by the episode with the faulty breech on a gun.

From Ervillers a secondary road branched off in the direction of Mory, a village a little over a mile away. About 500 yards before the latter place was reached a farm track led off in a southerly direction. It was on this track that Major Tomasson decided to place the battery and here we spent the next seven weeks, the most miserable of my life. It had been evident for some time that there was no love lost between the CO and his second in command and it is possible that Capt Sanderson, having selected the Ervillers position, Major Tomasson promptly vetoed it. Be that as it may, the Captain's scheme of short reliefs was at once jettisoned, all hands without exception were set to work and there was to be no rest for anyone until the guns were in action. For our accommodation the Major had obtained two large tents, oblong in shape and brown in colour; an Armstrong hut[1] was used for the Officers' Mess while Major Tomasson himself lived in state in a bell tent some distance away. While a party was erecting the tents the main body set to work on the gun pits.

The farm track was in the form of a sunken road and lay like an open trench some five feet below ground level. Running north to south it would afford excellent protection against enemy gun-fire. The emplacements each about twelve feet square were formed by cutting into the bank. No.4 pit the left handed gun lay 10 yards from the main roads while the others were dug at 25 yard intervals.

The work of construction was most elaborate. The sites were laid out and excavated until a firm foundation of chalk was found. Then parties were sent into the village for bricks which they obtained by demolishing houses. The bricks carried to the pits in sandbags were broken and laid on the chalk foundation, the surface being tested by a spirit level. Three planks

10 feet long by 15 inches wide were now laid lengthways, one to take the weight of each wheel and one in the centre. The spaces between the planks was filled with broken bricks well rammed. Five ten foot planks were now laid crossways across these supporters and so became the platform on which the gun was to rest. A ramp was now constructed to hold the trail of the gun steady when it was fired. This could not be completed until the gun was in position but was advanced as far as possible. The ramp was made by digging a trench six foot long by four feet deep in rear of the platform. In this trench six baulks of timber were inserted so that they rose three feet from the ground. Then they were rammed in so as to be immovable. Thirty sand-bags filled with chalk (care being taken to discard any flints which might buckle the trail) were built like a wall in front of these timber posts so that when the gun fired, the spade underneath the trail would dig in and hold it firm. All this time the work of camouflaging the pits was proceeding. Posts were erected at each corner of the gun pit and on this a framework was made. Over this frame was stretched wire netting to which were tied bits of rag. The netting was stretched down at the sides to make an irregular intervals, the idea at Mory being to preserve the outline of the lane. The camouflaging we had brought from Auchonvillers was green and unsuitable for the dirty white of Mory, so the original rags had to be untied and bits of sandbags substituted.

When the emplacements were ready the tractors brought up the guns as far as they junction of the farm track, whence they were manhandled into position. The ramps were then completed, the Lines of Fire laid out and the guns made ready for action. The tractor officer wished to draw the guns right on to their emplacements but was prevented by Major Tomasson. Guns must always be man-handled into position.

There was trouble at Mory from the very beginning. We arrived there practically exhausted after the long march from Albert, followed by the intensive work at Ervillers. Work on the gun-pits at Mory started early on the morning of March 23 and continued throughout the day and the same night without intermission. The emplacements were ready for the guns by the later afternoon of the 24 but we were kept at work doing odd jobs until they arrived. The first gun arrived at 10pm. Its weight exploded a mine at Ervillers crossroad. No casualties resulted but the crater formed by the explosion delayed the other guns and it was not until 4am 25 March that the last gun was in position.

There was now the ammunition to be dealt with. The whole convoy was waiting on the road and had to be dealt with before dawn. Each lorry held 30 shells, the same number of cartridges, together with boxes of fuses and friction tubes. Over 700 rounds were unloaded and dumped near the top of the track. It was at this stage that the Sgt-Major encouraged us by promising a good night's rest after the day's work, a promise repeated by Major Tomasson at morning parade a few hours later.

After the lorries had dispersed, the worst of the work began getting the ammunition to the gun emplacements. There was no other way but rolling them on the ground and as the guns were up to 150 yards distant from the dump, this presented some difficulty. The ground was very soft and the shells gathered mud as they rolled, growing in size like a snowball until they could be rolled no longer and had to be scraped. After a time we managed to get some old planks – wood was very scarce – and rolling on these made the job easier but occasionally shells would slip off the planks onto the mud. Then two or three of us had to gather round and lift the shell onto the plank, getting well muddied in the process. By the time the shells had arrived at the pits they were covered in mud and had to be first scraped and then washed – a loathsome job. It was well into the evening when the ammunition was in position. At midnight we were dismissed and, making our way to the tents, sank down to enjoy the promised sleep after nearly 70 hours continuous work.

Fuzing shells and unpacking the charges during a bombardment witnessed by Captain Francis Vernon Lyne Redman MC RGA (Firepower Museum AL/517.16)

At two o'clock in the morning we heard Bdr Pateman's strident voice *"turn out everybody."* Asked the reason, he didn't quite know but it had something to do with stowing the cartridge cases. At any rate it was the CO's orders. Angry protests were made; we had the definite promise made on parade and now this was to be broken. Someone said *"I report sick"*. *"Does this mean that you refuse to turn out,"* said Pateman. Fortunately the Gunner kept his head and replied, *"No but I am unable to turn out and ask to be taken before the medical officer"*. The ruse spread and some fifty of us reported sick for the same reason. Bdr Pateman went for instructions and returning presently proceeded to take our names. At this stage a few waverers gave in and wearily turned out but the bulk of us were determined to see the thing through, heedless of the consequences. The news of the revolt spread to the other tent but here the rebels were not so numerous. In all, however, there were over sixty names in the book and these, myself among them, turned over determined to have our sleep and damn the consequences.

But in the morning we were more apprehensive, the more so when Bdr Pateman put his head in the tent and told us that on no account were we to move; the CO had telephoned the medical officer who was on his way to see the sick men. This move on Major Tomasson's part proved to be his undoing. We learnt afterwards that he had telephoned the brigade doctor in a towering rage saying that his men had mutinied and had demanded to see the MO *"Let the medical officer certify them fit for duty and he* (the CO) *would deal with them"*. The RAMC was, however, a law unto itself. The medical officer came over and without seeing the Major, walked straight to our tent. He looked none too amiable and brusquely asked the first man what was wrong with him. The rebels were now inventing all kinds of imaginary complaints but they did not seem to be carrying weight. I was sixth on the list and I thought it best to tell the truth, *"I was exhausted last night – we had been working continuously for 70 hours and I felt that I could do no more without some sleep"*. *"And do you feel better now that you have had your sleep?"* said the MO. *"Yes sir."* *"Of course you do – then there is no need to examine you."* *"No, sir."* The others followed suit and before the MO left us the whole of the wretched business came out. The MO said nothing until we had all been interrogated – then he gave his decision *"light duty"*. The victory was ours; technically we were all sick men, the refusal to parade was fully justified and Major Tomasson was unable to inflict any punishment on our revolt. What happened at the subsequent interview with the Major we did not know but the MO's orders were strictly obeyed and for the rest of the day we rebels were given such light jobs as camouflaging the guns, much to the disgust of the loyal troops. The incident was now closed and never referred to again by anyone.

It is only fair to say that never again were we kept so long without rest, although constant interruption was the rule rather than the exception and we considered ourselves lucky if we got one unbroken night in four. We endeavoured to snatch sleep whenever we could, in meal time particularly. The food was revolting anyway and I regarded the break for dinner better spent in sleeping than eating and would readily sacrifice a meal so that I could enjoy half an hour's nap.

Water fatigue so hated at Auchonvillers was now eagerly sought after and men detailed to drag the water cart to the tanks at Hendecourt were deemed fortunate by those compelled to remain at the battery position. All the original wells were befouled by the retreating Germans and at first, water had to be brought up by motor lorries from tanks many miles in rear. In an incredibly short time, however, deep wells had been sunk in the chalk at Hendecourt and the water cart was again brought into action, although at Mory it had to be dragged over open fields and was consequently harder work. Water fatigue, however, meant the chance of a sleep at the water point. In addition, a canteen had been opened at Hendecourt and I spent most of my money on tins of apricots and evaporated milk. This tasted wonderfully clean in contrast to the horrible stew served at the cook-house. The same routine was followed in the afternoon and again after tea, after which we were available for odd jobs about the battery. We would usually retire at ten, then we would be roused at midnight for ammunition until three or four in the morning, after which we would resume our sleep until the 7am parade.

Another job for the spare men was the construction of cartridge recesses. Several loads of sandbags and corrugated iron arrived at the battery and we thought, not unnaturally, that these would be used for making dugouts. A number of us were detailed by the Sgt-Major to construct shelters in the bank side some little distance from the guns. It was only after a number had been erected that we realised that the shelters were not meant for men but for cartridges. All the personnel were huddled in the two tents and there we stayed the whole time we were at Mory. Had the position been shelled the number of casualties would have been appalling, for there was no protection of any kind for the men. Nevertheless roomy dugouts were erected for the Sergeants' mess, the battery office and so on. These and the cartridge recesses soon used up all the material that had been sent for our protection.

On completion of the recesses Major Tomasson found a job for Bdr Poulton which nearly drove that unfortunate NCO insane. Poulton had been posted to the battery while in training as Acting Corporal BCA. Like Cpl Tudhope in 221 Siege Battery he opened a BCA class and among his pupils was a young NCO, Acting Bdr Jackson. The pupil made such good progress that at the end of the course Major Tomasson promoted him Corporal and refused to confirm Poulton's acting rank with the result that he reverted to Bombardier. At Courcelles, Corpl Jackson took over the BC Post while his former instructor wandered aimlessly about the battery doing any odd jobs that showed up. Now his work was to segregate the cartridges into 'lots'. These lot numbers were stencilled on the cases at the munitions factory. On arrival, cartridges were dumped in the first vacant recess, no easy job on a dark night as the recesses were over 200 yards from the unloading point. Then in the morning half a dozen spare men were sent to help Poulton to separate the 'lots'. Sometimes as many as thirty or forty lots would arrive in one night. Those bearing identical numbers would be stored in the same recess, the oddments being thrown together for night firing. For long shoots the guns had to be supplied with cartridges bearing the same number and any leftover had to be withdrawn and odd lots substituted. The job was of course an endless one, for no matter how the cartridges were stacked they could always have been better arranged. Sgt-Major Cavalier was merciless and gave Bdr Poulton no peace; Major Tomasson would inspect the recesses and tell him that unless he arranged the cartridges more systematically, he would lose his chevron. After five weeks Bdr Poulton saw the CO and that afternoon he paraded without his stripe. *"Bombardier Poulton,"* bellowed the SM who had not been told of the reversion but no-one stepped forward. *"Bombardier Poulton"* was repeated but still no response. Then the SM looked down the ranks and saw what had happened. *"Gunner Poulton,"* he called and smartly came the reply, *"Sir"*.

Poulton now joined the ranks of the spare men and Bdr Maxon took over the cartridge job. He was at once regarded as an expert on ammunition and his work was made easy for him by the Sgt-Major and the CO. The segregation of cartridges continued until we left Mory when it was quietly dropped.

From the first there was a lot of heavy firing at Mory. The enemy were in a very strong position in their Hindenburg Line and considerable artillery preparation was necessary before an attack could be launched. The gun crews were kept hard at work during the day, night firing being taken by the right and left sections in turn. As we expected, the quick motion gear was out of action on all the guns and elevating and depressing the guns by means of the slow motion screws threw a considerable strain on the Gun Layer. The recuperation of mechanism which took the recoil of the guns was also giving a good deal of trouble and pumping up the guns was a daily occurrence. This was done by means of a portable air compressor which was clamped to the trail. Six men took to the handles, three a side, and pumped away until the dial registered the required pressure. The main thing was to keep the compressor going, for once we stopped the pressure would rapidly fall. One man in turn would drop off the handles while another took his place so that pumping never stopped. On occasions we would tie ropes to the handles and twenty men would pull on each rope but this method was not favoured as the action tended to be jerky.

Ammunition was received in enormous quantities by lorries which arrived nightly. There was the usual dispute between the rolling school and those who preferred to carry the shells, but in the main they were just pitched out of the lorries into the mud for the spare men to sort out in the morning.

Later we learnt that a light railway was being run through the battery position and forward to reach the field batteries further up the line. These light railways, 'Decauvilles'[2] as they were called, did very good work. Of 15 inch gauge they ran from the ammunition dumps to the forward positions and at night petrol and sometimes steam trains ran on them. A train load consisted of four to six wagons each carrying 100 rounds of 8 inch shells (or its equivalent to other ordnance). Spurs were run to each battery position so that wagons could, if necessary, be run direct to the guns. In practice the heavy locomotives could not travel on the lighter tracks in the batteries and the procedure was for the engine to shunt the trucks on to the sidings, retire while they were being unloaded and call back for the empties later on. There was trouble about our spur; the engineer officer came to see Major Tomasson who flatly refused to have the Decauville run to his guns and the engineers had to be content with constructing a siding just long enough to clear the main line. The Major set his face firm against any easier methods; the shells still had to be rolled to the guns and seeing that the railway siding was further away than the lorry dump, we lost over the change.

Actually the light railway ran between No.1 gun and the living tents. We had as neighbours a 9.2 inch howitzer battery on the opposite side of the line whose No.4 gun was just outside our second tent. These people had their own siding and had no hesitation in having a line to their guns connected up with the result that they received their shells clean and ready for loading and it was with our considerable chagrin that we observed their business-like methods of taking ammunition while we were rolling our own shells through the mud and cleaning them with scraper and brush, our own Decauville track laying meanwhile in a ditch unused.

Altogether the 9.2 inch battery gave us every cause for envy. The men lounged about playing cards, built themselves comfortable shelters and when action was called, they were quick on their guns, fired off their rounds and returned to their billets. Their guns once set needed no adjustment and it gave them considerable amusement to see us heaving on the drag ropes. They did not limit themselves to the three fused shells per gun ordained by Major Tomasson. Instead, when things were quiet, they would all set to and fuse as many as they thought were necessary, forty or fifty at a time. They mimicked our Sergeant-Major's high pitched voice and roused the battery orderly to fury. *"Bombardier Pateman"* the BSM would call out. *"Bombardier Pateman"* came the mooching echo from the 9.2 inch battery.

As for our own gun teams the life of the Gunner was no sinecure but it was infinitely to be preferred to that of the spare men. If he were not fortunate enough to get on the water fatigue, chop wood for the cook or help Bdr Poulton with his endless cartridge sorting, he was detailed for shell rolling and washing. Two men were sent into each pit to clean shells and the others would roll them from the dumps to the respective emplacement. Either job was revolting. Shell rolling meant bending down and frequently getting on hands and knees in the slime. The weather being very wet and our long greatcoats and puttees became plastered with mud. The unfortunates in the pits would scrape off the mud from the shells with their knives and then wash them with a brush and water. It was heart-breaking to think that all this foul work might have been avoided if only the Major had allowed the Decauville track to be laid to the guns.

The arrogance of the gun teams knew no bounds. Their business was to fire the guns and they would do nothing else. They would not help with the shell dumping and the shell washers were under the supervision of their loading numbers, who would report if the ammunition was not clean enough. Between shoots they would sit on the gun trail and watch us work. Rapid firing only meant that we should have to work harder to keep them supplied. When guns required to be pulled out, which was pretty often, they would not attempt the task until all the spare men were on the ropes and even then some of the team would find odd jobs to do in order to dodge this hard work. We were bundled from one gun to another. *"Lend me your spare men,"* one Sergeant would say to another *"I want a pull out."* The gun teams always had their meals first. On one occasion, my boots being very worn out, I went to the Quartermaster's Stores for another pair. There were plenty in stock but I was not allowed to draw mine. The gun teams might want them, they must come first, and I had to wait another fortnight until their prior needs were met. At night when ammunition arrived, the section on duty would start unloading and the orderly Sergeant for the night would take charge. The rest could sleep on, except of course the spare men – they were always on duty.

"Turn out all the spare men" by day and night the hateful cry rang through the battery. The 9.2 men next door echoed the call in mockery until to them the joke grew stale. And so one day followed another, water fatigue, cartridge segregating, rolling and washing shells, camouflaging and fetching wood and every night ammunition. I looked back to the days at Ewshot and at Lydd when I was training to be a BCA and not content with that was even aspiring to the commissioned rank. Now I was not considered fit to fight a gun – how I envied and at the same time detested the regular gun crew!

Ammunition was now arriving much quicker than the guns were firing it away and it was obvious that we were preparing to attack the Hindenburg Line. Signallers, cooks and servants were pressed into service for the fatigues, much to their disgust. The Signallers were particularly vociferous in their protests and it was hard on men who had been patrolling the telephone line all night to be called to assist with such work during the day. The result was inevitable. The whole battery became adept at the gentle art of swinging the lead and indeed we were abetted to some extent by the Sergeant-Major himself. *"Fetch the water,"* he would shout and in a lower voice *"and don't hurry back."* If we were lucky at the water tanks and returned to the battery by say 11.30 there was trouble. Work must be found for the men, even with only half an hour to dinner time. If the CO found six men idle, the Sergeant-Major suffered. The result was that we spun out the journey and returned late. Similarly Signallers on patrol would cut the telephone cable and spend hours ostensibly searching for the fault but actually dozing in shell holes.

The aeroplane spotter, now a man of consequence, would sound the alarm whenever an enemy aircraft was to be seen; even through it was miles away and so gave us all a few minutes grace. When there were insufficient enemy machines he would mistake one of ours to be on the safe side. The breaks meant a rest for the gun crews for they would cover up and stop firing but for the spare men shell washing could be carried on just as well under the camouflage.

Major Tomasson seemed completely deceived by these tactics; so long as every man was accounted for and had a job to do he was satisfied. Not so Captain Sanderson. The Captain knew every man's capabilities and was well aware that malingering was rife in the battery. He rarely appeared on parade but when some special job wanted doing, he would always be there and would storm and rave at our slowness. He would throw off his coat and show us how the work should be done and, in truth, he performed two or three times as much as an ordinary man.

While Major Tomasson rarely issued rum[3] and a large number of jars were accumulating in the Quartermaster's Stores. Captain Sanderson on the other hand would issue it on special occasions very freely indeed. On one occasion when a gun broke down, another spare man and I were detailed to help the Sergeant Artificer with the repairs and the Captain gave us three large issues, one every hour, with the result that while the gun was restored to working order in record time, the two helpers were in a hopeless state of intoxication and I was never able to remember how I eventually returned to billets.

With the warmer weather a new trial was encountered – lice. Lice were always with us in France and existed from the base to the front line. All ranks suffered to a greater or less extent and, until the end of the war, I never remember being completely free from these vermin. The best one would wish for was to be relatively clear. This could only be done by taking baths as often as possible, boiling all the underclothing and most important hunting down the lice when they became troublesome. Unlike the flea, the body louse is easily tracked down and only the man who could devote an hour or so daily to the examination of his clothes and particularly of his undergarments, killing the lice and burning out the nits, could hope to keep at all comfortable. Let him neglect this duty and they would breed apace, producing an itching which would give their host no peace day or night. If scratched the punctures festered and there was the unpleasant consequences of scabies or trench fever. It was not until a number of men had been admitted into hospital with scabies that we were allowed any time off for washing our clothing. It was now April and the bulk of us had no opportunity for washing ourselves or our clothing since our arrival in France early in January. The time for washing did not last many days however.

About the beginning of April we received some assistance in the shape of a party of twenty men of the Royal Marine Artillery who were posted to us temporarily to help with the ammunition. The RMA normally manned the largest guns (as opposed to howitzers) that were used in the field, i.e. 9 inch, 12 inch and 15 inch. Those attached to our battery normally fought a 12 inch gun on rail mountings. This had gone down for repair and the men were detailed to help various RGA batteries until it was ready for action again. The marines being with the army and yet not of it were in a peculiar position. Those posted to us seemed to be prepared to help but only on their own terms. First they must be found reasonable accommodation. They selected a spot on the bank side, commandeered the Major's precious corrugated iron and sandbags and built themselves a first rate dugout. They drew their own rations and appointed one of their number as cook. They paraded under their own Corporal and at 9am reported for duty to Sgt-Major Cavalier. Their business was to get shells to the guns and they would do nothing else. They soon found the Decauville railway track where it had been hidden and attempted to connect it to the railway siding but Major Tomasson objected. As a compromise he obtained some good 10 foot planks and they made a runway from the shell dump to the gun pits. They had their regular dinner hour and at 5pm were finished for the day. Their own officer visited them daily and took up their complaints with Major Tomasson.

242 Siege Battery had been depleted by sickness, although no casualties (beyond the first at Auchonvillers) had as yet been sustained and the help from the marines made little if any difference to the spare men. We had all the night work to perform and the tasks of water fatigue and shell washing fell squarely on our shoulders. Gunner Mason and I were all that remained of the transferees from 221 Battery. Mason had become thoroughly demoralised. I knew him in England as a tall dark man of about 30 years of age. He knew all about horses and would have made an excellent officer. Now dirty and unshaven, he slouched about, his only ambition to get out of sight and to rest. I expect I was in the same condition.

It was at 5pm one evening that the CO sent for me. The night previously I had been up with the ammunition. Today I had made three journeys to Hendecourt for water; the weather was wet and the track particularly muddy. I was soaked with mud and water, unshaven and filthy and now the Major wanted to see me. What had I done wrong now?

To do Major Tomasson credit he started off with an apology. He looked me up and down and said, *"I'm awfully sorry, Hall, I had completely forgotten it until this moment. The papers about your Commission have come through and you have to see the General at half past six."* Then he showed me my application which had been sent by the War Office to the OC 221 Battery, then back to Bristol, then to 242 Battery, through the hospitals, back to base and back again to 242 Battery at Mory. *"What have you been doing today?"* *"Water fatigue,"* I replied. Then he turned to the Sgt-Major, *"What can we do to make him presentable?"* *"We can't get a spare uniform from the Quartermaster's Stores now,"* came the reply. *"Well, do what you can for Gunner Hall and I'll explain things to the General."* I went with the Sgt-Major and I verily believe he did his best for me. Hot water was obtained, I washed and shaved; some Gunners were called in who scraped the mud from my greatcoat and puttees, brushes were brought into action, the Sgt-Major found a button stick and polish and so at last, with Mr Tharpe fretting and fuming that we should be late for the interview, I went with him in the battery car to headquarters.

Headquarters were situated in an orchard some twenty miles back and when Mr Tharpe and I arrived there were some twenty candidates along with their escorts awaiting interview. My heart sank. I saw twenty young men, including several NCO's mostly wearing breeches and the short British warm overcoat, all cleaned up and smart as if for a ceremonial parade. They were by no means all confident it is true but they were all dressed up in the best uniform available to create a good impression. Many were wearing Observer's or Layer's badges.

My turn came. I discarded my still wet and muddy greatcoat which would only make my appearance, bad as it was, even worse and accompanied by Lt Tharpe marched in for interview.

The General was considerate enough but I realised from the first the hopelessness of the situation. The interviews started with an excuse and finished with an excuse. Lt Tharpe first put in an excuse for my appearance – the CO's forgetfulness. The General laughed but seemed satisfied. Now he started with the application. I had to give an excuse for leaving the secondary school prematurely – in order to obtain a special post, which never eventuated. Then I had to make an excuse for being so late at joining up – I was detained by John Brown & Co; an excuse for changing Batteries – 221 Battery was over strength. I was trained as a BCA Was I then in the BC Post? – no – the positions had been allotted before I arrived in 242. *"I see"*, said the General. *"So, of course, you are on the guns, a Gun-Layer?"* *"No, sir."* There was a nasty pause at this, well exactly what was I doing on the guns? I had to admit that I was not on the guns at all. Lt Tharpe interposed to explain Major Tomasson's arrangement of permanent gun crews and spare men. *"I see,"* said the General and the interview terminated, the General courteous to the last. I waited for Lt Tharpe who had been to see the adjutant. Later I asked him how he thought I had fared, *"I think things will be alright,"* he replied but in my heart I knew they were not. I put myself in the General's place; could I possibly have passed a Gunner of such an appearance and with such character? I reached the battery at 8pm, finished what remained of my morning's bread for tea was long since over and I had nothing to eat since noon. Then I sat to await the too familiar call *"Fall in all spare men"*.

Officially I heard no more about my application but later rumours came floating about the battery and once I overheard Bdr Maxton telling Corpl Cole that Hall's application had been turned down because ------. But they stopped talking when I approached and as I was still hoping against hope that some miracle might happen, I dare not pursue the matter further.

But if I needed confirmation it was to be found in the attitude of Sgt Peake. His attitude towards me had become positively venomous. Water fatigue, bad as it was, was too good for me; whenever possible he would have me washing shells for his team. *"It will be good training for you and when you have become an officer"* he would jeer and to the hateful call *"turn out all spare men"* he would add in his vile Staffordshire accent *"Coom on Hall"*. In this Bdr Pateman, the battery orderly faithfully imitated his master.

I was now seized with black despair. I loathed every man in the battery from the commanding officer to my fellow spare men. It was at this time that I actually prayed for death and, as if to mock my prayers, enemy shells continued to burst short of the battery position, away to Ervillers in the rear, to the valley on the right, over the hills to the left but the position itself might have been enchanted; never a stray shell fell near the guns. Oh God! For some fierce destructive shoot to grind that damnable battery into the mud and slime where it rightfully belonged. Then and only then might the survivors crawling painfully out of their shattered gun emplacements emerge with some semblance of humanity in their hearts!

My misery might be said to reach its climax on Easter Monday April 9. It was then that the Canadians captured Vimy Ridge[4]. A supporting attack was launched on our sector which had been preceded by artillery bombardments a few days before. On the day itself a barrage was laid down in the early morning and the infantry advanced, capturing a few villages. We had the unaccustomed sight of German prisoners marching down the road on their way to the cages. The inevitable counter attack took place in the afternoon, SOS messages were sent up by the infantry and all guns were brought into action to repel the enemy. The net result was that the Germans re-took some of the captured trenches but had been forced to give ground to the extent of a few hundred yards but not sufficient to justify moving the battery forward.

On the day in question I had been washing shells for No.1 gun. We had been firing heavily all morning and in the afternoon were maintaining a desultory fire on enemy strong points. No.1 gun was running hot, the obturating pad had swollen with the heat and Sibley the Limber Gunner had difficulty in closing the breech. A red line was drawn on the breech ring and on the breech block and our instructions were that these must always coincide before firing, otherwise the breech would not be properly closed and on firing might blow out and destroy the gun. The results would be fatal for anyone standing by. Sgt Peake called up the Sergeant Artificer who promptly put the gun out of action and started dismantling the breech block in order to change the pad. At this moment the SOS call went up. Major Tomasson ran up and asked why No.1 gun was not firing. He was told of the trouble. *"Put No.1 gun back into action,"* he ordered. *"But I can't, she's dangerous until the obturating pad is changed,"* replied the Artificer. *"Do as you're told,"* said the CO, *"It will be on your responsibility then, sir,"* replied the Artificer. *"All right then,"* said the Major, *"carry on firing Sgt Peake."* Whereupon the Sergeant looking very pale about the gills gave the order to load. I now saw Sibley the Limber Gunner whisper something to Peake. Then the Sergeant shouted to me, *"Now then Hall, you want to get on a gun team, here's your chance, take over No.2"* and threw over the lanyard. *"Don't fire until I tell you,"* he roared. There was nothing for it but to take up my position to the right of the gun. I attempted to close the breech but the block stuck half way. Sgt Peake picked up the wooden maul and, swinging it over his head, struck the closing handle with all his might. The safety lines nearly but not quite, met. *"Now put in the tube and fire when I tell you."* I obeyed and on the command, fired the gun. Then I saw what had happened. The whole of the team had taken cover in the cartridge recesses alongside and it was from the shelter of these that the order to fire had been given. I alone was exposed, tied to the howitzer by the lanyard a piece of rope a yard long. If the gun had exploded there was a chance for the team under cover; I should certainly have been blown to pieces. And so the shoot went on, the gap between the safety lines becoming wider and wider after every round. Even Sgt Peake and his maul could not bring the lines any nearer. Willy nilly I had to stick to my post of honour alongside the gun, watching with contempt the men in their funk holes. Then at last the attack was repelled, the firing ceased. The Sergeant Artificer proceeded to dismantle the breech, Gunner Sibley ever jealous of the privileges attached to the post of Limber Gunner resumed duty while I was set to my old task of washing shells.

But from this point onwards my condition started to improve. The following day Sgt Peake did not appear on parade. Rumour had it that he had lost his nerve. True or false he was never seen on a gun again. For some days he lay in a dugout watched over by his friend BSM Cavalier; then he was sent down the line. Corpl Cole took his place on No.1 gun although he was not actually promoted until much later. Cole had been extremely jealous of Peake and particularly disliked anyone he considered to have been the Sergeant's crony. He hinted at drastic changes in the gun team. The regular hands were not so easily deposed but the controversy made things easier for me as spare man. Sometimes when of the team was sick, I would take his place and always to Corpl Cole's satisfaction and so began my long struggle for rehabilitation.

After the attack Major Tomasson followed his usual practice of having us on parade and lecturing us on the progress of the war in general and on our part in particular. We were now approaching a lull in the battle and would be able to take things a little easier. In the first place there was to be a wash day for each sub-section in turn and he hoped that we would take full advantage of it. I think the medical officer had something to do with this arrangement as quite a number of cases of scabies had been reported. When our turn came we boiled water in cartridge cases and soon shirts, pants and socks were all boiling merrily. While these were during we washed ourselves thoroughly and soon experienced the job of being tolerably clean again.

In other ways life became easier. The weather became clearer, the mud was drying up and on dry days it was possible to get the shells into the pits in fairly clean condition so that it was only necessary to brush them before firing, instead of having to wash them in water. An April shower, it is true, would bring on the mud with its attendant discomforts again but on the whole work on the ammunition became much lighter. Wells had been sunk in Mory itself and the long trail to Hendecourt with the water-cart came to an end. Instead we fetched the water in petrol cans from the village. This was a mixed blessing – we missed the YMCA and the military bands which were always playing at Hendecourt.

Major Tomasson now decided that as water was so plentiful he would make a swimming bath for the troops. We dug a hole ten feet square by six feet deep and in this laid a tarpaulin. We now set to work to fill the tank. As everyone was supposed to benefit, all had to help and anyone with an odd half-hour to spare had to fetch a couple of cans of water. At first the tank leaked a good deal but at length we got it filled. Yet another well, nearer to the battery position, made the task lighter. The bath on completion was freely used but it is questionable whether the work was justified.

In mid-April we got a lot of reinforcements. The CO had some trouble with Cpl Jackson, his Battery Commander's Assistant, whom he relieved of his post but he would not call upon the services of either Poulton or myself. Instead he started a school of no fewer than six of these new men instructing them himself. Only one qualified however and the rest soon found themselves among the spare men. Another three men had been members of a sixty-pounder battery having all been wounded by the same shell. On recovering they were given the opportunity of transferring from Heavy to Siege and incidentally from horse to motor traction. When they arrived they were wearing their mounted uniform (breeches and the short British warm greatcoat) which the SM promptly called in. They objected and appealed to the CO pointing out that our Sergeants, though not entitled to breeches, were wearing them. They carried their point to the Major, stipulating that they would have to wear slacks once their breeches were due for replacement. The jubilant trio now joined the ranks of the spare men. This they did under protest and had fought 60 pounder guns, a much more difficult weapon for two years *"before we came up"*. They appealed to the Sergeant-Major, to the officers and finally to Major Tomasson himself. But what was to be done?

The gun-crews stuck to their posts like limpets and no-one became a spare man by choice. And so they stalked about in their breeches, grumbling all the time and comparing this rag-time battery to the one they had left. To me they became a tower of strength; I was no longer alone, I had three allies men in the same position as myself, my manhood was returning and I determined to struggle on.

First I came to grips with Bdr Pateman, the battery orderly. This NCO had developed the habit of adding to his call *"Turn out all spare men"* the words *"come on Hall"* – a trick he had learnt from Sgt Peake. One night I challenged him and demanded why I should be this singled out. (I had anticipated his visit and had been the first on my feet when he called). I said this was victimisation and if it did not stop I should report the matter to the CO. To my surprise he climbed down at once. He was sorry but he had to obey orders and call men out. *"Yes"* I agreed, *"but why mention my name in particular?"*. He said that he meant nothing by it and would not do it again. I had no further cause for complaint.

There was a peculiar episode at this time which brings out the Major's character. It was rumoured that he suffered from insomnia. Whether this is true or not he decided to walk round the vicinity of the battery in the small hours of the morning. In a field some distance away were some particularly fine poppy heads, the remains of last years' crop. Major Tomasson evidently thought these would do splendidly for camouflaging the shells and immediately called on Bdr Pateman to turn out the whole Battery. The spectacle of 100 men being roused at three o'clock in the morning to gather poppy heads may seem ludicrous. At the time we were conscious only of the brutality of the order.

At the end of April we again started accumulating ammunition and it was evident that a big attack was developing. It was at this time that we had trouble with the fuses and a serious matter it was too. I have tried to find the inner history of the matter in various documents concerning the war, all without avail. But while the scare lasted it set the whole of the artillery shivering in their shoes. It appeared that in 1917 premature, that is shells bursting either inside the guns or immediately after leaving the barrels, had become too prevalent to be accidental. It is possible that the incident in which I was involved in Auchonvillers was an early case. After much investigation the trouble was traced to faulty fuses imported from America. The Zenith Company, the contractors in question, marked their fuses with three letters "z" thus "zzz" followed by a lot number. The Zenith Company were blameless but certain of their sub-contractors had been subject to enemy machinations and all lots from 63 upwards were suspect. By the time the trouble had been traced, the fuses had been distributed to the batteries. Urgent messages were sent for all fuses to be examined and those bearing the marks zzz lot 63 and upwards removed to a special centre for destruction. It was at first thought that big batches of the suspect fuses would be located but this proved not to be the case and all the boxes of fuses had to be undone, the tins opened (one fuse to each tin) and the fuses passed by the gun Sergeants before firing. Later it was ordered that officers were to be employed on the job and I can remember poor old Lt Horner scrutinising fuses at night by the light of an electric torch. Later still it appeared that all Zenith fuses, irrespective of lot number, were suspect and had to be returned. Altogether we found about 20 dangerous fuses among our ammunition all in different boxes.

Other things were found in fuse boxes in the shape of letters from girls in munition factories addressed to *"Lonely soldiers up the line"*. One or two men communicated with the senders but I do not know with what result. Later the practice was frowned on by the authorities. There were also little pads of felt with the fuses which proved useful in plugging the ears to avoid gun deafness. The practice was to face the gun when it fired; if one turned sideways and caught the blast in one ear a nasty crack was felt which might even burst the eardrum.

Of the attack on Bullecourt[5] I remember very little except that it was a long drawn-out affair lasting from May 3 to 7, when the village at last fell into our possession. There was almost constant firing the whole time. We saw tanks[6] on the move for the first time. We were busy one evening when Major Tomasson called us up and showed us the slowly moving monsters in a hollow exclaiming dramatically, *"Look at these you men – and God help the man who says anything about them"*.

Bullecourt, at length in our possession, we did a little firing but were practically out of range. We did not follow up our success however; the Hindenburg Line proved a very hard nut to crack and no more attacks were launched in the sector – the Battle of the Somme[7] was over. Later in May the Major let it be known that we were going to Belgium.

On May 1 we pulled out the guns and sent them back to Albert. Then we proceeded to demolish the battery position; shells were rolled back to the dump and reloaded on lorries, the cartridge recesses were pulled down and the corrugated iron recovered. Even sandbags were opened and salvaged after the earth had been shaken out. Finally the bathing pool was drained, the tents struck, the lorries loaded and sent on their way. Then we set off on the long march to Albert.

So we marched away glad to leave this unhappy position; a nightmare situation, made almost unendurable. Not by the enemy, for the whole time we were there very few shells fell anywhere near the guns, but by the inhumanity of our fellow countrymen.

---

1   The Armstrong hut probably owes its name to a major in the War Office's Directorate of Fortifications and Works, which on 12 August 1914, was asked to submit plans for a standard hutted camp that could house one battalion at a war strength of 1,000 men. Having already done some preliminary work, the Directorate's design branch under Major R.H.O. Armstrong produced plans within two days. These embraced seventeen different designs, including those for officers' and sergeants' messes, a recreation hut and a large central cookhouse with a dining-

hall for a half-battalion on either side. The staple unit was a hut, 60 feet by 20 feet and with an average height of 10 feet, providing sleeping quarters for 24 men and an NCO. Forty such huts catered for a battalion's rank and file and could be built for an estimated £15,000. (In fact in February 1915 the Government was to claim an average actual cost that was lower, of £13 a man, of which £4 was for the hut, the rest for stores, lighting and recreational facilities.) By 17 August Armstrong's proposals had been approved by the Army Council and a construction programme set under way. (Source – The Great War Forum.)

2   Decauville railways (named after the Decauville manufacturing company was founded by Paul Decauville (1846–1922), a French pioneer in industrial railways) were light, narrow gauge railways used to bring men and stores closer to the front line than standard gauge lines could operate. Steam and petrol locomotives were used to haul small wagons. The tracks could be re-laid easily. Rails from these lines frequently can be seen today in use a fence posts in fields along the former Western Front.

3   Rum was issued in earthenware jars and fragments can be found easily on the battlefields today. It was regularly issued to troops typically before an attack, as a reward or in cold weather but was subject to abuses such as hoarding and there were opponents to the issue among temperance groups and some influential officers; their stance was not popular among the rank and file! Rum jars were made by a variety of manufacturers and were marked SRD – the precise meaning is unclear but suggestions include Special Red Demerara and Service Rum Distribution. The soldiers inevitably had their own acronyms such as Seldom Reaches Destination and Soon Runs Dry.

4   The capture of Vimy Ridge by British and Canadian troops was part of a major offensive in April 1917. Vimy Ridge is a huge chalk escarpment overlooking the Plain of Douai. It is now a memorial park and visitors can go undergrounds through one of the many tunnels dug to assist the advance of troops. The Canadian Memorial to the Missing is located here.

5   There were two battles at Bullecourt marked by atrocious weather and difficulties with tanks which were used in quite large numbers. The objective was to break through the Hindenburg Line but the Germans had defended the line in great depth and, as on the Somme, used fortified villages as a key part of their defences.

6   Tanks had been introduced on the Western Front in September 1916 with limited success. As with other technological developments, tanks and the tactical use of them improved in 1917 and again in 1918.

7   The Battle of the Somme in fact ran from 1 July to 5 November 1916. The operations described here by Gnr Hall were part of the Battle of Arras.

CHAPTER 12
THE CAPTURE OF MESSINES

In this chapter Gnr Hall draws attention to one of the most famous stretches of road on the Western Front, the long Roman road from Bapaume to Albert which cut through the scene of very heavy fighting in the summer of 1916. If you drive along that road today it is easy to imagine the battery travelling through the ruins of Pozieres, past the site of the windmill and Gibraltar blockhouse, the Glory Hole and, nearby, the huge crater at La Boiselle before descending to Albert still with the Golden Virgin hanging precariously from the spire of the basilica. The war had not yet finished with this sector as in March 1918 the Germans would retake the ground won by the imperial and colonial troops at such a high price. At their destination in French Flanders the terrain changed. Again we find the Germans on the high ground, this time it was Messines Ridge, a long clay formation running north-south. The preparations to dislodge them had started in 1916 with the digging of long galleries deep beneath the ridge and the planting of huge charges of ammonal ready to be blown at 3.10am on 7 June 1917. Hall's diary records the incorrect date but the scale of this offensive easily enables identification of the action he describes. The arrival of 242 Siege Battery was a late addition to the plan for this tumultuous offensive and an example of artillery being moved to where it was needed. Gnr Hall had served on the Somme, one of the places synonymous with the Great War, and now he was to enter the Ypres Salient, a huge bulge in the line that had been fought over bitterly since the German advance was halted in 1914. Sir Douglas Haig, C-in-C of the British Army, wanted an offensive in Flanders to push the Germans back from the coast and make a strategic advance eastwards but the Messines operations were deemed a necessary precursor to secure a strong southern flank for this subsequent offensive. The explosion of mines witnessed by Hall enabled the infantry to take the enemy front line and capture the villages of Messines and Wytschaete. Later in the day the advance continued down the east side of the ridge. The success of the Messines operation was in stark contrast to British offensive operations in previous years of the war.

As soon as the Mory position was cleared, Major Tomasson set off by car to Belgium, leaving the battery in charge of Capt Sanderson. Led by the Captain we started on the long march to Albert. Familiarity made the going somewhat easier but the Bapaume–Albert road with its dreary expanse of shell-holes seemed interminable. At length Pozieres was reached and the ruined tower of Albert cathedral showed ahead, the step quickened, someone struck up a tune and we began the long descent to the town. Once there the Captain led the way to our billets, very similar to those we had previously occupied and brought out his usual medicine, the rum issue. Soon we were happy enough and were determined to make the most of our welcomed holiday.

We remained at Albert for a week, a time of complete rest, that is with the exception of guard duty and it goes without saying that I managed to click one of these. We enjoyed the comfort of a really hot bath in an old brewery. There were the usual amenities; the YMCA and a couple of canteens and we were at liberty to go about as we wished. Not that there was much to see in Albert – the town had been badly knocked about and the cathedral was in ruins; that is except for the famous hanging Virgin which leaned out from the tower at an angle of 90 degrees.

On the 18 May we were on the move again, this time to the neighbouring village of Aveluy where, on the railway sidings, awaited the train that was to carry us to Belgium. First we hauled the guns up on to the flat wagons then the tractors crawled up under their own power. This accounted for the eight open wagons painted with the text 40 hommes 8 chevaux (40 men or 8 horses) and a third class coach for the officers. An engine coupled up and our long journey commenced. By now the twenty four lorries forming our convoy had gone off on their own by road to re-join us at our destination.

The train journey was an adventure in itself. There was much amusement about the wartime trains in France. Ten miles an hour was express speed, more often we travelled at four, so that when we tired of sitting on the hard floor one would often get off and walk alongside the train but, with a perverted sense of humour the driver seemed to wait until most of the passengers had alighted and then start off at a brisk pace, leaving us all running behind. The pace did not last long however and somehow we would always manage to re-join the train. Sometimes we would alight from the carriage, take a sprint to the locomotive and ask the driver for a tin-full of hot water to make tea. This was rarely refused. Sometimes we would buy hard boiled eggs and chocolates from peasants at the stations and the troops were not averse to picking up unconsidered trifles on the way. Occasionally we would pass troop trains going in the opposite direction with many of their passengers riding on the top of the carriages and on the buffers, or walking alongside. We would stop to exchange greetings and then have to sprint to catch up with the departing train.

At length we came to our destination, a station called Abeele on the France/Belgium frontier. The French town of Abeele lay some little distance from the station and we did not pass through it but a few hundred yards from the railway track was the frontier and a cluster of cottages. Painted on the wall of one of these in large white letters was the name Boeschepe. A peasant woman was standing at the cottage door, the smell of roasting chicory permeated the air, a tree-lined road leading into the distance, a peaceful enough scene – this then was Belgium. This picture is one of the most vivid of all my war experiences and the smell of roasting chicory always brings it back to me. It is afternoon, I see the cottages, the watching woman and the train standing in the sidings ready for unloading. Then I see us as we fall in and drag the guns from the trucks, the Caterpillars hook up, the battery is ready and so we move slowly up the lane. Our new adventure had begun.

After the waste and filth of the Somme this part of the front seemed singularly peaceful, although we could hear the guns rumbling in the distance.

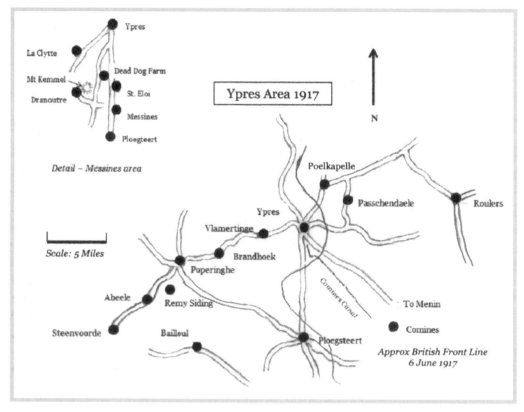

Ypres Area 1917

We did not advance far that day but soon reached Poperinge, the railhead for the sector and here we parked the guns and retired for the night in an old hop warehouse. Poor old Poperinge, "Pop" as it was called, a charming old town, it was bombed nightly and always being shelled by long range guns. The square in front of the railway station could tell some ghastly tales of troops with their leave chits in their pockets waiting with excitement for the train that was to take them to the port on the first stage of their eagerly awaited leave. But for them the train never came, a long range shell landed along them and they were buried in the ever increasing military cemetery. But the brave old town stood its punishment well and trade was carried on as usual. I visited Poperinge on several occasions and every time found that some well-known landmark had disappeared.

The following morning May 21 we left the guns behind and advanced not on the straight road to Vlamertinge and Ypres of evil reputation but turned right through Reninghelst, a peaceful old town with its lopsided church, then through La Clytte, a hamlet by the crossroads, which was to figure largely in my later adventures. Civilians were still in occupation and after the Somme and the evacuated land it gave us considerable surprise to see them working so close to the line. But soon after the crossroads a notice posted to a tree informed civilians that they must not pass east of this point without a special permit. Then came Kemmel village with its chateau beautiful still in ruins and another crossroads with the words on a huge board "Hell Fire Corner", calm enough now but large shell holes showed that the name was well earned. A little way on the road to the right we passed through Lindenhoek, a village deserted but still intact and soon afterwards we halted. Here was to be the battery position.

We looked at one another in surprise. We had heard so much of Ypres that pockmarked mass of mud and shell holes we had seen pictures of its ruin and desolation. Yet here was a peaceful country lane, no sound of firing, no shell holes, farm buildings still intact and fields that seemed to have been neglected for only a little while. Yet across the road was the entrance to the main communication trench and we were nearer to the enemy than we had ever been before. Actually it was just over a mile to our front line trenches. It was not until later that we realise the cause of this apparent contradiction. Ypres lay ten miles to the north. Successive advances by the British had driven the enemy back east of the town until a huge salient had been formed but here at the right flank of the salient a condition of stalemate prevailed. The secret of this lay in the hills. Whereas the ground round Ypres was quite flat, here to the right flank were hills, of little elevation it is true but sufficient to hold up operations from both forces. We held the highest hill Mount Kemmel and the Germans on the other hand were in possession of Wytschaete[1] Ridge some four miles to the east. The battle front lay in a valley midway between these two elevations. The British held the most favourable position for with Mount Kemmel in our possession we could observe the enemy in comfort. Observation posts were constructed on the face of the hill, actually well behind the batteries, a most unusual state of affairs and from here the country opened up like a map. With Kemmel Hill in our possession the Germans could not possibly hope to advance. Actually they did little but fire at Hell Fire Corner[2] where all traffic was bound to pass. The enemy, for his part, was not so fortunate but he had a good view of our lines from Messines and Wytschaete Ridge. It is no wonder that the civilians in the neighbourhood felt secure. However the fierce tide of battle might ebb or flow on the Ypres Salient, here on the right flank the ripples were hardly felt.

Where we halted was a deserted farm, the buildings adjoining the road, intact as they had been left by the fleeing occupants, although the furniture had long since disappeared. Perhaps the farmer had obtained permission to remove his goods and chattels. Like our British farms and unlike the French, the farm was divided into fields by thick hedges. An orchard now overgrown with weeds lay alongside the road and a large pasture sloped gently from the orchard. Towards the side of the field could still be discerned a faint track formerly used by the farm wagons. One could imagine a farm hand at the close of the day leading his horses to the stables, little dreaming that the next to use his tracks would be 8 inch howitzers. At the bottom of this field and about 200 yards from the roadside was another field divided from the first by a thick hedge about six feet high. Behind this hedge we were to place our guns.

The ground continued to slope in the second field until at the foot was a tiny rivulet where cattle drank in the far off days of peace but one or two shells had fallen into the stream and by causing an obstruction had turned the ground into something of a marsh. On the far side of this marsh were to be the officers' quarters.

Major Tomasson met us in the orchard when we arrived and proceeded to lecture us about our changed conditions. He stressed our proximity to the front line and told us that every care was to be taken to conceal the position. We must always walk about cautiously under the cover of the hedges – under no circumstances were we to run. (This seemed strange to us for a while; at Mory the cry had been *"double",* now it was to *be "don't double – walk!"*) We must not make tracks; leave no tins about and so on. But the most welcome news was that henceforth reliefs were to be worked. Billets had been secured at Kemmel and detachments would work turns about so that at any rate we could rely on one full night's rest in two.

Preparing the Lindenhoek position was not nearly such a formidable task as at Mory. The weather was good; the ground fairly level, there were one or two shell-holes about but these could easily be avoided. While some of us were laying planks others were at work making artificial hedges. Bushes obtained from a distance were threaded into ten foot pieces of wire netting mounted on a framework and when these were ready gaps were cut in the real hedge and the counterfeit article substituted. From a distance they looked sufficiently like the real thing. The idea was to remove the framework when firing and to replace it quickly whenever enemy aircraft appeared on the scene. The camouflage brought over from Mory was no use as this was a green position as opposed to the dirty white prevailing at Mory. Accordingly we tore out the bits of sandbag and replaced them by tufts of grass. In time, of course, the grass withered and had to be replaced – this was one of the constant chores at Lindenhoek. Under the camouflages we erected shelters for the detachments on duty who were to sleep on the guns and for cartridges and fuses.

The guns arrived on the evening of the 21 May. The transport officer wished to bring them right into the emplacements and there was quite an argument before he was over-ruled by Major Tomasson. Accordingly the tractors deposited their guns in the orchard and withdrew.

As usual Capt Sanderson now took charge. Standing on the gun trail, a most dangerous position incidentally for if the piece had got out of control, he might well have been thrown and crushed to death. With fifty men aside on the drag ropes and others in rear with levers and hand spokes, he alone directed the operations. He had an eye for everything and a tongue that wheedle that bit of extra effort or if anyone was not pulling his weight could bite like a lash. When the task was too much for a direct pull, we would get more purchase by passing the ropes over the rims of the wheels. Sometimes the gun would sink in the soft ground. Then planks had to be fetched, the wheels dug out and run on to them. Shell holes required careful negotiation. Whether we liked the Captain or not, we could not but admire his handling of the guns and his stentorian voice as he bellowed his orders will ever remain in my memory *"On the ropes,"* he would shout. *"Take the strain – now, taut heave – heave – heave – heave – now, walk away with it – Jackson you're not pulling – come on – keep her going – heave – heave – she's stopped – quick Corporal Coleman take a purchase over the right rope – now then don't let her sink – taut heave – heave – now she's coming – that's fine – now pull on the left rope while we take another purchase – mind that shell hole – heave – heave – heave."* Sometimes he would jump from his position on the gun, seize an iron shod lever and with a tremendous effort, throw the trail right over and so extricate the gun from an awkward position.

At Lindenhoek we manhandled all four guns, distances varying from two to three hundred yards over soft ground and with two right-angled turns. Often we could manage only six inches to each pull and sometimes not even that. A nasty shell-hole lay in the way of No.4 gun and in spite of all our efforts, one of the wheels sank up to the axle and had to be dug out. It should be remembered that the ordnance weighed over ten tons each and had great iron shod wheels six feet in diameter. The whole operation was the most difficult we ever undertook and looking back was quite unnecessary; the tractors could have done the job in a fraction of the time. Once the guns were in position, we carefully obliterated all traces of the tracks that had been made.

The Sergeant-Major had now drawn up the schemes that would provide the promised relief. Eight detachments of eight men each were provided. To accomplish this water-fatigue and double guard were abolished and the interminable sorting and re-sorting of cartridges disappeared, while a number of employed men were relieved of their duties to serve on the guns. The first detachments as they were called were led by the four Sergeants while the Corporals were in charge of the second. The personnel was completely rearranged and thus I became No.7 loading number on No.3 gun, second detachment under Corporal Coleman. My association with No.1 gun and Sergeant Peake's cronies was at an end.

At 9pm on May 22 the guns being ready for action and a reasonable amount of ammunition brought up, the first detachments marched off to billets at Kemmel leaving the Corporal's reliefs on duty. We did some firing during the night and managed quite well on our own, despite the smaller number on duty. The first detachments returned to take over at 9am May 23 but in the night there had been an unfortunate occurrence at Kemmel; one of the men having been killed[3] by a long range shell. This was our first casualty by enemy action (the death of Gunner Rees on February 22 was regarded as an accident) and Major Tomasson was genuinely distressed. He had us all on parade and explained the circumstances. He said he had made full enquiries before selecting the rear billets and had been told that there had been no shelling on that part of Mount Kemmel for the past eighteen months. He could not explain the isolated shot that had killed our colleague except that it might have been a case of the enemy emptying his guns at extreme elevation. He was arranging to shift the billets to another part of the hill which he felt certain was safe. The Major's concern over the casualty certainly threw a fresh light on his character.

After the parade we handed the guns over to the first detachments but we remained at the position doing various fatigues until evening, when we marched away to rear billets were we arrived at 9.30pm tired after a hard day's work. The canteen was still open however and we were able to get a good supper, stroll round Kemmel Hill, watch the gun flashes in the distance and go to bed with the glorious feeling that now we should sleep content and the terrible cry *"turn out all spare men"* should trouble us no more. We rose at 7am, breakfasted and set off down the hill to relieve the first detachments at 9.

For myself I was delighted with the new arrangements. I was now a regular member of a gun team, taking my part with the rest and no longer subject to the indignity of waiting on others. There were some men however who were by no means satisfied. Major Tomasson was determined that the Decauville railway should not be used and the lines that we had brought from Mory were hidden under camouflage in the orchard. It was the main job of the detachment off duty to see that the guns were supplied with ammunition. Compared with Mory this was child's play. The ground was hard and dry and downhill all the way to the guns. The shells only needed guiding on their way with sticks. When the shells reached the pits they were clean and dry and needed only brushing to be ready for use. Nevertheless many of the men who had been on the original gun crews now objected to doing their share of shell humping, formerly the duty of the spare men. Moreover the guns were of course being fought shorthanded which made harder work; there was still a considerable element in favour of a return to full gun teams and spare men.

Concealment of the battery position was very difficult. The artificial hedge had to be kept in good condition, all faded branches had to be removed daily and replaced by fresh and the flash patch in front of the guns where the blast of firing tended to wither the grass had to be watered continually and fresh grass had to be woven into the camouflaging netting daily. The strain of constantly having to walk close to the hedges was considerable and the greatest care had to be taken when hostile aircraft were about. When firing in the daylight, two men on each gun were always on the alert to replace the gaps in the hedge at the shortest notice.

In spite of the apparent calm we could never forget the proximity to the front line; field guns were now our close neighbours and the crackle of machine guns a familiar sound. Hostile aircraft circled overhead, enemy kite balloons seemed very close, the glint of sunlight on an empty cartridge case might have brought into action every hostile battery that could bear on the position.

But the weather was glorious; we could work in our shirt sleeves and with the system of reliefs, had time to concentrate in keeping down the lice. Parades were few and discipline relaxed to some extent. Firing was not particularly heavy and even the detachment on duty could snatch a few hours' sleep during the night in the recesses alongside the guns. Sometimes we would wander off during the day, never out of sight of the guns, to the springs where water bubbled out of the ground. It was at a spring by the roadside one day that, listening to the drone of the insects and seeing the wild flowers that grew in profusion, I felt deluded that the war simply did not exist and that I was merely on a visit to a familiar and pleasant countryside.

But, early in June, it became evident that we had been brought into this strange battlefield for some definite purpose; ammunition kept arriving in ever increasing quantities; a battle was imminent.[4]

At 9am June 8 we, the second detachments, arrived from Kemmel and took over the guns until 9am the following day.[5] The first detachments went on fatigues until nightfall when according to plan, they returned to rear billets. Soon after they left we started on a long slow shoot, one round every two minutes until further orders. Then at 2am June 9, Major Tomasson visited each emplacement and in a most dramatic manner warned us to be ready for something happening at 3am. We continued with our slot shoot. A few minutes before 3am the first detachments arrived from Kemmel and came into the gun pits. Evidently they had been brought back for some purpose. Meanwhile we continued firing. Then came the Sergeant-Major's order: *"Sergeants to take over"* and I saw Sgt Sturt take the clinometers from the hands of Corpl Coleman who, in turn, went to the dial sight.

Then came the explosion. Mines had been sprung under the enemy lines at Messines, Wytschaete and St Eloi. The shock was terrific; the ground trembled like jelly – for a moment we were all stunned.[6]

Then the Field Artillery opened out while an instant later with a roar like an express train a shell passed over our heads as a 12 inch gun whose presence we had never even suspected joined in. Meantime the cry *"gun fire"* (fire as rapidly as possible without waiting for orders) went up. Sgt Sturt yelled out *"first detachments take over and start loading"*. Some sprang into action at once but others seemed too bewildered to do anything. Then Sturt, frenzied at the delay, called out *"come on, anybody, only load and let's get going"*. This was just what I wanted. On the first order I had stood aside to give way for the first detachment, as had my opposite number on the other side of the loading tray. He had been properly relieved but Gunner Weeks, loading number on the Sergeant's team seemed bewildered and slow to take his cue. On the words *"Come on anybody"* I resumed my post even as I saw him coming forward to take over and pushed him out of the way. The new No.5 and I now lifted the tray between us and were carrying the shell to the bore. I saw Weeks pick himself up and assume a threatening attitude but now I was helping to ram home the shell. As we jumped clear to reload the Sgt–Major appeared *"Now then, all spare men out of the pit and on to the ammunition dump"* but by then I was on the gun trail with another shell and I saw the disconsolate Weeks leave the gun emplacement. I was no longer a spare man.

So we fought the battle of Messines and when Sgt Sturt came to take stock in the morning, he found a very mixed team on No.3 gun. He, as the Gun Captain, with our Corporal as his Gun Layer, I partnering one of his men on the loading tray, another second team man on the cartridges, while two of his team were dejectedly making their way down by the hedge rolling shells.

The billets at Kemmel were never again occupied. The gun teams were brought up to full strength again and spare men reintroduced but while we were at Lindenhoek, I always managed to keep my precarious hold on No.3 gun team.

Fierce firing continued well into the morning of June 9, after which we maintained a slow fire at five minute intervals for some days and nights without cessation. During this time we managed to work some form of unofficial relief; spells of four hours on the guns and four hours sleeping in the gun-side shelters. The spare men of course carried on as usual but I was not now concerned with them. I managed to sleep on my off spells although troubled with terrific nightmares caused by the constant firing of the gun within a yard of my head. On one occasion we were sitting on the trail waiting for the time to fire but one of us had dozed off. Sgt Sturt looked at his watch. *"Times up,"* he said and we all took post except the sleeping man. *"Hello,"* said the Sergeant when he saw what had happened. *"Watch me wake him up."* And before anyone could say a word of protest he fired the gun. But he failed in his object, the sleeper did not wake and we had to move him before we could reload.

The slow firing dragged on until midday June 9 when it suddenly came to an end in response to a sarcastic enquiry from the infantry as to why a certain 8 inch siege battery was firing at regular intervals at precisely nothing. On investigation it transpired that certain orders had been misread and the slow shoot should have terminated on the morning of the 7. The battery was now unable to perform any further useful work from Lindenhoek and was put out of action and the Major went to find a more suitable place for the guns.

On the morning of June 10, he gave us a lecture on the conduct of the battle and announced a day's holiday which he recommended we should spend on Mount Kemmel, where we could see for ourselves what had happened. I jumped at the opportunity. Though only 185 feet high, Mount Kemmel towered above the otherwise flat countryside. In front lay the Messines-Wytschaete Ridge and the Comines Canal, mostly dry but with pools of water in places. Beyond the canal could be seen the ground east of Ypres of evil memory. The front line now stretched north to south and it seemed difficult to imagine that the Germans had occupied that terrific bulge only a few days ago. Occasionally we could see enemy shells bursting over our new front line like bits of cotton wool and we realised that, before the battle, every shell the enemy fired could be traced to its source by the watchers on Kemmel Hill. The taking of Messines Ridge had mattered for our comrades before Ypres. The southern part of the salient had virtually ceased to exist.

So ended the most spectacular attack of all times; all our objectives had been taken and the attack was a greater success than the most optimistic ever imagined. We ourselves were shaken by the magnitude of the explosion but never have I seen such trembling wrecks of men as were the prisoners taken on that occasion. Many critics believe that the attack on Messines should have been followed up and that the victorious troops allowed to go forward to Roulers and beyond. Certain it was that all opposition had been crushed for the moment and it is possible that had sufficient troops been thrown into the gap, the enemy might have been forced to withdraw from Belgium altogether. Against this caution said that on such a narrow front it would have been suicidal to allow our troops to penetrate into the hinterland.

The front straightened out, the Salient eliminated, the ridges in our possession. All that remained was to launch a grand attack over the widest front possible, the catchwords 'grand attack' caught on and was echoed from one end of the line to the other.

And now a new battery position had been found for us and we proceeded to demolish Lindenhoek. Shells were rolled back to the dump in the orchard and reloaded onto the lorries and we realised it was a much more difficult job rolling them uphill than down to the guns. Then, as we were well out of sight of the enemy, we threw back the artificial hedges and pulled the guns forward just clear of the emplacements and this time the tractors were allowed to pull them up the field on to the road and so to the next position.

Thus we evacuated Lindenhoek.

1   Wytschaete is a village along the road winding up the ridge from Armentieres passing through Messines and then St Eloi and into Ypres. Being on the high ground it was well defended by the Germans.

2   Hell Fire Corner was a very dangerous road junction just on the road south from Ypres to Zillebeke under constant observation by the Germans.

3   The only casualty that may match this one described by Hall is 111727 Act Bdr Henry Holdsworth Whitear, killed in action on 30 May and buried in Dranoutre Military Cemetery, plot 1, row J, grave 15.

4   The accumulation of ammunition would also be a sign of an impending attack that enemy aircraft would seek while patrolling above the lines.

5   Gnr Hall recorded the incorrect date. The offensive at Messines which started with nineteen huge mines being exploded under the German lines commenced on 7 June 1917. The objective was to push the line forward south of Ypres from where German troops had been withdrawn to strengthen the Arras and Aisne sectors. It was also a prelude to the far large scale offensive known as Third Ypres which started on 31 July 1917. The battle was very successful at a cost and a severe setback for the Germans in Belgium.

6   It was said that the sound of nineteen huge mines being fired at 3.10am could be heard in London. Three other mines were not blown that day and one exploded in 1955 after a lightning strike.

CHAPTER 13
THE JULY ATTACK

Following the Messines operations in June, 242 Siege Battery moved two miles south of the ramparts of Ypres to take a new position on the lane running SW between Voormezeele and St Eloi close to the site of Bus House Cemetery[1] where the ground was well marked by a series of mines blown in March 1916 and still visible. The July attack was Third Ypres, an offensive running from 31 July to 10 November 1917 often referred to simply as 'Passchendaele'. This part of the front was favoured by Haig for a major offensive as it was nearer his base of supply and had the potential for a more important strategic outcome. By this stage of the war the lessons of previous operations had been well learned, infantry tactics improved and the artillery had better guns and ammunition. The objectives were to capture certain ridges in the Ypres Salient to enable the major railway junction at Roulers to be taken and, secondly, to clear the enemy from the section of the Belgian coast that they held. The front was 13,700 yards wide and initially it was successful especially around Pilckem Ridge but German counterattacks frustrated the British and, when the rain came, the battlefield turned into the quagmire so often depicted in scenes of the Great War; the attack came to a halt by the end of August. In late September/early October further assaults were made and on 6 November the Canadians captured Passchendaele.

We had been dilatory in moving and it was not until June 13 that we were established in our next position outside Voormezeele. We had moved northwards rather than in a forward direction and were now 5 miles south of Ypres. In fact we were fairly close to St Eloi, which before the advance had been the most southerly point of the salient and from whence the line took a sharp right-handed turn to the quieter Messines sector. All this had been straightened out by the attack of June 6. Further from the protecting eye of Mount Kemmel and nearer to the fiery salient it was natural that the buildings had suffered more than at Lindenhoek. We were gathered round what had been a large farm a few hundred yards east of the village. Some troops had previously been in occupation and had built some very strong shelters in the vicinity. The farmhouse had been un-roofed but was capable of protecting the gun stores and the cook-house, which faced a large pond covered with green scum where lived a great number of large green frogs who croaked incessantly. The guns were widely separated, No.1 being in the orchard and the others, masked by a hedge, faced the narrow lane running between the villages of Grout Vierstraat and Voormezeele. This country lane bordered by deep ditches on either side was later to prove considerable trouble, for it was the only way of reaching the advanced posts in this part of the line. That is without going through Voormezeele village, which was very dangerous owing to enemy gun fire.

We were by no means so close to the enemy as at Lindenhoek and it was obvious that the comparative comfort of the former position was due in no small measure to the proximity of the Germans. In the first place the scheme for two reliefs was definitely abandoned, the fixed gun crews were reintroduced and spare men again paraded for duty. I was most disappointed at not being chosen as a regular member of a team; the old hands were too well entrenched for that but later it appeared that I was destined to drift about from one gun to another, officiating for any member who was absent from duty and it was rarely I was called upon to perform the menial tasks of the spare men. In this connection a large number of supernumery NCO's had been created to work on the double teams at Lindenhoek and now that single manning was in operation again they crowded into the pits. On one occasion I worked on one detachment with another Gunner and nine NCO's.

Accommodation at the battery was very restricted. Although the shelters were secure, a space of fifteen inches by six feet was all the space allowed for each man and his equipment. In addition they were very verminous and after a severe outbreak of scabies, they were inspected by the medical officer who ordered them to be thoroughly disinfected. The spare men were billeted in dugouts which had been found in an old communication trench some 500 yards in rear of the guns. Direct access to these forbidden owing to the possibility of making tracks across the field and a wide detour to secure the protection of hedges had to be made, with the result that it took half an hour to reach the battery. This meant that the unfortunate spare men had to carry all their valuables about with them as they were quite unable to reach the billets without being missed. After the rear billets had been raided by some marauders, it was decided to fix an informal guard to protect the property and this proved to be the only soft job provided by 242 Siege Battery. It became the perquisite of the formal battery guard. After being on duty all night it was thought they might as well retire to the rear billets and sleep there, thus protecting battery property during the day.

The rear billets were mere shelters in the trench, each capable of holding a couple of men and comfort depended in a large measure on the sleeping partner. One night I returned from a spell of officiating and was compelled to join forces with Dungworth, a new reinforcement. I should have known better for he was verminous and dirty in his habits that he was more or less sent to Coventry. The following morning I took off my shirt and found myself in a terrible condition. The Sergeant-Major appeared on the scene and asked why I was not on the ammunition. I pleaded extraordinary circumstances and was allowed to continue the delousing while Dungworth was hauled off to account for his filthy condition. That night I fixed up a shelter of my own. There were a number of eighteen pounder ammunition boxes about, each containing four live shells and from these I constructed a tolerably comfortable if decidedly dangerous shelter. As I expected it was condemned next day but by then I had a place on another gun team. There was a deep pond near the rear billets and in this we would bathe at night, members of the gun teams being liberated in turn. A pleasant sensation although ten o'clock at night was hardly the best time to bathe.

With guns so widely spread out Voormezeele proved a most difficult position to work and we were thankful when Major Tomasson at long last capitulated in the matter of the Decauville railway. We were allowed to lay one track and use the little wagon for bringing up shells but only on condition that the lines were covered with grass when not in use. The farthest pit was some 400 yards from the ammunition dump and it was some time before we could lay the rails the whole distance owing to a little stream between Numbers 3 and 4 guns, which had to be bridged. When at length the Decauville was finished, Major Tomasson decided on a much more ambitious scheme, that of camouflaging the whole battery position. Hitherto each gun had its separate camouflage shelter. The object now was to connect the camouflages together in one long passage so that it would be possible to travel from one end of the battery position to the other away from prying eyes of hostile aircraft. Hundreds of poles were used and all kinds of wire netting. As much as possible was obtained from the stores already threaded with green rags but when this supply ran out we made our own camouflages by threading tufts of grass on to plain wiring. When the job was completed we could run our trucks from the dump to all the guns without having to stop for enemy aeroplanes.

But the grand attack was not to be hurried. We bombarded enemy strong points vigorously, collected a prodigious amount of ammunition and continued our work of camouflaging. And now the enemy began to retaliate. One night towards the end of June he gave us a good gassing (the first we had experienced) and we were ordered to retire to the flank which we did to such purpose that many did not return to the battery before morning. We had not long been issued with the new box respirators – these gave adequate protection but were unpleasant to use.

Other preparations for the attack were being made and one of these was the Main Overland Track. This was just a rough path which cut across the front of our position towards the front line and was intended for infantry, pack mules and Field Artillery so as to relieve the congested lanes. Large signboards[2] bore the directions *"Main Overland Track leading to Swan & Edgars, The Brasserie, Dead Dog Farm, Moated Grange, Shelley Dump, Oosthoek Farm and the Damstrasse"*. Swan & Edgars, where the track started, was an old trench system some way behind the battery position, the Brasserie a former estaminet with a brew house attached further down our lane on the way to Grout Vierstraat whence the track ran parallel with our lane to Dead Dog Farm, after which it turned sharply eastwards towards the front line. The other places were landmarks on the way and the terminus of the track was at the Damstrasse,[3] a notorious sunken road captured at the same time as Messines. Passing so close to the battery position the Overland Track certainly attracted enemy fire but worse was to follow. One morning towards the end of June a party of pioneers arrived at the lane in front of our No.2 gun and started laying a corduroy road straight across the hill towards the German lines. This was a trick learned from the Canadians. Logs of timber were laid on the ground securely spiked together. Later when the road got worn out either by hostile shelling or heavy traffic, it was covered with stones until the road became eventually fully metalled. There were many such roads laid in this sector. And we now saw a gleaming white road being laid in full view of the enemy. The casualties suffered by the pioneers were terrific and it is no exaggeration to say that each plank cost a life. They would lay some planks in the morning, the Germans would shell them and destroy a good number and then the pioneers would return replace the damaged planks until by the end of the day the road had advanced a little further. At last it led right out of sight over the hill.

The work undoubtedly drew shell fire on us for, however carefully the battery position was concealed, it lay just at the point where the new road started. The first day of the new work a Gunner sitting in a wheelbarrow eating his dinner was killed by a shell which threw him out of his seat.[4] There was an aversion to sitting in wheelbarrows after this. Three men were seriously wounded the following day and so on. At Voormezeele we lost ten men, one killed the rest wounded, among the latter Sgt Sturt. The casualties had a subduing effect on the troops; the immunity from shell fire we had hitherto enjoyed had gone for good. Gunner Waddington and some of the more arrogant members of the original gun-teams had been wounded and were evacuated down the line. The replacements were of a very different type from the original personnel, mostly youths, willing enough to help but of very indifferent physique and quite incapable of doing the heavier work on the guns. Sgt Sturt on the other hand was replaced by Sgt Green, a wounded NCO of considerable experience who was to prove a pillar of strength in the days ahead and one or two junior NCO's were introduced into the battery who, like the Sergeant, were men of experience.

The weakening of the rank and file made matters more difficulty for those of us who were left. Voormezeele was a difficult place to supply with ammunition on account of the new narrow lane and the deep ditches alongside. There seemed to be no alternative but to carry shells from the lorries. The ditch was spanned by narrow planks and across these it was necessary to pass. The newcomers gamely enough tried their hands at carrying but often collapsed when the shell was laid on their shoulders, as I had done months before at Auchonvillers. There was not the contempt shown for these failures as had been meted out to me but the strain on the remaining Gunners was considerable when it is realised that only a third of the men were capable of dealing with the shells. The work of carrying cartridges and fuses devolved on the weaker men.

I had not been long at Voormezeele when I joined the shell party. Spurred on by some sarcastic remark by the Sergeant in charge, I left the cartridge men and joined the queue for shells and was gratified to find that I was now quite capable of the heavier work. Later on when ammunition began to arrive in greater quantities, work became more severe. Even when the whole battery turned out the shell party numbered only 30 against twice that number of cartridge men. On one occasion after a particularly exhausting day, thirty lorries arrived with ammunition. Only one at a time could be dealt with owing to the restricted space and we thirty lay in a row on the grass. As each man's turn arrived he would walk to the lorry tail, take a shell on his shoulder and stagger across the plank bridge to the dump. Here he would pitch off his shell, rouse the next man and immediately drop asleep until his next turn arrived. Not a few collapsed with their load that night but fortunately no accident occurred. For shell carrying we would pack our shoulders with empty sandbags. Great care had to be taken to balance the shell properly, for once the weight was taken on the shoulder, it could not be shifted and many a man was pulled over by an ill-balanced shell. Now that I had shown my capabilities, I advanced in the esteem of my colleagues. I had the satisfaction of knowing that my treatment, if hard, was at least no worse than my fellow Gunners and it was rarely that I was without a job on one or other of the guns for the most part as one of the loading numbers.

Many were the rumours about the grand attack. We had the ammunition in readiness long before the date and we enlarged the pits so as to fire at wider angles. And so the days wore on, the glorious summer weather continued and still we waited.

But as July advanced a disconcerting matter became apparent; we seemed to have lost our supremacy in the air. From the earliest dates we had seen duels in the air and aeroplanes brought down in flames, sometimes ours, sometimes the enemy's but it was difficult for us groundlings to understand what was happening above us. We knew, however, of the slow moving machines on patrol over the enemy lines, how they would be attacked by bodies of enemy fighters and have to make for home. We also saw enemy observation planes flying over our position taking photographs until driven away by a flight of our own machines. We watched the anti-aircraft guns open fire on marauders, firing with such rapidity that there were sometimes a hundred or more puffs of smoke in the air at once, like balls of cotton wool where the shells had burst. We had always been told that our aircraft were superior in all ways to the enemy's and who were we to dispute it? Then suddenly he started his attack on our kite balloons.[5] On our sector one day he destroyed two in the morning and when they were replaced, he destroyed them again in the afternoon and again at night. Another day he shot down four, one after the other, while the day following no less than six were in flames at the same time. And our airmen seemed unable to protect our balloons and when they went over the German lines to retaliate, he drove them away.

Little had been said about the kite balloons. Every mile or so they were suspended about four miles in rear of the front line. From their elevated position two officers watched the enemy line reporting any movement that took place. From the observation point of view it is possible that they were overrated and the one or two shoots we conducted with their help were anything but a success. They were the most helpless thing in the war. There were no means of protection and when attached the Observers had to jump for it and hope that they would not get caught in the bag of flames falling with them. Shooting up kite balloons was good sport for all concerned. Aeroplanes delighted in the job, long range guns would fire at them and there were occasions (during advances) when they had to contend with machine gun fire. When attached by hostile aircraft, our anti-aircraft guns dare not fire for fear of harming the balloons and the task of protecting them was laid solely to the fighter aeroplanes. When these failed the balloonists were in a sad plight.

But if their use was small and their upkeep heavy, the moral effect on the troops was enormous. They were the only instruments of war that could be plainly seen by the opposing troops. To us they represented eyes and from our battery position we saw two series of eyes, the protesting eyes of our own kite balloons ever watching over our interests and over the German lines another malignant eye intent on mischief. When attacks were staged the kite balloons would be brought up overnight and in the morning they could be seen high in the heavens and almost over the enemy lines always watching. Then if the German eyes withdrew we knew the day was ours. And so on that day when six of our observation balloons were brought down in flames we felt blinded and in the distance we saw not the one baneful eye to which we were accustomed but three larger and more daring for the enemy had brought them forward to see what preparations we were making for the grand attack. So it seemed that if our aeroplanes were unable to protect our observation balloons, where was our supremacy in the air? We watched and saw that in the duels in the air our men seemed to be coming off second best and that enemy reconnaissance planes flew over our position without let or hindrance.

So we continued camouflaging, watered the flash-patches and never ventured beyond our screened corridors. Not only us but it seemed every battery in the sector. Roads were screened for miles back, sometimes with netting twenty feet in height. Dummy guns were set up and false tracks leading to nowhere were made. On one occasion I saw a strange battery at work. Drawing fire they told me. They moved into a vacant field some distance from our rear billets and promptly opened fire on one of the German sensitive spots. When the inevitable German aeroplane came round to investigate, they did not cover up but continued firing as if in defiance. Their Gunners did all the things we had been told to avoid; they made tracks, ran about while the aircraft was overhead, threw about tins to catch the sun, lit fires and so on. In a short time the enemy dropped a few shells on the position and the battery seemed satisfied. They withdrew, leaving four dummy guns, logs laid across old cart wheel in the field. It seemed a bit too obvious to me but a few days later I noticed a goodly number of fresh shell holes on the pitch and the counterfeit guns had been destroyed so the subterfuge was successful.

July 13 was probably the most important day in my Army career. I had been fighting No. 1 gun for some days but the Gunner for whom I had been officiating had returned to duty and when the gun teams were called out I was again left with the spare men and not feeling too pleased. The Sgt-Major noticed, however, that there was a man short on No. 2 Gun. The firing number or Limber Gunner as he was called had been casualtied the day before and it was evident that he would not return to the battery. The SM called me from the ranks. *"You have done Limber Gunner, haven't you Hall?" "Yes Sir, at Mory,"* I replied with some bitterness, for I remembered the last occasion when I had been allowed to fire the gun. *"Very good then,"* he directed. *"You had better take over Limber Gunner on No. 2 Gun permanently. I shall transfer you to the Sub-Section."* I fell in with the team, marched to gun and took up my post. After seven long months I had at last become a permanent member of a gun team.

Targets were soon coming in merrily and I performed my duties to the best of my ability and to the satisfaction of the Gun Captain, Sgt Green, opening and closing the breech, elevating and depressing and of course firing the gun. Between shoots I followed the Limber Gunners' usual practice, oiling up, cleaning the breech block and generally messing about while the others were working the ammunition. I had now my regular job and felt that life was worth living.

As the day wore on it was evident that the gun was not working properly. She was, as we say, knocking badly – that is, after firing the barrel, instead of returning in an orderly fashion, would rush back with a rather alarming jar. I called Sgt Green's attention to this and he soon had the Staff Sergeant Artificer on the scene. Tiffy diagnosed the trouble as low air pressure, a frequent cause of complaint with 8 inch howitzers. The air compressor was brought into use and pressure brought up to normal. After this the gun should have lasted for a week at least without further attention but in the afternoon she started failing again and by tea time the pressure had gone down like a punctured tyre. Tiffy now decided that the business was beyond him and reported that the gun must go into ordnance workshops for repair. This meant a big job of pulling out for the team but it also meant a few days holiday for two of us, for it was the usual practice for the Limber Gunner and another of the team to accompany the gun to the workshops to attend to the brakes when travelling and to help the RAOC[6] with the repairs. There was some argument as to who should go but Sgt Green was obdurate; although I had been in the sub-section only that day I was properly appointed Limber Gunner and so should enjoy the privileges attached to the post. After some discussion it was agreed that Gunner Reed, an elderly loading number, should accompany me.

Soon after 6pm Major Tomasson had another outburst. He had been examining the camouflaging and had discovered that some tufts of grass had withered and had not been replaced by fresh. Without more ado he called out every man in the battery to the work, that is with the exception of No.2 team, who were working on the emplacement preparatory to withdrawing the gun. Some men were set to work cutting grass from in the meadows, while others were extracting the withered grass from the wire netting and then started the weary work of threading in the new. Each tuft of grass had to be threaded through the netting and tied and as they were six inches apart and there were many hundreds of feet of camouflaging, the task was of some magnitude. Everyone was impressed for the work and on this occasion Major Tomasson even violated the immunity of the cook, for Big Bill Turner, much against his will, had been requisitioned. The immovability of the cook had hitherto been respected; his job was a hard one and on active service the comfort was largely dependent on him. Hitherto none had dared to dictate to Turner as to how he should spend his leisure hours (if indeed he had any) but we knew that there were such jobs as cutting up bacon and preparing the meat for tomorrow's dinner and though it might afford some satisfaction to see him at work with the others, we knew that we should suffer for it in the long run.

By dark we started pulling out the crippled gun. Reed and I packed our belongings in sandbags and strapped them to the trail. We drew rations from the cookhouse; a piece of bacon, a couple of tins of Maconochies and some tea, bread and cheese. Then we realised that we were short of ready money so we decided to beard the lion in his den. Major Tomasson, however, was in quite a jovial spirit and readily acceded to our request. We were well in credit and so he advanced us twenty francs each. Then he gave us, of all things, a stiff glass of whisky from his private supply. He told us not to be long with the gun as it would be needed for the attack. We never saw him again.

When we returned to the gun emplacement the howitzer was hitched to the tractor ready for the road. We started off, Reed and I following in rear ready to apply the brakes if necessary. Once out of sight we left the brakes to look after themselves and heedless of the perils of the situation, clambered on to the trail of the swaying gun and promptly went to sleep.

Our fiery steed drew up at an estaminet near Abeele. It was morning of July 14 when, refreshed with sleep, we descended from the gun trail. The Army Service Corps men knew the estaminet well. We handed our rations to the innkeeper and in exchange were soon enjoying a substantial breakfast, fried bacon with a couple of eggs and plenty of coffee. After breakfast we continued our journey until we reached the Royal Army Ordnance Cops workshop at Steenvoorde.

The Lieutenant in charge was glad to see us as they had no guns under repair at the moment. Our howitzer was run into the workshop while the Caterpillar tractor returned to its park. The ordnance men were a friendly lot, gave us another breakfast and showing us our quarters, told us to have a sleep for we must be tired after that long march behind the gun. We were roused for dinner, a very good meal too; fried steak and boiled rice with jam, a pleasant change after seven months of stew. Then we went into the workshop where about 30 men were dismantling our gun while some 20 others were making bed frames out of wire netting. We were given a free hand, could hang about the workshop or go out and see the country as we wished but if we expected to be absent all day it would be best to tell the Staff Sergeant beforehand. Breakfast was at 8, dinner at 1, tea at 5 and last but by no means least, supper at 9.

We spent the next few days exploring the district, jumping lorries and visiting the delightful old world towns in the back area; Poperinge, Bailleul, Dranoutre and the rest. We called at estaminets and talked with other troops, infantry on rest, RAMC men, lorry drivers and others. Everywhere the air was seething with excitement and we saw for ourselves the vast preparations that were being made for the grand attack. Hospitals were being advanced to receive the wounded, cages erected for the prisoners that were sure to be taken and already, sites were being marked out for graves. But there were misgivings about our position in the air and camouflaging was being developed to an enormous extent. Roads were masked for miles but the prying eyes of enemy aircraft seemed to be everywhere.

Our friends at ordnance hung out the job as long as they could but at length the howitzer was re-assembled, charged with oil, pumped up with a good pressure of air and pronounced fit for service. Our convoy was informed and on July 20 a tractor appeared to take us as we thought back to Voormezeele.

But the driver had different instructions. Things were stirring at the battery and he understood that all the guns were being changed. Meanwhile we were to proceed to the lorry park to await orders. Our convoy was parked at a small village called La Clytte at the foot of Kemmel Hill where there were crossroads running north, south, east and west. The twenty-four lorries forming the convoy were stretched out alongside the southern road while the Caterpillars were in a farmyard nearby. Our driver brought us to the crossroads and told us that this was our destination. We uncoupled the gun, the tractor withdrew and we were left to our own devices.

Our first thought was for accommodation for the night. We were told that the lorries were at our disposal. For rations we had Maconochies supplied by ordnance before we left and these were warmed for us on the lorry drivers' spirit stove. We spent an enjoyable evening at the neighbouring estaminet and eventually turned in for the night in an empty lorry. For that night at any rate the gun had to look after itself.

The following day July 21 No.3 gun arrived with a Bombardier and a Gunner in charge. They drew up behind our No.2 gun. There were now three Gunners and an NCO and the latter, acting on prior instructions, proceeded to mount a guard.

Next day July 22 saw the arrival of No.4 gun with two more Gunners one of whom was my old friend from 221 Battery, Gunner Mason. The gun took its place in the queue while the two Gunners joined in the guard. Then we were told what was happening at the battery; the original 8 inch howitzers were being replaced by a new type of gun of the same calibre but with a longer range and with a specially designed platform which would eliminate the heavy work of pulling out and enable targets to be changed much more rapidly. The shells for use with the new guns were the same weight, 200lbs but much more tapered, streamlined we would now say and the cartridges were much larger. Altogether the effective range of the howitzers would be increased by as much as 5,000 yards.

The next news brought by the lorry drivers was that the battery was preparing an advanced position at Spoil Bank some three miles east of Voormezeele. Not content with our extra range, we were advancing some 3,000 yards. We were now going on counter battery work and would in future engage enemy artillery and strong points well in rear of the enemy front line.

On July 23 orders came for Numbers 3 and 4 guns. Tractors came and towed them away presumably to some gun park. The two Gunners last to arrive returned to Voormezeele while the Bombardier with Gunners Mason, Reed and myself remained to guard the original No.2 gun. No orders had yet come for us and it was evident that there was a hitch somewhere. It transpired later than no replacement could be made while the original gun was at the workshop being repaired and this upset all the calculations. For the moment we were nobody's children.

Guarding an 8 inch howitzer at La Clytte crossroads was beginning to get a bit of a bore despite the fact that we were drawing double rations, that is from the convoy and those sent up daily from the battery.

I am afraid the guard got rather slack and early in the morning of the 26 July we were horrified to see a real, live General, red tabs[7] and all. Some of us were washing but Reed and I had sense to cut down some foliage before the great man spotted us. He was in a towering rage. *"Who was in charge, where was the guard and what the devil are we doing?"* *"Camouflaging our gun, sir,"* I replied. This appeared to mollify him considerably but he asked who we were and exactly what we intended doing with the gun. We informed him of the circumstances that had brought us to La Clytte crossroads; how we had been there six days and were still awaiting orders. The great man now seemed to see the humour of the situation. *"But,"* he said, *"Get the damned gun out of the way somewhere; we can't have you blocking up the road like this. There's going to be an attack any day now!"* We promised to do our best and informed the tractor men of the General's not unreasonable demands. They pulled the gun into a neighbouring field and left us there.

Whether the General had taken up the matter or not things at last seemed to be straightening out. The following day 27 July a new type howitzer replacement for No.2 was taken direct to the battery position. All that remained was to dispose of the old gun and re-join the battery. We hitched up to the tractor, the guard was disbanded and Mason and the Bombardier prepared to depart. Mason looked particularly glum and we chipped him a bit about this. He turned on us almost savagely, quite unlike his usual good natured self. Whether some second sense had told him, I do not know but he never actually reached the battery position. He was mortally wounded on his way to Spoil Bank.[8]

Reed and I took up our posts behind the gun, expecting this move to be our last but the driver had apparently got his orders mixed up, for after travelling some miles he pulled up at another ordnance workshop, this time outside Abeele.

We sought the officer in charge and explained our mission. He was somewhat indignant; this was a repair shop, not a dump for unwanted guns but since we were here we might as well stop and he directed his men to start dismantling the gun in spite of our protests that it had been repaired a few days ago. We were detained at Abeele until August 4 and it is through this extraordinary chain of circumstances that I missed the early days at Spoil Bank and did not participate in the attack of July 31.

At the battery they expected us to return soon after the Bombardier and some enquiries were made when we failed to appear but there were other things to think about besides a couple of Gunners and they knew that we could not disappear forever with an eight inch howitzer. They lost all track of us however and did not locate us again until August 4 when we the ordnance officer reported that the gun sent for repair was now ready for removal. We had been pretty comfortable at the workshop although compared with the Steenvoorde crowd, they tended to be autocratic and with all our money spent it was not so pleasant roaming the back areas. After a day or two we appealed to the officer in charge and he advanced us another twenty francs.

With July drawing to a close the long delayed attack was expected at any moment. And now came tragedy; it was evident that the long spell of glorious weather we had enjoyed since Messines could not last indefinitely – the barometer was failing steadily. From Abeele we had a splendid view of the immense preparations that were being made and finally on July 30, we saw a sight that made the blood leap in our veins – the cavalry were moving up. How glorious they looked, their lances gleaming, their horses wonderfully groomed. Once they broke through they must strike terror in the heart of the flying foe, for this must surely be the end. After such preparations, victory quick and decisive must surely be ours. But, would the weather hold out? On fine weather depended glorious victory or terrible disaster. And the sky was overcast and every omen predicted rain.

On the early morning of July 31 we were awakened by such a terrific bombardment that we crowded out the huts to see the spectacle. Fascinated we watched the sight; the flashing of the guns as far as the eye could see. The noise was terrific. The Third Battle of Ypres had begun. Soon it became evident that the enemy was putting up a stiff resistance. And then came the storm. All day it rained, pitilessly, incessantly, the thunder drowning the noise of the guns. We thought of the men fighting out there and what of the cavalry? Next day the cavalry returned, what was left of them. Man and beast a picture of hopeless misery. Unable to break through, many had been caught in the barbed wire. Shell holes soon became full of water through which they were unable to pass. The watchful enemy was well prepared to beat off the attack. We had dallied too long. The grand attack had failed.

On August 4, the gun being reassembled, we were told to get our kit together. The tractor arrived in the afternoon and in a short time we were on the road again. Once away from the workshop the driver explained the mistake of the previous week. Our purpose was now to dump the gun and return to the battery as soon as possible. This proved easier said than done, for we tried several likely looking depots without avail. At length we arrived at a field near Goedwaersvelde where, behind a camouflage screen stood a considerable number of guns, all calibre, some new others badly damaged. After some parley the Sergeant in charge of the dump agreed to accept our gun but would not let us depart until his action had been confirmed by higher authority. We passed the night in a hut in the gun park. The Sergeant's misgivings at last were satisfied and after breakfast we were allowed to depart, so clambering aboard the tractor we started our uneasy way up the line. We soon discovered that marching behind a tractor was probably more comfortable than riding on one but we stuck it out until we arrived well shaken up at Westoutre, the destination of the tractor. Here we congregated all the heavy transport required for drawing the guns of all kinds, Caterpillars for the 8 inch howitzers and steam traction engines for the still heavier guns. All these had been bustled to Westoutre out of the way for the attack. Our next step was to reach La Clytte where the lighter part of the convoy was still stationed. Jumping lorries part of the way and walking the rest, we eventually reached the familiar crossroads where we were greeted with ironical cheers from the lorry drivers. The Sergeant in charge decided that the best thing was to send us forward with the ration lorry which was leaving for the battery position at 6pm.

Accordingly we lounged about until tea time, picking up news about the battery and of the attack.

Of the attack the lorry men added little to what we already knew. The cavalry had been unable to advance on account of the rain. At Messines the Germans had held firm but we had gained some ground before Ypres. The net result for the troops was even worse than if they had been repulsed on all fronts, for the Salient which had been straightened out on June 9 again appeared on the map as bad, if not worse, than before.

As for the battery they were now in a terrible place known as Spoil Bank alongside the Ypres canal, a position they had occupied towards the end of July. They had suffered very heavy casualties at first and men were still falling every day. In fact as one driver gruesomely remarked, *"We take up the rations every night and bring back the 'returns'"*, by which he meant dead men sewn up in blankets being returned for burial. When the tractors had brought up the guns, the enemy had been gassing heavily. Gas masks were donned and attempts were made to pull in the guns. But it was slow work thus hampered and after some time Major Tomasson tested for gas and found the atmosphere comparatively clear. He ordered gas masks to be removed and almost at once received the contents of a gas shell full in the face. He collapsed in agony and was carried away apparently blinded. The enemy were now shelling vigorously, mixing high explosive with gas. Somehow the guns were dragged into position but not before five men had been killed[9] and twenty wounded or gassed. Next day Captain Sanderson was badly wounded along with many others. With both senior officers gone a young officer, a certain Major Guy, had been rushed up to take charge.

Such then was the end of Major Tomasson and of Captain Sanderson,[10] his second in command, surely a most unhappy combination. Captain Sanderson the bluff, quick tempered officer who would drive us unmercifully should the occasion require it but with sense of humour and a gift of humanity that made us almost love him. He would have made a first rate Battery Commander but with Major Tomasson in charge, he had no chance.

But of Major Tomasson, that remarkable man. From the first I hated him and all his ways. I detested his method of promoting recruits so that he would be able to carry his plans without the opposition he would have expected from experienced NCO's; his mania for camouflaging, his opposition to the Decauville railway, the water cart that made us the laughing stock of all the units that saw us, how at Mory he kept us from sleep for three nights in succession until in desperation, we practically mutinied. How he turned us out in the middle of the night to gather poppy heads and above all, how he set up that iniquitous system of fixed gun teams and no reliefs, which condemned many of us to a position of inferiority from which there was no escape. But with the passage of time I am not so sure. Might not our seven months' practical freedom from casualties be due in some respects to his care? I can see him practically in tears when a Gunner was killed by a stray shot at Kemmel and he was explaining the care he had taken in selecting the rear billets. Would it not have been easier to have adopted the attitude of so many commanding officers, popularity at all costs? Of one thing I am convinced; Major Tomasson followed the dictates of his own conscience and behaved in the way he felt to be right, regardless of any man's disapproval.

1   Bus House Cemetery was created about the time that Gnr Hall was located near Voormezeele. It was named after a farm on the opposite side of the lane and contains 266 burials from the Great War (plus 79 from the Second World War). Many of the casualties date from June-November 1917 and one is from 242 Siege Battery — 31927 Bdr S.G. Turner who died on 16 July 1917. The names of cemeteries reflect a variety of themes — place names, units that started the cemetery, names of trenches, personalities, prominent landmarks and many other sources.

2   In view of the profusion of trenches and other battlefield features, as with war cemeteries, a wide range of names was used — streets of London, Glasgow and other cities, a sequence of words commencing with the same letter and so on,

3   Damstrasse was a lane running in a NE direction about ¾ mile south east of St Eloi passing Damm Wood and Pheasant Wood. Leading to White Chateau or Bayershof as the Germans called it.

4   The CWGC records do not enable identification of this casualty.

5   Balloons were used by both sides for observation across enemy lines. Inevitably they were a target for aircraft often necessitating Observers to descend by parachute as their burning balloons fell to earth.

6   Royal Army Ordnance Corps. In 1917 it was still the Army Ordnance Corps (AOC) and did not become 'Royal' until 1918 when it merged with the Army Ordnance Department.

7   Red Tabs — staff officers so called as they wore red tabs with a central red cord on their lapels. Intelligence officers wore green and is the other commonly seen variation though there were others for the RFC, medical etc.

8   Spoil Bank was part of the canal that ran SE from Ypres to Comines.

9   CWGC records do not show five killed on or about this day for this battery. However, in the period 3 July to 14 August the battery did lose five men killed — 98716 Gnr H.H. Bridges; 166204 Gnr Charles Lovelock; 39594 Gnr James Lyons; 111657 Gnr William Reed; and 126540 Gnr John Townsend.

10   It appears that Major Tomasson and Capt Sanderson survived the war.

Major Tomasson and by mounting one at Spoil Bank the Sgt-Major had merely followed precedent. The Spoil Bank guard served no useful purpose whatsoever, it was situated in the most dangerous part of the position, against a main road constantly exposed to gun fire and far distant from any form of shelter. It seemed that there had been previous casualties and the guard room had been destroyed twice before.

The feeling against Sgt-Major Cavalier now intensified. He belonged to the old gang it was argued and would take the first opportunity to restore the old ceremonial and its attendant miseries. *"Once we can get rid of him we shall be alright"* was the talk. We had not long to wait. On the morning of August 8 he took the parade under the cover of some trees near the deserted guard-room. Major Guy, who rarely attended parades, was not present. An unknown soldier was buried near the parade ground and one of our reinforcements walked over his grave. He was pulled up sharply by the Sgt-Major *"Don't go over there, don't you realise that this is a man's grave?"* *"Alright, Sgt-Major,"* came the light-hearted reply. *"Sir,"* would have been the title a few weeks ago. The parade was soon dismissed to the guns. Before the SM could retire there came a sharp burst of shellfire. The Sgt-Major was wounded. His leg was very badly broken, much of the flesh having been torn away. Then as we went to attend to him we noticed that the same shells had desecrated the unknown soldier's grave and his naked corpse was exposed. Soon the ambulance arrived for the Sgt-Major. He attempted to say goodbye but no answer came from the crowd of Gunners. Some went so far as to call uproarious remarks after him. The passing of BSM Cavalier marked the end of all ceremonial. All parades were cancelled. Even the harmless corpse was left as it had been torn from the grave until some days later in common decency, it was re-interred.

Major Guy was now in full charge of the battery with no other assistance save that of Lt Tharpe. All the other officers had been casualties and now his Sergeant-Major had gone. And such a battery in such a position! On this young man of twenty-six devolved the Herculean task of restoring us to health. His rank was only an acting one, his substantive rank being that of Lieutenant. The product of the English public school at its best, he was tall and handsome of splendid appearance. He remained with us only a month. When he took us over we were hysterical, malingering cowardly lot who would do nothing unless driven but in that short time he changed us into a self-reliant body of men who could think for themselves, endure hardships, stand shell-fire without flinching and, above all, who loved him as a commanding officer had never been loved before. He spoke but little and the key-note of his words was that we should *"play the game"*. He would never intrude in the gun pits when things were quiet but always seemed to be present when shells were flying. He taught us the subtle difference between shoots that were our concern alone, when we could pack up when things became too hot and others when the infantry were depending on us and we must stick at all costs. Whenever it was necessary for us to take cover he would always be the last to enter the deep dugout and his tall figure strolling about the position in spite of the heaviest gun-fire, inspired many a timid heart with courage.

It was said that when he first took over command he could be heard stalking about the officers mess muttering *"poor devils, poor devils"* and indeed we must have been in an unhappy state when he first arrived. The shock of that first night at Spoil Bank seemed to have paralysed the battery. Men had no confidence in their NCO's and the reinforcements from England could not look to the old hands for guidance. Even the guns were new and the Vickers platforms were not functioning properly. Every time we opened fire the enemy retaliated; the terror of all Gunners was realised, the battery was well and truly spotted. Major Guy tackled all these problems in a calm, serene manner that won the respect of all.

His first step was to evacuate from the battery position every man not actually required for fighting the guns and maintaining lines of communication. Casualties had been too severe to allow the working of regular reliefs but the detachments were fixed at seven men as against the official team of eleven and any in excess of this number were sent down to Voormezeele. The old rear billets were re-occupied but material for building a couple of Nissen huts was obtained and once these were erected there was a shelter where the troops on rest could live in comparative comfort. No restrictions of any kind were placed on these men except that they were expected to keep themselves as clean as possible and with the bathing pool at hand this proved no difficult task. The troops would rest a couple of days and then would be brought up to relieve another batch of their fellows at Spoil Bank. More valuable still, men were being sent to a rest camp on the coast, half a dozen at a time, the holiday being of six day's duration. Major Guy may not have been altogether responsible for this but it was felt that he had pulled some strings to secure this valuable concession for us.

At the battery everything possible was done for our comfort. Night firing was reduced to an absolute minimum (it was said that the CO had intervened for us in this) and when it was necessary, measures were taken to render the duty less onerous, as for instance one section turning out to do double firing instead of the whole battery.

To avoid night work Major Guy adopted the very risky practice of bringing up ammunition in daylight rather than at night. The lorries would rush up the hill; one at a time would back into the gun emplacements and unload right onto the gun platforms. First the cartridges and fuses were unloaded and thrown into trenches, then two or three of us would stand round the lorry tail at once and with a peculiar movement, allow to run right down our bodies until they dropped on their bases between our feet, whence other members of the team would trundle them away. Lorries were dealt with in this manner in an incredibly short time and as soon as one empty lorry started on its return journey, the next waiting under cover would rush up the hill at full speed.

We were allowed great relaxations in the fusing of shells. When shells arrived they had a safety screw inserted in the nose. Before firing this blind screw had to be removed and the fuse inserted. Major Tomasson had made a rule that only three shells were to be kept fused at a time and this meant that the fusing number was kept hard at work fusing shells the whole time the gun was firing. Indeed he could hardly keep up with the firing and this led to the employment of spare men at busy times. With the reduced gun teams this practice was clearly impossible and all hands had to fuse shells in odd moments between shoots. We kept as many as a hundred shells fused behind each gun but although the practice was considered dangerous and the enemy ignited many of our cartridges, none of the shells were exploded although some were so badly damaged, particularly on the soft copper bands as to be unfit for use. We had to keep a sharp look-out for damaged shells which might have prematured the guns.

Major Guy next turned his attention to our food. The Sergeants' mess which had functioned ever since we arrived in France and which catered not only for Sergeants but also for some hangers-on of other ranks, was summarily disbanded, Major Guy expressing indignation that such a practice had ever been tolerated on active service. The Officers' Mess continued but in name only the food being drawn from the same cooking pots as the men's but served on plates instead of mess tins. Big Turner had gone but his successor was shown how to make a good thick stew instead of the rubbish that had previously been issued. The NCO in charge of rations was closely questioned and a word in season spoken to the Army Service Corps men at the ration dump. As a result our food improved considerably, both in quality and quantity. Boiled rice and raisins, luxuries previously unknown, appeared on the scene. A welcome addition was vegetables which came dried in large tins ready for the stew. Potatoes were peeled instead of just washed and we often had Maconochies meat and vegetable rations, one tin per man, much appreciated though somewhat hard to digest.

The young Major was prodigal with his rum issues. Major Tomasson had hoarded the rum to such account that scores of bottles were carried about whenever we moved. Major Guy proceeded to squander these reserves and although it was August, the close season for rum, liberal doses were given with one proviso that if there was any night firing to be done, the parties concerned had to wait for their issue until they had finished. The men fighting the guns had best keep sober.

But this was an infrequent occurrence. Most evenings, the day's firing finished, the ammunition unloaded and fused up, the guns laid on their night lines ready for any emergency and a couple of good men at the sap entrance sniffing for gas, we lay on our bunks drinking the fiery spirit neat until we were drunk as lords and heedless of the enemy shells pounding on the canal bank above us. Sometimes he would send over extra heavy ones, even armour piercing shells were used. Then the ground would quiver like a jelly, the electric light would go out and equipment thrown over the place. But candles would be lit until the electric light could be restored and the only complaints were from the unfortunates whose rum had been knocked over.

Gunner Moody, the sanitary orderly, would often regale us with a song but after a time he grew wary and would only oblige after he had received an extra rum issue. Major Guy would put his head through the curtain dividing the Officers' Mess and call out, *"Isn't Gunner Moody with us tonight?"*. *"Yes, sir, but not feeling too well,"* was the reply. *"Come inside Moody"* and a few minutes later he would emerge beaming, prop himself up in the gangway and reel off song after song, the whole battery joining in the chorus. The Bonny Banks of Loch Lomond was prime favourite and the evening entertainment would wind up with what Moody called a new song, although we had heard it dozens of times before. The chorus ran:

> *"It's hard to say goodbye to your own native land,*
> *Hard to give a farewell kiss, a farewell shake of the hand.*
> *It's hard to leave your sweetheart in foreign lands to roam….".*

…while for the last line Moody would substitute one of his own, the spirit having now taken full effect and causing tears to roll down his cheeks:

> *"…but it's a damned sight harder to leave your wife and children dear and your*
> *dear old home".*

Major Guy, who thoroughly entered into the spirit of the entertainment, would now call *"Time gentlemen please"* and we would all turn in regardless of the German's ferocious attempt to bury us alive. Sometimes when the gas guard found it necessary to lower the gas curtains, we would wake up coughing and spluttering as if in danger of asphyxiation but on one occasion a far more serious thing happened. The look-out went to sleep at his post and a fair quantity of poison gas penetrated the sap before it was realised what was wrong. The guard was promptly relieved of his duty and the Major had a few choice things to say to him in the morning. There was really no excuse for this guard's dereliction of duty but no punishment was ever meted out. Probably Major Guy told the culprit that it was damned bad form to allow ones comrades to be gassed. The man had, of course, been guilty of a cardinal offence *"while a sentry sleeping at his post,"* the penalty for which under military law could be death.

The guns lay half a mile from the protection of the canal bank; to reach them was an adventure in itself. After Sgt-Major Cavalier had left us there were no fixed parades. Major Guy would look out of the entrance to the sap and, if satisfied, would say, *"It looks fairly clear now. You'd better get to the guns and don't loiter on the way"*. We would make a dash across the intervening ground some half a dozen at a time. Sometimes we would get across safely, sometimes not. There were five or six enemy kite balloons in the sky, probably they could not see us but their presence was far from reassuring. The Major had obtained for us, without difficulty, the right in an emergency to take shelter in another deep sap on the roadside nearer the guns. Should the enemy open fire on us when we were on our way we could either make a dash for this sap or return to our own, whichever was the nearest. We lost quite a number of men this way. When a shell burst we would all duck or drop into a shell hole. When a man failed to rise afterwards we would investigate and, throwing him on another's shoulders like a sack of potatoes, march off to the nearest shelter, the others helping to steady the burden as far as possible. I myself have carried off a number of wounded men in this manner.

An early morning "shoot" by a battery of 6 inch 26cwt howitzers. September 1917. (IWM Q11621)

The deep sap on the roadside was by rights the property of my old friends 221 Siege Battery who now occupied a position slightly in front of our own. The entrance was by some fifty or sixty slippery wooden steps leading to a main chamber, which was very wet and required constant pumping to keep it at all habitable. 221 Siege Battery had been given a better dugout on the canal bank and this old sap was now used as an emergency shelter by both batteries. It was remarkable that when we had to rush for safety, those who reached the bottom of the sap first were reluctant to proceed further for fear of getting their feet wet. Consequently late comers could not get very far down the steps. Major Guy noticed this state of affairs on one occasion. As a matter of principle, he was last to take cover and said a few choice words about *"playing the game"*. There was no further cause for complaint.

As stated, two guns under the shelter of the few trees to the left of the road and the other two lay in a bare field to the right. In addition there was in this field an eight inch howitzer of the old type. Evidently the confusion in changing the guns had not been straightened out even yet. It was not long, however, before the old gun was taken away.

In the early days it was self-evident that our battery was not pulling its weight. There could be no doubt that the position was well known to the enemy who tried to silence us every time we opened fire. For the few targets that we engaged we would make elaborate preparations.

Everything would be got in readiness, shells ready for loading, cartridges taken out of cases, the guns laid and, on the word of command, we endeavoured to get a burst of fire as quickly as possible. If we were lucky we could get ten rounds off before the enemy replied then we threw the camouflage over the guns and bolted for the sap. On one occasion he must have been waiting for us, for we got our change before the third round had been fired.

It was obvious that this state of affairs could not be allowed to continue. Major Guy had the position surveyed by aeroplane and it was revealed that the left section guns were distinctly visible from the air. The left section had suffered considerably more than the right and had we been obliged to remain on these two guns for any length of time, we should certainly have been annihilated. I was on No.3 gun and when we turned out for action in a morning, we would discover that the shells so carefully stacked the night before had been knocked about like a row of skittles, the cartridges exploded overnight, the camouflages in ruins and masses of still smoking shell–holes showed how determined was the enemy to put us out of action. On one occasion one of the gun wheels had been blown completely off. We expected a rare job but this did not prove to be the case; a new wheel was obtained from ordnance and was fitted without much trouble, the broken wheel dumped in a shell hole.

Another cause of the discomfort to the left section was not realised for some time. Some fifty yards in rear of No.3 gun stood a large brick barn, still in a reasonable state of repair. The enemy would often fire at the barn but would never bombard it to the point of destruction. Only one gun would fire at a time and only a few rounds would be fired. Then after a few minutes another would take over. Guns of all calibres would fire at the barn. At length it dawned on us the Germans had such an excellent view of the barn that they were using it for calibrating their guns. The left section stood directly in their line of fire and as calibration meant bracketing the targets, any shorts tended to fall in the proximity of the two gun pits. At one time it was considered whether we should demolish the barn altogether but Major Guy decided against this.

The CO decided on the bold course of concentrating all the guns in the bare land to the right of the road. As regards the right section, following our usual practice, we had erected a camouflage framework over No.1 and No.2 guns and built a dwarf parapet of sandbags around the front and sides of the emplacement to afford some protection from enemy shellfire. The position of these two emplacements could be traced, though faintly, in the aerial photographs and Major Guy ruthlessly ordered the parapets and framework to be pulled down, the guns being concealed merely by a rough piece of coconut matting thrown over them. The next stage was to bring over the left section.

Even with the small amount of firing done up to now the new Vickers platforms were causing trouble. The platforms consisted of three enormous baulks of timber about 20 feet long arranged in the form of a triangle with an oblong block 10 feet by 6 feet in the centre, on which the gun wheels rested. A groove in the form of a segment was cut in the rear block. The gun itself possessed no spade and so could not dig itself into the ground after firing. In place of the spade was a flange which engaged the groove, the idea being that the gun could be swung round to any angle with the touch of a handspike. But practice proved different from theory; as was a common occurrence, most of the target lay at a considerable angle from zero line. The effect of this was to slew the platform round bodily, drive it backwards into the soft ground and tilt the whole arrangement with the result that after a long shoot in one direction, it was quite impossible to engage a target on another switch without relaying the whole platform. As the transoms weighed some 7cwts, each end would now be firmly embedded in the soil. This meant a formidable job besides putting the gun out of action for twelve hours or more. The designers had provided a device to enable the guns to be fired from an extraordinary flat platform in an emergency and this the CO decided to use.

Our first step was to lay two rough platforms between Nos.1 and 2 guns. This did not take long and we expected to have the job of man-handling Nos.3 and 4 guns across the road to their new emplacements. To our intense delight however, Major Guy obtained a Caterpillar tractor which came up at twilight, did the job for us in half an hour and went on its way. Under the old regime, moving the guns would have taken six hours of intensive effort. Once on their platforms the emergency device was brought into operation. This involved screwing a large iron shoe over the flange in the gun trail and placing wooden scotches on both sides of the gun wheels. The rear scotches were five feet long by three high and were lined with iron. The front ones were not so large; all were wider than the wheels themselves. When the gun was fired the recoil would first run her up the heavy rear scotches and back again up the front ones, after which she would settle down for re-loading.

Firing from scotches proved a tricky business. The noise was terrific. If the brakes were left off the gun might run over the scotches and injure the gun crew. If applied too tight, the gun would jump in the air. If one brake were applied tighter than the other, the trail would swing round with great force and the gun run off the platform altogether. After the guns had run off the platforms once or twice, we learnt how to handle them and by easing the scotches after each round, managed to keep the guns central. So the Spoil Bank rocking horses came into being and great interest they caused to passing infantrymen who had seen heavy guns before but never ones that jumped about like bucking mules.

The stratagem proved successful. The Vickers platforms were dug up from the evacuated left section gun pits and the enemy allowed to vent his fury on empty camouflages. So much easier did the emergency method of firing prove that the Vickers platforms on Nos.1 and 2 guns were also removed. We had now four rocking horse guns huddled together so closely that on occasions we would load from each other's shell platforms. The ground was kept as bare as possible; all shelters were knocked down, all protecting walls destroyed. The sole concealment for guns and shells was the coconut matting, which toned with the colour of the ground. The cartridge cases were placed in the disused trenches which we were forbidden to alter in any way. One well directed 12 inch shell would have destroyed the whole battery but fortune smiled on us. We had moved out of the enemy's line of fire. When we started a shoot he promptly replied but his shells fell in a line to our left with barely the width of the road away from us so narrow was the margin of safety. It was fascinating to realise that our safety depended on the good shooting of the Germans. Had his Gun Layers been negligent and strayed from their line if fired we should certainly have been caught; while they fired accurately we were immune.

There were still casualties but they diminished considerably on the change-over and by the end of August we were conducting destructive shoots on enemy batteries. Counter battery work, while more dangerous than bombardment, was certainly less fatiguing than the class of work we had hitherto conducted. About ten per cent of the batteries were engaged and took orders from their own headquarters, corps counter batteries. Our business first to last was to fight enemy guns; the work of providing barrages and bombarding crossroads was left severely alone. In order to reach the enemy positions we had to be well forward. At Spoil Bank we were in front of many of the field guns. The main compensation was the comparative absence of night firing. Counter battery work was conducted mainly by aeroplane observation and a dull day meant little work for us. Once we were settled it was remarkable how quickly we dropped into the routine. Each morning we would go to the entrance to the sap to see what the observation was like. We found one infallible test; Mount Kemmel lay well to the rear. If its outline showed up sharply we could count on the aeroplane being able to conduct a shoot. If, on the other hand, it was barely discernible, we knew it was an off day. I am afraid I was responsible for the following piece of doggerel which was widely taken up by all ranks:

> *"If Kemmel Hill shows bright and clear,*
> *An aeroplane shoot is very near.*
> *If Kemmel Hill seems dull and grey,*
> *There'll be no aeroplane shoot today".*

In any case we would make out way to the guns and, if the weather seemed favourable, would start fusing shells and preparing cartridges. About ten o'clock the aeroplane would call us up and we would start ranging on the selected hostile battery. We would start with a salvo so that the airmen could identify us and carry on slowly correcting the guns after each round until we were ranged to his satisfaction. At about eleven the airman would direct us to carry on and bombardment would begin. This meant firing 400 rounds, 100 per gun. If one gun went sick the others had to make up the number. At noon we would break off for dinner and continue the shoot in the afternoon. About three o'clock the airmen would have another look at the target and might rearrange us if we had fallen off the mark. There would be another break for tea. Then we would complete our shoot, sponge out the guns, lay them on their night line and cover up. The ammunition lorries would now arrive and would be quickly disposed of. Four or five hundred rounds meant nothing to us now that the lorries could run right up to the gun emplacements. Work over for the day we would adjourn to the deep dugout; the cook would probably have some supper for us. In any case there was the rum issue and the concert to follow. Truly a great change had occurred in little over a month.

There were still some difficulties to be faced. The worst the matter of the cartridges. Cartridges were supplied in silk bags, the old type being about two feet long and they arrived packed two together in long green tins. The tins had to be ripped open to extract the cartridges but with the full team of eleven men the cartridge number was much sought after as being a bit of a sinecure. Things were more difficult now we had the new guns. The cartridges were much longer and were at first supplied in long brass cases, each containing a single cartridge. The new cases were of elaborate construction and took a couple of minutes to unscrew. The guns could fire twice as quickly as this so it was obvious that there was going to be trouble in keeping up the supply of cartridges particularly with our depleted teams. It was also found that the new cases were not watertight and cartridges were being damaged by water and could not be used. After a short time the brass cases were discontinued and tins (longer than the old style of course) used again. The polished tins gleamed in the sunshine like so many mirrors. Our cries of indignation must somehow have reached the munition factories in England for we were soon supplied with the familiar green cases again. Further, each case contained two cartridges so the problem of supply was solved.

Now that heavier firing had commenced, complaints were being received from 221 Siege Battery that we were drawing fire on them. This was probably correct. Since we had moved the left section across the road we had escaped to a large measure the fury of the enemy but 221 Siege Battery whose position lay to the left and a little in front of us seemed to be feeling the full effect of the enemy's fire. It is probable that the complaints from 221 Siege Battery eventually caused us to leave the position. There was obviously not room for two 8 inch batteries on Spoil Bank.

One afternoon things being rather slack, I determined to see how my old friends were getting on. My visit was inopportune; I found the battery office a little way up the hill. There was no-one in but I noticed on the table a pair of binoculars, just the ordinary field glasses used by the aeroplane spotter but so shattered that it was evident that had the spotter been wearing them at the time he would have been killed. Presently BSM Netherway came in. He recognised me at once but when I stated that I had come over from 242 Battery, he was furious. *"That's the bloody battery that's drawing fire on us. Look at these field glasses. That's Winter[4] gone west. You can go and tell your CO that he's killing us."* Presently my old companion Gunner Turner arrived, a portable telephone on his back. He explained to the Sgt-Major that he had found a break in the wire. *"More of 242's work drawing fire"*, I heard him mutter. When he saw me he became sullen and morose. I did learn however that they were suffering badly from shell fire. In fact they had suffered ever since they had landed in France but nothing like Spoil Bank. Corporal McHugh (Little Ernest) was now their Battery Commander's Assistant having taken over the post when Tudhope had obtained his commission. That was the last time I attempted to get in touch with my old battery.

By now August had drawn to a close and Major Guy's task was finished. He had restored the battery's self-respect and made us a fighting unit once more and he had done this practically single-handed for he had neither officers nor Sergeant-Major to assist him. That is with the exception of 2/Lt Tharpe and to that youngster's credit he fully entered into the new spirit that prevailed. Mr Tharpe spent most of his time with the men and would take his turn on the guns doing the heaviest work, loading and fusing shells. Once we had finished firing but our gun wanted pumping before we close down for the night. We had fixed the air compressor to the trail but the enemy started shell-firing and we had to take cover. After some time Mr Tharpe looked at me. I was the only old hand that was left and he said quietly, *"What about it Hall, shall we show them how to pump it up?"*. There was no resisting such an invitation so the subaltern and I took a handle each and started work. It was hard going but we got the pressure up after a fashion. Then the others took the compressor away and we retired for the night.

By the end of August reinforcements had overtaken casualties. The original members of the battery now represented less than 15 per cent of the establishment. The reinforcements were a mixture of ex-casualties from the base and recruits from England. The former were welcomed for they brought their experience to us but the recruits were something of a proposition. With only four months training these were thrown into a fiery position willing enough as a rule but with most extraordinary ideas about the war picked up from soldiers on leave and from highly coloured newspaper accounts.

It was to one of these youths that our first decoration was awarded. It was evening and a party of the newcomers had crossed the canal to look at the batteries on the other side. On their return an enemy battery opened fire. Major Guy came to see what the trouble was about and enquired if they were all right. It then transpired that one of their number was missing. Some had seen him fall but assumed he would follow them to the sap. Johnson, one of their number thereupon exclaimed *"I'll fetch him in Sir, we can't let him stop like that,"* and dashed out of the dugout along the foot of the canal bank until he came to a shell hole where the man was lying down with a not too serious wound in the fleshy part of the leg, smoking a cigarette and awaiting the arrival of a stretcher party. Heedless to the wounded man's protests that he was quite safe and comfortable and in any case preferred being carried on a stretcher to being dragged along, Johnson managed to pull him to the sap. He got no plaudits from the assembled Gunners who considered this a blatant case of *"playing for a decoration"* and we were astonished when on Major Guy's recommendation he was awarded a Military Medal a few days later. Many of the troops who had been at Spoil Bank from the outset were particularly sore about this. The men had no right to leave the position in the first place. There was practically no danger in creeping back along the foot of the canal bank and it was felt that it would have been better if Johnson had remained with the wounded man when he fell rather than bolting for the dugout and then going back for him. Johnson did not wear his decoration long however; a fortnight later he himself was wounded.

Soon after this we got our new Sergeant–Major. BSM Walker was a tall quiet man with two wound strips and a vast amount of experience. He would go round the guns giving hints to members of the teams and could pre–judge the effect of hostile shelling better than any man I have ever met. *"It's all right boys,"* he would call out as a shell burst close at hand and we began to feel alarm. *"What did I tell you – its miles away."* On rare occasions he would shout *"look out"* and then we knew the shell was really dangerous. We all developed the faculty for analysing the direction and calibre of the hostile shells while they were still in the air. There seemed to be a slowing down of the senses. One heard the shell whistling through the air and the process would start. *"That's the 5.9 gun that fired yesterday afternoon – it's going to land behind the trail of No. 1 gun – Gunner West had better look out – no, he's safe."* And sure enough, the shell would burst just where predicted.

And now a strange thing happened; another Major appeared on the scene and for some time we had two Majors in the battery. The newcomer, Major Austin, was to be our new CO but what was to happen to Major Guy? We knew that his rank was not substantive, would he revert to rank of Captain and remain with us? The wish was father to the thought and was not to be realised. Early one September morning some of us were at work on the guns. Sgt–Major Walker pulled us up to attention and saluted us as Major Guy appeared on the scene. Major Guy returned the salute and spoke a few words to the SM. Then they shook hands and we knew the dearly loved Major was leaving us. He said *"well goodbye men"*, hesitated a few moments and shook hands all round. We stood to attention as the tall figure walked down the hill and so passed out of sight. It was said he was returning to headquarters but exactly what that meant we did not know – all we knew was that we had lost a friend.

Major Austin was now in sole control of the battery. We saw very little of him at first but understood that we were to leave Spoil Bank and that he was already prospecting for a new battery position.

1   One of the tasks of Royal Engineers Field Companies was the preparation of dugouts and other shelter for the infantry and others. The war underground was extensive and battlefield archaeologists have excavated many such examples often well preserved. These shelters gave some protection to the troops.

2   A field battery would belong to the Royal Field Artillery. The RFA, organised into brigades, was equipped with medium calibre guns and howitzers deployed close to the front line and was reasonably mobile.

3   111657 Gnr William Joseph Reed, aged 39, 242 Siege Battery, Royal Garrison Artillery, killed in action 9 August 1917, buried in Klein Vierstraat British Cemetery, Belgium, plot 3, row A, Grave 11. He was the son of William and Martha Reed; husband of Alice Emily Jane Reed, of 69, Shortlands Rd., Kingston-on-Thames.

4   100104 Gnr A.W. Winters, 221 Siege Battery, killed in action 9 August 1917, buried in Klein Vierstraat British Cemetery, plot 3, row A, grave 15.

CHAPTER 15
THE NEW BATTERY POSITIONS

2*42 Siege Battery's new position at St Eloi was by the mine blown on 7 June 1917 in the fork in the road where it divides heading south to Messines and to Warneton The mine crater, now filled with water, can still be seen today. Again his diary records a period of moving the guns, establishing new positions and casualties as well as two periods away from the battery, one at a rest camp and the other as a consequence of a mishap while handling shells. The latter incident also brought about his transfer to another battery with which not only would he see out the rest of the war but also experience his most intense periods of action.*

Work commenced on the St. Eloi position early in September, action being continued at Spoil Bank until it was ready.

The new position lay in open country about a mile to the south. We were to place our guns in the main street of St. Eloi, one of the places where the mines had been sprung on June 9.[1] When the enemy held the village they dug their front line trenches alongside the street and through the churchyard at the top of the hill. Street and church alike were unrecognisable and the trenches themselves were so broken up as to resemble holes in the ground connected by a straight line. A huge crater occupied the site of the church, a pool of water[2] had formed at the bottom and on the sides we started erecting shelters for the men. Here we should be safe from observation and the walls of the crater would afford some protection from shell fire. The shelters were rather flimsy structures of Monk's Expanded Metal, a kind of steel netting of extremely fine mesh. We dug into the loose earth on the side of the crater and erected the inner wall, then we fixed up the outer wall and piled loose earth. For some reason sandbags were unobtainable at St. Eloi and six inches of loose soil did not give a great sense of security compared with the deep sap at Soil Bank. We erected bunks in the shelters in this case only two deep.

Altogether we erected three large huts for the troops on one side of the crater, and a small one for the Officers' Mess on the other. We noticed that Major Austin had selected the dangerous side of the crater for the officers.

The gun pits lay 200 yards further down the road. By this is meant that they were separated from the crater by a mass of tangled barbed wire, broken trenches and shell holes that made it impossible to trace the road at this point. At the spot selected for the guns however, faint traces of road metalling were visible between the shell holes. To maintain communication a totally new corduroy road had been laid bypassing the remains of the village as it was utterly impossible to repair the old one. The point where the new road left the old was selected as an ammunition dump, and the line of the guns followed the old road and the trenches alongside.

A good deal of latitude was left to the Sergeants in selecting the actual sites. Sgt Green on

No.1 gun levelled up a piece of ground and had his gun boldly on the surface after the manner of Spoil Bank. The other three guns were actually in pits below ground level. This was made possible by making use of the shell holes made when the trenches were bombarded on the fateful night of June 9. No.4 gun, the left and most northerly, was sunken about 3 feet, No.3 about 4 feet, while No.3 whose Gun Captain had selected a particularly fine shell hole made by a 12 inch shell, was no less than 6 feet below ground level. The old trenches were cleaned out to some extent to use as funk-holes. We came across traces of dead Germans while doing this.

It was known that we were to make another experiment with the Vickers platforms. There had been overhauled in ordnance workshops, strengthened in the weak places and the strained parts adjusted. The platforms were brought up by lorry and laid in the new emplacements. This work proved much easier than anticipated, and was done much more quickly than the old style platform. The ground was soft but dry in the shell-holes and the huge baulks of timber were soon in position.

Major Austin meantime had obtained assistance from the Royal Engineers who ran a Decauville railway from the ammunition dump, passing in rear of Nos.1 to 4 guns whence it took a sharp right angled turn to join the main light railway track half a mile away. The task involved levelling the ground for a considerable distance and made such an obvious track as to make one wonder whether there was anything in Major Tomasson's mania for concealment.

The work of constructing the new position was done by parties sent from Spoil Bank. Through it all Major Austin maintained his predecessor's practice of sending men to the rear billets for a rest, although there might have been an excuse for employing every possible man. A couple of day's rest at Voormezeele was much appreciated after the hard work up the line.

At length the new position was completed to Major Austin's satisfaction. On September 10 we fired out last shots from Spoil Bank and at dusk the Caterpillar tractors made straight for the emplacement, hitched up the guns and went off with them. In a short time they were in the new position.

Getting the guns into action at St. Eloi was rather more difficult. Numbers 1 and 4 guns were taken straight into the emplacements by the tractors but owing to the considerable depth of the other two pits they had to be lowered by rope. Sergeant-Major Walker was ready with his advice. He obtained a set of pulley blocks, fixed the tackle round the stump of a tree and in a short time the guns were run down planks like beer barrels into a cellar.

A few men had been left at Spoil Bank to keep an eye for marauders but they were not sharp enough, for 221 Siege Battery were in the emplacements the moment the tractors had left and they went off with all our ten foot planks. The following day the lorries brought over what stores were left and we abandoned Spoil Bank to the rival battery.

Once in position reliefs were fixed on the recognised principle of 24 hours on and 24 hours off duty, the changeover to take place every morning when the relief teams were brought over from Voormezeele, the lorry returning to rear billets with the tired men. The fresh reliefs would parade in the crater. The roll would be called by the Sergeant-Major who would bark out the order *"Battery 'shun'"* and as if he had not been obeyed smartly enough, he would go through the orders again. *"Stand at ease – easy – 'shun'."* Then Major Austin would appear outside his shelter in gum boots and a wonderfully decorated dressing gown, rather a strange combination. The SM would report the battery present and correct and the CO give the order to *"Carry on Sergeant-Major"*. BSM Walker would now give the order *"Battery, to your guns, dismiss"* and forthwith would be off parade ready to give a word of advice to NCO and Gunner alike.

To fix up the reliefs Major Austin was almost ruthless. Every employed man was called upon to give an account of his duties and if not satisfied the CO would post him to one or other of the teams. Some jobs fixed by Major Tomasson had been continued under the beneficent command of Major Guy but none escaped the searching scrutiny of Major Austin.

Sergeant Rowbottom was called from the battery office to justify his stripes. In most units the battery clerk was an acting (or full) Bombardier but Major Tomasson had created the post of Staff Sergeant clerk in the early days of the battery and Rowbottom had been appointed within having done hardly a parade let alone having been on a gun. Major Austin sarcastically remarked that now was a good chance to learn but if the Staff Sergeant did not feel competent to charge of a gun crew he was at liberty to serve with the rank and file but, in any case, to the guns he must go. Sgt Rowbottom floated about No.4. The men on No.4 gun were a particularly rough lot and at first pulled his leg unmercifully. On first attempting to load the Sergeant gave the order *"Halfway – home"* in the approved manner but the shell would not enter the bore. Rowbottom was perplexed and after keeping him in suspense a considerable time, one of the team suggested that they might do better if the grummet (the thick rope at the base of the shell to protect the driving band) were removed. Fortunately Sergeant Rowbottom took the ragging in good part and appealed to the men not to let him down. But however good he may have been as battery clerk he was hopeless as a Gun Captain. Entirely in the hands of his team who were able to throw the gun out of action without his knowing the cause and would load dirty shells unchecked he was a fat good natured man who demonstrated the fallacy of Major Tomasson's practice of indiscriminate promotion. Having been confirmed in his rank he could not be downgraded except for misconduct which he would certainly avoid, and so he continued at best a passenger and at worst a positive menace to the battery.

Sergeant Rees on No.3 gun was the only other surviving Sergeant who had accompanied the battery from England, and unlike Rowbottom, he was highly competent and very much respected. Even at Mory he was popular for it was thought he was the only NCO who tried to shield his men, even at the risk of getting into Major Tomasson's bad books. He was to gain the Military Medal at St. Eloi for turning out under heavy shelling to extinguish a fire which was in danger of exploding some ammunition.

Sergeant Green of No.1 gun was a happy go lucky cockney who introduced the gentle art of scrounging into the battery and himself led many an expedition. Since 221 Siege Battery had purloined our planks at Spoil Bank we were very short of skidding (artillery term for timber) but there was a good supply nearby which had been brought up by the Royal Engineers for the purpose of repairing the corduroy road. An RE Corporal kept a watchful eye on the stack but was no match for Green's strategy. The Sergeant engaged the Engineer Corporal in conversation and gradually enticed him away. At the crucial moment he gave a signal and a dozen Gunners marched down the road. On reaching the stack each pair of men seized a ten foot plank and bore it away in triumph, later to emerge front of the two NCO's who were still engaged in earnest conversation and pick up another load. Timber troubled us no more but nothing escaped Sgt Green's marauders; picks and shovels left unguarded by the pioneers, expanded metal, corrugated iron and, most valuable of all, sandbags. Sandbags were still scarce and were used for many purposes other than the official one, as for instance kit bags, shoulder pads used when shell carrying and when the weather was wet we would wrap them around our puttees to protect them from mud.

St. Eloi proved a much safer position than Spoil Bank. The enemy was by no means as active and the deep gun pits gave a sense of security. It was however a much harder position to work. Ammunition was received by lorry at the dump near No.1 gun and was also brought up by the light railway but the heavy trucks could not run on our lightly constructed track and the ammunition had to be reloaded onto the light wagons and pulled by hand to the battery position. The Decauville gave us a good deal of trouble as it had been laid down very hastily, and the trucks frequently ran off the line in which case the shells rolled off on to the track, or worse still into adjoining shell holes from which they had to be recovered and the truck reloaded. Often it was easier to fetch another load from the dump and the Decauville track was lined with shells that had fallen off en route. The right angled bend at No.4 gun required particular care in negotiating but one this was passed we could run the wagon down the hill to any gun that required ammunition.

Our great care was to keep the shells clean and so avoid washing them. To make matters more difficult we were now receiving two kinds of shells; the original blunt type and the stream-lined variety, the former being used for near targets and the new ones for more distant ranges. Try as we would we always seemed to be stocking up the wrong type of shells. There would be a run on short shells but no sooner had the loading platforms filled up with them than orders were received to change over to the long variety of which perhaps we had only half a dozen ready for use. That meant running the wagons to the dumps for more shells, and when they arrived the gun pits would be so choc-a-block with shells that we could hardly move. After some hours we would, in desperation, trundle away the old shells and fill up with new when another target came through requiring old shells again. The shells delivered by road were simply thrown off the lorries and formed a huge stack. Here again the type of shells wanted at any time always seemed to be at the bottom of the stack and it was tricky work extracting them.

There was a pleasant interlude for me at the end of September when my turn came around to go to the rest camp. Four Gunners and one NCO were selected, the three men from the 60 pounder battery who joined us at Mory, and myself with Sgt Rowbottom in charge. We obtained a clean change of underwear from the Quartermaster's Stores and by easy stages made our way to Bailleul. Here we joined a large body of troops from many different units and after some delay, boarded a train composed for a wonder of third class carriages of ancient design. After many hours the train halted at a station on a high embankment not far from Boulogne and we read the name Wimille-Wimereux. We formed up outside the station and after a sharp four mile march, reached our destination, a camp on the downs facing the sea between the twin villages of Ambleteus and Audresselles. Here we were to stop for the next ten days and a pleasant time we had on the whole. We were under canvas but the tents were not overcrowded, the food was good and there were concerts at night.

Every morning we would parade and march down to the beach headed by the Camp Commandant, a genial Lieutenant Colonel too old for service at the front but still determined to do his bit by giving the troops a good time. The Colonel evidently believing that example was the best encouragement, proceeded to strip and called upon us to do the same and follow him into the water. Officers and men alike, rank being abandoned for the moment at any rate. After a time we would emerge and lay on the sands to dry while French peasant women quite un-bashed would sell us apples at an exorbitant price, two pence each I believe. Then at length we would return to camp for dinner.

There was another parade in the afternoon, not so popular, for physical jerks or a route march. Poor Sgt Rowbottom had to take a party of squad drill on one occasion and had the mortification of trying to instruct a party of men, mostly infantry who knew the drill from A to Z without being acquainted with the first element of it himself. His first order *"right turn"* when he obviously meant *"left"* evoked roars of laughter. *"Some Sergeant"* said the men to one another while the Gunners and I attempted to defend the NCO. One of the Staff Sergeants on the camp staff must have seen his plight and got him off the parade ground on some pretext, substituting an infantry Corporal who soon put is through our paces.

The afternoon parades were dodged so blatantly that we four determined to try our luck and lay behind a hut ignoring the whistle. Alas, the commandant had ordered a general roll-call on this occasion and later in the afternoon we were hauled before him to account for our default. There were some twenty delinquents in all. The word must have gone round about the roll call for on previous occasions there must have been a hundred or so absent from parade. Fortunately, as it happened, none of us attempted to explain away our absence. We all expressed our very deep regret and hoped he would deal with us as leniently as possible. At first he threatened to send us back to our units but our contrite attitude must have touched his heart and discipline was satisfied by detailing us to various camp fatigues instead of being allowed out for the evening.

My lot fell to opening tins of food for the cooks – an easy job I thought at first, afterwards I was not so sure. I started off with pork and bean tins and did not think there were so many tins in the world. I had been instructed to separate the pork from the beans and I noticed that while I filled several pails with beans there did not seem to be much pork in the receptacle provided. The cook told me I could help myself to the beans but somehow I had no wish to avail myself this kind offer. After the pork and beans there were Maconochies and finally jam tins to be dealt with. Neither I nor my comrades who were cleaning pans in the kitchen missed any more parades.

Most evenings we would scour the countryside and sometimes went to Wimereux and Boulogne. On one occasion Gunner Bolton and I found a little farm some way off the beaten track where we had brown bread and some coffee served in little basins. We were served by two exceedingly pretty girls, the only good looking girls I ever saw in France as a matter of fact. One blonde and the other with jet black hair. Bolton was attracted by the blonde while I was equally fascinated by the brunette. We spent all our time which was not much, at the farm, talking to them in schoolboy French. We may have held hands but it was a pretty innocent affair. I know that Bolton fell genuinely in love with his blonde, and when it was time to leave he sobbed bitterly and unashamedly. Probably I was in no better state.

On October 2 we returned to the battery. Things had not altered much; there had been one or two casualties, nothing very serious. The position seemed reasonably safe and comfortable enough so long as the weather continued fine. But with October came the rain and we soon discovered the drawbacks of the St. Eloi position.

Once rain fell the pool in the crater increased until it reached the door of the Officers' Mess and Major Austin, still taking the parade in dressing gown and gum boots across an expanse of water, looked more incongruous than ever. All the shell holes between the crater and the guns were full to the brim but worse conditions prevailed in the pits. Being on the slope and connected by trenches, water poured from one pit to another. No. 4 gun at the top of the slope kept fairly clear, and Sgt Green who had scorned the protecting shell holes could now say *"I told you so"*. The condition of the centre guns, however, was deplorable. Water poured into the pits until they were knee deep. Baling had to be resorted to between shoots and empty fuse boxes laid down for the gun teams to stand on. When at last the water was bailed out the floor was a sticky mass of mud, and if a loading number stepped off the narrow line of boxes he sank almost knee deep and would be unable to move until relieved of his heavy load.

In this mud the Vickers platform slipped and slid about. Luckily the firing was fairly well distributed so after they had sunk badly on one side, a shoot in the other direction would restore equilibrium but slide backwards they never failed to do. Every day the gun and its platform retreated a few more feet; the trail would bury itself in the soft ground and had to be dug out. The two pits accordingly became larger every day.

When first laid out the loading platform was as near to the trail of the gun as possible so as to afford a straight run up for the loading numbers. With the continual retreat of the guns, the shells were now stacked almost level with the muzzle and it was a considerable effort to load. The teams were frequently changed for No. 7 on the team could not bear the strain for long. There was only one practicable way of loading. The loading tray was taken to the shells, upended, and a shell wriggled on. It was now lowered; two men instead of the four laid down in drill, would take hold of the tray and its load, No.5 walking forward and No.7 backwards until they reached the trail. No.7's truly frightful journey now began. Looking over his shoulder and still walking backwards carrying the shell tray with its two hundred pound burden, he stepped upwards on to the trail a matter of eighteen inches. He then walked over the trail and took another step downward on the other side. No.5 on the other side of the tray was meantime slowly pivoting round. A third man No.3 seized hold of the back of the tray while it was being carried over the gun trail, the other two men tilting the tray backwards with the double object of throwing as much weight as possible on to this man (he being in the best position to bear it) and also to prevent the shell from slipping off the tray. Once over the trail came a straight run forward and No.7 could enjoy a few moments rest while the others were ramming the shell home. The arrangement was bad enough when the three men worked in unison but was intolerable when No.5 could not, or would not, pivot round in tune with his opposite number, and I have known men refuse point blank to work with others. Bad enough in day time, in the dark of night when the steps of the loading numbers had to be guided by the light of the Gun Captain's torch, loading was infinitely worse, and it was a good man who could act as No.7 for twenty consecutive rounds without being relieved.

It was not surprising in the circumstances at some grumbling about continuously working short-handed, which was the price we had to pay for the double reliefs. Between shoots we had to bring up the ammunition and it was laid down that before the reliefs took over at least 50 fused shells were to be left on the loading platforms. There was considerable irregularity in shooting and it sometimes happened that one team would spend its 24 hours in continuous work while its successor would not fire a single round. On one occasion our Sergeant flatly refused to take over until the requisite number of shells was brought up, which, as the other relief were firing at the time, they were obviously unable to do. Meantime the lorries were waiting to take the men back to the rear billets and the Sergeant-Major came to see what the trouble was. Some compromise was affected in this instance but there always seemed to be the belief that the relief detachment was not pulling its weight.

There were still some men who would have welcomed a return to the system of full gun teams plus spare men. These found a spokesman in Sergeant (late Corporal) Coleman and consisted mostly of the old hands, Gun Layers whose position on any gun team was assured, and disgruntled ex-employed men whom Major Austin's ruthless policy had dislodged from their relatively soft jobs. It was argued that the battery position was as safe as the rear billets at Voormezeele and certainly more comfortable. Why then should seven men have to do the work of eleven while the others were idle? After all, night work was the exception rather than the rule. The spirit of Mory was not quite dead. Major Austin however was adamant against this insidious doctrine; the reliefs must continue. The only concession he would make was to change the normal time of changing over to 2pm on the understanding that in the exceptional case of heavy night firing, the relief teams should report in the morning to take over from the tired men.

Work at the battery usually ceased at dark and we retired to the shelters. We were allowed to sleep in the bunks provided that we did not take off our clothes and were ready for immediate action. We managed to obey this order by scraping off as much mud as possible from our boots and pulling sandbags over them to keep the dirt from our blankets. Sometimes we would be forewarned of night firing in which case we would be roused a quarter of an hour in advance and could walk down the new corduroy road, the longest way but the cleanest. More often, action would be called without warning. Then we would jump out of bed, pull the sandbags off our boots, snatch up gasmasks and steel helmets and make a dash for the guns over the broken ground that was formerly the village street. Stumbling into shell holes, slipping in the mud, we ran to the guns, the air resounding with curses. On dark nights it was quite a common thing for some to get lost and find their way to the guns only after the first round had been fired when they had the flashes to guide them.

Each morning before breakfast, if not actually firing, we would spend an hour or so tidying up the position and pulling up the dank vegetation to cover up the shells. The work was not popular.

There was a spell of dry weather and it was decided to relay the Vickers platforms of the two centre guns. This meant pulling the guns out of the pits – pretty hard work with the small number of men available. No.3 platform was in such a bad state as to necessitate it being sent back to the workshops. A flat platform was laid, the emergency shoe fitted and she was fired from scotches again much to the disgust of Sgt Coleman. In spite of their drawbacks, the Vickers platforms certainly did speed up firing and Coleman's gun was unable to compete with the others, even with Sgt Rowbottom's rag-time team. But repairs took a considerable time and whether they liked it or not, the rocking horse gun remained in action.

As regards No.2 gun, the platform had been driven backwards nearly ten feet and Sgt Rees determined, if humanly possible, to anchor it down this time. After the transoms had been lifted the pit bottom was scraped until a solid foundation was reached. The platform was now re-laid and poles driven in at each corner in an attempt to peg it down. Not satisfied with this, the men obtained a tree stump which they buried near the apex of the triangle and anchored the platform to this with a strong wire hawser. Nothing on earth would move the damned thing now. Alas for fond hopes. The weather broke again, water filled the trenches and poured into the gun pits. We partly filled the trenches to keep back the water but the defences broke down and the gun pits were again flooded. They were bailed out but after firing it was found that No.2 gun was sliding backwards again. The apex of the triangle was uncovered and it was found that the hawser was broken. In desperation a heavy chain was obtained and with this we fastened the platform to the tree stump. This at last seemed to anchor the platform permanently.

Another thing that gave us a lot of trouble at St. Eloi was richly deserved. One night early in September a large number of shells arrived by light railway. Somehow Major Austin had obtained the help of a party of infantrymen to help us with the unloading. At first the shells were properly stacked alongside the track ready for removal by our light wagon but when our men saw the job being properly performed they promptly went back to bed leaving the infantry to it. This so enraged the latter that they pitched the rest of the consignment into the surrounding shell holes and made off. When the bad weather came the shell holes filled with water and we had the unpleasant task of recovering the shells. We put off the task whenever possible and obtained fresh supplies but there were occasions when there was no alternative but to take out drag ropes and fish for shells.

Both the light railway and our Decauville track were exposed to hostile shelling and occasionally the enemy secured a direct hit and the track had to be re-laid. On one occasion a rather strange thing happened. We had gone to fish for shells and had got a truck load ready which some of us were running down to the battery while others were getting a further supply. When we reached No.4 pit we noticed the enemy had started shelling the dump and one shell seemed to burst right among the men we had left. We thought that some of them must have been caught but as it happened they were all safe, the only casualty being one of our party who was injured by a long flying shell splinter.

In mid-October there was more trouble with the guns. First No.3 in one of the deep pits failed and had to be sent to ordnance workshops. A 'strafe' was on and it was essential that the gun should be back in action as soon as possible. The gun failed at night and a tractor was ordered for dawn. The other guns were firing and so could give little help. They spared us one or two of their men however and in all we numbered twelve, not many to extract an eight tonne gun from a pit over six feet deep. The Sergeant-Major took charge of operations and at 9pm divided us into two parties of six men each. One party he sent straight off to bed until midnight the others being sent to work digging a ramp for the gun to be run up. At midnight we were changed round and while the first party enjoyed their three hours rest the others completed the ramp and laid down planks. At three in the morning we were all on the ropes, a seemingly hopeless task but pulley blocks were brought up, twenty foot levers used and at last the gun began to move. Inch by inch she was brought up the slope, wedges were thrust behind the wheels to prevent any running back. We twelve had the gun half way up the slope when a lull in the firing enabled the Gunners from the neighbouring emplacements to help and with a few vigorous heaves she was high and dry on the surface well in time for the Caterpillar. Although this was the most strenuous task I have ever performed, it proved once and for all how unnecessary it was to employ huge droves of men on work of this nature.

The heavy rainfall at the end of October proved conclusively that we should be unable to remain at St. Eloi throughout the winter and Major Austin again had to search for another position. He found a suitable spot not far away from the crater shown on the map as Bus House. All traces of the mansion had disappeared but the drive was in fairly good condition, its hard gravel surface little marred by shell holes. The ground was fairly level and here we should at any rate be dryer that at St. Eloi. Work began on November 1 fighting being continued at the old position. There was no violent hurry to move the guns and the task of preparing the place was undertaken by the reliefs on duty the teams being reduced accordingly. Great hopes were set on Bus House. It was to embody all the latest improvement known to battery positions. The shelters were again made of expanded metal but were much nearer the guns so as to avoid the long walk as at St. Eloi.

Meantime at St. Eloi the crippled gun had been repaired and returned to duty. Some changes were made in the gun teams and I was allocated to No.1 gun under Sgt Green. I was very pleased for I liked the Sergeant and the gun being on the surface was easier to work.

We were experiencing some amusement at this time by the enemy's strange tactics. At 10am precisely he would start his morning's hate. We had a good view of the surrounding country and could follow his movements. He would start on the Damstrasse well over to our right, work down the road as it lay in the valley and up the new corduroy track leading past our battery position. When he reached a certain point we would gracefully retire to our left flank and watch his shells bursting over our guns. After working his way methodically through the position, he would follow the track of our Decauville railway. About this time we would return to our guns to see what damage had been done, usually very little for he was using only light guns. The same thing was happening all along the track of his fire, troops retiring when the firing became too close and returning as soon as the danger was past. Day after day this happened, the half hour needed to evacuate the position became a regular interlude and we would laugh heartily at Jerry's love of order and lack of imagination which gave us a not unwelcomed break in the morning's work.

On the afternoon of November 3 the relief of which I was a member came up from Voormezeele in accordance with the usual practice. Sgt Green took over the gun and we learnt that the enemy had followed his usual practice that morning. Something had gone wrong with No.1 gun however and the Artificer was working on it. He now pronounced it beyond his capabilities; the gun must go to ordnance workshops. Being on ground level the gun needed little preparation to get ready for the road, so we were a detachment of seven men surplus. We worked at Bus House until dark after which we returned to St. Eloi. It became known that there was to be heavy firing that night so Major Austin arranged to send some of the surplus men to the remaining guns to reinforce their teams; the rest could make themselves comfortable for the night. It fell to my lot to be drafted to No.2 gun.

This was an unwelcome change for me as the gun was in the deepest pit and the hardest one to fight. The Vickers platform had slipped back so far that the loading stage was almost level with the muzzle of the gun. When shells were taken off the truck they were stacked on ground level near the gun, then they were rolled down a sloping plank to an intermediate level where they lay on their sides. The next stage was to get them down to the loading platform on the level of the gun where they were fused and placed on the loading tray. There was a difference of three feet between the intermediate platform and the gun level. The distance had not been so great at first but had developed after the bottom of the gun pit had been scooped out after being flooded. The way of bringing down the shells was to stand astride on the loading platform, grasp the shell on the intermediate platform by the nose and twist it round until the base faced the body of the operator. Then with a quick jerk pull it forward when it would topple over and fall neatly on its base between the Gunner's legs after which it could be trundled away and fused. The capacity of the loading platform was limited to six shells, so this meant that during a heavy shoot one member of the team would be continually pulling down shells.

As anticipated there was heavy firing throughout the night and we experienced every conceivable trouble. Just sufficient rain to make the planks and the gun trail as slippery as glass, awkward targets and continual changes from long to short shells and vice versa. No sooner had one target been engaged, the gun sponged down and ammunition brought up, than we were told to stand by for another shoot until we gave up hope of getting any rest that night. As was now customary, we had been regularly been changing post on the gun and in the early morning of November 4, I was acting as fusing number, pulling down shells from the intermediate platform to the loading platform and fusing and placing them on the loading tray. Being so close to the muzzle of the gun the roar and flash were terrific. The Sergeant would give the words *"Stand by"* before firing and we would all shut our eyes and turn facing the gun so as to avoid any possible effects. Whether it was the flash of the gun, the slipperiness of the timber or whether I was getting tired and losing my dexterity I do not know but I pulled down a shell and it dropped on this occasion not between my legs on to the loading platform but with the full force of its two hundred pounds fairly and squarely on my booted foot.

It was three o'clock in the morning when the accident happened. It was witnessed by two Gunners who passed the word to the Sergeant. I sat on the bank for a short time and fused a few more shells. There were only half a dozen rounds to complete the shoot. Then Sgt Coleman came round to investigate. He told me that I had better get back to billets and would have sent another man to help me but another target was coming through and all they could do was to assist me out of the pit, give me a pick handle as a walking stick and put me on the road.

I made my way slowly and painfully along the corduroy road to the crater. Several times I rested by the roadside. It was now fine and the stars were shining. At length I reached the shelter and stumbled into a spare bunk. One of the surplus Gunners awoke and enquired what the trouble was. I told him and asked the time. It was half past four so it had taken me and hour and a half to get from the guns, a distance which took about ten minutes. They carefully removed my boot and blood poured from my foot. I remember no more until roused by Sgt Rowbottom. It was eight o'clock. He took full particulars of the accident and told me I should have gone to the Dressing Station immediately. My heavy boot had saved me to some extent but the great toe was crushed and this might have serious consequences. Someone fetched my breakfast, others collected my kit or rather what I had with me, for the bulk had been left at Voormezeele. Big Reid volunteered to carry me to the Dressing Station if someone would help to steady me, so off we went.

The Dressing Station was not far away but Big Reid was puffed when we arrived. The RAMC men cut off my stocking. Yes I was one of the lucky ones – probably a blighty wound. In any case it would keep me out of action for a considerable time. Strange I had not looked at it that way before but the news was comforting. They bound up the foot, gave me an injection of ATS (anti-tetanus-serum) and a bowl of soup and told me to lie down until the ambulance arrived. I lay there thinking that it would soon be ten o'clock, time for the enemy to start his morning hate. As usual he would start at the Damstrasse, go down the hill, up the corduroy road and when he reached the lone tree it would be time to clear until he passed over the battery position. How typically German and how utterly futile.

Ten o'clock and a crash outside told me that something was happening that was not according to programme. An RAMC man spoke, *"Son, you're well in there, they're shelling your battery"*. So that was the game. By following the same route day after day the enemy had lulled everybody into a sense of security. Now he had simply reversed the order and started shelling from the other end of the line and with heavy guns too.

The bombardment of the battery continued for some minutes and stopped abruptly. Soon the motor ambulance arrived at the Dressing Station but it was required for more urgent cases than mine. Big Reid and another carrying a man face downwards on a stretcher. They were white faced and their burden was groaning badly. I recognised him as the man who had taken my place as fusing number on No.2 gun. He must have been bending over pulling down shells when he was struck, for half a dozen pieces of shell were still sticking in his back, hence his peculiar position on the stretcher. Three more badly wounded men were brought over; two at the battery were dead.[3] The badly wounded men were given precedence on the ambulance. My turn came later when I was joined by other walking wounded cases from various units up the line.

Looking out of the open door of the ambulance, I saw Cpl Pateman as we passed the battery position. I called out to him but he did not hear. Then following the corduroy road that had cost so many lives in the making, we passed the rear billets at Voormezeele, then the abandoned position, the broken camouflages flapping in the wind, and so along the Main Overland Track past the well-known landmarks, Moated Grange, Dead Dog Farm, the Brasserie and finally Swan & Edgars and the main road.

Although I did not realise it at the time, that for me was the end of 242 Siege Battery.

---

1   The mine to which Gnr Hall refers was blown on 7 June but three at St. Eloi dated from March 1916.

2   The debris from mines blown in the clay of Messines blew upwards and came down again in close proximity and the mine craters filled with water whereas the chalk on the Somme tended to blow outwards leaving huge dry craters (e.g. Lochnagar at La Boiselle).

3   The CWGC database does not list any fatal casualties for 242 Siege Battery for 4 November 1917.

CHAPTER 16
DOWN THE LINE TO THE BASE

G nr Hall was fortunate to incur a relatively minor injury while manning the guns but his experience thereafter shows the reader how wounded troops were handled as they were passed back down the line and received treatment at intervals then spent time recovering before being sent back to a unit. This is one explanation why troops' records often show service with multiple battalions etc.

My journey down the line as a casualty was very involved. First I was taken to the Main Dressing Station at Lindenhoek, not far from our first position in Belgium. I was detained only a short time, an RAMC orderly merely giving a cursory examination to see that the bandages had not slipped in transit. Having satisfied himself on this point and verified that I had been inoculated against tetanus, I was allowed to proceed, no account being taken at this stage of the blood oozing through the bandages – that could be dealt with later. A crowd of minor casualties had now gathered at the Main Dressing Station but we had to wait while the more serious cases were rushed through.

As last our turn arrived and a motor load of us were sent forward to the Field Ambulance at Dranoutre. Here, in a large barn, it was possible for a more detailed examination to be made. The rough dressing was removed, the injured member thoroughly cleaned, and a medical officer proceeded to assess the extent of the damage. Contrary to expectations no bones were broken. Had such been the case that would have meant the end of my military career, as I should have been unable to march and would have been discharged from the service. As it was, the root of the nail had been forced right through the flesh. This was the first opportunity I had of seeing for myself what had happened. My foot was re-bandaged, so much cotton wool being used that it looked as if my whole foot had been injured let alone my toe. A small Scots orderly carried me pig-a-back out of the examination room and laid me on the floor. It was now tea time and I was to make myself comfortable for the night.

Somewhat to my surprise I remained at Dranoutre until the 6 November. I was quite unable to walk but made myself as comfortable as I could round the coke fire and ate the rather thin meals provided. There were quite a number of minor casualties in a similar state and we lay on the straw exchanging yarns and wondering what was going to happen next. Orderlies would occasionally look in to see if we were alright, otherwise we received no further attention.

On the morning of November 6 we were conveyed to the Divisional Rest Centre at Bailleul. There were now a large number of casualties at Dranoutre and it took some time getting us through although here our wounds were examined and again dressed. The rest centre proved to be merely a continuation of the condition at Dranoutre, although we were now in huts instead of a barn. The whole business was getting frightfully boring. Naturally my injured toe was making its presence felt and I was beginning to think that something should be done about it. However I had to endure with patience for a couple of days more until on the evening of November 8 I was moved to the Casualty Clearing Station.[1]

The Casualty Clearing Station stood in what had been a large lunatic asylum outside Bailleul, an imposing brick building in extensive grounds. I had often passed the place on my excursions round Bailleul and had admired its splendid appearance, for it was the finest building in the neighbourhood. In peace time it had accommodated a large colony of females and there had been a lot of trouble in evacuating the poor lunatics in the early days of the invasion.

The whole staff looked worn out when we arrived, now over a hundred strong. A jaded looking doctor examined my foot and said, somewhat to my surprise, *"That's going to be a rather long job. Would you like to go down the line?"*. On my agreement he continued, *"All right then, we'll evacuate you tomorrow"*. We were getting a move on at last. We were taken to the ward or rather to an annex for there were only three beds in the small room. I was helped to undress, my clothes were removed for the first time since the accident, pyjamas were donned and I experienced the glorious feeling of being in bed again, the first time for eleven months.

An orderly came to see us and became quite communicative. The reason for the long delay was explained. Owing to the offensive in front of Ypres, the Casualty Clearing Station had become congested with serious cases requiring immediate operations and the medical officers had been working day and night. They had therefore to restrict the intake of the minor casualties who were in the Field Ambulance and Dressing Stations. It was now possible to take most of these but it had been decided that any whose stay was likely to extend over a day or two should be evacuated to the Base Hospitals. At all costs the CCS must be kept clear.

The following morning November 9 I was helped into my uniform and taken to the ambulance train which was waiting in a railway siding in the CCS grounds. After the stretcher cases had been loaded we minor casualties were assisted into the ordinary carriages.

The ambulance train was one of the English corridor trains which had been transported bodily to France. The front portion had been converted to hold stretcher cases and there were two or three carriages in rear. Such trains were painted white with the red cross on sides and roof. They were given priority over all other traffic and consequently travelled at a fairly brisk rate. En route we had an issue of the very thin stew which seemed to be a speciality of the RAMC.

We drew up at Camiers, a small town on the coast where the 22 General Hospital[2] had been established and it was not long before we were escorted to the wards. The hospital covered a very large area and consisted of both tents and wooden huts. Like most large establishments, it teemed with efficiency but had very little heart – a reversal of the Casualty Clearing Stations up the line.

First we had a hot bath, much appreciated in my case, for it was only the third that year. Then our injuries were examined. Nothing said in my case and it was obvious that it was regarded as trivial and in the normal way should not have been sent to them at all. A much smaller dressing was applied and I was given a pair of slippers in which I could hobble about. Our uniforms were left outside the bathroom and everything was taken away from us except such personal belongings as we could cram into the small bag provided. Then we were supplied with a clean set of underwear and given a suit of the hospital blue.

I was retained at Camiers only three days. The MO gave a searching examination of all cases in the ward with the evident intention of evacuating as many as possible in readiness for more casualties from Ypres. My foot was pronounced to be progressing satisfactorily, all I wanted was a few weeks rest and this could be provided in a Convalescent Camp quite as well as the hospital. In order to get to the camp I should need footwear, so in order to accommodate the bandages I was supplied odd boots, one my ordinary size and the other size 12, for my injured foot. I looked rather odd walking about with different sized boots.

On November 12 many of us were evacuated from hospital. Still technically wounded men we were entitled to travel in the ambulance train provided we still wore our hospital blues. Thus the train could be used to carry troops instead of returning empty up the line. Our destination was Etaples and as soon as we arrived at the 6 Convalescent Camp we handed in our blues and were issued with uniform.

The Convalescent Camp was rather a formal place, the commandant seeming to have the fixed idea of getting the troops ready to return to the line as soon as possible. There were parades at 9am and 2pm and pretty strenuous physical drill was given. Those with injuries to feet and legs were put in a squad to themselves and were given a special drill which imposed no strain on the injured members. No-one was allowed out of camp. On the third day after my arrival a searching medical examination was held and I must give the medical officers credit for being scrupulously fair although they had certainly did not err on the side of leniency. Most of those examined were pronounced fit for return to their units; in my case it was thought a little more rest was desirable. I must go to the new Convalescent Camp at Trouville.

On November 16 a large party of us travelled by ordinary train to the station of Trouville/Deauville, and soon afterwards reached the 14 Convalescent Camp which had been established outside the former town. Trouville proved to be a very different camp from the one we had left, and the memories of my stay are among the pleasantest of the war.

The camp was pleasantly situated and consisted largely of Nissen huts and three large dining halls. The commandant was evidently a man of character. He had us all on parade as soon as we arrived and explained his scheme. He wanted us to have a pleasant time but to leave the camp a little better than we found it. The camp was a new one and everyone up to now had done their share to improve it. He urged us to continue the good work until it became a thing of beauty and joy for the countless number of convalescents that were to follow us. A singularly beautiful idea.

Gardening – the first day we loathed it; afterwards we gloried in it, particularly when the commandant came round to see how the work was progressing. My party were engaged for the most part in laying turves on what had been a barren piece of ground between two huts.

Later we were fixing trellises. Even in November the camp looked beautiful. There were no asphalted parade grounds so beloved of the military authorities, simply grass with neat patches and flower beds. Some group before us had planted ferns against our hut and in a part of the camp creepers were already growing. Perfection was aimed at, nothing was hurried and we lived as a community dedicated to do our share in the work of steadily beautifying the camp.

In the evenings we were free but somehow the artificiality of the two famous watering places seemed to pall, and we were glad to return to camp.

Trouville is separated from its neighbour by a small creek round which clustered some rather squalid property. The celebrated plage was deserted and the hotels empty. With the fashionable throng absent, the twin towns were in a sorry plight and I understand the Convalescent Camp was established in response to an SOS from the inhabitants. The cafes on the front now sold cheap wine to the soldiers. Now when I read of the gay scenes in these famous Normandy pleasure resorts it brings to my mind those November days in wartime. Yarmouth certainly bore its days of trial with more dignity.

If there were no pleasures in the town there were certainly excellent concerts organised within the Camp. Here incidentally I first heard Elsis Janis[3] and many other music hall artists who came over to entertain the troops.

The last week of my sojourn was as an employed man – a waiter in the large dining hall. It was a full time job and rather strenuous work.

The dining hall was in three bays and half a dozen of us were on duty at each bay. We started work at half past six. Breakfast was at seven for the first mess and half past for the second for there were too many troops to be accommodated at one sitting. Our first job was to place mugs on the end of each table and lay plates, knives and forks for each man. The troops meanwhile would be lining up outside the doors. These would be thrown open at the stated time and they would pour in when our work would start with a vengeance. Some of us would fill the mugs with tea from galvanised pails while others would bring round the bread and bacon. As soon as the troops had breakfasted they left the hall and the dirty plates were rapidly cleared away and places laid for the second sitting. The second sitting away, we tidied up the dirty plates and joined the cooks for our own breakfast, staff mess as it was called. Here we were recompensed for our labours for it was not one rasher per man but as many as one could eat, followed with lashings of bread and jam. Often the cooks prepared porridge for the mess.

After breakfast came the washing of hundreds of plates and mugs, cleaning the hall and washing down the tables ready for the commandant's inspection. He came round about eleven o'clock and had an eagle eye for any dust or litter. Inspection over, came a few minutes rest and then preparation for dinner.

Dinner was harder work than breakfast and the serving of stew, potatoes and greens to hungry troops always ready to point out any irregularity in the portions was no sinecure. One experienced a sinking feeling when, half way down the table with peas, it was realised that some curtailment was essential if supplies were to do round. Where should we start, for the occupants of the table being served would inspect the plates of their fellows and actively resent any economy at their expense? Before the bottom tables had been served with their first course the top tables would be clamouring for pudding and an eye had to be kept for scroungers who would make a pretext of going out only to fall in again with the second mess and thus secure double rations. The cooks and their satellites did themselves royally for dinner. This over there was the washing and tidying up to be done but as is usual, the cooks and their mates managed to find time for an afternoon siesta. Tea was a comparatively easy meal after which the hall had to be cleared for the evening concert.

It was while shifting tables one evening that I received a scar on my upper lip which I still carry and which is the only visible mark of my service. Hanging to supports to the roof were rows of fire buckets, fortunately empty. In swinging a form out of the way one of these became dislodged and fell on my face, cutting the lip very deeply. This happened soon after I had been certified fit for active service and was awaiting a draft to the base. In the circumstances it would have been awkward to have to report sick. I found the NCO in charge to patch up the cut. Eventually he poured a lot of iodine into the cut and fixed some sticking plaster over it. I was unable to shave for some weeks and when I reached my new battery, I had quite a passable moustache. The scar had afforded me a good deal of amusement as friends, knowing I had served in the war, have remarked that it was a nasty place to be wounded, little knowing that the injury had been caused by a falling fire bucket. The medical service at the Convalescent Camp was conspicuous by its absence and seemed to exist for the sole purpose of passing troops for the line. My foot was never examined from first to last but it was obviously getting better. The old nail dropped off and a new one was forming. I myself reduced the bandaging until at last I discontinued it altogether.

On December 1 a large number of us were summoned and there followed the most farcical medical examination I have ever experienced. We fell in outside the dining hall and simply marched through it. The medical officer was seated at a table and watched us as we passed. On the strength of this examination we were all certified fit for active service. For myself I had no grounds for disputing the verdict but there were some who considered that they had not fully recovered from their injuries and protested, they merely wasted their breath. The wholesale posting of troops gave a nasty flavour to what had otherwise been an enjoyable convalescence. I feel that the conduct of the doctor on this occasion to be a disgrace to the medical profession. After all, we had been sent to the camp not for a holiday but to recover from wounds and other injuries. Surely the injured parts might at least have been looked at.

On December 2 the whole crowd of us left the camp by train for the reinforcement camp at Rouen. The reinforcement depot was merely a goods shed in the Maritime Station adjoining River Seine where the troops could be sorted out and returned to their respective bases. We hung about the shed until the names of the various divisions were called. The troops concerned would come out in front and be told the location of their base and when the next train left. The turn of the RGA came last for we were not attached to a division but were known merely as corps troops. There were some twenty of us all told and we were informed that our base was at Harfleur and that our train would leave sometime the following morning. We were not allowed outside the precincts of the station and spent out time walking moodily along the bank side watching the river. Then we made ourselves as comfortable as we could in the goods shed.

Troops seemed to be leaving all night for one centre or another but I did not hear my own party called out. When I looked round in the morning however I saw that I was the only Gunner left. Something had evidently gone wrong so I made enquiries of the Sergeant in charge. It seemed that the Gunners had left at 6 o'clock in the morning. The NCO said that he called out for RGA men and had roused all he could find but I must have been sleeping heavily and had been overlooked. There was nothing for it but to find my way to Harfleur by myself. Timetables were consulted and it was found that a civilian train left Central Station at 3pm (December 3). I had better go by that and make my peace with the authorities on arrival. I dined off biscuits and tea in the canteen for no rations were provided and at 2pm was allowed out of the Depot precincts to find my way to Rouen Central Station. I boarded a tramcar, managed to convey to the conductor where I wanted to go and in due course I reached my destination. Once in the station there were plenty of RTO[4] men to advise me and when the train arrived I was put into a compartment with a number of other soldiers bound for the same destination.

On the morning of December 4 we arrived at Harfleur station and I had little difficulty in finding my way to the base. I was in some trepidation when I arrived but I had no need to be for when I reached the Orderly Room and explained my mission, one NCO turned to another and said, *"How many reinforcements are we short from the lot that arrived yesterday?" "Eight,"* came the reply. *"Well here's one of them at any rate,"* replied the first man and with that he delivered me to the charge of a Bombardier who detailed me to one of the innumerable tents.

My arrival at base marks the end of the first part of my story. Had I been discharged from the Casualty Clearing Station I should most probably have returned to my unit but once I entered the General Hospital, Camiers, the chance became much more remote and now at base there was little or no possibility that I should ever see 242 Siege Battery again.

---

1   This CCS was either No 3 CCS and it was based at Bailleul from 15 May 1915 to 31 March 1918 or No 53 (North Midland) CCS located there from 23 July 1917 to 28 March 1918.

2   22 General Hospital was based at Camiers from June 1915 to January 1919, the location being close to a main railway line and to the coast for onward evacuation to Britain. At various periods of the war Nos. 4, 11, 18 and 20 General Hospitals and 42 Stationary Hospital were based at Camiers.

3   Elsis Janis was an American singer and actress who worked tirelessly providing musical entertainment for British and American troops on the Western Front.

4   Rail Transport Officer.

CHAPTER 17
FROM THE BASE TO THE SALIENT

With his injured foot recovered, Gnr Hall was transferred to a battery with an interesting history. As he explains, it had served pre-war in India where the guns were hauled by bullocks; now it was one of very few on the Western Front that used horses (Clydesdales) and this was a source of pride to the men. When the unit history was published in 1919 it bore an escutcheon showing associations with India such as a bullock and the type of gun it used there. Hall also encountered a close knit band of Regular soldiers that perpetuated customs of the battery but whose numbers were dwindling as casualties were incurred. He also returned to the Ypres Salient, to Frezenberg, a destroyed village on the road from Ypres eastwards to Zonnebeke amid a devastated landscape that had been fought over since 1914 and particularly during Third Ypres. His description of the mud and human remains give some idea of the condition of the battlefield and why there are so many 'missing' soldiers from the Great War commemorated at places such as the Menin Gate and Tyne Cot. The battery was equipped with 6" Howitzers (26cwt) rather than the 8" Howitzers he had worked on with 242 Siege Battery.

Coincidentally, Hall drafted the history of 81 Siege Battery in late 1918. Its story up to this stage of the war informs us that on the day war was declared, 4 August 1914, the battery was in Rhoorki, India, armed with four 6" 30cwt howitzers, drawn by bullocks. It was partly demobilised in September and some personnel transferred to other RGA batteries but they were recalled in November prior to the unit moving to Bombay. It sailed with 59 Siege Battery on the SS Kenilworth Castle arriving at Devonport on 23 December. In January 1915 the unit moved to Clarence Barracks in Portsmouth and then sailed from Southampton on 4 March arriving at Le Havre the following day. 81 SB moved to Laventie and saw its first action in the Battle of Neuve Chapelle on 10 March. In May it participated in the fateful Aubers Ridge action and in September in the Battle of Loos. In March 1916 the battery was in the Vimy sector and then in June at Engelbemer in readiness for the Somme offensive where it was engaged in shelling targets in Beaumont Hamel. The battery had a ten day period over Christmas and New Year in rest at Doullens and, by March, was at Fonquevillers at the time the Germans fell back to their new Hindenburg Line positions but they moved to the Arras front for the Easter 1917 offensive. On 23 June it entrained to move to Abeele and Poperinge and into the line at Dead End, Ypres, where it suffered heavy casualties from gas shells and again when a shell exploded prematurely killing three and wounding two gunners. In the period from 1 July to 20 September casualties (according to the unit history) were 11 killed and 90 wounded mainly by gas.[1] On 4 October, 81 Siege Battery was at Bavaria House on the Frezenberg-Zonnebeke road and took part in the Passchendaele offensive incurring several battle casualties plus the loss of the unfortunate 23321 Gnr P. O'Rourke run over and killed by a lorry. On 6 December the battery moved to Frost House and it was located here when Gnr Hall joined it.

The much dreaded Harfleur Base was in two parts, the main portion consisting of the living tents and dining hall being on a plain at the foot of the cliff while the exercising ground was on a high plateau reached by a steep path up the hillside. The whole camp was under canvas, eighteen men to a tent. There was no comfort of any kind; food was particularly bad and half cold and the canteens were so poor that it was difficult to supplement our rations. There was no YMCA and the shelter run by the Salvation Army seemed infected with the same spirit of general discomfort.

Our first parade was at five in the morning and we had to stand at least an hour on the parade ground with the regimental Sergeant-Major bellowed out the names and numbers of those selected for draft. I observed that the names were not always answered. With so many on parade it was difficult to hear one's name. Whatever the cause the discrepancies did not seem to bother the authorities overmuch. The absentees were certainly not in the tents for the staff went through them before roll call and there was no exception from the early parade even for newcomers like myself who could not possibly have been selected for draft. Second parade was at 8am when we were inspected by the Camp Commandant before being marched to our respective duties.

The first day after arrival we were marched to the Quartermaster's Stores to draw kit and equipment, a straightforward job but I encountered a snag with regards to my boots. I was still wearing odd boots, a size 8 on my right foot and size 12 on my left. I was of course no longer wearing my bandages and I wished to return to normal footwear. The Quartermaster objected to changing the boots on the grounds that they were in perfectly good condition. After we had drawn our equipment we were inspected by an officer whose attention I drew to my feet. The Quartermaster still protesting was directed to give me a new pair.

At 2pm we were marched up the hill for physical exercise. These were taken under experts, Staff Sergeant instructors they were called. There were about a dozen of them and each took a squad of men and put us through our paces. They were all short, stocky men, wonderfully agile and with squeaky voices. Why all PT instructors should have squeaky voices I do not know but it seems to be a hallmark of the fraternity. In addition to the physical jerks there was the notorious course to be negotiated. This was in an enclosed part of the parade ground and there were many obstacles to be taken, a ditch to jump, a wall to scale and then we had to walk along a narrow plank twelve feet long, through a drain pipe and then run home. Some stoutish men were unable to negotiate the wall while others jibbed the plank. The object of the course I am unable to conceive; there was no training for it, it was simply the accepted state of affairs. Just as a man had to draw his equipment and go through the gas chamber, so had he to drop into a bed of sand.

Another formality was the reading of camp orders. We newcomers were lined up in a square by a particularly unpleasant looking Bombardier who delivered an oration at great length, largely concerned with our conduct when on pass in Le Havre which, considering that we were not allowed in the town at all, seemed somewhat inappropriate. During his speech it began to rain so we were marched into another position where the NCO could obtain shelter for himself under a veranda while we troops were still exposed to the rain.

Next day, December 6, we were given instructions in gas warfare. We paraded in shirt-sleeves but carried ground sheets in case of rain. Then we drew rations for the day, bully-beef and biscuits. We were then issued with box-respirators, all the same size, size 'O', which would be a good fit for a boy of 12 but was not merely useless but positively dangerous for most men to wear. *"That's all right,"* said the NCO *"They'll change them up the hill."* And so it appeared for once we arrived the Sergeant looked at our tiny masks and changed them for the proper size. It appeared that the small masks had been issued and rejected at least fifty times already and at the end of the day they would be returned to the main stores only to be reissued on the morrow.

The gas instructions were thorough enough however. Every care was taken to ensure that the mask finally issued was a good fit. Then we had the usual gas drill, the alarm being given when we had to don the masks in the shortest possible time. We were marched about wearing the respirators and had various lectures on gas warfare. There was a short break at midday during which we ate our bully and biscuits and in the afternoon we had to pass through the gas chambers. First we passed through the comparatively harmless lachrymatory gas wearing our respirators, a good test for them. The few who could taste gas through their respirators had them changed. Then there were the lethal chambers where we had to remain resting on forms for some minutes, wearing the respirators of course, although at the end we were told to lift them a little to get a sniff of the gas and then pass out of the chamber. It certainly smelt like the real stuff.

The serious part of the job was now over and as a comic relief came the job of putting a gas mask on a horse. The horse was brought up, a well-trained animal with a gas helmet rolled up over its nose. Our instructor showed us how delightfully simple it was to fit the helmet. Someone was told to call out *"gas"* whereupon the instructor pulled down the mask over the horse's nose and mouth. It was observed that the sagacious animal thrust out its face to receive the mask and remained behaved in precisely the same manner at the front. This being the concluding item we were marched down the hill to the camp.

I was now ready to be drafted up the line and it was only a matter of time before my name would be called out in the morning parade. Meantime there was the camp routine of gun drill, physical training and squad drill. There were also classes for specialists and it was more out of curiosity than anything else that I stated that I was an Observer and a BCA. For a few days I enjoyed a refresher course, outdoor on the director and in a hut where the instructor went over the elements of gunnery with a few of us.

But life at the Base was exhausting work and it was with disappointment that I returned from early morning parade without my name having been called. This happened several days in succession. Many of us were now feeling fed up with the base and a soldier who had been through the procedure before gave me a useful tip. The idea, it seemed was to hang about the

Orderly Room at about 7 o'clock at night. The drafts were then checked over and there were nearly always some men short. One could then volunteer to fill the vacant place and with a bit of luck might get a really good battery.

I determined to put the scheme into operation. On December 9 my name not having been called at parade I joined a group of men assembled outside the Orderly Room. Soon names were called out. After each batch the reinforcements were told the number of their new battery. There were, as I anticipated, a number of absentees. The NCO would then call out, *"Any volunteers for 351 Battery?"* Sometimes where would be a rush for a battery with a reputation for being *"cushy"*, at other times the call would be received in silence. Then there would be a bit of auctioneering like *"It's a twelve inch battery"*. This would usually do the trick, or for a change *"A six inch howitzer battery in a jolly fine position"*. Most of the batteries had been detailed when my turn arrived. Thirteen names were called out but only twelve responded. *"Any volunteers for 351 Battery?"*. There were no takers at first, thirteen men looked ominous, too many casualties to be filled. There was, however, only one thing I wanted to know; what was the calibre of the guns? Six inch howitzers. My claim was undisputed for 6 inch howitzers were regarded as dangerous, 12 inch were the prime favourites followed by the 9.2 inch howitzers. But so long as they were not the damnable 8 inch howitzers I did not mind. I was accepted for the draft and after my number and name were taken I went off to fetch my kit and fell in with the others for my new adventure.

Leaving Harfleur was a long drawn out business. We paraded for the Sgt-Major's inspection, the commandant's inspection and a final inspection before leaving the base. Finally we marched off headed by a band until we reached Le Havre station. We hung about for a long time until the train arrived. Then we boarded the trucks and by 10pm the train began its weary journey up the line.

The journey was really uneventful. It was so late when we started and we had such a tiring day that we were all soon asleep on the wagon floor. The long journey was half over when we awoke the following morning (December 9), and began to take stock. This was very necessary in order to see how we fared as regards rations for when we lined up before entraining every fourth man had been given a loaf, every fifth a tin of jam, every sixth a tin of milk and so on but with shuffling into different trucks the rations had got hopelessly mixed up so that some carriages had tea but no bread, others an excess of milk but no jam and so on. Exchanges with neighbouring compartments were affected to more or less mutual satisfaction and we were able to get breakfast.

After this we enquired about each other's destination. So many seemed bound for 351 Battery that one of the party, a Scotsman who had inscribed his name Whitla[2] in huge letters on his gas mask, said, *"Hands up all bound for 351"*. Thirteen men bound for a life, nine from England and four including myself casualties. Someone passed the inevitable comment *"Thirteen – unlucky number,"* and conversation flagged for some time.

We arrived at Poperinge on December 10, mustered in the station yard and were quickly marched to the reinforcement billets, the same hop warehouse where I had stayed with 242 Battery on my first arrival in Belgium.

Motor lorries came for us the following day (December 11) and some fifty of our number were taken to Caterpillar Park outside Ypres. Here were assembled a large number of tractors belonging to various batteries in the Ypres Salient and here we remained until the respective units sent escorts for us.

An NCO arrived at the park on December 12, took charge of the thirteen of us and marched us to the centre of Ypres. Here on the canal bank were the rear billets of 351 Siege Battery. They looked fairly comfortable and I noticed among other things a bath, doubtless scrounged from the town and now decently camouflaged. The Sergeant-Major who inspected us told us, however, that there had evidently been some mistake as his battery were up to strength and certainly not in need of thirteen reinforcements.[3] We had better make ourselves comfortable while he made further enquiries. We were directed to a disused dugout which we were told to clean up and here we spent the night.

The following day (December 12) a job was found for us. It appeared that they had erected a Nissen hut in what had once been intended as a battery position. The position had been abandoned and scroungers had been detected in trying to remove the hut bodily. Our business was to occupy the hut until its future could be decided. We were left with sufficient rations for the day and wondered what would happen next. But on December 14 our fate was decided; we were claimed by 81 Siege Battery who had suffered severe casualties some days previously. We returned to the rear billets where a Bombardier from that battery was waiting for us. We marched through the town, through Menin Gate and straight up Frezenberg Road until we came to some farm buildings which we became later to know as Potije Farm, the rear billets of 81 Siege Battery, and here we were handed over to the Sergeant-Major.[4] He took our names and enquired if we had any qualifications. I told him I was trained as a Battery Commander's Assistant. Somewhat to my surprise he informed me that there was no vacancy at present but that he would make a note of it; I should have to go on the guns for the time being.

Then came the question of allocating us to the various gun detachments and of finding us accommodation. There were, it seemed, eight detachments so I was satisfied to learn that here at any rate reliefs were being worked. Seven of our number were told to proceed to the battery position in the morning to join the detachments on duty there, while the rest including myself were allocated to the reliefs now on rest. I was posted to No.1 gun Sergeant McIlroy[5].

There was difficulty in finding room for so many of us. The rear billets consisted of a single Nissen hut and the out-buildings, and what remained of the farm. As many as possible were sent to the hut which was now crowded to suffocation. Some were fixed up in the battery office and the canteen while Sgt McIlroy said that being as I was on his detachment I could stay with him in the kitchen.

The kitchen at Potije Farm. All that remained of the original farm house was a wall in which stood the chimney breast. The fireplace had long since disappeared. To make this into the semblance of a room a wall of sandbags had been erected and connected to the chimney breast with its corrugated iron roof. Access to the kitchen was through a rough cloth hung from the roof. Small cubby holes made of curved pieces of corrugated iron led off from the main building and here the occupants slept at night. In the chimney breast a huge log was burning, a trestle table was fixed in place by the fire, while in the corner was box full of cordite and NCT.

Here in this so-called kitchen I was to spend many happy hours seated in front of the fire with my companions ever and anon, throwing the cordite on the log where it would burn fiercely with a blue flame giving out an intense heat. The cordite (or NCT) was brought from the battery where it seemed they were firing exclusively third charge. The propellant was made up in bags loosely tied together, the full charge consisting of all four portions. When firing less than this the requisite number of spare bags were detached and came in useful for the fires.

From my colleagues I learnt much of the history of the battery. It seemed I had joined no ordinary unit. At the outbreak of the war the 81 Company RGA, as it was then called, had been stationed in India where it was armed with four 6 inch 30cwt howitzers drawn by bullocks. In December 1914 the battery was recalled to England and refitted for service in France. They took part in the battle of Neuve Chapelle in the spring of 1915 and had been in action ever since. It had first been intended to re-name the company No.3 Siege Battery but the then CO had been allowed to retain the original number which now became 81 Siege. The wisdom of retaining the number was a matter of controversy.

Of one thing they were intensely proud. On re-fitting they had been converted to horse transport; along with Numbers 1 and 2 Siege, had been allowed to retain their horses ever since. These together with our sister battery 59 Siege were the only horse drawn siege batteries in action. All the others were drawn by a peculiar type of lorry, the FWD, an American which drove on the front as well as the rear wheel. There was no use for horses on the Salient it seemed, all the ammunition arrived by light railway and the animals were at present eating their heads off at Poperinge. So I was among a battery of regular soldiers. Very few of the original men who came over from India were left but there were sufficient to carry on the tradition and soon I was to learn that now I belonged to the Royal Regiment of Artillery – the Right of the Line and the Pride of the British Army.

The farm kitchen was the rendezvous of the old hands. Here they would congregate and spin yarns about India and the early days of the war. This was my first experience of regular soldiers; like most of the New Army I had fought shy of associating with them and the few I had met occupied for the most part the exalted ranks of Warrant Officers. Here at Potije were men of all ranks, the remnant of the company who left India three years ago. Somewhat exclusive, they naturally preferred each other's company to the newcomers yet because one of their number Sgt McIlroy had introduced me to their midst they accepted me as one of themselves. They had a rather strange manner of referring to one another by the rank they had held in India as if the world had stood still when they left. The Sergeant-Major was still known by them as Corporal Spratley[6] and he would often call in for a chat with his old comrades. Advancement had been available to all who cared to accept it but they seemed to regard with most respect those who remained in their original rank. Somehow they seemed to consider promotion in the field as a back door method of advancement.

The doyen of the little band was Gunner Wheeler, the Major's groom. A tall man of dignified appearance and ponderous mode of address, Wheeler ruled the kitchen with a rod of iron. He occupied the corner seat nearest the fire, an upturned box, while the rest of us had to be content with a seat on the form. He alone decided when the fire needed replenishing. Of an evening he would call the party in turn for a song, he would have the last word in any dispute and finally he would decide when we were to retire for the night. He would pull out his watch and in a stentorian voice call out *"Bed time"* and like obedient children, we would all rise, say *"goodnight"* and pass out into the darkness. Gunner Smith, the second groom, was a cheerful little cockney and being on more familiar terms with Wheeler did not regard him with such awe as the rest of the party. Sometimes he would even answer the great man back but a dignified rebuke would eventually reduce him to silence.

Another of the party was Gunner Chinnery, the dispatch rider. Unlike the others he was not a regular but must have joined up very early in the war as he seemed to have been in all the battery positions with them. Anything unlike the traditional dispatch rider, it was impossible to conceive. An elderly Norfolk farmer with a heavy moustache, slow of speech and of slovenly appearance, nevertheless he fully justified his selection for the post. Equally at home on horseback or bicycle, he mostly plodded his way on foot between the battery, the rear billets and the Horse Lines. Whatever mode of travel he adopted he could always be relied on to deliver his message. He must have had dozens of escapes from death but he said little of his adventures except perhaps that there was heavy shelling at the crossroads. Later I was to see him walking through the heaviest barrage with as little heed as if he were going out in a rather bad thunderstorm. At Potije the chief topic of conversation was of farming and his beloved Norfolk.

Somewhat akin to Chinnery was Driver Seeley, the water cart man. Seeley was in charge of two beautiful white horses to which he was passionately attached, and his duty was to make one delivery daily to the battery position and another to the rear billets. As the journey was performed in broad daylight his white horses showed up prominently on the way up the hill to the battery and he was told repeatedly to leave his white horses behind and use dark horses for his work. In spite of all orders Seeley never failed to bring the water with his conspicuous team to the battery position at 10 o'clock sharp each morning.

There were two other members of the clique who had *"got into trouble"* soon after my arrival; Driver Swan[7] and Sergeant Quillinan[8], both regulars from India.

Swan was an extraordinarily smart little chap, always spick and span and a credit to the battery. However bad things might be Swan always managed to shave every day, to polish his buttons and clean his boots. He would rise early in the morning and have a cold bath in a cartridge box even when snow was on the grounds. If ever a man worshipped cleanliness it was Driver Swan. Alas he had one failing, the usual with regular soldiers, drink. Normally of the most temperate habits he would break out usually every other month and then become most beastly and disgustingly drunk when every sense of decency would disappear. On such occasions his comrades would guide him to a shelter to sleep off the effects and early the following morning he might be seen having his usual cold bath after which he would report for duty, spick and span as ever.

Driver Swan seemed to have no regular duties but rather was the general utility man equally at home with the horses or on the guns. He would work as a Gun Layer for some weeks and suddenly disappear to emerge as a leading driver. He acted as officer's servant, battery cook, dispatch rider, even telephonist, and was an expert in every task he undertook. He wore the French Croix de Guerre which he had earned in 1915 in an extraordinary manner. In charge of the water cart at the time, he had taken the opportunity to get drunk at an estaminet. Returning to the battery, quite oblivious to a heavy bombardment, he delivered the water to a French 75 battery either in a spirit of bravado or more probably by mistake, it was never quite known which. At any rate he had to make another journey to his own unit and on arrival was promptly put under arrest for being drunk in charge of horses. The following day a French Colonel called to see about making some award to the *"brave Englishman"* who had brought water to his sorely tried battery when none of their own men dare make the venture. The fact of Swan's arrest was suppressed and in due course he received the decoration of which he was intensely proud.

His companion, Sgt Quillinan, was an Irishman, wonderfully efficient but very quick tempered. One never felt quite certain of his current rank for he was promoted Sergeant several times but always lost his stripes for the same thing – drink.

One of my first tasks in 81 Siege Battery was guarding these two men. They had been to Poperinge and had got gloriously drunk. Swan had been apprehended by the military police and Sergeant Quillinan had come to the rescue of his companion. The NCO affecting the arrest was like all military police, a Lance Corporal, and Quillinan as a Sergeant ordered him to be released. This interference with police duties was bad enough but when the Lance Corporal expostulated, Sgt Quillinan struck him for *"not obeying orders"*. The outcome of the business was that an officer was fetched who put both culprits under arrest and sent them to the battery under escort. Everyone at the battery from the CO downwards was furious at the military police for touching our men, nevertheless discipline had to be maintained, and a guard mounted to take charge of the delinquents until they could be tried by the Colonel. Sgt McIlroy with another Gunner and myself formed the first guard and our instructions were not to let the men out of sight but not to interfere with them in any way. This meant a few days in the kitchen spinning yarns and when they wanted a drink we had to go too. Quillinan knew of a canteen run by a unit some distance away so off the whole party went. When we got there Sgt Quillinan maintained that in no circumstances were prisoners under escort to treat their guards but there were no orders against the reverse procedure. As a matter of fact they had spent all their money but they were reasonably temperate now and when they were satisfied we all marched back to the billets.

A week elapsed before the prisoners were brought to trial and the duties of the guard were taken over by another Sergeant and his men who were pleased of the chance to a rest.

The result of the trial was that Sgt Quillinan was reduced to the ranks but the following day he was promoted again to Bombardier, it being the intention of the CO to raise him to his former ranks as speedily as possible. To pass through all the stages took two months and no sooner had Quillinan been restored to the rank of Sergeant than he broke out again and the same punishment was meted out. Once again he started climbing the ladder as he had done so many times before and long before armistice he was again Sergeant. I have no recollection of Driver Swan's punishment but it would not be so severe.

Of the other old hands there was my own Sergeant McIlroy, a most likeable and efficient NCO, and Sergeant Rolfe[9], the popular Sergeant in charge of the Horse Lines who often came to visit us. Then there was Corporal Brazier[10], the youngest of them all who had accompanied the battery from India as a trumpeter. A strikingly handsome youth of eighteen he might, he had wished, remained at the Horse Lines but he preferred to take his turn on the guns and was now in charge of a detachment. Finally there was the Sergeant-Major or "Corporal" Spratley as the regulars persisted in calling him; a stoutish, rugged faced easy going man who admittedly preferred the quiet of the rear billets to the glory of the forward position. He kept himself well informed of the happenings there by judicious questioning everyone who returned and he accordingly gleaned a mine of information which he was at pains to impart to newcomers like myself. I was completely deceived by this subterfuge, and thought the Sergeant-Major must have spent most of his time at the battery position whereas he has never visited it at all and had obtained all his information at second hand.

Such then were the men who carried on the traditions of the regular army, a round dozen men out of the hundred odd who had come over from India. The more I associated with them the more I appreciate their nature. Simple souls they were, in spite of all their swaggering and boasting. They loved the army, the regiment and above all their battery. They never questioned the orders of their superiors, they worked together in a remarkable way, and their belief was a peculiar mixture of fatalism coupled with a deep religious feeling. They accepted death as a natural consequence of their calling, to attempt to escape would be futile for it had been pre-ordained who should be taken and who left. If a shell bore your number it would be bound to find you whatever precautions you would take. There was however a profound belief in immortality. On occasions I heard it said *"I wonder what Billy Button's doing now"* and it took me some time to realise that Button[11] was a deeply loved Sergeant who had been killed with the whole of his gun crew when the enemy secured a direct hit on their dugout the week before my arrival. They took great care to see that all the dead were interred with the proper religious rites and such profane jests like *"any returns?"*, as had been made at Spoil Bank, would not have been tolerated for a single moment.

The battery had, it seemed, at the same time as I had been at Spoil Bank, passed through such an inferno of fire as to make my experience there seem more child's play. They had been located at Dead End on the canal at Ypres before the advance of July 31 and in a few weeks had over a hundred casualties, the entire personnel being at one time reduced to sixteen. In addition two of their guns had blown up in one case killing the whole team. All these experiences they had related in a most calm and detached manner.

But in some ways 81 Siege Battery compared unfavourably with the one I had left. Food was badly cooked and accommodation left much to be desired. As stated I had found quarters in the kitchen. When it was time to retire for the night, I was directed to a cubby hole leading off the main building. This was about two feet high by three wide and held two of us. The first night I felt terribly cold and in the morning I discovered the reason. At the far end of the cubby hole was a small door about eighteen inches square, part of the original fixtures of the farm. In my sleep I had kicked open the door and my feet were exposed to the snow. My comrades were quite apologetic about this and we found some sandbags with which we barricaded up the door the following night.

A canteen of sorts was run in the rear billets. Critics maintained it was positively the worst canteen in France.[12] Gunner Wiley in whose charge it was had a genius for obtaining merchandise that no-one was likely to want but was aggrieved when he did not make a sale. When one went for a packet of cigarettes he would apologetically state that he was sold out but had been fortunate in securing some excellent bootlaces. He was jubilant when he managed to dispose of some tins of sausages that had been on his shelves for months to some of us newcomers who has asked for writing pads and chocolate.

At the time of my arrival two reliefs of forty-eight hours each were being worked it being considered that the distance from the battery was too far to justify the normal twenty-four hour shifts. The detachments off duty were absolutely free without discipline or parades of any kind. This concession lost some of its value when it is realised that it was winter, there was considerable snow and the ground was frozen hard. The nearest town, Poperinge, was over ten miles away. The troops off duty remained for the most part in their billets; those of us in the kitchen had undoubtedly the best time.

And a happy time it was sitting in front of the fire throwing cordite on the blazing logs. I remember saying that those of us who were spared to return to civilian life might in later years wish ourselves back at the ruined farm. For myself, prophesy proved only too true and for years I would look back with envy at those days at Potije.

On December 18 four days after my arrival, Sgt McIlroy took his detachments up to the battery position. Five men were chosen to accompany him, the method being to ask different men if they would like to *"Go up the line"*. Being a newcomer it was desirable that I should be one of the party. The detachments could have been made up to eight if necessary but it was considered that six were adequate to fight the guns and it would do no harm for the others to have a couple of days of rest. With the smaller guns there always seemed to be a surplus of men.

We had dinner at 1pm. The reliefs paraded under the Sgt-Major and we marched or rather walked up the hill to the battery position at Frezenberg.

It had been truly said that a soldier who had not served on the Ypres front had no idea what warfare really meant. As we advanced up the hill all signs of civilization disappeared. Not the ruins of a house nor the remains of a tree or even a blade of grass was to be seen. Nothing but a mass of shell-holes full of water was visible as far as the eye could see. Over such ground it was impossible even for the infantry to pass on foot and when at last the road petered out, a special duckboard track had to be maintained to enable the troops to reach their advanced positions. The duckboards themselves consisted of two pieces of wood six feet long, across which slats were nailed making the width of each board two feet. The elevated track on which we passed consisted of three duckboards fastened together thus being six feet wide, and was supported on piles about four feet above ground level. Woe betide any who fell off the track. If they were lucky they might escape with a ducking in the icy water but many were drowned or suffocated in the mud. Naturally the tracks came in for a good deal of shelling. The enemy preferred to use shrapnel which was ideal for his purpose. He had the tracks perfectly registered and would open up day or night without the least warning. When he fired on the track there was nothing for it but to bolt for there was no shelter of any kind. In parts the track had been damaged by a direct hit and these points required careful negotiating. Most terrible of all was the sight of dead men lying in the shell-holes all along the track. There were literally hundreds of them and some had been there for months. Parties proceeding up the line had been caught by enemy gun fire and many of the dead had been left where they fell. Also there were those killed in previous actions for the battlefield had never been cleared. Pioneers were constantly at work replacing damaged duckboards and the cost of life maintaining communications must have been terrific. Yet these tracks and the light railway were the only ways up the line.

Our battery position was typical of many in this part of the front. It was situated near Frezenberg Ridge which had been wrested from the enemy in one of the later battles of Ypres. The actual spot we identified as Borry Farm[13] although all traces of the farm itself had disappeared. Here the elevated track and the light railway ran side by side. Two guns were on the right of the track and other two on the left a hundred yards away.

The other relief awaited our arrival. They were not firing at the moment. Handing over was the work of a few minutes and they were soon on their way down the duckboards anxious to leave while it was still quiet. Sgt McIlroy introduced me to my new quarters. First of all the dugout. This was about eight feet square by three feet high. The floor was about twelve inches below ground level, this being the maximum depth that could be obtained in the water-logged ground. The walls were cartridge boxes filled with earth on which rested the curved pieces of corrugated iron that formed the roof. A hole in one of the boxes formed a rough stove in which NCT could be burned to warm the shelter. This was rarely necessary as with five or six men in the place it became very stuffy.

Map showing Borry Farm

Next the Sergeant showed me Sgt Button's dugout which had received a direct hit a few days earlier when all the occupants had been killed; a shelter of precisely the same construction as our own and about five yards away. Acting on the superstition that it was unlucky to rebuild a blown up dugout, it had been abandoned and another built nearby.

Sgt McIlroy explained vividly and at considerable length how the bodies had been recovered through the broken roof.

Graves of Bradley, McNamara and Button, Ypres Reservoir Cemetery

I was, however, delighted with the guns; after the eight inch howitzers they seemed like toys. The shells were stacked in neat heaps behind the guns all fused ready for firing. The hundred pound shells could be lifted with ease, the cartridges were twenty-four to a box. Later it seemed that some ammunition required re-stacking and after tea I started on the job single-handed – the team thought I had gone mad but I gloried in the work and felt that I could carry on all night if needs be.

The gun rested on a rough platform composed of three planks of wood while I noticed another plank at the right angles under the trail. I enquired its purpose and was told that it was to prevent the spade from digging in. As the first thing we were told in 242 Battery was that the spade <u>must</u> dig in to hold the gun firm when firing, this seemed strange to me but I was assured that it worked all right. Sgt McIlroy gave me a handspike and told me to throw the trail over. This I did with the greatest ease while memories of Mory came back to me of spare men going from gun to gun pulling them out when they got off their line. Forty, fifty or even sixty men on ropes, tugging and heaving until when it was felt that human effort could do no more, the gun was dragged inch by inch from the tenacious hold of the ramps. Thank God I had finished with the 8 inch and while the lighter gun was supposed to be more dangerous, anything was better than the misery associated with these monstrous howitzers.

Action was called at 3pm and I was astonished at the ease of fighting the howitzers and the rapidity of fire. Three rounds a minute could be maintained with a team of five. In practice the pace was set by the time the Gun Captain took to centralise the bubble on his clinometer and not by the loading time as with the 8 inch. There was no hard and fast way of working and Sgt McIlroy let me try my hand at all the different jobs, including

Iken war memorial showing the Button brothers

gun laying which I managed competently. The only thing that distressed me was the harsh staccato bark of the guns after the dull roar of the 8 inch. I never became quite used to the noise of the six inch howitzer. After the shoot all hands sent to work fusing shells which we made up to about a hundred a gun. Cartridges in boxes of 24 presented no difficulty but we loosened the screws of a few in readiness.

For tea we walked up the duckboard track to the cookhouse which was situated in what remained of a concrete gun emplacement (captured from the enemy of course). On the way I saw a terrible sight. In a large shell-hole full of water were the bodies of a Scotsman and a German as they had fallen months before. Apparently the Scot had bayoneted his enemy but he himself had been killed by a shell, for he was without a head, or perhaps he had been decapitated later. Now the two corpses rested on each other with the Scotsman's hand and arm above water level beckoning, as it were, passers-by to see what horrors the shell-hole contained. As we passed by the bodies it was agreed that it was disgraceful that they should be left in such a state – something should be done about it. But whose job was it to clear up the mess? Perhaps it was ours; every man in the battery position had passed the horrid sight at least half a dozen times a day but no-one volunteered for the task of dragging the decomposed bodies out of the water and sending them for interment. Some said it was a job for the labour company, others that it was a crying shame that the Scots battalion had left one of their number in such a condition. We congratulated ourselves that all our own dead had been decently buried with appropriate rites. But with these strangers nothing was done and a few days later the shell-hole was frozen over but ever the dead hand stretched forth above the ice as if to remind us of what lay under the water. There were many such horrors on the Salient but no-one was worried about them; on one occasion I picked up what I thought was a stone but I put it down quickly – it was a human skull.

At night a guard was mounted, four men taking two hours each. As a newcomer I was not surprised to be selected. I was on duty from midnight to 2am. Guard was quite informal but full of responsibility. I was roused at midnight by my predecessor, stumbled out of the dugout and made for the BC Post, a concrete blockhouse or "pill-box" as it was called. This was a legacy from our friend the enemy and was the only strong point in the battery position. Whenever shelling became acute all hands would dash for the post and remain there until the danger was over. I took my position outside the BC Post watching the front line. It was comparatively quiet. The field guns were in action however, and from their flashes the front could be traced curving round like a gigantic horseshoe. It was not a comforting thought that the battery position could be engaged from both flanks as well as the front and that it would be virtually impossible to silence hostile guns so widely separated. Occasionally the Germans would shell the duckboard track and the light railway but none of the shells came near enough to cause alarm. The whole of the hillside was on the que vive, however, none slept soundly on the Salient. The officer on duty came out on several occasions and spoke a few words to Sgt McIlroy and some other Gun Captain also came out of his dugout to see that all was well.

I had been specially warned to look out for the SOS signal. This was a rocket fired by the infantry when pressed by the enemy. The signal was frequently changed but on this occasion consisted of three coloured lights red – green – red. If ever I saw this signal I was to call out *"Battery Action"* first and then report to the post.

As night advanced the activity seemed to be on the increase and soon after one o'clock it became evident that something was afoot. I called to the duty officer who came out of the BC Post and stood beside me while we watched for the warning signals. The gun crews were by now making their way to the guns; all round could be heard the sound of voices. A signal went up, the golden rain, a signal used by the Germans for their own artillery. Then came the crashing of enemy shells and at last the expected rocket red-green-red. *"Battery Action,"* I yelled and was not alone for in every direction the words echoed as called to their respective guns *"Battery Action, Battery Action."* Then, crash, crash, crash. *"Gun fire – let 'em have it, thick and heavy."* All guns responded, the hillside was aflame with gun flashes and the cries of the Gunners as the shells were being rammed home could be heard from all directions. Then the tumult ceased as suddenly as it had started. We had fired ten minutes from the time of receiving the SOS signal; now we paused for confirmation or for further orders. But the signal was not repeated and after a few minutes the guns were sponged down, the spent ammunition replaced and the Gunners returned to their dugouts leaving me alone outside the BC Post. I finished my tour of duty, called out my successor and returned to the shelter. Nothing further of moment occurred but the night was typical of many spent on the Salient.

The rest of the spell was uneventful but something was giving me more trouble than enemy action – a raging toothache. I had broken a molar over a particularly hard biscuit some weeks previously, and had experienced trouble with it off and on ever since. I tried to have it removed during my stay at hospital but no dentist was available. I had obtained some dental cement from home and was hoping that I would be able to last out until my leave, which I knew was not too far distant when I could have the tooth extracted privately. The last two days had however brought matters to a crisis and I was determined to have it out at the earliest opportunity. I consulted Sgt McIlroy who advised me to report sick as soon as I returned to rear billets. I could then have the tooth extracted by the dentist at Ypres Prison and would be all right in an hour or two.

It proved not to be so easy as we thought. We were relieved on the afternoon of December 20 and quickly returned to billets. I reported sick the following morning (December 21) and was marched to the Advanced Dressing Station outside the Menin Gate at Ypres. After I had told them of my trouble I was sent down to the Main Dressing Station at the old prison. So far things were proceeding according to plan and I screwed up my courage for the forceps. It was not to be however for as soon as I told the medical officer of my trouble he said *"Oh, dental is it, have you got your kit?"*. I replied in the negative whereupon I was directed to return to my unit for my kit and report again. I walked back to Potije, collected my belongings, told the Sgt-Major what had happened and returned to the Dressing Station. After some time I, with a few others, were taken off in a motor ambulance. Our journey was of only a few minutes duration for we were taken to Ypres railway station a few hundred yards away.

Here in a sandbagged shelter was the Collecting Station of the RAMC. We were told that we were too late for that day's ambulance train and should have to spend the night there. My tooth had now stopped aching but I had brought up all the ponderous RAMC machinery into operation and nothing would stop it until its task had been performed.

At 10am on December 22 we were told that the ambulance train had arrived and that we had better be slippy because they wanted to get it away. It seemed ludicrous that the railway line had been extended to the town of Ypres right into the firing line so that a Red Cross train could move a dozen or so trivial medical cases including one or two for dental treatment.

The train pulled away and we were ordered to alight at Brandhoek, the next station a couple of miles away. We did so but here at the Divisional Rest Station there was still no dentist and all cases requiring his attention were segregated and sent to a hut on their own. We joined some others who had been here for several days. The dental party now numbered twenty, every one of whom would gladly have backed out of the adventure for there did not seem to be an aching tooth among the lot of us.

The following day December 23 the ambulance train went its weary way from Ypres, discharged another party of minor casualties and picked up, among others, the twenty dental cases. Excitement was rife; to which base hospital were we going? Optimists were speculating on Blighty. The RAMC again took our particulars, name and number rank, religion, next of kin and the rest. At length the train moved down the line.

But not for long for at Remy Sidings outside Poperinge and three miles from Brandhoek, we were told to alight. We had reached our destination, the 17 Casualty Clearing Station.[14] It was tea time. We marched off to a ward under canvas and were given the familiar stretcher beds. Nothing more could be done that day.

On December 24 however we dental cases were informed that the dentist attached to the Casualty Clearing Station had gone home on leave but luckily one was available at neighbouring Clearing Station, 2 CCS (casualty clearing stations usually worked in pairs).[15] After breakfast we marched across the railway line to that unit. We formed up in a queue outside a small hut having two doors. Other dental cases had been collected from our various sources and we now numbered about 50. The men entered by one door and emerged from the other a few minutes later spitting blood and giving hair raising accounts of their treatment to the others waiting their turn. My turn arrived at last and after several attempts the molar was extracted. The dentist was a cheery soul. I remember his words *"Well, that's one piece out at any rate,"* as the tooth broke in his forceps and he continued his search for more. He seemed disappointed when I declined to have any more teeth extracted. The business was now over and I was discharged forthwith, without, I remember, anything to eat.

I had a little money so with another man made my way to Poperinge where at a little restaurant a particularly loathsome old woman served us with eggs and chips. Then by means of lorry jumping I made my way to Ypres and walked through the Menin Gate and up the hill, not forgetting to partake of the hospitality provided by the YMCA a can full of soup for all men proceeding up the line and very acceptable on that cold winters evening. And so along the road until I reached the familiar rear billets at Potije on Christmas Eve 1917. My friends wondered where on earth I had been. My detachment had spent another spell of duty at the battery during my absence and had returned to the rear billets for rest so I was just in time for my Christmas dinner.

Much preparation had been spent on the Christmas dinner and the detachments off duty were considered doubly fortunate, although those at the battery position did not fare so badly, although necessarily more rough and ready. The Nissen hut had been decorated with holly and mistletoe, trestle tables had been borrowed for the occasion (with much difficulty for they had to be returned the same night) and a special field oven had been erected to roast the meat. The oven had given a great deal of anxiety. It was built of bricks scrounged from a great distance and plastered together with mud. Hitherto there had been no attempt at roasting meat but it was felt that the occasion merited special treatment. A vast quantity of cordite and NCT together with small sticks and the joint, a huge piece of beef, was placed in the oven. It speaks well for our oven to say that it drew and the joint was cooked to a turn. There were at least a dozen cooks on duty; potatoes had been carefully peeled and some greens had been obtained from Poperinge. At 1 o'clock dinner was served, the Sergeant-Major carved and there were liberal helpings for all. After meat came the Christmas puddings which that year had been distributed by a fund in England, it being the intent that all serving soldiers in 1917 should have their pudding. They were of good quality and a liberal supply of army rum helped them down. Toasts were now drunk in copious draughts of neat rum; the King, sweethearts and wives and the rest. We were now all in high spirits and it was decided that the time had arrived to broach the barrel of beer. This had been obtained after considerable trouble from a brasserie in Poperinge and stood outside the cookhouse. At first Sgt McIlroy deemed it advisable to keep some check on the liquor and doled out the beer in mess tin fulls. But it was flat and of very indifferent quality and soon the Sergeant called on us to be sports and help him to drink the stuff. The barrel remained in the open all Christmas and the remainder froze. On Boxing Day some hardened spirits could be seen about the billets sucking pieces of frozen beer.

On Boxing Day our detachments went up to Frezenberg to relieve the party there for a couple of days. This time we took Gunner Williams[16] with us. Williams was a regular soldier but unlike most of them, was rather nervous; "windy" as we said, and made no pretence to hide the fact. It was the very sensible practice at 81 Siege Battery to keep nervous men away from danger whenever possible. This was not out of consideration for the men themselves but because blue funk was highly infectious and one windy soldier might upset the whole battery, a fact not realised by all commanding officers.

The battery position at Frezenberg had by now quietened down considerably and it was thought safe enough to admit sending up Williams on this occasion. He would have been better in the rear billets. We had no firing to do during the night and were trying to doze in the dugout. We should have slept more soundly except that Williams kept us awake with his anxiety. At last the enemy landed a heavy shell some little distance away and Williams jumped up with the words *"That's the ------- I've been waiting for all night, where's my --------tin hat?"* He snatched up his steel helmet and respirator and made a dash for the concrete pill-box. The rest of us promptly became infected and followed suit much to the protests of the occupants who were very overcrowded. We soon returned to our shelter except the "windy" one who insisted in remaining in the BC Post all night. The words of Williams caused a good deal of amusement in the battery and were often recalled. It is only fair to say that he took the matter in good part and enjoyed the laugh as much as the rest of us.

---

1   The CWGC records list twelve killed or died of wounds in this period.

2   95243 Gnr Thomas Whitla, (his medal index card shows A/Cpl) 81 Siege Battery, Royal Garrison Artillery, killed in action 21 March 1918 aged 34. He has no known grave and is commemorated on the Arras Memorial to the Missing. Whitla came from Greenock and was a park keeper in civilian life and was married with three children. (Source: Great War Forum).

3   In November 351 Siege Battery had lost three men killed.

4   The battery was located at Frost Farm/Frost House close to Borry Farm and at this time was equipped with four 26cwt 6" Howitzers. Other battery members of the Heavy Artillery Group at the time were 59 and 351 Siege Batteries, 1 Canadian Siege Battery, 133 and 147 Heavy Batteries.

5   29013 Sgt Edward McIlroy 81 Siege Battery, RGA.

6   27379 Sgt Maj Harry F. Spratley DCM. First theatre of war was France and Flanders from 5 March 1915; he was discharged on 14 May 1919. The award of his DCM is recorded in the war diary (WO95/225 48 Brigade RGA) on 8 June 1918 and the ribbon presented at Vauchelles on 23 June. The unit history refers to it being awarded for actions at Arras and at Dead End, Ypres.

7   30825 Dvr Cyril Swan, awarded the French Croix de Guerre 1915. This was recorded in the unit history for the water cart incident which occurred in the Vimy sector in March-June 1915. He was also hospitalised January 1916.

8   27723 Sgt Patrick Quillinan was posted to the battery from the Divisional Ammunition Column. His medal index card notes that he was reduced from Bdr to Gnr by General Court Martial on 27 December 1917. His first theatre of war was France and Flanders from 21 April 1915.

9   Probably 37418 Sgt Rolfe. The unit history (p13) does refer to a Gnr Rolffe (sic) gassed on 22 July 1917.

10   37224 Cpl William James Brazier, 81 Siege Battery, Royal Garrison Artillery, killed in action 23 March 1918. He has no known grave and is commemorated on the Arras Memorial to the Missing. Brazier came from Chailey in Sussex and is listed on the village war memorial.

11   33789 Sgt William Thomas Button, aged 33. 81 Siege Battery, Royal Garrison Artillery. His first theatre of war was France and Flanders from 5 March 1915. He was the son of Mrs Jemima Button, of 21, Iken Common, Tunstall, Suffolk. Killed in action 11 December 1917 near Frezenberg Ridge. Buried in Ypres Reservoir Cemetery plot 4, row B, grave 1. Sgt Button's two brothers were also killed in the war and all three are commemorated on the memorial in Iken church. The brothers were 33610 Pte Reginald Button (4/East Surrey), died 9 October 1917 and buried in Godewaersvelde British Cemetery, plot 1, row H, grave 12; and 326935 Gnr Sidney Button (X1 Trench Mortar Battery, Royal Field Artillery), died 23 July 1918, buried in Terlincthum Military Cemetery, plot 1, row F, grave 22. The other casualties in this event were 37553 Gnr John Diprose, aged 25, son of Mr. and Mrs. A. Diprose, of 13, Leyton Rd., Wimbledon, London, died of wounds 11 December 1917 and buried at Lijssenthoek Military Cemetery plot 27, row DD, grave 8A. His first theatre of war was France and Flanders from 5 March 1915; 106320 Gnr George Bradley, plot 4, row B, grave 3; and 65791 Gnr J. McNamara, plot 4 row B, grave 2. This is a good example of how casualties from a single incident can be found in multiple locations.

12   The term 'France' often seems to be the generic term for 'the Western Front' regardless of whether in France or Belgium.

13   Borry Farm was about half a mile NE of Frezenberg.

14   17 CCS was based at Remy Siding from 15 July 1915 to 8 April 1918. The area handled thousands of casualties and today the surrounding countryside contains many war cemeteries including some of the largest on the Western Front.

15   Hall is incorrect. At this time No 10 CCS was at Remy Siding.

16   128437 Gnr Frederick Joseph Williams.

CHAPTER 18

APPOINTMENT AS BATTERY COMMANDER'S ASSISTANT

Periods of leave were cherished by the troops although several days could be required to get home despite the best efforts to move troops to and from the ports and across the English Channel. During his absence a new CO was appointed, a long serving soldier who had seen action in South Africa and had been part of the original British Expeditionary Force in 1914. Major Warren stands out among Hall's pen portraits as a much respected officer who was a great loss when he died of wounds during the German Spring Offensive in March 1918. Also during this period the battery changed from being a four gun to a six gun unit. When Gnr Hall returned from leave the Salient was a bleak place with heavy snow falling some days and a constant duel taking place between opposing artillery units. The Ypres Salient was certainly a fearful place but the battery was soon to be moved south to Third Army sector where it would be caught in one of the most dramatic periods of fighting on the Western Front.

I alternated between rear billets and battery position until January 3 1918 when I was told that my long expected leave had been granted. I returned from Frezenberg about 3pm when the news was conveyed to me. My first step was to secure some clean uniform from the Quartermaster then I had a hot bath in a cartridge box. After this I examined my equipment; my bandolier looked shabby so I exchanged it, for a consideration, with the cook. Next I drew as much pay as I was entitled, for me a considerable amount. There was nothing else to do but get to Poperinge for the leave train due to leave any time after 10pm. I set off at 7pm. The first part of my journey was by the ration wagon. I remember driving through the Menin Gate, the silent streets of Ypres and across the Grand Place. The driver of the wagon happened to be a Sheffielder and was most anxious that I should find his sister and tell her that all was well and most important of all that he was serving on the Ypres front. Later I was able to deliver the message and while she was delighted to hear from her brother, the question of the actual sector interested her not in the least. Perhaps just as well.

I went a good way by ration lorry and jumped a lorry for the rest of the journey, reaching Poperinge by 10pm where I joined an anxious crowd in the station square. The anxiety was due in some measures to the fact that none of the buildings were intact, the enemy having a long ranged gun trained on the spot. He was apt to open out periodically and it was not pleasant to be casualtied when proceeding on leave.

We entrained about midnight and started on our way at 1.30am (January 4), arriving at Boulogne at 7am – pretty smart travelling for wartime. On arrival at the port we moved to a Rest Billet to wait for the boat to take us to England. This day actually counted as the first of the fourteen day's leave, so everyone was anxious to get home as soon as possible. A large number of troops had been held over from the previous day and these naturally had priority for the morning boat which was due to leave at 10am we latecomers had to be content with the meal provided by the Expeditionary Force Canteens and await our chance on the afternoon boat with as much patience as we possessed. To prevent our rushing the boat we had all been provided with checks and were called out in numerical order. There was an enormous number of troops going on leave at this time and when the afternoon boat arrived, the first to be embarked were the remainder of yesterday's men who had failed to find passage on the morning boat. There did not seem room for many more men and several hundred were disconsolately marched back to billets for the night. This meant going without tea so I purchased the most substantial food obtainable from the canteen which meant a packet of biscuits and a tin of cherries, and made my way to the quay. The boat left at 5pm and we arrived in Folkestone two hours later. The leave boat was packed and the crossing rough but nobody seemed to mind.

A train awaited us at Folkestone and brought us into Victoria station, London at 10pm in comfortable time for me to catch the midnight express from St. Pancras. I was setting off to walk to the latter when I was stopped by a kindly disposed civilian belonging to some organisation or other who suggested I should go by underground. I thanked him for his consideration but reiterated my intention of walking to St. Pancras as I knew my London well and wished to take this opportunity of seeing the city by night. He retired but returned with reinforcements until I became the centre of a crowd, they pleading with me to travel by underground and I equally determined to go on foot. I learnt something of their anxiety. It appeared that many provincial soldiers proceeding home on leave were so attracted by the lures of the metropolis that they never reached their native villages and it seemed that the only safe way was to buttonhole the warriors as they attempted to leave the terminus and gently but firmly guide their steps to the entrance of the underground. Here they were safe and would reach their northern terminus without encountering the temptations of the outer world. A good advertisement for London's underground. However I carried my way and stepped out of the portals of Victoria station leaving a group of sad faced men staring after me. I arrived at St. Pancras in time for the train and arrived at Sheffield Midland at 5am (January 5). The town was not quite awake but I caught a workmen's tram for part of the way and then walked along the silent streets. At last I reached home where I roused my parents who had no idea I was due for leave. I enjoyed a good breakfast for I was very hungry and the tinned cherries were not particularly satisfying.

Leave passed all too quickly and the time arrived for my return to France. Technically I suppose I overstayed leave by one day for I had been told that the boat train left Victoria at 7am, as my pass was dated from January 4 to 18, that is fourteen days, and I had lost the whole of the first day in travelling, I saw no reason why the final day should similarly be sacrificed. Accordingly I left Sheffield by the morning train on January 18 and reported to the railway transport officer at Victoria at 11.30am. That official was inclined to be shirty but I stood my ground and argued that as my pass did not expire until midnight, I could hardly be blamed if there were no trains to convey me to the port. The RTO thereupon told me that while he would accept no responsibility for my delay, I had better stay at the Buckingham Palace Hotel for the night and be ready for the Dover train at 7am the following morning and make sure that this was endorsed on my pass. I booked a room, told the clerk of my intention and handed him my pass which he promptly stamped with the date of my arrival and their words "Delayed in London". I am quite convinced that I had frustrated an attempt to filch a day of my leave and later I related my experience on others with the result that they followed my example with equal success.

I made the most of my last day of liberty seeing, among other things, St Paul's Cathedral, where I was taken round the galleries by a gentleman who showed me many parts not usually shown to the public. A charming act and there were many in London who devoted their time to such acts of kindness. With another soldier I went to the London Coliseum in the evening and at midnight returned to the hotel where the booking clerk asked me what train I was catching in the morning so that I could be called.

At 6am the following morning (January 19) I was roused, breakfasted and arrived at Victoria in time for the boat train. I reached Dover at 12.30, obtained something to eat at the canteen and was soon aboard the waiting ship. We left Dover at 3pm and at 4.30 disembarked at Calais where we were marched to a most dreary looking camp on the top of the hill. Here we were told the time of departure of the trains to the various fronts and left to our own devices. The Poperinge train was due to leave early the following morning so I wandered about the wretched camp trying to get something to eat from the canteen only to find them sold out except very weak tea and some most unappetising pastries. Ignoring the lures of the wet canteen where a group of soldiers were trying to drown their sorrows in drink, I made my way to my tent. I was the first to arrive and must confess to shedding many bitter tears before my companions came in and put me to shame. Others came in later but few words were spoken, we merely wrapped ourselves in our inadequate blankets and tried to sleep while the wind howled round the canvas.

Morning (January 20) came and we drew our rations for the day, the bully beef and biscuits that seemed to constitute the sole diet of these Base Camps and so we marched to the station. The train left at 9am and one could not but contrast the smart business-like way with which we were being returned to the front with the long drawn out way on going on leave. Once we left Calais we brightened up considerably. We were in one of the famous French covered wagons but the journey up the line was by no means the miserable affair that might be imagined. We de-trained at Poperinge at 2.30pm and went our various ways. It was confirmed that my battery had not moved and I was left to find my way by myself. I took the opportunity of spending a few hours at Poperinge and obtained a meal there, the usual eggs and chips, for no good purpose was served by returning to the battery too early. Then following recognised practice I jumped a lorry and afterwards enquired its destination. My luck was in – they were going as far as Ypres. Here I alighted, made my way through Menin Gate,[1] had the usual tin of soup from the YMCA and soon reached the familiar kitchen at Potije and right glad I was to reach my second home and see the familiar faces once again. I cast off my equipment and went off in search of the Sergeant-Major. I showed him the endorsement on my pass and he seemed quite satisfied. Then I re-joined my friends round the blazing log fire.

There was much to talk about. First I had been lucky to miss a heavy bombardment on January 13 when the enemy opened out on the battery position at Frezenberg and had given the teams on duty a severe gassing, very uncomfortable as there were no gas-proof shelters there. Two of the reinforcements had been wounded and another casualty, a very severe one, had been reported from Frezenberg that very morning.

Then a Major Warren[2] had taken command of the battery. It appeared that we had been without a commanding officer for some months. The previous CO Major Murphy[3], an Australian, had been sent home on prolonged leave last October. During his absence the unit had fallen into easy-going and somewhat slipshod ways; Major Warren was altering all this. He was voted a fine fellow, a disciplinarian and every inch a soldier, a type that particularly appealed to the regulars. He was certainly gingering things up. A deep dugout was being constructed at Frezenberg and, appalled by the gross over-crowding at the rear billets, he had ordered another Nissen hut to be erected at Potije. Gunner Wiley had been given a choice of running the canteen in a business-like manner or of relinquishing his post. As a result there was a greater variety of provisions on show and he was negotiating for a regular supply of beer.

The following day (January 21) saw me at the battery position with my detachment. On the way up the hill I noticed that the Labour Corps were at work draining the shell holes and generally cleaning up the hill side. Later they were to start digging trenches in the cleared ground. This was the first I saw of the new spirit that was a road from one end of the line to the other. We were no longer preparing to attack, from now on we were to be on the defensive.

At Frezenberg I had to help with the new deep dugout. The actual excavation was being done by a Tunnelling Company of the Royal Engineers who were working eight hour shifts on the job. We had to supply six men to act as labourers for them and to dispose of the debris. All that was visible of the work was a square shaft near the BC Post with a windlass on top under camouflage. We reported to the Sergeant in charge who, seeing that I was wearing rubber boots which I had brought while on leave, suggested I should work underground, two others manning the windlass and the rest disposing of the spoil by dumping it in shell-holes. It was strenuous wok for all concerned. The sappers had all been miners and were attacking the pit face with unbelievable vigour. They put the clay into sandbags which they flung across the floor in my direction. My job was to hook the bags on to a rope which the others would wind to the surface. Bags of wet clay came sliding towards me from all directions until I was almost barricaded with them. Periodically I had to cease work on the sandbags and send up buckets of water which overflowed from the sump at the bottom of the shaft. The sappers were in two parties, one extending the gallery while the other was digging upwards in a sloping direction making steps as they advanced, the object being to form the main stairway to the shelter. They suspected that they would come to light in a big shell-hole and water was pouring down on the workers causing them to curse furiously and to attack the clay with redoubled effort. We all worked hard. The men on the windlass were moaning at the amount of spoil that was being sent up and the sappers were grumbling because the bags were not being removed quickly enough. Sometimes the rope would swing and the bags of clay became lodged on the side of the shaft when I had to climb up and release them, a tricky business. None of us were sorry when our tour of duty came to an end. The two who had been turning the windlass continuously for eight hours and the others who had been carrying slimy bags of clay over the rough ground joined me in cursing the Royal Engineers and all their works. We retired to our shelters and slept for hours.

The entrance to the deep dugout was finished some days later. As suspected the surface was reached through the medium of one of the largest of the shell-holes. It had been full of water and the size of a small pond. The dugout was never occupied by us, our successors may have done so. It seemed far too wet to live in and I do not remember it even being used as a bolt-hole in time of danger, the troops preferring to use the concrete BC Post. The enemy knew better than us, the concrete pill-boxes were the only proper protection on the Salient.

Soon we had an unpleasant surprise. We were ordered to construct a reserve position and the spot chosen was within a stone's throw of the notorious Dead End at Ypres. Detachments off duty were set to work levelling the ground and erecting shelters. It was quiet enough now but if Passchendaele were evacuated and the new trenches at Frezenberg became the front line, it would become very dangerous. It was disheartening to think of abandoning Passchendaele Ridge after all the casualties in its capture.

Then I had a complete surprise. On February 1 I returned from a spell at the battery position. It was afternoon and I was lying in my shelter at the Potije billets. For some reason there was no-one in the kitchen and I was amusing myself by extracting square roots of the lot numbers stencilled on the cartridge cases which formed the walls of the cubby hole, when the Sergeant-Major appeared and called me. *"You said you were a BCA didn't you, Gunner Hall?" "Yes, Sergeant Major,"* I replied. *"Well you'd better go to the battery and report to Bombardier Bush – Dale has got his commission and they want another man."* It appeared there had been two BCA's at Frezenberg and now that there was a vacancy, the Sgt-Major looked up my credentials and seeing that I was qualified, posted me as a replacement. I picked up my kit and, leaving the kitchen where I had spent so many happy hours, set off up the hill to the battery position.[4]

I cannot say that I was particularly pleased that the long delayed opportunity had arrived for I was very comfortable serving the guns and the thought rankled that I was to replace a candidate more fortunate than I in obtaining his commission. However I reported to the duty officer at the post and told him that I had been fully trained as a Battery Commander's Assistant and had been passed out by Major Wyllie commanding 221 Siege Battery but then came a change of batteries and I had as yet no chance of practising. I deemed it inadvisable to refer to the cause for the change of unit nor was I asked. Indeed I only once referred to my abortive attempt to obtain a commission. That was months afterwards when a young officer assured me that the then CO Major Bennett[5] would be pleased to support any application I might make. I then revealed the circumstances to Major Bennett who, after consultation with his superior officers, advised me that, *"although he would have been delighted to help me, he felt that, in the circumstances, no good purpose would be served by resurrecting the matter and I would be well advised to let it drop"*. I agreed; it was too late.

Dale was busy packing and soon left. I then made acquaintance of the occupants of the BC Post who were responsible for the control of the battery. First of course was the duty officer usually rotated daily. The Major lived at Potije but visited the position daily. Major Warren was at this time a very busy man and spent his time between the battery position at Frezenberg, the billets at Potije, the Horse Lines at Vlamertinge, and the new position being built at Ypres, to say nothing about visiting the brigade headquarters for orders. Then there was the rank and file. Sergeant Clarke[6] in charge of the Signallers spent all his time at Frezenberg and had his bunk in the BC Post. An extraordinary man who seemed to bear a charmed life, he had been promoted in the field and won two decorations for bravery, the Military Medal and the Distinguished Conduct Medal (later he was awarded a bar[7] to this). He had absolutely no control over his men who always addressed him as Nobby and often disputed his orders when he would curse them heartily and do the job himself. He had not been trained as a Signaller but had joined the battery early on and just picked things up. It was questionable whether he had ever mastered the theory of signalling, and newly appointed Signallers were surprised and sometimes annoyed at being placed under the charge of an NCO who could read the Morse code only with considerable difficulty. It was said that all Nobby lived for was for repairing telephone lines under shell fire. At any rate when the telephone went dead he would sling his portable telephone over his shoulder and be out of the BC Post like a shot, quite oblivious that there were two of his men detailed for such a purpose. Sometimes the officer would recall him and send the proper Signaller, in which case Nobby would return exceedingly grumpy and bad tempered. His second in command Bombardier Daly, a young Signaller from the training school, was in a peculiar position. Sgt Clarke certainly relieved him of nearly all the work but laid on his shoulders the task of maintaining discipline among the Signallers, which went to pieces as soon as the Sergeant arrived. Bdr Daly was rarely at the battery position as Sgt Clarke made it a whole time job for himself.

The Signallers maintained a telephone exchange at the BC Post and two men were in charge, one sleeping while the other worked. In addition there were a couple of men whose job it was to maintain the lines, that is if they were not forestalled by their Sergeant. Periodically the telephone operator would test the lines and if he got no response, a linesman would have to go out to repair the break. The usual way was to follow the line and from time to time plug in the portable telephone and call the battery. At last the break would be located, the lines joined up and voices from both ends of the wire would indicate that communications had been restored. When interruptions occurred frequently Signallers might stay near the danger points and tap in periodically. The main lines of communication from the BC Post were to the Observation Post, brigade headquarters, the rear billets at Potije, and also two other batteries in the brigade. As all four batteries in the brigade were linked together and each maintained its own line to headquarters, it followed that we were rarely, if ever, isolated. The Observation Posts were similarly connected to several batteries. With such a network of lines it followed that the Signallers' roster of duties was very involved and disputes were frequent and acrimonious. Some thought that Sgt Clarke would be better employed in directing his staff rather than trying to maintain all the lines himself. However, because of his splendid record and his obvious disappointment if kept from his post of honour, the officers were content to let the Sergeant control his staff in his own tin-pot way.

So much for the Signallers. The wireless operators also maintained a station in the BC Post next to the telephone exchange. There were two of them, Air Mechanic Thomas of the Royal Air Force[8] and his assistant, one of our Signallers. Their work varied with the seasons and at present, owing to the dark days, they were having a very easy time and could always rely on a full night's rest. As soon as it was light one of them would sit with the headphones on listening to any signals sent down by the aeroplanes. At busy times when we were shooting with aerial observation both would be in action so that they could check each other. Their receiving set, which was guarded with great care, was a crystal set of cumbersome design although it was at that time regarded as a wonderful pieces of apparatus and there was nothing that fascinated me so much as to be allowed to sit with the headphones on listening to the faint Morse signals from the skies.

At that time, although the aeroplanes could transmit signals to the ground, they were unable to receive them and we communicated with the airman by means of strips of linen laid on the ground. An elaborate code had been devised. Thus when an aeroplane shoot was about to begin the airman would call us up by wireless and ask if we were ready. If ready to fire at once we would put out the letter "L"; a triangle meant ready in five minutes and a triangle with a bar ten minutes. A cumbersome method with the added disadvantage that the linen strips were visible to prowling enemy aircraft as well as our own. One of my first duties as BCA was arranging these linen strips.

But of more interest to me was Bombardier Bush, the senior BCA, for it was with him I should have to work. A school teacher 25 years of age, self-opinionated and apt to be dictatorial with an infinite belief in his own capabilities, he was nevertheless a remarkably efficient man, calm under shell fire and quick in action in an emergency. I think we were somewhat alike in temperament so that frequent clashes were inevitable. Undoubtedly we mistrusted one another, I thinking he was always planning to have me superseded and he feeling that I would take the first opportunity to step into his shoes. Probably we were both right. The easy going Bdr Dale whose position I had filled was content to play second fiddle to the domineering Bush and so the two had got on fairly well together. I soon learnt that it was no thanks to Bdr Bush that I was in the BC Post at all and that he was both willing and anxious to carry on single handed after the departure of Dale. It was Major Warren who had insisted that a second man was essential and Bush then suggested that one of the Signallers might act as his assistant rather than risk applying for a trained man who might well be his senior. It was Sgt–Major Spratley who, noting my qualifications from his records, sent me to the BC Post. Bdr Bush was quick to define and to limit my duties and if I had wanted a soft job I had no grounds for complaint. Like Sgt Clarke, he preferred to do all the work himself rather than trust to a subordinate. So far as I could see all that was required of me was to resolve the Meteors (meteorological reports submitted every six hours) and shout out orders to the guns. Bush himself would work out all the targets and take the night firing. I was in no mind to accept such a sinecure. However in a few days, another aspect presented itself. Bush appeared one morning very jaded after a disturbed night and Major Warren, noting his appearance, asked if Gunner Hall was not yet capable of working out targets. Bush attempted to explain that I had not yet sufficient experience to be trusted, whereupon the CO caustically remarked *"Well it's about time he had"* – a most unsatisfactory position for all concerned. After this I consistently badgered Bush until he revealed to me the methods employed in working out targets and laying the Line of Fire which differed considerably from the theoretical methods learnt at school but many weeks were to elapse before I could consider myself as capable as my master.

The other occupant of the BC Post was Gunner Proud, the officers' cook, so eleven of us lived, worked and slept in those confined quarters about ten feet square. Day and night the telephone exchange was running and two or three Signallers would be asleep in bunks near the instrument. The wireless operators dismantled their receiving set at nightfall and this left a little more room for them to sleep but the firing map or planchette board as we called it, always rested on a table ready for instant use. Bush and I slept under this table where Proud had fixed a couple of shelves in a corner, one for his pots and pans and the other as his bed. Then of course there had to be room for the valise of the officer on duty, to say nothing of spare telephones, reels of wire, the BCA's instruments and the like. It is not to be wondered that the occupants of the post were none too pleased when the enemy started shelling and another two dozen men, the detachments on duty, dashed in for shelter.

The pill-box however, was wonderfully well constructed and suffered many direct hits with no more effect than to blow out the candles. There was a sump against the doorway which needed pumping out every few hours for the floor was two feet below ground level and the whole building was sinking under its enormous weight into the unstable ground. Many pill-boxes were already out of use owing to subsidence and stood at crazy angles half sunk into the mud. What infinite trouble must have been taken in their construction heaven only knows. A farm building had been destroyed by shell fire, the merest fragment of a wall remained but this fragment would form the nucleus of the enemy's defence system. Concrete and still more concrete was added until the wall was two feet thick. Finally a roof was added until an almost impregnable fortress resulted in which the Germans placed their machine guns. That the blockhouse was captured at all was little short of a miracle, and the toll of life before they fell into our hands must have been terrific. Once the pill-boxes fell into our hands they were adapted for a variety of purposes, control posts for batteries, first aid posts, telephone exchanges, etc. But little or nothing was done to repair any damage that might have been sustained beyond perhaps throwing a few sandbags over any broken parts. Certainly no concrete was used. From our point of view they all possessed the disadvantage of being built the wrong way round. The Germans had constructed them with the entrance in rear so that once they passed into our possession, the position was reversed and the door faced the enemy. Gunner Proud was injured while standing in the doorway of another pill-box.

Life at the BC Post proved very congenial, even allowing for Bdr Bush's somewhat condescending attitude. We were in the closest contact with the officers on duty who proved to be excellent company and particularly friendly. Every night the cards were brought out, there was always plenty to drink and there were such little courtesies as for instance the censoring of letters. I would write my letter, pass it over to the officer unsealed, whereupon he would sign the envelope and return it to me unread. Although Bush still insisted in taking the bulk of the targets, I had to turn out for the Meteors at two and six in the morning. At first I found it more difficult to be plunged into a complicated mass of figures at these unearthly hours than to turn out for action on the guns but I soon got used to it. Then there were the mass of returns to be tackled. At one time there were nineteen daily reports concerning targets engaged, details of hostile shelling, stock of ammunition and a host of other matters. We had nothing to do with Orderly Room work, matters concerning pay, casualties and staffing were dealt with by Bdr Lowe[9] at rear billets. We were solely concerned with fighting the guns and our occupation ceased whenever the battery went out of action.

There was another aspect to the BCA work; we were always "in the know". I had not been in the BC Post very long before I knew that our days at Frezenberg were numbered, a thing never suspected by the rank and file. There was never any leakage of information from the BC Post and although I was often greeted by *"What do you know?"* from my old comrades, I knew when to keep my mouth shut.

The business of moving was complicated by the difficulty of shifting the guns. It would have been a lengthy job to have constructed a path across the shell-holes in order to get the guns to the light railway, as we knew to our cost when an odd howitzer had to be sent to the shops for repair. It was arranged therefore that we should first change guns with 250 Siege Battery and, when we eventually moved out of the line, we should take their guns with us. We had been on counter-battery work for a long time whereas 250 Siege, being on bombardment duties, occupied a more healthy position on Godley Road, well to our rear. It was decided that the time for a change had arrived and that 81 Siege, after being in action so long on the Salient, were entitled to a spell on a quieter front.

The change-over took place on February 8. Bush went down to Godley Road to take over from the BCA there while I remained at Frezenberg to meet the newcomers when they arrived.

A particularly gloomy lot of men arrived at Frezenberg that afternoon. We were firing at the time and they grouped themselves disconsolately round our guns until the shoot was over. Meanwhile the officer accompanied by his BCA and signalling Sergeant came into the BC Post and were by no means pleased to see such confined quarters. I handed over the log-books of the four guns and the planchette board showing our position on the map and indicated to my successor the Lines of Fire. Then gathering up the remainder of our instruments (the heavy stuff had already been removed) abandoned the pill-box to 250 Battery. The Gun Captains were not long in handing over and we all set down the duck-board track for the last time to see how things fared at Godley Road.

There was not much individuality about the new position for Godley Road was simply a corduroy track leading off at right angles from the Ypres–Passchendaele road and was lined with guns of all calibres from one end to the other. Actually it was difficult to identify one's own guns among such a company. The dugouts behind the guns were much more soundly constructed than at Frezenberg following the corollary that the further from the front, the stronger the shelter. The BC Post, a long way from the guns, was situated in a large concrete blockhouse known as Rat Farm. It was much larger than the one we had left and there was a separate room for the telephone exchange. Like all captured pill-boxes, the entrance faced the enemy and it was here that Gunner Proud was wounded. There were disadvantages in having the post so far from the guns; orders could not be shouted to them and a Section Post connected by telephone had to be established. All the CO's of 81 Siege disliked Section Posts intensely and avoided them wherever possible. Another disadvantage from our point of view was that it was impossible to get our meals from the cook-house in a warm condition, so that the few of us whose duties kept us at Rat Farm had to draw our own rations and cook for ourselves.

We were not long at Godley Road for on February 12 the gun-limbers were brought up and we pulled out retiring for the night to the rear billets at Potije. Here the guns were parked and temporary Horse Lines established for the teams concerned. On the morrow both the Potije billets and the Vlamertinge Horse Lines were evacuated and the whole battery moved into billets into what had formerly been a monastery outside Poperinge.

It was while we were here that we were re-equipped and brought up to strength, the guns were overhauled, the horses tended and fresh stores were poured into the battery while physical training and light route marches restored the troops to fitness. The strain of warfare relaxed for the moment, Major Warren proved himself the most genial of men and considerate of CO's and the days passed all too quickly in this the first rest the battery had enjoyed since 1915. The great change in our constitution was deferred until February 20 however when, with the arrival of Lieut Page[10] and 76 other ranks, we were converted from a four gun to a six gun battery.

This was something new for Siege Artillery although six gun batteries had been the rule with the Field Artillery for some years. On the line of march we looked imposing enough and the new arrangement certainly involved a considerable saving in personnel, while with six guns bearing on a target the effective power of the battery was much enhanced. In practice however it was to prove much more efficacious to concentrate four guns on the main target leaving a couple of guns for sniping and other odd jobs. In February and early March many batteries were converted into six guns but by the end of the year, the old rule of four gun batteries was restored.

81 Siege and our sister battery 59 Siege were among the first to be converted and the personnel was obtained by the simple expedient of breaking a battery in formation, 454 Siege, and allocating the members among the two older batteries. The newcomers were pretty raw for training had been speeded up considerably since I enlisted and they were for the most part youths of eighteen with three or four months' service to their credit. They brought with them only a very few NCO's, a good thing for the old timers for it opened up a fresh avenue of promotion for them, and Major Warren, after inspecting the reinforcements, very wisely decided to pool them with his own men and so form twelve detachments each containing a majority of experienced men along with some of the recruits. The move was not appreciated by the men from 454 battery who wished to man their own guns but events proved it was instrumental in saving many casualties.

The new officer 2/Lt Page was a tall arrogant type whom the newcomers informed us was a terrible martinet, completely dominating the easy going CO who had been in charge of the unit. The old hands laughed when they heard of the dark doings of Mr Page – *"We'll tame him,"* they said, and the long struggle with this unpleasant officer began. Well Mr Page never really was tamed, although he was never in a position to work his will on the troops. The other officers detested him and I have heard him referred to as *"that cad Page"*. Major Warren snubbed him in public and on one occasion ordered him to stand to attention and another time supported Bdr Bush who had point blank refused to obey one of the subaltern's orders which he thought irregular. Whatever reputation 2/Lt Page might have brought with him he certainly cut no ice with 81 Siege Battery.

Among the few NCO's that came over from 454 Battery was Sgt Salter[11], a very efficient Sergeant who had seen plenty of active service. There was also a young Bombardier Observer Perry[12] with whom I was to have a great deal of contact later on. Perry had been posted direct from the Observers' school where he had obtained a second class.

And now reconstruction was complete and we were ready for the line again. It was to be in another sector, a quieter one it was said, for which relief much thanks for we knew that whatever the future had in store there was only one Ypres and nothing could be worse than that terrible Salient.

On February 26 we packed up our multitude of stores and, early in the morning of the 27, we succeeded in getting safely aboard a special train at Poperinge sidings, not such an easy task with six guns and close on a hundred horses, particularly when it is remembered that Poperinge was always liable to long range shell fire from enemy lines. Anyway we felt a lot more comfortable at 11am starting our journey southwards to Bapaume.

---

1   The Menin Gate was one of the old gates in the town walls and as thousands of troops passed through it was thus a fitting location for the Ypres (Menin Gate) Memorial to the Missing (one of four memorials to the missing in Belgian Flanders which cover the area known as the Ypres Salient) to be constructed.

2   The Brigade war diary (WO95/225 48 Brigade RGA) notes on 8 January 'Major Warren posted to 81SB, formerly Capt in 177 HB'. He joined 81 Siege Battery on 9 January.

3   Major Francis Power Murphy. A member of the Australian Imperial Force. As a lieutenant aged 35 he left Australia with HQ 1st Australian Division on 22 October 1914 on board transport ship A3 Orvieto in the company of famous soldiers such as Maj-Gen William Bridges, Lt Col Neville Howse VC, Lt Col C.B.B. White and Major John Gellibrand. According to the unit history he was appointed to command the battery with effect from 1 August 1917.

4   On most days in January and early February the battery fired 10-20 rounds but on Hall's second day on the guns the war diary records that 300 shells were fired.

5   Major William Bennett transferred from 303 Siege Battery.

6   51489 Sgt Charles Edwin Clarke DCM, MM and Bar. The Bar to the MM appears in the London Gazette on 12 July 1918 p8307. According to the unit history, as a Gunner, Clarke won his first MM for services in the Vimy sector march-June 1915. The unit history mentions Sgt Clarke being awarded the MSM (Meritorious Service Medal) for actions at Arras and at Dead End, Ypres, but this appears to be an error and should read MM.

7   A 'bar' denotes a subsequent award of the same decoration.

8   At this stage it was Royal Flying Corps as the RAF did not come into being until 1 April 1918.

9   Bdr Lowe – this is 127050 Bdr James Low, aged 43 from Durham.

10 2/Lt Page transferred from 454 Siege Battery when 81 SB was made up to a 6 gun establishment.

11 162705 Sgt Walter Salter.

12 Possibly 162825 Bdr Reginald Perry, later 25069 Army Pay Corps.

CHAPTER 19

THE BEGINNING OF THE GERMAN OFFENSIVE

The German plan was to transfer resources from the Eastern Front when Russia collapsed and initiate offensives against the French and British which would force them to seek peace terms. The British sector was believed to be vulnerable following the British operations in 1917 – Arras, Messines, Ypres and Cambrai. A further reason for striking now was the arrival of American troops, not yet ready for front line service but very soon could make a decisive difference to Allied capability. Thus the scene was set for Kaiserschlacht – the Kaiser's Battle. Their plan was to break through on the Somme and move northwards to create a pocket enclosing British forces in northern France and Belgium and force their surrender. Initially the Germans would seek to destroy key features of the British line plus railways and other important locations; an infantry assault would follow. British intelligence knew that an attack was imminent and proposed a deep defensive zone rather than the trench line used to-date. The main German thrust was on the Fifth Army which was to the right of the Third Army in which 81 Siege Battery was at this time. Nevertheless, it was to be a tumultuous period and Gnr Hall's account captures the drama of those traumatic weeks. The battery arrived in Bapaume, a town that had been an objective in the July 1916 offensive and which now lay in ruins having been destroyed by gunfire and by the retreating Germans.

Gnr Hall's notes capture the spirit of his battery's predicament when the German attack was unleashed. The war diary[1] confirms his story with entries such as "Boche planes ranging battery on 81SB" and "Enemy barrage commenced at 5am and continued till 11am. Enemy came over the top at 10am. All our batteries active. Outskirts of Vaulx reported to be in hands of the enemy about 3pm" and then later "all batteries moved back to Beugnatre in the afternoon. 81SB had two guns knocked out at Vaulx one of which they left behind". Losses were noted – "Batteries had a good many casualties 81SB having 14".

We arrived at Bapaume at 10pm (February 27). The town looked more desolate and miserable than ever. A rough sort of platform had been erected alongside the railway line but that was all. The ruins of the sugar factory with its tangled mass of machinery showed up as ghastly in the moonlight as it did when the town fell into our hands a year ago. But now to work, the horses were taken from the wagons and led away to be watered and fed and the guns were unshipped from the flat bottomed wagons and run down to the railway platform where they were left for the night. Then we dealt with the GS[2] wagons, limbered wagons, water cart and the rest of the impediments. Our work completed we found some wretched billets and it was not until late in the morning that we rose for breakfast. When it was dusk (February 28) we had tea, fed the horses and made ready for the road. Major Warren was very proud of his horses and most particular that the column should be in order before we started. At last we were ready. The CO mounted, placed himself at the head of the column and gave the order *"Walk march"*.

Never have I felt so proud of the battery in which I was privileged to serve than on that march and I could not help feeling contempt for the wretched mechanised units. At the head of the column road Major Warren on his black mare Bess closely attended by Wheeler, the groom on his brown horse. Fifty paces behind rode the Sergeant-Major and the Quartermaster-Sergeant. Next the sub-sections led by the Lieutenant and Sergeant riding together, then the gun itself pulled by eight magnificent heavy draught horses with twenty Gunners following in rear on foot. After the gun came three GS wagons each drawn by four light horses, two Gunners riding and two following in rear of each wagon. There were six sub-sections so constituted. After the sub-sections came the Signallers, Lt Lakin[3] leading with Sgt Clarke, both on horseback, then their store wagon with twenty four Signallers marching in rear. After that the BCA's Bush and I following the limbered wagon which contained our stores, the cook's wagon and two or three with miscellaneous stores, Driver Seeley with his famous white horses pulling the water cart. At the tail of the column were the few sick horses fit to travel but not capable of heavy work each led not ridden by a driver, the Farrier-Sergeant and the veterinary – riding together but ready to move forward should their services be required, while Captain Fletcher[4] as second in command brought up the rear. Driver Chinnery, the dispatch rider, was continually galloping from one end of the column to the other maintaining contact.

We travelled light, all our kit being carried on the wagons but wearing the bandolier without which no Gunner could consider himself properly dressed and with gas masks and steel helmets slung loosely over our shoulder. The going was easy and halts frequent when we stood round in the moonlight and made much of the horses. So in the early hours of March 1 we reached Vaulx-Vraucourt.

There was never a battery position so easily occupied. We advanced along the road leading to the twin villages until we came to an empty building which we later knew as the distillery; here we halted. A few hundred yards further on a farm track led off from the left. One by one the guns were called up, the teams went forward up the track and dropped their guns into already prepared positions; it was the work of a few moments to run the howitzers under the camouflages. The ammunition wagons were quickly dealt with. Then without bothering to lay out the Lines of Fire, the troops were mustered and detailed to some Nissen huts in rear of the guns. Nissen huts five thousand yards from the firing line! If we had been directed to a first class hotel we could not have been more astonished.

There were more surprises in the morning. The farm buildings were practically intact, not a shell-hole could be seen anywhere, not a gun could be heard – the silence of the place was uncanny.[5] After life in the Salient we were in clover and yet there was something sinister about it all – we didn't like it.

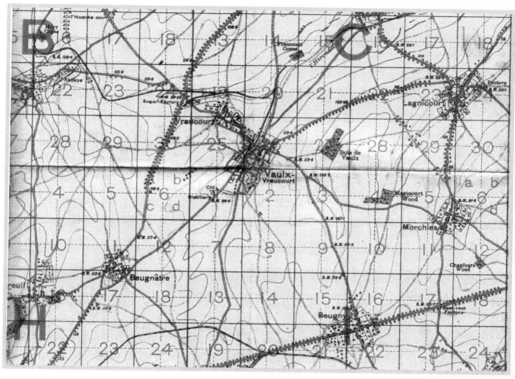

Map of Vaulx Vraucourt

And so on March 1 we leisurely set to work. The director was brought out and Bush and I set to work on the Lines of Fire. Pickets were planted and the guns well and truly laid on their zero lines, due east or as we said 90 degrees grid. The ammunition was neatly stacked in the emplacements while Sergeant Clarke and his merry men connected up the telephones. Their task was an easy one for the telephone lines were already in position, neatly tied to poles and running in every direction. Nobby growled about this, he hadn't been used to overhead cables – he liked them buried, the deeper the better. Exposed lined were only tempting providence.

Who had prepared the Vaulx-Vraucourt battery position? I do not know. There was no ammunition left about but there were signs of previous occupation. It is possible that it was used by a battery some twelve months previously when the fierce attacks were being made on Bullecourt and the Hindenburg Line. As a matter of fact we were not far from Mory where I spent so many unhappy days with 242 Battery. The position too bore a striking resemblance to the Mory one. We lay in rear of the village on a sunken farm track leading off the main road, while similarly the pits were dug into the chalk banks and covered with a permanent camouflage, so the place was well protected from aerial observation. Two saps, one between 2 and 3 and the other between 5 and 6, had been driven deep into the chalk by the Royal Engineers. All the donkey work had been done before our arrival and all that remained to be done was to drive a gallery connecting the two entrances when we should have a first rate deep dugout, dry as a bone and to all intents impregnable against any explosive. The BC Post however was not as good as could have been desired. It was a small corrugated iron shelter about 10 feet square, dug into the opposite bank and directly in rear of No.3 gun. There was about six inches of earth covering the roof and the front faced the enemy and was quite exposed. I would have preferred a larger shelter slightly to the right but this had been appropriated by the Sergeants as their mess. The Sergeants' mess received a direct hit on March 21 so it was perhaps as well I failed in my choice.

Sunken lane where 81 SB was located 21 March 1918

After the first two hundred yards the farm track curved first towards a large barn in which we placed the heavy stores and where the cook had established his quarters and then towards sundry farm buildings where 59 Siege Battery and an 8 inch howitzer battery were located. We were to see much of this lane and the barn later on. The two sixty pounder batteries in the brigade were somewhere in the vicinity. We had other neighbours off the Vaulx road opposite to the entrance of our lane. A 9.2 inch battery was located while a little further south was the aristocrat of the RGA – a twelve inch howitzer on rail mountings.[6] I paid a visit to the 9.2

battery and had a few words with their BCA, an excellent fellow. They had, it appeared, been in position twelve months and fired on an average once a week, although he admitted that a fortnight had elapsed since their last shoot so they must expect being busy again soon. How many rounds? Well twenty or thirty as a rule. There had been a certain amount of sickness but no casualties of any sort, and from what I could see, no shell-holes. *"No,"* he agreed, *"we don't bother Jerry and he doesn't bother us, so we hope you won't come stirring up trouble."* Shades of Ypres and Passchendaele Ridge! The utter stagnation of the front was inconceivable; the whole land was as peaceful as an English countryside. Five thousand yards away the Germans were securely entrenched in their impregnable Hindenburg Line, complete masters of the field. We had given up all hope of dislodging them and the Germans were too comfortable to exchange their concrete trenches for a few miles of the worthless territory they had so cheerfully evacuated a year ago – hence the complete deadlock. I was told that the twin villages were quite intact and well worth a visit and contained excellent canteens where good beer was sold.

The 12 inch howitzer was rather more active and we saw them in action several times. A shunting locomotive was in attendance as after every round the gun would run back twenty yards or so when the engine had to push her back. Whatever they were firing at it did not appear to annoy the enemy over much and after twenty rounds had been fired the engine withdrew and the Gunners presumably sank to rest.

Into this Arcadian atmosphere 48 Brigade (2 six inch howitzers and 2 sixty pounder gun batteries) had been introduced but it seemed we were not to break the peace. All were silent batteries not to fire except in grave emergencies.

The troops were jubilant at the prospects. In the Nissen huts was room and to spare; the officers claimed one as a mess and another for sleeping quarters. In another an Orderly Room was established, while in the remaining huts the rank and file sprawled like millionaires.

But in a few days arose the eternal problem of finding occupation for the men. The pits and guns were in perfect condition, shells were oiled, counted and stacked then recounted and re-stacked. Camouflages were adjusted and stores laid out and checked. Except for the drivers, the whole personnel was living in the Nissen huts for no rear billets could be more comfortable or safer than those at the battery position. A double guard was mounted and parties set to work excavating at the foot of the two shafts to form one deep dugout but the job was unpopular and progress was slow. No attempt was made to drive the work forward. It seemed so unnecessary in that quiet countryside and work on the saps developed into a glorified scrounge, smoking and talking at the foot of the shafts and sending up a load of chalk very, very occasionally. Work for the day ceased at four o'clock.

Then there was the reserve position at Beugnatre two miles in rear. Since the beginning of the year the order had gone forward that all batteries were to prepare reserve positions in case of a German attack and so a party of men was sent daily to work on this. But here again the work was done in a half-hearted manner, and it was surprising how little so many men could do in the time. The fact of the matter was that no-one from the CO downwards took the threatened attack seriously. One day followed another and still the enemy gave no signs of his presence. He might have been three hundred instead of a bare three miles away. A few rounds of hostile shelling would have been a Godsend at this time. We might have seen things in their true perspective, realised how vulnerable were the Nissen huts and pushed on with the deep dugout. Beugnatre might have been a duplicate position instead of the sham it was, and the battery have been divided and rear billets established. But with such a feeling of security nothing was done. A Lewis gun[7] had been sent to afford some protection against hostile aircraft and a Gunner trained in its use but the gun was never unpacked let alone set up. Had it been in position on March 21 some casualties might have been saved.

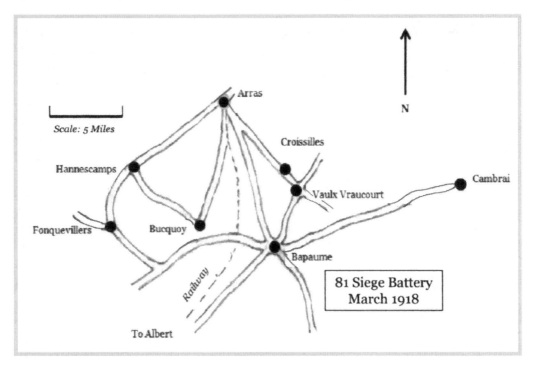

81 Siege Battery March 1918

An aerial photograph of the battery position showed the guns well concealed but the Nissen huts showed up prominently. What madness had led to their erection in the first place I have never been able to conceive. At any moment a burst of shelling could have blown the lot to smithereens but, after all, they had stood twelve months without injury so why not for the duration of the war. Others had used them so why not us?

But the height of absurdity was reached in the middle of the month when it was ordered that physical and squad drill should be carried out in the battery position. Who gave the orders I do not know but I feel sure that it originated from higher quarters than Major Warren. And so the troops marched about and formed fours in full view of several politely watching German aeroplanes. The aircraft made no attempt to interfere, perhaps they were too busy taking photographs.

One serious preparation and one only for the attack was made. Sergeant Clarke insisted on removing the telephone lines from their standards and burying them. As I have said he detested the overhead wires from the start. Sgt Clarke's decorations proved him no coward and when the Signallers saw that he was in earnest and it was either that or squad drill, they set to work and all the wires were well and truly buried. As a result of these precautions we had no Signaller casualties on the day of the attack and were the only battery out of eight to maintain communications throughout the day.

That the authorities realise the danger of communications breaking down was seen in their attempt to establish visual signalling stations. The forward Observation Post was in a hollow near the front line but some little distance away on a slight elevation the Advanced Visual Station (AV) was set up. Then the brigade Signallers established another station BV some little distance from the batteries. The two stations were able to communicate by means of heliograph by day and signalling lamps by night. The visual stations were linked up by telephone but at intervals this means of communication was forbidden and messages were transmitted visually from the Observation Post via AV and BV. Sgt Clarke was contemptuous of these new-fangled ways and prophesied its breakdown in an emergency. Future events proved him correct.

I was thrown very much on my own resource at Vaulx-Vraucourt. The first night Bush and I slept in the BC Post together but after the Lines of Fire had been laid, we parted company and he took up his quarters in one of the Nissen huts to do some special work for Capt Fletcher, mainly painting and recognition marks of wagons I believe. The Signallers had now fixed up their telephone exchange in the post and my job was to work out the meteors as they came in and give the necessary corrections to the Gun Captains. I had plenty of time to make the shelter a little more presentable. First I blocked up the wide opening and made a door of kinds with a window of oiled canvas. It was still cold so scrounged a fine French stove from one of the deserted houses in the village and some lengths of stove pipe from another source. With these the Signallers and I soon fixed up the heating apparatus. There was fire wood in abundance in the vicinity and soon a fire was blazing up the chimney.

My bed took several days in the making. First I used an old stretcher I found somewhere. I was alone at night for at first no attempt was made to man the telephone after dark. This state of affairs ceased on March 4 when Sgt Clarke ordered that the exchange should be double manned day and night. I therefore decided to make a bunk bed for myself and the Signaller off duty. I drove four posts into the ground in the form of a rectangle, fixed crossed pieces two feet from the ground and stretched some good German wire netting to form the bottom bunk. The old stretcher was pressed into service as an upper bunk for the Signaller off duty; in the day time it was folded up when the bottom bunk became a comfortable settee. A rough table completed the furnishing.

I now set to work on the floor. Day after day I visited one of the farm buildings and after infinite trouble worthy of a better cause, succeeded in removing the tiled floor which I carried over in sandbags and re-laid in the BC Post. At the time of the German offensive I was contemplating white-washing the interior of the shelter.

On March 7 Capt Fletcher carried off the planchette board and the fighting map to the Nissen hut which was being used as an Officers' Mess. Major Warren was away at the time but when he returned the same evening he paid a visit of inspection before turning in and noticed the absence of the map and asked me what I had done with it. When I told him about Capt Fletcher he was furious. *"Does he think he can run the battery from the Officers' Mess?"* he roared. *"Well he damned well can't and what's more, an officer must sleep in the BC Post every night."* He left but in a few minutes 2/Lt Lakin appeared on the scene with the map and planchette board. Mr Lakin was full of praises for the comfortable shelter and particularly admired the bed. The inevitable result was that I turned over my bed to the officer on duty and occupied the upper bunk; the displaced Signaller had to be content with the floor and incidentally complained about the tiles striking cold. I soon discovered drawbacks to the upper bunk – the Signallers would persist in putting large pieces of wood on the fire and keeping the covers open, the result being that the top of the room was full of smoke. It was adding insult to injury to see the duty officer sleeping peacefully on my comfortable bed well out of the smoke while I was nearly suffocated.

It was at this stage that a most charming and likeable character arrived who nevertheless was destined to cause us all an infinite amount of trouble - Bombardier Reginald Perry. When the half of 454 Battery had been merged with us, Bush and I appropriated the additional BC stores and pleased we were with the shining new instruments after the battered mud-stained articles we had hitherto been using. We polished up the directors, the prismatic compasses and the binoculars with loving care. We did not concern ourselves with the fate of the man who accompanied the stores and so Bdr Perry the trained plotter of 454 Battery finding no place for himself in the BC Post, drifted to the guns just as I had done when I joined 242 Battery. But he was more fortunate than I his rank had been made substantive and when the CO saw a full Bombardier walking about the battery utterly incapable of controlling men and completely ignorant of everything pertaining to the guns, he made enquiries and discovered that Perry held his rank by virtue of a second-class pass at the BCA school. Perry was sent to Bush, now busily occupied in painting elephants (our recognition mark) on the GS wagons and the latter brought him over to the BC Post.

I never forgave Bush for the way he introduced Perry to the BC Post. Had Perry proved efficient he would undoubtedly have supplanted me and I should have returned to the guns then and there. Bush knew this and was obviously gloating. After saying *"This is Bdr Perry, the new BCA,"* he ignored me altogether and proceeded to show the newcomer the ropes. I sat on my bunk and glared at the couple of them.

After a few minutes Bush returned to his painting and when he had gone, Perry extended his hand and asked, *"Can't we be friends?"*. After this what more could be said? Perry and I did in fact become the firmest of pals. Perry was not a bright lad by any means and how he secured even a second class pass at the school was a mystery. So long as he was with us he never succeeded in working out a meteor let alone a target and he always seemed to have the most hazy ideas as to whether a switch was left or right of zero. It was obvious that he would never be able to control the fire of the guns and that I had no fear of any competition from that source. Major Warren let him stay as a sort of supernumery to deliver messages between the BC Post and the guns and make himself generally useful. Then Bdr Bush made an unpleasant discovery. Perry was the senior NCO; Bush had been promoted in the field and his rank had been made substantive later than Perry's. The fat was in the fire with a vengeance. Perry made the most of his seniority (he grew to detest Bush) in such ways as pulling us up to attention when the Major was present and refusing to take orders from his junior. Bush turned to me for sympathy and would moan for hours on being supplanted by a *"youth of eighteen who was incapable of adding a couple of figures"* and this after all the work he (Bush) had done at Ypres.

The parade ground atmosphere of Vaux was suddenly dispelled. It was 10pm on March 12 when the troops were preparing to retire that we were suddenly called into action, not only for us but all the batteries silent as well as active in the sector. For a couple of hours we pounded enemy positions chiefly with gas shells, the first time that we in 81 Siege Battery had been in action. The false attack as it came to be called was a one sided affair. The enemy refused to be drawn. Not a single hostile gun replied and so far as I could see, the only effect of our fire was to reveal to the enemy the entire strength of our artillery. At midnight we ceased fire.

After the false attack we continued as before, drilling, cleaning the guns and, as slowly as ever, completing the deep dugout but on March 17 enemy shells were observed falling on the village. Compared with the bombardments that were a daily experience on the Salient, this was a mere fleabite but Major Warren passed the word round that we would be well advised to keep away from Vaulx for a time.

Desultory shelling of the twin villages was continued on March 18 and 19, and during the two nights we slept in our uniforms, though not our boots, in order to be ready for prompt action if necessary. The firing ceased on the afternoon of the 19 however, and on March 20, the front was as silent as the grave. In the evening Capt Fletcher came to the BC Post for night duty. We discussed the situation and the officer professed himself certain that the scare was over, asserted that he for one was going to remove his clothes, and advised me to do the same. Following his example we retired for the night.

At 2am I was roused for the usual meteor. According to practice I worked out the necessary adjustments noting with pleasure that weather conditions had changed so little since ten o'clock that it was unnecessary for me to correct the guns. Before resuming my broken rest however I glanced outside the post. The night was calm and the front practically silent. The sentry was marching down the sunken road for in this quiet sector we indulged in the luxury of a guard. Inside the post the stove was burning well, the telephonist on duty was reading a magazine, his companion curled up in a blanket on the floor. Captain Fletcher was sleeping comfortably in bed, in "my" bed, I thought. Taking care not to disturb him I clambered on to the stretcher above, little thinking that this was the last time I should sleep at Vaulx-Vraucourt, or for that matter that the era of trench warfare was so rapidly drawing to a close. In a few minutes I was asleep.

The next thing I remember was a violent commotion outside. Capt Fletcher was sitting up in his bunk and I heard him say quietly as to be almost a whisper *"You'd better get up Hall – it's started"*. As we looked at one another we realised that here at last was the long expected German offensive. It was only a matter of seconds before we were out of bed pulling on our clothes, nor were we fully dressed when the door burst open and the tiny shelter was filled to over-flowing – Major Warren and the rest of the officers, Nobby Clarke, Cpl Bush, not to forget the faithful Perry all came rushing in. Meantime the Gunners came tearing from the Nissen huts into the sunken road in all sorts of disattire and grabbing what personal property they could. The reason for this sudden exodus was apparent. When the enemy opened fire he seemed to regard the Nissen huts as a sensitive point worth a single gun to search and sweep at any rate. The shelling had the effect of clearing the huts in record time quicker than any call to action would have done. It was 5am March 21, a thick mist covered the entire front. Up the line a heavy bombardment was in progress and the active batteries were responding. The CO went to the telephone to find out what was happening. Observation post reported heavy bombardment all round but could distinguish nothing in the heavy fog. The visual stations were unable to communicate with one another or with the Observation Post. Plainly visual signalling had broken down. The Colonel at brigade headquarters was aware that something was happening but had no news as yet – we must stand by for further orders. The troops, now more or less dressed, lounged about the emplacements or fused shells. The solitary enemy gun meanwhile continued its work among the Nissen huts; the target was wide and the range good and even before our guns had spoken, the officers' mess was reduced to matchwood.

At 6am orders came through from Brigade to open fire on our SOS lines, the same sensitive points we had engaged on March 12. No sooner did we come into action than the enemy brought his guns to bear on us. Plainly our attempted concealment had been for nothing. Within ten minutes the Germans had registered a direct hit on No.6 gun, wounding several of the crew. The less serious casualties were bandaged up and sent down the road to the Dressing Station. No-one seemed to know where this was but all they had to do was to join the procession of walking wounded making their way from the front line. Two cases were not disposed of so easily, Gunner Whitla one of the thirteen who came with me from the base and Dewey[8], a Signaller who happened to be passing No.6 gun at the time; both received such terrible injuries that there was no hope of recovery. They were removed into the shelter of the barn and made as comfortable as possible. Soon it was necessary to lay them on the ground as their bloody stretchers were required for other cases. The two men endured terrible agony from their abdominal wounds until the afternoon. The officers, Lt Saville in particular, visited them whenever possible but could do nothing to relieve their sufferings and it was not until 4pm that Whitla expired. Dewey in full consciousness that he would soon follow his companion lasted a couple of hours longer.

Grave of 162834 Gnr G. Beaver in Vaulx Hill Cemetery

Immediately the first casualties had occurred Major Warren telephoned to the Colonel asking to be put out of action, this being the usual practice when it was apparent that a battery had been spotted. His application could not be granted in this instance for quite apart from the seriousness of the attack, it was evident that all the other batteries in the brigade were in the same situation and none could make up the shooting for us. Major Warren had frankly only one thought to save his battery and as the day wore on and casualties mounted up, he appealed time after time to be allowed to cease fire. It was pathetic to hear the hardened old soldier pleading on the telephone for his men to be spared. *"They're killing all my men,"* he said on one occasion. It was solely as a result of his entreaties that we were allowed short intervals of respite during which we retired down the shafts of the half-completed deep dugout. In these intervals the enemy ceased firing on the position only to resume again once the guns had been manned.

At 8am Lt Lakin and a party of Signallers returned from the Observation Post and reported to the CO It was particularly fortunate that this officer had been on duty at the time for he was the most calm and collected officer in the battery. He had considerable experience in telephony and always took charge of the Signallers when on parade. At the OP all had been quiet until 5am. When the attack opened up Mr Lakin put his two Signallers under cover and went to the front line trenches to investigate. It was too misty to observe anything but it was only too apparent that the enemy was bombarding our trenches vigorously. About 7am the barrage started advancing and it was evident that the Germans were coming over. Mr Lakin had no hesitation in abandoning the Observation Post which was in the second line trench, and picking up the men at the Advanced Visual Station, the whole party returned to the battery.

The barn where wounded were placed

Mr Lakin telephoned to the Colonel and volunteered to return to the trenches and try and get in touch with the now fast retiring infantry. The OP had gone and in any case it was still too hazy to distinguish anything but there was always a chance that the weather would clear and he might be able to pick up some targets later on. The Colonel agreed, whereupon Lakin made a dash for the officers' mess where he succeeded in recovering his revolver. Slinging a portable telephone and a reel of wire on his shoulders he discussed certain technicalities with his henchman Sgt Clarke and set off up the line, whistling merrily. That was the last we saw of him for a week but his voice would come through the wire on most unexpected occasions. *"This is Lakin speaking – there's a good target for you at (giving the locality). Going on all right? Yes, I'm having a grand time, cheerio."* Sometimes he would contact the battery by most diverse means, via wires that the infantry had laid down to their own headquarters when half-a-dozen voices could be heard on the telephone at once but overall would be heard Lakin's voice calling for Sgt Clarke. *"Nobby"* he would call out and there was an angry buzz of voices *"Get off the line,"* he would shout to the interrupters, then, *"Nobby, I've pinched the General's line and they'll cut me off in a minute, run a line to the ruined mill at -------- and plug into the wires there"*. Off would go a couple of Signallers or more often the Sergeant himself, unreeling the cable as they went, until they reached the rendezvous. Then they would plug into the line indicated and there would be a babble of voices but over all would come Lakin's voice loud and clear and as cheery as ever, *"I've got a target for you,"* and so on until the temporary line was shot to pieces by the enemy.

Sgt Clarke in action was a sight to be remembered. He took charge of operations on the telephone exchange from the first. The minute the line became dead he would hand the instrument to a satellite and rush out to mend the break. Code letters had been assigned to all batteries early in March and much to Clarke's disgust those allocated to 81 Siege had been YMA which rival wags naturally rendered as YMCA. But on the fateful day Sergeant Clarke got his own back. When a call came through from headquarters *"Is that YMA?"* he replied *"No, this isn't the bloody YMCA, this is Nobby Clarke of 81 Siege Battery, call word 'Nobby', got that?" N.O.B.B.Y. – Nobby"*. The official call word was thereupon dropped and for the next few days the buzzer was constantly calling N.O.B.B.Y.

Sgt Clarke's determination to bury the cables in the vicinity of the battery proved a blessing and it was a pity that we were unable to have them covered all the way to brigade headquarters. This was impracticable, particularly where the line crossed roads. The authorities would not allow the roads to be disturbed and at these points there was nothing for it but to carry the wires on telegraph poles. The inevitable result was that once the enemy started his bombardment the lines were cut at these points and the Signallers spent hours mending them. The operator on the exchange was testing the line almost continuously and immediately he was unable to get a reply he would call out to the Sergeant *"Nobby, the line's 'dis' again"*. Sgt Clarke who had not the least idea of what any of his men were doing would turn to the first man he could see and call out, *"Well, Jones, what about it?"*. That would start Nobby off, *"Was ever a Sergeant cursed with such a miserable, selfish, windy lot of ------- whenever there's a job wants doing, poor old Nobby must do it himself,"* and snatching a portable telephone he would start off. Ten minutes later his buzzer would be heard on the exchange. He had located the break and joined up the broken pieces we were again in communication with headquarters. A few minutes later Clarke would tap in and call the exchange, *"I'm stopping here for a bit. Jerry's shelling like ------ and it looks as if he'll cut the line again"*. A deadness on the line proved Nobby's prognostication to be correct. Then the familiar call N.O.B.B.Y. would come through, followed by lured oaths indicating that he was only too well aware of what had happened and was endeavouring to locate the break.

About 9am word went round that the cook had managed to prepare some breakfast. This proved to be the only meal we were to receive that day.

By 10am the mist had cleared considerably but improved visibility brought fresh horrors in the shape of enemy aircraft. One of these flew over the sunken road ranging enemy guns on our position. The signals to his battery were so loud that they blocked all others on our wireless set. Never have I seen an aeroplane fly so low, the features of the occupants were plainly visible and not content with ranging his gun the Observer turned his machine gun on us wounding a couple of our men. Some snatched up the rifles that had been used by the guard. The officers fired their revolvers at the intruder; in desperation some men were throwing stones at the machine!

The enemy were now in possession of most of the trenches and orders were received for us to bombard our old front line.

By 11am we had the unpleasant sight of infantry retreating past the battery position. A few minutes later one of our neighbours, an eight inch howitzer battery, passed the sunken road near the barn. They had dismantled their guns and were carrying away their breech blocks. *"We're off!"* they shouted as they went by. *"How much longer are you going to stick it?"* The conduct of this battery came in for some adverse comment. Their lines had been cut and they were unable to communicate with their brigade. Seeing the retreating infantry they thought it was time for them to be going. They were sent back however and returned very sheepishly with their breech blocks a couple of hours later.

Meantime our casualties were mounting up and we had some very nasty cases. I saw one man have an eye torn completely out by a shell splinter. Lt Saville took upon himself the care of the wounded men. This young officer was a wealthy man and very much of a dandy. His kit was enormous and it was said that among other things he had eight greatcoats. His main topic of conversation was what clothes he should wear and it was known that Major Warren regarded him as an empty headed ass. Nevertheless he rose to the occasion. He had some knowledge of first aid and he set to work on the wounded men plying them with whisky and bandaging up their wounds. When they complained of being cold he would dash to the Nissen huts and return with blankets and his own clothing which he wrapped round the casualties until it looked as if all the wounded men were officers. At the end of the day all his beautiful clothes were soaked in blood and Mr Saville himself looked like a slaughter man. Later he admitted the loss of *"several hundred pounds worth"* of kit which being unofficial and over the recognised standard he dare not reveal.

Most of the officers were very calm and collected. Capt Fletcher took over the BC Post. Lts Page and Morkill[9] were out on the guns, one of Major Warren's first orders being that they were to remain near the emplacements checking the lay and in general help in steadying the men. Mr Saville bustled about carrying the wounded safely while Mr Lakin, somewhere with the infantry, would periodically telephone targets. There was one officer the CO decided to keep out of the way. This youth Mr Rimer was only eighteen years of age and had arrived at the battery only the night before. He asked if he could do anything but Major Warren told him to sit in a corner and keep his mouth shut. It was as well that he did so for 2/Lt Rimer was obviously scared and could only have had a bad influence on the Gunners.

It was obvious that the Major was feeling the strain. He would walk up and down the sunken road talking to the men on the guns and trying to cheer up the wounded. He would telephone the RAMC trying to make them send up an ambulance so that we could evacuate them. Then again he would beg the Colonel to let us take cover.

In the afternoon the battle intensified and respites became fewer. The enemy had the exact range of our guns and it seemed only a matter of time before we would be wiped out. At 2pm No.1 gun received a direct hit completely severing the trail. Fortunately this happened during one of our spells of respite or our casualties would have been higher. The range of our guns had now dropped considerably and we were firing on open ground between Vraucourt and Lagnicourt. It was evident that none of the lost ground would be regained that day.

But if our battery had fared badly it was certain that others were in a worse plight. Our Signallers were having trouble with the line but at any rate they were keeping it open which was more than could be said for the three other batteries in the brigade. Orders were given for these to abandon their lines to headquarters and link up with 81 Siege by telephone if possible otherwise by runner. Nobby Clarke was to concentrate in keeping his lines open, now the only means of communication. Nor was that all for later other batteries asked if they could use our line until no less than eight were connected to our BC Post. *"What do they take us for, a bloody telephone exchange?"* said Nobby Clarke but secretly he was delighted to take the responsibility for maintaining the lines of communication.

Soon news came through that Vaulx Wood and Vraucourt Copse had been taken and we fired on these on second charge. My experience as BCA was getting a bit too realistic for by following the map and working out the ranges, I was only too well aware of the German progress. On the guns they were of course conscious of the constantly falling elevation but here in black and white I saw one familiar landmark after another fall into enemy hands. So complete had been the surprise that even now we were not all fully dressed. I remember searching for my steel helmet at 4 o'clock in the afternoon (up to then I had been wearing a soft cap) but in the confusion it was nowhere to be found and there was no alternative but to take one from a dead man.

At 6pm the range was dropped to its lowest level, 1,500 yards which meant that the enemy were less than half a mile away. Actually they were in full possession of Vraucourt and in the outskirts of Vaulx itself. This was actually the last target we engaged and novelty overcame any fear that we may have felt of the strange situation. The howitzers seemed to be practically level and with the low (first) charge we were using fired with a feeble pop instead of the accustomed roar. Many climbed the bank side to get our first and only view of the battlefield.

A few of us got a grand stand view from the top of a water cart. In front lay the twin villages now in enemy hands, in the open figures could be seen, our infantry, but quite what they were doing we could not make out except that they seemed to be constantly moving about firing their rifles. There were other figures in the background, the Germans, among whom our shells were bursting without much effect. The flight of our shells could be traced from muzzle to target.

It was now growing dark; the Germans had definitely won the day. Orders were coming through for a general evacuation of battery positions. The first to be ordered out was the 8 inch battery who had prematurely withdrawn in the morning. Their position lay slightly in front of ours but so close were the enemy that every yard told and they were now in a most perilous state. They had ceased firing for some time and had been constructing ramps preparatory to withdrawing their guns but as I knew only too well, pulling out 8 inch howitzers was a very different matter from the lighter 6 inch and when their Caterpillar tractors, belching flames and making enough noise to wake the dead, endeavoured to reach them they were unable to do so. All six guns fell into German hands intact, the Gunners themselves were dispersed to replace casualties in other units – the battery had ceased to exist.

The big 12 inch howitzer had been firing all day from the railway line in the valley. About 8 o'clock a strange voice on the phone asked if we could possibly get in touch with them as the direct line had gone "dis" and they had been trying to communicate with the battery for hours. Sgt Clarke, pleased with his ever-growing reputation, volunteered to go himself and soon returned with the CO of the 12 inch. The conversation as the strange Major spoke to his Colonel was illuminating. The big gun was intact and behaving perfectly, they had comparatively few casualties in the battery itself but so many in trying to maintain the telephone line that they had been obliged to let it go and trust to luck. Yes, he would prepare to pull out and be ready for the locomotive. With this he left the BC Post only to return a short time later. It would be no use sending up the locomotive he said enemy shellfire had destroyed the railway track. So his new instructions were to continue firing as long as possible and then abandon the gun.

Our own orders came soon afterwards and were repeated to the other three batteries in the brigade. Cease firing, get under cover and retire to reserve positions as soon as possible.

Major Warren got in touch with the Horse Lines and told the waiting teams to start for the battery position. The RAMC had promised to send an ambulance to remove the wounded men as soon as they could get through. There was nothing to do except remove the telephone exchange to the deep dugout where most of the troops were now congregated. Soon after this the line was again broken but the CO gave instructions that it was not to be repaired. The whole front quietened down for a time the silence being broken only by the solemn boom of the 12 inch howitzer as every few minutes it swept strong points of the enemy's rear. A few daring spirits made a dive for the broken Nissen huts and emerged with their belongings. We were awaiting the arrival of the teams but knew that while we were preparing to withdraw, the enemy guns were already advancing and the question was whether we should be able to get the guns away before the Germans resumed fire.

At last dim forms could be seen – the horses making their way across the plain. It was too dangerous to trust the road which the enemy still had under shell fire. They halted some little distance from the battery position, all seemed quiet; everyone spoke in whispers. *"First team"* the word was sent back and the eight noble horses advanced pulling the gun limber behind them. Following the torches the drivers cautiously rounded the barn and backed down the lane. *"No. 1 team. No time for ceremony now – take the guns in any order – leave No. 6 for the time being, she's a cripple anyhow – take No. 5."* We all stood round, ran out the gun, lifted the trail, hooked up to the limber and led the horses on to the plain when they silently moved away to safety. One gun out of the way, thank God. A torch flashed and the second team moved in – No. 4 gun was disposed of. Meanwhile a couple of GS wagons were hastily loaded with ammunition and stores. Would we succeed in getting away safely?

No. 3 gun next but scarcely had the gun been limbered up than like a hurricane the enemy opened fire. Pandemonium raged, the terrified horses plunged and would have bolted but for their heavy load. The quick eye of Major Warren saw that to leave the sunken road at either end was impossible. Orders were given, the team was swung round, some of us manhandled the wheels while others closed round the horses, the drivers applied their whips unmercifully and with one mighty heave the gun and limber plunged right up six feet of bank side into the comparative safety of the plain whence the horses galloped away. A more terrifying sight than the heavy draught horses accustomed to nothing but a slow walk plunging up the hillside with a five ton gun behind them I have rarely seen. In the manoeuvre a driver was struck by a fragment of shell and fell from his horse mortally wounded while a Gunner was wounded but not so seriously.

Once the enemy had resumed shelling we knew that he would continue for a long time, so the CO directed that No. 2 gun should be removed without delay. An easier way up the bank side had been found but the horses were unwilling to advance under shellfire and had literally to be dragged to the gun. Once the howitzer had been limbered up the poor beasts were only too glad to depart and followed the other teams across the plain. There were two more gun teams standing by but Major Warren decided not to risk pulling out the crippled No. 6 gun, while No. 1 with its shattered trail could not be moved without a crane so the teams were sent back to the Horse Lines. The remaining GS wagons also were sent back empty. One was being loaded at the time the enemy opened fire. The horses bolted and the wagon ran over a Gunner breaking his foot.

The fact that we had been discovered pulling out (always a Gunner's nightmare) completely upset Major Warren's plans for evacuating the position. He now detailed a party of 20 men to remain at Vaulx and ordered everyone else to follow the retreating guns to the reserve position.

It was at this point that the final tragedy of the day occurred. The enemy had been bombarding the Nissen huts intermittently all day but some of the Gunners had taken advantage of any lull in the firing to rescue their personal belongings. He was now completing his work of destruction and those who had been unable to salvage their property had to reconcile themselves to their loss. Two inexperienced men however decided to risk the shelling. They were called back but were probably out of earshot. At any rate they were seen making their way to the ruined huts – the next instant both men had completely disappeared – a heavy shell had burst between them and literally blown them to fragments. Sometime later I stumbled against an object a considerable distance from the scene. It was the booted foot of one of the lost men.

Bdr Bush decided to accompany the guns to their new position in order to lay out the Lines of Fire. Accordingly it fell to my lot to remain at Vaulx for the time being. Altogether there were twenty of us, Sgt-Major Spratley in charge, Sgt Salter of the damaged No.1 gun, two or three Signallers and myself as BCA and the rest Gunners. Our duties were first to evacuate the wounded. There were a dozen or so serious cases in the deep dugout, some of whom had been there since morning. The RAMC had informed us that as last an ambulance was on its way. Next there was the crippled No.6 gun and the remaining stores to be dealt with; No.1 gun must be abandoned. Major Warren had informed us that he would send a gun team and as many GS wagons as possible, as soon as it had quietened down. Meantime we retired to the deep dugout.

It was ten o'clock at night. The 12 inch howitzer was still firing, determined to inflict as much damage as possible before finally being abandoned. Far away to the rear a few field guns were firing over our heads but in a very ragged manner. None of our other heavy guns were in action. The enemy was methodically shelling the road.

At eleven the motor ambulance arrived. The firing on the road had abated somewhat but the drivers were apprehensive lest it be resumed. We had much difficulty in getting the wounded men up the steep stairs as we had insufficient stretchers but eventually they were crowded into the ambulance which set off down the road at high speed, regardless of shell-holes and of any subsequent discomfort to the injured men.

We returned to cover expecting the return of the gun team and the GS wagons and settled down to snatch a little sleep. Now and again a few of us would emerge to see if there was any sign of the horses.

Midnight. The 12 inch howitzer still booming away, otherwise the front was much quieter. The horses should not be so long now.

Two am March 22. The 12 inch howitzer was silent at last and there was but little activity on either side – still no sign of the horses. Twenty four hours had elapsed since I was called out for the meteor the last we were to receive for some days for this refinement of gunnery was discontinued at the first attack and we had to guess the force and direction of the wind as best we could. It was now safe to walk down the sunken road. The gun emplacements were in a state of indescribable confusion, shell holes everywhere, ammunition scattered all over the place, cartridges burnt out and camouflages in ruins. Large craters bracketed the BC

Post and I shuddered to think what difference a single yard would have made. No.6 gun had been pulled out ready for the team but No.1 was hopeless its broken trail stuck up at a crazy angle. Under cover of the barn our fatalities had found peace at last. Incidentally our boast that all our dead received a christian burial no longer applied. And only half a mile away the Germans were in full possession of both villages.

So we passed the night alternately dozing and looking out until with the morning it was evident that the plan had miscarried and we were not receiving the horses after all.

Morning March 22. What was the enemy doing? As usual he had brought out his observation balloons which loomed over our heads, huge and terrifying. Still he was making no hurry to resume the attack – he was evidently not going to make the mistake of pushing his troops to the point of exhaustion. Later it transpired that fresh troops were at that moment enjoying a hearty breakfast in the Hindenburg Line before making their way to relieve their comrades, who had occupied the villages the night before. The German troops engaged on March 21 had spent the night in the reasonable security of the cellars and the captured trenches while our own infantry had no protection on the open ground save what poor trenches they had been able to scratch during the night. Here they awaited the inevitable attack.

It was late in starting for the enemy was evidently waiting for the mist to clear. There was no need for concealment now and he might as well have good observation. He opened out with a standing barrage on the shallow trenches in front of the sunken road that had housed the battery. Then after half an hour the barrages started advancing. There were two of them, a barrage of heavy guns preceding that of the Field Artillery. Slowly but surely the barrages advanced until from the dugout we could hear the heavy guns pummelling the sunken road. Then it grew calmer and we emerged. The heavy barrage could be seen slowly advancing on the plain to our rear while in front could be seen the bursts of the smaller shells. We were between the two barrages.

Naturally we began to get anxious. It was 10am and we had received no orders for twelve hours. There were only two rifles between the twenty of us and no-one knew when the enemy would overrun the position. On the other hand we were in charge of two six inch howitzers and a large quantity of ammunition. Both guns were out of action it was true but a few days in the workshops would soon put them to rights and we knew that to abandon them without orders might be serious. Some talked glibly of destroying the guns but exactly how no-one knew. Again if we succeeded in destruction and the ground was subsequently recovered, it might be awkward. The Sergeant-Major decided to proceed to Beugnatre for orders and, calling on me to accompany him, left the party in the charge of Sgt Salter.

Sgt-Major Spratley and I walked across the plain until we approached the point where, like a wall of smoke and fire, the barrage blocked our path – a seemingly insurmountable obstacle. The Sgt-Major however seemed unperturbed and proceeded calmly to calculate the fall of the shells. They seemed to be from 5.9 inch howitzers falling at two minute intervals. They were keeping well in line but jumping up and down owing to the zone of the guns.

We always allowed 2 per cent of the range for this and assuming the howitzers to be firing at 6,000 yards, this meant a length zone of 120 yards in which the shells might be expected to drop. The fall of the shells seemed to be following a pattern working from one extreme of the zone to the other and back again so that if we kept our heads we could judge pretty accurately where the next shell would fall. The Sergeant-Major planned our course. We were to run the barrage in a diagonal direction immediately the gun in front of us had reached the farthest limit of its zone. Luckily the next gun was advancing on its zone while the one in front of us was retreating so between the two of them we might scramble through. He gave the word; we rushed forward, then dropped and rushed forward again. The strategy worked – we had run the barrage. All we had to do now was to make our way to Beugnatre which we judged to be a little to the south west.

We had no difficulty in finding the battery which lay in open country well in front of the village. When we arrived the four guns were in action firing on Vraucourt and on the eastern side of Vaulx. There was no cover of any kind nor attempt at concealment. A dozen yards in rear Bdr Bush had fixed his map on a plane table and was working out targets. This was the BC Post. Nearby in a shell-hole Sgt Clarke had located his telephone exchange. A party of men were digging trenches, partly for our own protection but also to help the infantry later on for a notice board stated that this was the front line trench. Our defence system existed merely on paper. The junior officers stood in a group talking, Major Warren stood apart like a man in a trance, dirty and unshaven, his hands behind his back. Sergeant-Major Spratley approached, saluted as smartly as on parade and in a few crisp words explained his mission but the CO seemed quite oblivious of his presence and answered never a word.

Then came the smell of frying bacon. The cook's stores had been one of the first things to be loaded on the wagons at Vaulx, and now a fire had been lit and it was evident that whatever the main party had missed they had not gone without breakfast. I was very hungry for I had nothing to eat since the previous morning so I made my way to the cookhouse. There was plenty of bacon left and some well stewed tea. Then I heard the news – how at midnight the gun teams and the GS wagons had assembled but the enemy opened fire securing a direct hit on one of the wagons but luckily without causing any casualties. On this Major Warren countermanded his orders and sent the horses away. So that was why we had waited in vain at Vaulx. Breakfast over, I washed and made my way to the BC Post to see if I could be of any assistance to Bdr Bush. I had heard the Sgt-Major report the facts about the men left behind to the CO and presumed that if it were decided to withdraw then Major Warren would take the necessary steps.

I was astonished therefore when Sgt-Major Spratley came over to me and said, *"For Heaven's sake, Hall, see what you can do with the Major about those men at Vaulx. I've spoken about them three or four times but I can't make head or tail out of him"*. I learnt later than the condition of the CO was causing great anxiety to the other officers. He seemed to have aged twenty years and to have literally broken down under the strain. As I had been accustomed to speak to Major Warren about targets and similar matters the Sgt-Major evidently thought I might get through to him where he had failed.

I walked up to Major Warren and as the Sgt-Major had said, had great difficulty in speaking to him. When I saluted he stared past me as if I did not exist. *"Major Warren, sir,"* I shouted repeatedly until at last he seemed to come of his coma. *"Well, what is it?"* he snapped. *"What about the men at Vaulx?"* I asked. *"What men?"* he retorted. *"There's twenty men left behind at Vaulx and the enemy is advancing,"* I said. *"Fetch them back,"* he ordered. *"And the guns, Sir?"* *"Bugger the guns."* *"Anything about the stores, Sir?"* *"Bugger the stores."* So that was how I got my orders. I told the Sgt-Major and set off on my way back to Vaulx.

And I certainly felt very much alone on that return journey. Not a soul was to be seen on the plain once I had left the battery behind. In front of me I could see the barrage through which I should have to pass but I was not to reach this point without event. As I was making my way in the correct direction I heard an angry zoom and looking upwards saw the black cross of a low flying German aeroplane. Immediately bullets splatted around as the airman turned his machine gun on me. I saw in the distance a number of flimsy shelters dug in a bank side and towards these I ran, pursued by the plane, until with bursting heart I sank exhausted in the nearest shelter. What a sport I thought to pursue a man with a machine gun from an aeroplane for there was no doubt I was the object of his attentions, there was no-one else on the spot. Soon I came out but he was only circling around and a burst of fire drove me in again. But when I left the shelter for a second time he was gone, doubtless he had better quarry than a solitary Gunner.

Then I continued my journey and ran the barrage for the second time that day. How I managed I do not know but, after my experience with the aeroplane, I was past caring. After a short time I stumbled into the sunken road where the eighteen men raised a cheer at my arrival.

They were in a most precarious plight. The enemy were advancing fast behind their Field Artillery barrage (the one I had been running was the heavy barrage). This had now reached the sunken road. Sergeant Salter and another man were now lying on the bank pointing the two rifles in the direction of the enemy; the others had provided themselves with pick handles and heavy spanners. So they were preparing to defend themselves against the Germans. It is very doubtful whether there were now any troops between ourselves and the enemy, all the infantry seem to have departed and I certainly saw none on my way from Beugnatre. I gave my orders exactly in the words I had received them *"Clear out and bugger the guns."* The troops needed no second telling. I deemed it advisable to call in at the BC Post to rescue certain instruments and maps and I called on a Gunner I knew to assist me. We slung binoculars, prismatic compasses and other instruments round our necks. I crammed all the maps I could find into a haversack and taking a director from its box, fixed it on its stand for easy carriage. Then Sgt Salter called out *"Come on Hall, we want you to show us the way"*. Shells had started to fall in the sunken road itself. So we departed. In quarter of an hour the enemy was in full possession of the place.

Then the nineteen of us made our way to Beugnatre. The heavy barrage had moved forward considerably and appeared a good deal thinner than before. Evidently the enemy had taken some guns off to deal with strong points but of course it still had to be run. However we all got through and were soon at Beugnatre where Sgt Salter reported the safe arrival of his contingent to Major Warren who seemed quite oblivious of his presence or of the fact that the party had escaped by a hair's breadth capture or worse.

---

1   War diary WO95/225 48 Brigade RGA

2   General Service wagons, a ubiquitous horse drawn vehicle used by the British Army.

3   Lt Edward Lyon Lakin. Landed in France on 9 August 1916.

4   Capt Francis Duncan Fletcher.

5   War diary WO95/225 48 Brigade RGA records that the batteries were ordered to remain silent. Registration of the guns began on 5 March.

6   This gun was probably located on the railway line that ran past Fremicourt just to the south; the remains of the line can be seen today.

7   The Lewis Gun was one of the standard machine guns used by the British Army. It fired .303 rounds, the same as the Lee Enfield rifle, from a drum mounted on the top. The drum held 47 rounds and was fired in short bursts. Aircraft also used the Lewis Gun but with a drum holding 97 rounds.

8   49446 Gnr A.E. Dewey, 81 Siege Battery, Royal Garrison Artillery. Died of wounds 23 March 1918. He is buried at Abbeville Communal Cemetery Extension (plot 1, row A, grave 28) which suggests that he was evacuated to the rear and did not die at the battery position.

9   Lt Alan Greenwood Morkill, formerly served as 245617 Gnr A.G. Morkill, RGA. Commissioned as 2/Lt on 21 January 1918. His first theatre of war was France and Flanders from 23 March 1916. His address, on his medal index card, is shown as Newfield House, Bell Busk, Yorks. If so, his father, J.W. Morkill, was to become High Sheriff of the West Riding in 1929. He was wounded on 9 September 1918 and rejoined the battery soon after the Armistice.

CHAPTER 20
THE END OF THE GERMAN OFFENSIVE

Since the latter part of 1914 the Western Front had been static for most of that time but the German offensive changed that as they advanced with alarming speed. Movement of batteries would be planned to allow time to undertake this operation in an orderly manner but we can see from Gnr Hall's account that they scarcely remained in one position for any time. His experience of bedlam, fatigue, close brushes with the enemy, the plight of refugees, death and devastation was typical of thousands of troops at this time. There were positive notes such as the destruction of an enemy gun and the awards made for good service during the retreat.[1]

The Beugnatre position was hopeless from the first. It was obvious that once the enemy had left his concrete stronghold, the Hindenburg Line, it would take more than our hastily dug trenches, mere holes scratched in the ground, to stop him and the idea of placing our reserve position little more than a mile in the rear of Vaulx represented the height of optimism. Considering the three weeks at our disposal surprisingly little had been done. Platforms had certainly been laid for the guns and 3,000 rounds of ammunition, most of which fell into the enemy hands, had been placed in readiness, but that was all. Work on the construction of the reserve position had in fact represented a glorious "mike"[2] – perhaps just as well. Then there was the usual trouble, lack of targets, the impossibility of knowing where our infantry was and what progress if any the Germans were making. However from this position we fired on Vaulx, where, if we could do no good, at any rate we were doing no harm.

But with the continued advance of the enemy Beugnatre clearly became untenable. Soon after Sgt Salter and his men arrived Major Warren ordered up the gun teams and by 4pm we were pulling out with the enemy a bare 500 yards away and advancing steadily. Unfortunately we were spotted by an enemy aeroplane which promptly proceeded to range a battery on us. The poor horses again had to gallop out of action but, with a position so open, we were able to get away before the German battery was correctly ranged and with only two casualties. A dozen GS wagons were hastily loaded with thirty rounds apiece thus 360 rounds were salvaged. Some 500 had been fired so the enemy secured a further 2,000 rounds to add to the 5,000 odd that had been left behind at Vaulx.

Thus in addition to the original position the second line of defence had given way and from now on we should have to make our plans as we retreated and pick up positions as best we could.

We pulled in behind a low mound to the west of Sapignies[3] some four miles in rear of Beugnatre as the crow flies although it had been reached by a devious route over twice that distance. At 7pm (March 22) we were in action again. Lt Lakin had telephoned a good target to us and we engaged an enemy battery now well established in our old position in the sunken road at Vaulx.

Battery position near Sapignies

In spite of the hurry in its selection, Sapignies was a surprisingly good position, much stronger than the one we had left. I was on familiar ground. The village of Sapignies lay on the high ground between Bapaume and Ervillers the path taken a year ago when 242 Siege Battery advanced into the evacuated country. The mound afforded some protection from shell-fire and from prying eyes, but for which our casualties would have been more severe. About 500 yards in rear was a broad sunken road and it was here that Major Warren decided to establish temporary horse lines for the gun teams might be needed at any moment. A party was sent to the permanent horse lines at Courcelles-le-Comte with an order for it to be dismantled and the few who remained there, the quartermaster-sergeant, the veterinary-sergeant with some drivers and spare horses to prepare to join the main party. When the party neared Courcelles however it was already in enemy hands and it was presumed that the occupants had been captured.

For some time the horses stood to their limbers but later when it became evident that the enemy would not attack further that night they were relieved of their harness and tied up to a rope that had been hurriedly put up.

The signalling arrangements were most primitive. A telephone wire, the omnibus line it was called, connected all four batteries for now brigade was moving together with their headquarters. It was very embarrassing when two sets of people wanted to use the 'phone at the same time. Speech was very indistinct for only one wire with an earth return was used and often we had to resort to Morse. The shortage of telephone wire was one of the first to be felt, so much had been used on the 21 March while on evacuating Beugnatre all the wiring had been abandoned.

As on the previous day fire moderated considerably with nightfall. The enemy had taken Beugnatre and the villages in the hollow while we still held the high ground on the line of the Ervillers–Bapaume road and the Germans were doubtless bringing up their artillery to carry the ridge on the morrow.

Tonight then we could make ourselves fairly comfortable. We found a dump of several thousand blankets. Some infantry men had passed the previous night on the hillside and had been ordered into action so quickly that they had to leave all their blankets and much of their kit behind. This was a very welcome find, for many of our gunners had lost their own blankets in the Nissen huts at Vaulx and the prospect of spending a night in the open without any covering at all did not greatly appeal. We divided the spoil between us, twelve I remember, fell to my share. When it became apparent that there would be no night firing for we had only 360 rounds of ammunition and could not afford to waste any on uncertain targets we wrapped ourselves in the blankets and slept in the open heedless of what the morrow would bring forth.

We were roused very early in the morning (March 23). A heavy dew had fallen and we stripped off layer after layer of soaking blanket. The cook was quick to prepare a hearty breakfast for the casualties had not yet been reported and we were still drawing rations for our full complement. Then we awaited orders.

Again the attack was slow in starting but enemy shelling was resumed at 8am. It was evident that we were in for a hot time and Major Warren decided to put as many of his men under cover as possible. The guns were quite exposed but the sunken track 500 yards back would afford some little protection. The CO decided on the drastic step of fighting with only three men per gun against the ten laid down in drill and five in actual practice. Every man beyond the actual twelve required was sent to join the horses in the sunken road. Similarly all the signallers that could be spared as well as the cook and his mate were evacuated. The cook was told to prepare a good dinner for 1pm after which another dozen men were to relieve their comrades on the guns. Thus by working six hour shifts we might be able to carry on for a time. Meantime, Bush, Perry and I were in a shell hole which we had elevated to the title of BC post when the Major's eye came upon us. Perry was bluntly told to clear out. Still the CO was not satisfied – trouble was expected. Was it really necessary to have two BCA's on duty; we had better work shifts like the others. We agreed and a toss of a coin settled the rota. It was now 9am Bush would carry on until 3pm after which I was to relieve him.

But the threatened attack did not develop after all, the enemy contenting himself with artillery preparation, engaging and putting out of action as many of our batteries (or what remained of them) as possible. For our part there was comparatively little firing and that at extremely doubtful targets. Counter battery work was almost at a standstill for the German aeroplanes drove all our machines away and we had to be content with such vague reports as *"Many guns firing east of Beugnatre"* when nothing but pinpointing the hostile batteries followed by three or four hours intensive bombardment would reduce them to silence.

Headquarters also sent up a few targets but no meteors were being received and without them accurate firing was impossible. Of course we guessed the force and direction of the wind but it was a poor substitute for the proper weather reports. Moreover we were now working on small scale maps which did not tend to accuracy.

Lt Lakin managed to send up two or three targets during the morning and these we shared with the brigade. We heard that the German aeroplanes had been ranging on one of the 60 pounder batteries and had inflicted many casualties. Our turn would no doubt come later.

Dinner was served at 1 o'clock and soon after the second reliefs mustered to take their turn on the guns. Four senior NCO's came forward and each called for two volunteers to accompany him. These were quickly forthcoming and the whole party went forward to the battery position. Then the first reliefs returned for dinner and rest. So far things had gone remarkably well.

But soon after 2pm it was evident that the battery was in trouble and from the horse lines we could see shells bursting over the guns. Then came the news of the tragedy. No.3 gun hit and its detachment wiped out. For some reason No.3 was always regarded as a treacherous gun and this time it had certainly lived up to its reputation. Corporal Brazier, that splendid boy, the youngest NCO in the battery was in charge with two volunteers Clinch[4] and Sandiford[5]. An important target was being engaged and although an enemy aeroplane was hovering about fire could not be discontinued. A hostile battery was at once ranged on us and almost immediately the enemy secured a direct hit on No.3 gun. The gun was being loaded at the time and by a remarkable coincidence the enemy shell landed on the tray exploding our own shell as well. The impact of the two exploding shells was so terrific that all three men were instantly decapitated while the breech of the gun was severely damaged and several spokes of the wheel broken. Clearly the gun was now out of action.

To shut out the horrible sight the other men rushed forward, hastily emptied the dead men's pockets for future examination, then matching the heads to the respective trunks, sewed up the corpses in blankets. Firing ceased for the time. Meanwhile the enemy aeroplane doubtless signalled *"OK"* to his battery and the bombardment continued. Later when Capt Fletcher went through the dead men's property he discovered a letter which Sandiford had written to his wife an hour or two previously and was awaiting an opportunity to post. It was assuring her that he was *"in excellent health and spirits"*. After a good deal of deliberation the Captain burnt the epistle and forwarded to the widow his own letter of condolence.

It was about this time that I realised that I was due to relieve Bdr Bush at the BC post at 3pm. The enemy was shelling the battery and maintaining a brisk fire on the ground between the horse lines and the position. Altogether things did not look too rosy. I had been with Perry all morning and told him that it was time for me to go. To my great surprise he insisted in accompanying me. I had some experience of barrage running and was prepared for some more but I had no wish to be burdened with a companion for whom I felt in some measure responsible. However there was no gainsaying Perry so off we started.

Owing to the direction of the shelling I deemed it advisable not to make direct for the position but rather take a detour by a point where lay the wreckage of one of our aeroplanes brought down in yesterday's fighting. As we approached the aeroplane Perry's nerves seemed to go and I had to grip his wrist with all the force at my disposal to steady him. However we reached the BC post at 3pm the appointed time.

But nerves were frayed at the post. *"What the Hell have you come here for,"* shouted Bush. Nothing loath I retorted, *"Clear out, it's my show now"*. Bush refused to budge, I refused to go back. We accused each other of *"playing for a decoration"* and squabbled until Capt Fletcher intervened that I should take over the BC post for the next six hours while Bush could remain but not interfere. Perry was also allowed to stay so long as he kept quiet. Strange that there should be such a demand to remain in the company of three newly killed men in a position that was still being shelled by the enemy. After this episode Bush and I remained on duty together. After he had silenced our guns the enemy transferred his attention to another battery although he would return periodically to let us know he had not forgotten us.

The CO surveyed the damage. No.3 gun was quite unworkable and would have to be removed to the workshops without delay. Many of the spokes having been broken Major Warren telephoned to the horse lines for a spare gun wheel to be sent over. 2/Lt Armstrong[6] who had recently joined us and suffered from gun-deafness took the call. He was not certain that he had got the message right so half an hour later we had the amusing spectacle of Gunner Wheeler the major's groom escorting two rear horses of a gun team "wheelers" as they were called to the battery position. Lt Armstrong evidently thought that one of his guesses must be right. The joke did us all good and everyone from the Major downwards laughed uproariously at the deaf officer's mistake. The groom took back the horses promising that a spare wheel should be sent without delay. This soon arrived and the damaged gun was made ready for the road if not for action.

At dark the damaged gun was sent back to the workshops but her adventures did not end there. When in the small hours the escort arrived at ordnance the personnel were preparing to depart to a safer place taking with them their machinery and a large number of damaged guns. The cripple was quickly handed over and hitched to a lorry but in the congested state of the roads the gun became ditched and no time could be lost extricating her. Thus our

No.3 gun fell into the hands of the enemy.

The three men were buried at midnight. The Brigade Chaplain heard of the loss and told us that he would conduct the service. The graves were dug and crosses made. Capt Fletcher oriented the position on the map and later sent the exact location to the relatives of the deceased. All the battery personnel assembled in that sinister little hollow where the fallen were laid to rest and the padre in his white surplice read the burial service in full. During the rites a prowling German aeroplane dropped a few bombs on the assembly and we all promptly ducked, that is all except the padre who never flinched. The sight of his standing there in his white surplice put us all to shame, one after another we abandoned our recumbent posture and stood proud and erect. The hostile aircraft still circled overhead but one felt that with our trust in God he could do us no further harm and, the service over we departed in peace.

The terrible loss of Corpl Brazier and his comrades had a profound effect on the battery. Brazier was a favourite of officers and men alike. He was just eighteen when he died. Altogether he was I think the most handsome youth I have ever seen with fair curly hair and the face of an angel. In addition he had a most generous and indeed a noble disposition. It was said that the battery was never the same since his death, our casualties were grievous but the loss of Brazier was something quite different from anything else.

After the funeral we dealt with a few lorries that had arrived from somewhere with ammunition. After that we settled to rest. The attack had not matured after all. We were spared for another day.

On March 24 the Germans have considered the artillery preparations of the previous day adequate attacked in force carrying all before them. From our battery position we could see the long procession of wounded men. Then came the infantry by the thousand retiring in good order in companies and battalions to take up positions in the rear. Then it was the turn of the field artillery, battery after battery all had suffered badly, two to three guns to a battery instead of the usual six being the rule. Meantime we continued firing rapidly from our remaining three guns not at any target in particular but searching and sweeping in an endeavour to check the enemy's advance. We felt terribly isolated for it was obvious that we were covering the retreat of the field artillery until the lighter guns came into action again. Till then we should have remain at our post. Would our turn never come? Major Warren telephoned for instructions. At 10am he got them and surprising orders they were too. We were to fight to the end and then when the enemy came on top of us we were to bolt. *"You mean we are to be sacrificed,"* said the Major and though we in the BC post could not hear the colonel's reply its import was obvious. Major Warren then turned to us in the BC post *"not a word of this to the men"*. Bush and I were not to leave the post in case we might spread the news. The officers went quietly out and stood behind the guns.

There is an interesting sequel to this. Some years after the war I got in touch with Gunner Frost a townsman who like myself had been demobilised. In conversation I mentioned that

Bush and I were the only ones of the rank and file who knew that the battery might be sacrificed. To my surprise he burst into laughter. It appeared that on the day in question he was linesman and in the course of duty tapped into the telephone cable when he overheard the conversation between the Major and the Colonel. Moreover he heard both sides of the talk which was more than we did at the BC post. And Frost told other signallers and soon the whole battery knew.

The feeling of utter isolation now became more intense. The field guns were not yet in action and we seemed to be the only battery firing. Yet with it all there was a remarkable calm in the waiting for we knew there would be no hope for us once the Germans approached. Further we knew that the artillery was not too popular with the German infantry who might not be considerate enough to take us prisoner.

By noon however the field artillery were in action again miles to our rear it seemed and their shells could be heard passing over our heads. Battery after battery opened out; there might be some hope for us after all. And so it transpired; after a time came the welcome order to pull out. We needed no second telling. We stopped firing and the guns were limbered up ready for the horses which even now were galloping across the plain for they had been harnessed up for some time in readiness. Willing hands attached the teams to the guns and in a few minutes we were galloping out of action. This time fortune was certainly on our side and we were able to get away without a single casualty and soon we left that sinister position with all its bitter memories. We had no idea of the next move but tension relaxed and the whole battery was in excellent spirits as we made off down the hill.

At 2pm we were in action again this time at Achiet-le-Grand an important railway junction some four miles in rear of Sapignies. Here the sergeant-artificer made the important discovery that No.4 gun must have been hit in the barrel and was in a dangerous state. A good deal of the rifling had been torn away and it was a wonder that she had not prematured for she must have been hit at Sapignies and the casualty had passed unnoticed so we had continued firing the damaged gun. Now she was definitely out of action and that meant that we had only two guns left not that that mattered much for we had only 60 rounds of ammunition. Then there was the usual trouble with targets. Headquarters had left us to our fate for some time. Mr Lakin pestered infantry colonels for targets but the higher officers had too much to do without bothering to find jobs for the siege artillery and frequently left the task to subordinates who had only hazy ideas of our function. I remember how indignant Mr Lakin became when he discovered that a young and enthusiastic subaltern was using our precious guns at a moment when every round of ammunition countered for the sole purpose of sniping at a man carrying a piece of wood.

Up to now the retreat had been orderly enough but by the afternoon of March 24 it became a rout. No longer were the infantry retreating in companies but in ones and twos and sometimes a dozen or so men who had lost their units and had no idea where they were going but all had the fixed motive of getting to the rear, anywhere for safety. And not only the infantry but a vast multitude of other units, Army Service Corps drivers who had lost their lorries, airmen who planes had fallen into enemy hands, men whose function it was to repair roads, to operate the railways and a multitude of jobs behind the lines. They drifted hither and thither with as little order as a crowd of ants whose nest is disturbed, pillaging as they went. Achiet-le-Grand was a big distributing centre and the troops ransacked the abandoned stores. One man passed down the road carrying at least 50 pairs of socks another a whole pile of shirts. Men would throw away their kits as impeding their progress and straightway take up burdens twice as cumbersome and utterly useless. The fever of looting and destruction quickly infected the battery. Nearby was a Casualty Clearing Station abandoned by the RAMC. We were feeling pretty hungry for Heaven knows when we had our last meal and many of us went in search of food. We broke into the stores and found plunder and to spare. Maconochies by the hundred were taken only to be abandoned again in favour of tins of chicken while those who had taken tins of jam scornfully discarded the plum and apple in favour of choicer varieties. Hundreds of bottles of Bass and Guinness were taken and soon more than one man was lying dead drunk. The offenders were moved out of sight of the officers who for their part turned a blind eye to the events. Hundreds of tins of jam, milk, butter, chicken, veal loaf and other delicacies were loaded on the wagons. Sometimes whole boxes were appropriated and these bore strange markings as for instance a case of Guinness was relabelled *"No. 4 Gun stores with care"* while I must confess to loading a case of tinned chicken on the BCA's wagon. Tinned chicken and Guinness formed the staple diet for some days and though the officers took no active part in the raid I noticed the proceeds were not unknown in the mess. The loot kept turning up for months afterwards. Then for want of something better to do we started breaking the hospital windows – it would make things more difficult for the advancing Germans.

At 4pm the situation had deteriorated considerably. Shells falling on the village and railway lines showed that the enemy had succeeded in advancing his artillery. Heavier and heavier became the bombardment as battery after battery came into action. And now staff officers and military police appeared on the scene rounding up stragglers on the road and sending them back to the line. There was a rumour that Major Warren had been approached to see if he could spare any men. I doubt the truth of this but the fact remained that we had only two guns in action and had run out of ammunition. Although the casualties had been severe there was a considerable surplus of manpower. A foraging party with GS wagons had been sent out to search for ammunition and there was considerable relief when they returned with a limited number of rounds and we were able to resume firing. Everybody tried to look busy even if they weren't and no one ventured out of the vicinity of the guns for fear of being picked up by the hated Red Caps.[7]

At 6pm came the orders to withdraw and not before time for the enemy was shelling the village vigorously and advancing behind his barrage. We had no sooner locked No.5 gun in the travelling position than she was struck by a shell. We were unable to ascertain the damage at the time but later when we attempted to fight the gun it was found that the elevating gear was hopelessly jammed and the gun was quite unusable. We were fortunate in sustaining only one casualty at Achiet-le-Grand a rather bad case of shell shock caused by a shell bursting at close quarters to the victim. We were able to get the guns away without much trouble. Progress along the narrow streets of the village however was very difficult owing to the heavy shelling and the horses had to be guided to prevent them bolting. There were rumours at this time that the German cavalry were in action. These proved to be false but at the time it was most alarming. The moral effect of the cavalry on dismounted troops was enormous.

We were not long on the road however when we pulled into an open field in rear of the neighbouring village of Achiet-le-Petit about a couple of miles away. At 9pm we were in action firing with our single gun on Achiet-le-Grand the village we had evacuated. It was a miserable night and the magnitude of the disaster fell heavily upon us. As usual the front quietened down considerably and most of us were able to curl up in our blankets for the night while our solitary gun kept on firing, a pitiful reply to the victorious Germans.

We woke early, breakfasted on our looted stores, packed up our kit and loaded them on the wagons for we expected moving again. This proved to be the case. At 8am March 25 the enemy resumed the attack and almost immediately we were ordered to withdraw. At 8.20 we were on the road again.

We pulled up behind Bucquoy a village some four miles in rear of Achiet-le-Petit. The solitary No.2 gun was unlimbered and Bush and I set to work laying out the lines of fire. Sgt Clarke started laying the telephone line but Major Warren told him to wait for a time. The teams stood behind Nos 4 & 5 guns and the stores remained unloaded. No news of any kind was received, we had no idea of the progress of the enemy or whether he was in range of our gun, whether the infantry needed our help or if so what targets we were to engage. It was now known that Courcelles-le-Comte had fallen. The spare drivers under the quartermaster had been stationed here and should have joined us by now but nothing had been heard of them and we could only assume that they had been captured by the enemy. Later in the day we fed and watered the horses and for ourselves had more of the purloined food, tinned chicken and Guinness's stout. It was not until 7pm that definite news was received. We were ordered right out of the line. No.2 gun was limbered up again and was joined by the crippled Nos 4 & 5. The major put himself at the head of the column and our long trek began.

The first part of our march was remarkably rapid considering the difficult country we had to negotiate and the narrow lanes across the old battlefield. These were in a terrible state of disrepair. Since the German withdrawal in 1917 they had not been used, indeed a good deal of the ground had purposely been left untouched. One particularly sinister looking place bore notices in French and English *"Nothing whatever is to be removed from this area – it is dedicated as a war memorial for ever"*.[8] Here there were old trenches and barbed wire entanglements. The dead certainly had been removed but ammunition limbers lay by the side of the road where they had been blown up eighteen months previously.

Sometimes we passed columns proceeding in the opposite direction and occasionally units faster than ours endeavoured to overtake. In either case the result was the same. At the best of times there was insufficient room for two columns abreast, now with the darkness of night some of the transport would be forced on to the verges and become hopelessly ditched. The war memorial scheme was responsible for much delay and loss of transport.

At one point a road forked to our left and here there were no less than three columns on the march, our own battery going westwards and endeavouring to pass another unit in the opposite direction, while a field artillery battery was trying to leave the main road and take the fork to the left. Complicated manoeuvres at the best of time for there was no traffic controller at this point and each column consisted of over sixty units to add to which it was pitch dark. There was much confusion as guns and wagons passed, each jostling the other in an attempt to keep on the hard road and avoid getting ditched. Just when pandemonium was at its height the enemy opened fire on the road junction, with shrapnel. Major Warren looking round at once gave the order *"81 Siege Battery – Gallop"*. The commanding officers of the other two units gave similar orders and three columns drew apart. By a miracle no one was injured but the orders came with dramatic and suddenness and the gunners marching behind their guns saw the terrified horses of the following team bearing down on them while any way to safety either to right or left was blocked by the other columns. There was only one thing to do, to clutch hold of the gun or wagon or failing that on the man in front and run as if one's life depends on it. As indeed it did, for any man failing to keep up would certainly have been crushed by the heavy guns or trampled by the horses. The incident seemed to me quite unnecessary. It was a pity that the order *"Gallop"* should have been given for a mere whiff of shrapnel.

Once past the road junction we halted and the gunners who were in little better plight themselves strove to calm the sweating and terrified animals. Once the march was resumed however the route became easier we drew away from the old battlefield and regained better roads.

At 2pm (March 26) we reached the village of Sarton. We gunners found a barn where we promptly went to sleep. The drivers had still to feed and water their horses, then they removed the heavier parts of their harness and left the animals tethered to the guns and wagons for the night for there was neither time nor opportunity to establish horse lines. This was I suppose the most severe forced march in which I have ever participated. In the seven hours we had covered 24 miles, the first six of which had been through the most difficult country and we had taken out three heavy guns through no less than nine villages with right angled bends and every conceivable obstacle to our progress. In the later stages the horses were driven as fast as possible and the attending gunners had to break into a jog trot to keep up with them. Fortunately we had plenty of horses and the teams were frequently changed although this meant some delay. There was only one other stop, when the River Authie was reached and all hands went off with canvas buckets to bring water to the horses. Gunners changed with drivers periodically, every one travelled light, all our kit being carried on the wagons. In the later stages even coats and caps were doffed. Bush, Perry and I travelled with the BCA's limbered wagon, two following in rear while the third took up a precarious perch on the limber pole joining the two parts of the wagon. In my travels here and later on I was to spend many hours thus and I became such an adept at balancing that I would even sleep on the swaying pole.

The village of Sarton reached by 81 SB on 26 March 1918

At the end of our long march we were all very tired and needed no rocking but I personally was unconscious of the extreme fatigue I had experienced on previous marches with 242 Battery, nor was there any evidence of exhaustion among my comrades. Undoubtedly Major Warren had saved his men as much as possible.

At 8am (March 27) we were on the road again. We had been allowed to sleep as long as possible and were roused for a hurried meal before march was resumed. No official breakfast had been provided, not that that mattered for there was plenty of plunder in the wagons and we regaled ourselves on the now familiar tinned chicken and cold oxtail soup washed down with a couple of bottles of Guinness. Then without bothering to wash or shave the column resumed its journey.

Now there we were on the main road and in daylight, movement was considerably easier and it was evident that we were only part of a continuous procession of units all moving back.

We were overtaken by motor ambulances evacuating wounded men from abandoned Casualty Clearing Stations, enormous air force lorries pulling on their trailers spare parts of aeroplanes and by mechanised batteries with their six-inch howitzers behind their four-wheel–drive lorries. For our own part we left behind RE[9] wagons with their clumsy pontoon bridges which they seemed to carry about wherever they went and Caterpillar tractors dragging eight inch howitzers and six inch guns to safety, traction engines plodding along with the heavy 12 inch, while even steam rollers used for repairing roads, painfully followed the westward trek. All seemed to have suffered and I saw not a single battery intact. Like ourselves most units had been pillaging for their lorries were loaded up with vast quantities of loot. It was noticed that most units had taken care to salvage their latrines.

But in addition to the military it was evident that the pitiful flight of refugees was again in progress. The unfortunate peasants were obliged to leave their homes a second time. On the German evacuation of 1917 many had been reinstated on the land, had patched up their ruined homes and were now living, as it were, under British guarantee that this part of France, at any rate, was clear of the enemy. Now we had failed them and were in headlong retreat before the victorious Germans so they had no alternative but to leave their homes again. Some naturally were bitter and as we passed through one village an excitable French blacksmith left his smithy to shake his fist in the face of our CO but for the most part they were too concerned with their own affairs to bother with us. Some wheeled their belongings in barrows, others carried them on their backs. One strange looking wagon was drawn by a horse and a cow yoked together while two more men were endeavouring to assist a broken down nag to pull an overloaded cart. The progress of the refugees was hampered by the fact that the whole of the hard surface of the road was occupied by the military while the civilians had to use the soft verges.

Then we reached Doullens which I had known as a headquarters of sorts. I noticed with some malice that the staff officers were evacuating the town and that their red tabs did not stop them from joining the ignoble retreat. Deputy Assistant this and that with their stupid titles and silly little flags were all represented, pushing and shoving trying to force their way in the already congested streets. We at any rate had suffered heavily before we turned tail but the staff were in flight long before their headquarters were within range of German guns.

Doullens was a bottle neck. Four main roads ran eastwards from the town, each road chock–a–bloc with traffic, military and civilian while to the west were two roads one on either side of the River Authie down which the converging forces would have to pass on their way to the rear. At one point we were held up for two hours while traffic from another direction was allowed through. What made things worse was that no convoy could be broken or the tail might be lost. As each convoy might consist of up to a hundred separate items and there were hundreds of such convoys converging on the town the task of traffic control was herculean.

But with all these troops retreating there were some going in the opposite direction. We noticed a battery of light artillery and a few battalions of infantry and all these wore the light blue uniform of the French. Everything was held up to give these advancing troops the right of way. The significance of the move was not lost on us. The British in headlong retreat and the French going forward to take our place and check the enemy where we had failed. The contrast between the men was remarkable, the British dirty, unshaven and dejected, the French spruce and full of confidence. This seemed the supreme moment of humiliation. The assistance that one army might be expected to give to a sorely pressed ally was one thing, the replacement of British by French troops was another. Nor could it be said that we had been particularly hard pressed. My own battery for instance, though we had suffered severely could have held up considerably longer had targets been notified and ammunition available nor were casualties one quarter as severe as on the Salient where we simply had to stick it. In any case there was no need for the staff to scuttle from Doullens a town which never came under enemy gunfire let alone occupation.

Once clear of Doullens the retreating forces were able to fan out into the country beyond. The roads became less congested. Occasionally we were held up at crossroads but on the whole we made much better progress. The horses, however, were feeling the strain and frequent halts were called while we patted the poor beasts and fed them with grass pulled from the road side. At intervals Major Warren would give the order to dismount. For many miles we walked besides the horses and a strange picture we must have presented as Major Warren with five day's growth of beard led his black mare followed by officers and men all leading their mounts.

A diversion occurred some miles after leaving Doullens. We were still following the River Authie and the CO called for a halt to rest the horses when 2/Lt Page was seen riding his charger to the river to give it a drink. Major Warren angrily called him back but Page evidently out of earshot and continued his way down the field. The River Authie was very deep at this point and had steep shelving banks. No sooner had the horse attempted to drink than it slipped into the river and horse and man were carried away by the swift current. At length they parted company and the charger relieved of its burden scrambled up the bank and made its way to join the convoy. Meanwhile the officer continued to drift downstream. A couple of men mounted and would have made their way to the rescue but Major Warren called them back and at once gave the order for the battery to *"Walk March"*. *"Let the bugger drown,"* he said. *"He's no bloody good anyway."* Lt Page was unpopular with officers and men alike but this action seemed somewhat drastic to say the least of it. However there was nothing for it but to obey. Mr Page drifted downstream for a considerable way but at last he managed to catch an overhanging branch and scrambled to safety more dead than alive.

His troubles were not yet over for he had still to regain the fast disappearing battery and the CO would not call a halt until Lt Page puffing and blowing and dripping with water at last rejoined the column. Then before the whole battery Major Warren proceeded to give the unfortunate officer such a dressing down as I have never heard before or since. His appearance, his dress, his speech his conduct in the field and his behaviour in the mess all came into criticism. Finally the CO gave Lt Page's charger to one of the gunners who had gathered round and refused to let him ride or even walk besides one of his own wagons. No, he had to get on the floor of one of the nondescript wagons forming the tail of the column and continue his journey among the drums of oil.

With this Major Warren took his place at the head of the column and the march was resumed. Mr Page was soon begging for the loan of a towel and some dry underwear for he dare not make any attempt to secure his own kit. After some time he was accommodated, then someone threw a spare pair of trousers into the wagon. So we enjoyed the discomfiture of the wretched Page for the rest of the journey and the incident was never forgotten. Mr Page must have been excessively thick skinned or he would have made early application for transfer to another unit.

And so alternatively riding and leading our horses we reached the village of Frohen-le-Grand some thirty miles in rear of Doullens. It was five o'clock in the afternoon of March 26 when we arrived. The village looked singularly peaceful for the tide of war had not reached so far. There was no question of falling in, we just crowded round the CO while he addressed us. *"You have done very well,"* he said. *"Now the cook will get a good meal for you. See to the horses, then get your dinner and turn in as soon as you possibly can. I am going to do the same for God knows what is in front of us in the morning."*

So we set to work. Some unharnessed the horses and led them to water while others fixed up horse lines on the village green. Meantime the cook and his volunteer assistants had got to work. They found meat and still more meat, jam and cheese galore, bread and biscuits in abundance. Rations had arrived daily, late it is true, but they always came and had simply been thrown on the cook's wagon and carried with us. Moreover there were rations for our full complement no account having been taken of the casualties we had suffered. With our constant movement no cooking had been possible and rations had accumulated while we lived on the plunder secured at Achiet-le-Grand. But a diet of tinned chicken and Guinness begins to pall after a time and we looked forward with eagerness to the huge pieces of beef now finding their way to the cooking pots for the cook had decided that the most satisfactory way was to boil the meat whole. But although enough meat was cooked to last us for several days there was still some to spare and the children who had gathered round to see the fun were packed off to mother with large pieces of raw beef. They returned with their parents who informed us that loaves of bread, though stale, were also acceptable so in a short time our supply of food was reduced to reasonable limits. For ourselves we fed well and few meals have I enjoyed more than the huge slices of hot boiled beef with slices of bread washed down with copious draughts of strong, sweet tea that we had that evening on the village green of Frohen-le-Grand.

After tea most of us adjourned to the estaminets but not for long for we were dog tired and the major's warning had not gone unheeded. Soon we returned to the village green where we slept under the wagons or bivouacs made of gun covers and pieces of tarpaulin.

We turned out early in the morning greatly refreshed. Major Warren appeared on the scene and we gathered round. It is noteworthy that no attempt was made to parade the troops. The major was in excellent spirits and remarked *"What about tidying ourselves up a bit?"* He passed his hand over his chin as he spoke and we all burst into roars of laughter. Like the majority of us he had neither washed nor shaved since the day preceding the attack. Razors were brought out and shared with those unfortunates who had lost their own. At our next appearance we looked a little more presentable. Breakfast over a sort of informal stocktaking began. Major Warren first of all drew attention to the horses. Like the men the night's rest had done them a lot of good but they were thinner than before the attack and badly needed grooming. On the whole they had survived the ordeal very well. Strangely enough no animals had been killed in the retreat although one or two had been slightly wounded. These casualties, their wounds bandaged, had followed in the rear of the column and were all progressing satisfactorily.

Then we turned our attention to the guns, one sound and two crippled. No.2 gun (Sergeant Norman's – lucky Norman as he was called[10]) was soon disposed of. A little oil in the buffers and a few turns on the air compressor and she was as good as new. The other two guns presented something of a problem. No.4 with her rifling torn away would never fire again while No.5 was jammed owing to the damage to her elevating gear. The artificer set to work to repair No.5 gun. The portable furnace was brought into operation, the damaged gear removed, the bent pieces straightened in the fire and replaced. Certain parts were removed from No.4 gun and fitted into No.5 to replace pieces smashed by the enemy. Thus after a few hours work we had a couple of guns Nos 2 and 5 ready for action. What remained of No.4 could be dumped into ordnance workshops at our leisure. Spirits were beginning to revive.

At 1 pm (March 27) to our utter astonishment who should arrive but the wagon line party from Courcelles-le-Comte. These people it will be remembered had remained at the lines when the majority of the drivers came to pull us out from Vaulx-Vraucourt of the evening of the 21 March. It was known that Courcelles had fallen into enemy hands and as nothing had been heard of the rear party there it was assumed that they had been captured. They had, it seemed, a remarkable escape. Cut off from all news of the German advance they were under the impression that they were miles away and when the veterinary-sergeant saw troops advancing towards the horse lines he thought they were our own men until they came near enough for him to recognise the German uniforms. Actually the British had been gone some hours previously and the enemy were cautiously making their way forward. The half dozen men abandoned everything but the horses and galloped the dozen animals, including some very sick, to safety. Then they tried to re-join the battery. After much trouble they reached Achiet-le-Grand but only after we had evacuated the position. From there they followed us to Sarton and afterwards to Doullens where a patrol told them that our battery, which he recognised by the 'elephant' mark[11] on the wagons was moving down the Authie valley. So at last they located us. Men and horses alike were famished and in an utterly exhausted condition for the party had been unable to obtain either rations or shelter since March 24 and with the sick horses progress had been slow and painful. When we left Frohen they had to be left behind some days to recover.

At 2pm Major Warren was able to bring us some news and great news it was. We were to return to the line. His words were greeted with an outburst of cheers. Without any claims to heroism we were glad to set our faces in the right direction again. The withdrawal out of the line had been most unsatisfactory for all concerned and the fact that we had been replaced by Frenchmen was galling to say the least. The rank and file appreciated the disgrace even if it was not apparent to the higher command and the sooner the blot was wiped out the better.

In this spirit we set out to prepare ourselves for the journey. With the natural perversity of the Tommy we started polishing our buttons and cleaning boots. Had we been ordered to do this the village would have resounded with complaints but, since on active service, polishing buttons was discouraged it was only natural that we should wish to do it. An early tea, a feed for the horses and at 4 o'clock we left Frohen-le-Grand to the surprise and somewhat to the relief of the villagers.

Although the return to the line was the longest march of all it was one of the easiest. All our equipment was carried for us and there was but little traffic on the roads, for, although the general retreat had been halted, few units were as yet returning to action. As we passed through the villages the locals turned out to wish us good luck, very different from the surly spirit evinced on our retreat.

So alternatively walking and riding we reached the village of Bienvillers[12] some thirty miles eastwards. Here were left the damaged No.4 gun and as many GS wagons as were not actually needed at the new battery position for here the CO decided to establish his horse lines. (Eventually it proved too near the front and the horse lines were moved back to Souastre a fortnight later.)

The main party continued on its way until the outskirts of the next village Hannescamps was reached. It was 2am (March 28) and we fully expected that the CO would lead us into action forthwith. Major Warren decided otherwise, however, a mistake that was to cost him his life. It appeared that the German advance had been arrested, petered out would perhaps have been a better term. Our instructions were to come into action in front of Hannescamps the selection of the actual position being left to the CO. Major Warren notified the colonel of arrival at the village but asked to defer putting the guns into action until the following morning on the grounds of the strain imposed on men and horses. The colonel agreed and Major Warren had the gun teams unhitched and sent back to Bienvillers with instructions to return in the morning and pull us in. We were then told to make ourselves comfortable for the night while the Major and Captain went forward to select the actual position.

Hannescamps itself lies on a ridge the ground falling steeply away to the west of the village. It was on this declivity that we rested for the night. Some trenches had been dug in the hillside and these would afford shelter from the weather and from the enemy should he start shelling. Some trees would screen the guns and wagons. Altogether this would have made a good battery position and in view of what happened later it was a pity that it was not selected. Perhaps the extra five hundred yards of range were essential. The trenches were dry and in them we made ourselves comfortable for the night.

At 8am the next morning (March 29) the gun teams returned. The first gun was limbered up and started advancing up the hill the Major leading the way to the selected position on his black mare. They had not gone many yards before the enemy opened fire (probably we were under open observation). Major Warren was observed to reel and would have fallen from his horse but for the fact that his groom Gunner Wheeler seeing what had happened galloped up and caught him, a remarkable piece of horsemanship. The CO was lifted from his charger and found to be terribly wounded in the chest.[13] Capt Fletcher came forward and bending over took his orders from the dying man. A GS wagon was quickly cleared, the major lifted on a stretcher and placed thereon. Gunner Wheeler galloped on ahead to find the whereabouts of a First Aid Post and the wagon followed bearing our deeply loved commanding officer. Major Warren was alive when the First Aid Post was reached but had lost a lot of blood. It was all a question of time. Could he reach the Casualty Clearing Station quick enough? But the CCS like everything else was in a terrible state of confusion. It was late before proper medical attention could be secured and although a blood transfusion was given he died the same day.[14]

Gezaincourt Communal Cemetery Extension burial place of Major Warren

On Capt Fletcher devolved the duty of getting the guns into action. He waited until the shelling had stopped and then cautiously advanced on foot with the first team the drivers leading instead of riding their horses. Bush and I followed in the wake of the gun. We went up the hill to the crossroads, then to the right along the ridge-way, until we approached a narrow lane at the foot of which was a large crucifix. We took the guns up the lane, a sunken road which afforded little protection as it ran from east to west and so was liable to enfilation. There was insufficient room to place all the guns in the sunken road itself so one had to be placed in the open. The first gun in position, the second was sent for and then one by one the ammunition wagons. We laid out the lines of fire but it was not until two more men were killed that we were able to put the guns into action.[15]

There were a number of shelters in the sunken road and the largest Bush and I claimed as the BC post. I remember the feeling of disgust as we moved to our new quarters. The shelters had not been used for a long time, fungi grew on the rotting timbers while soil dropped from the roof. Later we were to find the place far from waterproof. We set to work clearing away the fallen rubbish and removing the vegetation. Then we fixed our map on the plane table and identified the position. Sgt Clarke and his men were busy with the telephone lines and the gunners were cleaning out their own dug-outs, wretched little places of corrugated iron on the bank side.

At 10 am March 29 we fired a salvo from our two guns. We were in action again.[16]

Such then was the part we played in the March retreat. From first to last we had retreated some twenty miles. The brunt of the attack fell on General Byng's Fifth Army, on our right, who were driven back considerably further. We in General Gough's Third Army escaped comparatively lightly and it was I think too readily assumed that we had retired in good order so as to preserve the continuity of the line. The fact remains that, on our front, the retreat commenced immediately the Germans opened fire on the morning of March 21 and continued with ever increasing momentum for six days. Why the Germans did not follow up the attack when all the heavy artillery was withdrawn remains a mystery. Had they done so I feel certain that we should have suffered total defeat.

Our losses were on a par with most batteries in the sector. Three of our six guns in the hands of the enemy and another badly damaged in the workshop. Eleven killed including the CO and twenty one seriously injured, over six thousand rounds of ammunition lost, all six rifles and an immense amount of stores while most of the personnel had lost everything except the clothes they wore. It is safe to say that the artillery was reduced to one third of its strength in ordnance and one half in men.

Nor were we quick in returning to normal. Although we were back in action the various headquarters showed no particular hurry to return to their posts. The practice of picking up targets from the infantry continued for some time and Mr Lakin was now installed in a division HQ somewhere up the line. Of organised shooting there was none and Lakin was very much annoyed at the quality of the targets indicated. To be of any predictable use the fire of siege artillery must be properly directed which it certainly had not been since the beginning of the offensive nor was the machinery at corps headquarters in operation again until the middle of April.

Although we brought up but little ammunition to Hannescamps a fresh supply was fairly quickly obtained from emergency dumps down the line and in the course of a few days shells were arriving in the thousand by GS wagon and motor lorry. Even tanks were pressed into service, bringing up hundreds of rounds at a time and proving very difficult to unload. The ammunition proved to be of a very mixed variety, both cordite and NCT cartridges were sent up, every variety of fuze and shells fitted with both old and new type of driving band[17] (in the interest of the economy a new type of band was introduced in 1917, it used about half the amount of copper but caused more erratic shooting and reduced the range by as much as 1000 yards). As all these had to be segregated before they could be used Bdr Perry was found a job sorting out ammunition. He did not care for the job at first but once its back was broken became quite reconciled to his fate although he never seemed to know within a hundred or two how many rounds were in charge. On April 3 Bush and I were assured that were no more rivals for the BC post.

Two new guns were supplied within a few days but that was all and again we reverted to a four gun battery nor were we brought up to full strength for some weeks.

Stores and men's kit were not so quickly replaced. The signallers were handicapped through lack of cable and had only a couple of portable telephones, the larger instruments used for exchange work having been lost. All the heavy planks had been lost and no proper platforms could be made for the guns. Many essential gun stores were missing. One gun was without a rammer and shells had to be pushed home with a handspike an exhausting practice which considerably slowed down the rate of fire. Urgent messages were sent for replacement of the lost stores but without avail; we were told to carry on as best we could until our turn came for refitting and reorganisation.

Early in April it became known that certain decorations were to be awarded. Capt Fletcher now in charge of the battery was handicapped as Major Warren had kept rather aloof from the other officers. Certain names were found jotted down in a pocket book which Capt Fletcher took from the dying man but the exact purpose of these was never known and the Captain had to use his own judgement in making recommendations. Consequently it is not to be wondered that the selection did not meet with universal approbation.

No one grudged Nobby Clarke a bar to his Military Medal[18] while Gunner Shanks[19], a newcomer, did well in the dangerous job of runner keeping in touch with neighbouring batteries when we acted as a forward exchange. Sgt Norman had brought his gun through the retreat unscathed. The award to Sgt Salter was some acknowledgement for the party left behind at Vaulx–Vraucourt. All these were awarded the Military Medal. Sgt-Major Spratley received a bar to his DCM[20]. This award was not too well received. The BSM was a decent enough fellow but it was felt that even if he had performed conspicuous deeds of valour during the retreat he had never once visited the battery position while we were on the Salient nor would he have been at Vaulx at all but for its apparent safety. Now that some sort of order had been re-established he again took up his station with the horses nor did the battery position see him again until after the armistice. Strangely enough the officers received no recognition. This was a pity for Lt Lakin was with the infantry for a fortnight and did some remarkably good work finding targets for the whole brigade. Lt Saville was a great help to the wounded while Capt Fletcher ran the BC post and from there practically controlled the fighting of the battery for Major Warren concerned himself but little with the science of gunnery.

Many of the battery personnel were highly indignant that Major Warren did not receive a posthumous award. This was particularly true of the regular soldiers from India who formed the nucleus and who would constantly refer to the gallant man who gave his life leading the guns into action.

---

1   The war diary entry on 20 April notes "17 Military Medals and one bar awarded to batteries and Brigade sig sub-section for gallantry and devotion to duty 21st/30th April". The month was recorded incorrectly.

2   This term appears to mean loafing or being idle.

3   War diary (WO95/225 48 Brigade RGA) states 'Batteries moved to west of Sapignies'.

4   56351 Gnr Frederick Charles Clinch, aged 27, son of Henry James and Sarah Ann Clinch, of 4, Coleraine Cottages, Fortis Green Rd., East Finchley, London; husband of Grace Evelyn Philbey (formerly Clinch), of 189, Westbury Avenue, Wood Green, London. Killed in action 23 March 1918. Commemorated on the Arras Memorial to the Missing. His first theatre of war is shown on his medal index card as Egypt from 29 December 1915.

5   98039 Gnr Isaac Sandiford, aged 23, husband of Clara E. Sandiford, of 21, Devon St., Fishpool, Bury. Killed in action 23 March 1918. Commemorated on the Arras Memorial to the Missing. He had previously served in 239 Siege Battery.

6   2/Lt William Fortescue Armstrong. He had served pre-war in India.

7   Royal Military Police.

8   There had been a desire to leave part of the battlefield as a permanent memorial but this idea was overturned in due course as the land was required again for agriculture. Consequently, a few small areas such as Newfoundland Memorial Park remain giving the visitor some idea of the battle-scarred landscape.

9   Royal Engineers.

10   29558 Sgt Eugene Norman MM.

11   Various emblems were used on transport and on uniforms to enable identification of the unit. The elephant was a reminder that this battery had served in India and had used elephants to pull the guns. The pamphlet giving a brief history of the battery, drafted by Hall towards the end of the war, included an escutcheon depicting an elephant and a bullock.

12   Bienvillers-au-Bois.

13 The Brigade war diary (WO95/225 48 Brigade RGA) recorded on 28 March 'Major Warren of 81 SB seriously wounded in the chest. His horse being killed under him'. A supplement to the war diary then records 'Major Warren badly wounded leading a gun into position in sunken road in E.16.a.6.4'.

14 Major W. E. Warren 81 Siege Battery, Royal Garrison Artillery. Died of wounds 29 March 1918, buried at Gezaincourt Communal Cemetery Extension, plot 2, row H, grave 23.

15 Casualties identified on this day are 153680 Gnr Alfred G. Dowthwaite, Husband of E. N. Dowthwaite, of 9, Chatfield Rd., West Croydon, buried in Bienvillers Military Cemetery, plot 10, row A, grave 9; and 87077 Gnr W. Harper, husband of Mrs S.A. Harper of 1/36, New John Street West, Birmingham plot 20, row C, grave 14.

16 The Brigade war diary (WO95/225 48 Brigade RGA) states that the battery position was at E.16.a.75.20 (sheet 57d 1:20,000). The battery fired 100 rounds that day and 'knocked out an enemy gun at map reference L.26.a.

17 The driving band is a band of copper at the base of the shell which is forced into the rifling in the barrel of a gun and thus forms a tight seal so that the full force of the propellant is used to send the shell out of the barrel.

18 This award appeared in the London Gazette on 12 July 1918 p.8307.

19 158689 Gnr David H. Shanks MM.

20 Distinguished Conduct Medal. 27379 BSM H.F. Spratley's DCM was published in the London Gazette on 28 January 1918 p1407.

CHAPTER 21

THE ARRIVAL OF MAJOR BENNETT

D*uring April the line was steadied and the German advance halted. In their new position the battery spend day after day shelling enemy transport, gun positions and other targets spotted by aeroplanes and Forward Observation Officers. Gnr Hall now had an opportunity to act as BCA but this was short lived as a consequence of a very serious failing by a Bombardier – taking water for consumption from a shell hole polluted with gas. In time this would provide Hall with his material for his next chapter.*

A few days after our arrival at Hannescamps the front quieted down considerably and the enemy changed his attention to other directions. Corps headquarters returned and the direct link between the battery and the infantry was severed. Mr Lakin returned to us again. The Royal Engineers oriented the position and gave us a new planchette board (it was found that our rough and ready method of laying out Lines of Fire during the retreat was surprisingly accurate) dug-outs were cleaned, reliefs fixed up and we returned to normal again. Incidentally Bush and I both received promotion, he to Corporal and I to Acting Bombardier. Under Capt Fletcher's control we seemed to go straight back to the conditions that had prevailed at Ypres, alternate spells at battery and rear billets, a four gun battery, reasonably sound BC Post and small shelters for the detachments on duty. Vaulx, with its complacent make belief security while living on the edge of a volcano, remained only as a memory.

We had not been at Hannescamps very long before we found the BC Post uncomfortable crowded at night and it was arranged that one should sleep alternate nights at the Horse Lines at Bienvillers while the other remained on duty. But on Bienvillers all the reforms associated with Major Warren had gone by default. The drivers had taken over what had been a 1916 battery position with its covered gun emplacement and elaborate system of dug-outs connected by trenches. But the head covering had collapsed and the dug-outs were foul smelling and half full of water. The drivers being first to arrive had appropriated the best of the shelters and when I arrived a party of Signallers were baling out four feet of water from a big dug-out where they intended spending the night. I would willingly have joined them but there was positively no room. Moreover Bush had told me that Driver Crankshaw[1] the battery tailor had bagged a good dug-out which I could share. I found Crankshaw who showed me with some pride his new habitation. He must have been easily satisfied. An old cartridge recess alongside a fallen gun pit was all he had managed to secure. At best the recess had been only three feet high and now the supports on one side had fallen in while the rotten wooden posts covered with large fungoid growths that supported the other threatened to follow suit at any moment, the floor was uneven and covered with an evil smelling mould which even now was dropping from the roof. Most undesirable quarters which I was glad to leave the following morning.

On my return to the battery I informed Capt Fletcher of the difficulty in obtaining accommodation at the Horse Lines and suggested that I might be allowed to remain at Hannescamps. If there were no room in the BC Post I had no doubt that I could find a billet in the village itself. The easy going Captain readily gave his consent so searching out young Perry we two set out to find suitable apartments. We were soon successful. An isolated house stood almost opposite the crucifix. It had been occupied by civilians prior to the attack but when the enemy shelled the village the upper part had suffered considerably. What mattered most to us was that the house had a substantial cellar in which a number of trestle beds had been erected while some genius had removed the kitchen stove to a new position in the centre. This seemed to be the very place. We told some Signallers of our find and half a dozen of us appropriated the house on the spot. Incidentally the whole village had been pillaged before our arrival and the house itself had been cleaned right out. There was a trim little garden and we always took care to shut the gate before leaving. The original orchard adjoining the house had been destroyed early in the war but after the 1917 evacuation had been replanted with fruit trees which still bore tags giving the name of the English donor. These trees in turn were also destroyed.

On the evening of April 4 I was off duty but waited at the BC Post for the rum issue before retiring to my new quarters for the night. When this arrived I had my own ration and Perry and A/M^2 Thomas who were teetotallers also gave me theirs. My speech soon betrayed the effects of the fiery spirit and Capt Fletcher an inveterate practical joker now saw an opportunity of improving matters by insisting on my having a further large issue before he would let me go. Then bidding me good-night he watched me staggering down the sunken road to my billet. When I arrived Perry and Thomas had already turned in but the potent liquor was now having its full effect and I point blank refused to retire without supper. I remembered that a company of the Tank Corps had made a cache of stores about a mile away and to this I directed my uneasy footsteps. Then in a manner worthy of a better cause I crawled on my stomach eluded the guard in the darkness and emerged with a large piece of bacon and a seven pound tin of biscuits. I reached home safely without being detected, roused my protesting colleagues and proceeded to fry the bacon. We had a glorious meal, then flinging my gas mask to one end of the cellar and my tin hat to the other I threw myself on my bunk as happy as a king.

The next think I remember was a terrific nightmare. I was running down a street in Sheffield which the enemy was bombarding with terrible force. Familiar buildings to the right and left were falling like cards. Then I awoke with a splitting headache and realised the cause of the nightmare. The enemy were shelling the village and the battery position. There were now a dozen men in the cellar mostly passing infantry who had dived in for shelter. Everyone looked anxious. I tried to pull myself together. Shells were falling rapidly, heavy ones too by the sound of things. I recovered my steel helmet and groped for my gas-mask but my brain was still hazy. The cellar was in darkness for the blast had extinguished the candles and our extra visitors made movement difficult. At that moment a heavy gas shell burst right in the stairway bringing down a heavy load of masonry and two stone steps and filling the cellar with its noxious fumes. Someone cried *"Gas"* and respirators were donned. Mine however was the far end of the room where I had flung it the night before. The shock sobered me instantly and I remembered that a good way to clear a room of gas was to light a fire. Some spare cartridges were handy and there was plenty of wood available. In a few minutes the fire was blazing merrily. Soon the atmosphere was clear, respirators were removed and then and only then did I succeed in finding my own. Two of the party were badly gassed although they were well away from the shell and had donned their masks at the first alarm while I, who was unprotected and practically received the full force of the burst in my face felt none the worse. The only explanation for this apparent miracle I can give that I had an excellent constitution and was too full of rum to take hurt.

The bombardment started at 5am and lasted until 11. At least eighteen guns were firing on the battery position alone and 74mm and 4.2cm guns equivalent to our eighteen pounder and sixty pounder guns besides 5.9 inch howitzers were employed using a mixture of shrapnel, high explosive and gas. At least two thousand rounds of enfilading fire must have fallen in the vicinity of that narrow lane. The outcome of this destructive shoot was that three out of our four guns were damaged although one was capable of repair locally, shells were scattered all over the place and many boxes of cartridges set on fire. But most remarkable of all was that, although the gun detachments had no more cover than the flimsy corrugated iron shelters dug into the banks of the sunken road into which at least half the shells must have fallen, the only casualties sustained up to now were the two men gassed in my cellar.[3]

I say up to now that is up to 11am when the bombardment ceased and I made my way to the BC Post. The Gun Captains, too, went to the post to report the good luck of their crews to Capt Fletcher. But we were congratulating ourselves a bit too early for the enemy sent over a final burst of shot wounding in the hands two of the sergeants who were standing in the doorway. The wounds were not serious. Sgt Norman's luck still held but he staggered across the planchette board covering the map with blood which seemed to upset Cpl Bush more than the bombardment. The wounds were dressed and the injured men taken to the First Aid Post and now, the firing having stopped, the cook set to work to brew tea, a good strong pint of which restored our confidence.

Now the worst was over ill effects began to be felt. One of the officers had certainly taken a good dose of gas on his chest. Bush looked particularly seedy and Capt Fletcher suggested he should go to the Horse Lines for a few days' rest. At first Bush protested, he had been at the battery so long, Hall was only new to the job and so on. But Bombardier Hall as I now was felt full of confidence and was only too eager to take full charge of the BC Post so Cpl Bush with a last fond look at the beautiful new planchette board now alas desecrated with blood at last consented to go.

No sooner was he away that I started clearing up the post. I fixed a fresh map on the planchette board and took over Cpl Bush's bunk fetching my kit from the cellar. Now at last I had attained my ambition, I was Battery Commander's Assistant in full charge.

Capt Fletcher went out to survey the damage. The Sergeant-Artificer set to work on the gun that he was able to repair and a squad of men under Bdr Perry started separating the whole from the damaged shells. Two teams were ordered to remove the broken guns to ordnance as soon as it was dark. A belated dinner and all was well.

At three o'clock I was standing at the door of the BC Post when I saw an officer approaching. He had apparently been unnoticed by Bdr Perry's party at work sorting the shells down the sunken road and as he drew near I saluted him in a rather perfunctory manner. *"Is this 81 Siege Battery?"* he enquired. *"Yes, sir,"* I replied. *"My name is Bennett and I have been posted here,"* was the quiet rejoinder. I turned indoors, *"Capt Fletcher,"* I exclaimed horrified, *"the CO"*. Capt Fletcher bustled out of the BC Post and in a stentorian voice gave the command *"Battery, attention"*, while he saluted the newcomer. *"All right, all right, stand easy,"* came the reply and, the salute returned, the new Major followed Capt Fletcher inside the post.

In this unobtrusive manner did Major Bennett[4] take over command of his battery. Once inside the BC Post the Major was more at home. He shook hands all round not forgetting the telephonist on duty and myself and said that he hoped we would all get on well together. Capt Fletcher then suggested whisky and was obviously pleased when his offer was accepted; at any rate the new CO was not a teetotaller.

Over drinks Major Bennett referred to the morning's shelling and congratulated us on our escape. Then he got down to business and we quickly realised that here was a totally different type of CO from Major Warren. First and foremost Major Bennett was a businessman, one of the new army, not one whit did he care for tradition and no recruit detested ceremonial more than he. In private life he had been a consultant engineer from Nottingham and so seriously had he taken his training that he had been retained for some time at Lydd as an instructor of gunnery. At his own request he had been released for overseas service and had served as Captain with another battery before being posted to us. In appearance he was tall and dark of grave demeanour and about thirty five years of age.

To me he had much to say. How I worked out the targets,[5] what were the Lines of Fire for the guns, how the position had been oriented and so on. Capt Fletcher looked anxious and probably regretted having sent Bush to the Horse Lines. I was delighted at the opportunity to expand myself and the Captain could not say I had let him down. It was only later revealed that the senior BCA was sick at Bienvillers.

The following day the brigade chaplain visited the new Major and suggested that a religious service would not be out of place. Major Bennett agreed and the BC Post was cleared as far as possible. We were admitted a dozen at a time and rather surprisingly the Padre went straight on with a service of Holy Communion. I am unable to comment on the doctrinal aspect of the situation but can only state that all were invited, all participated and I am certain all benefited. We had just escaped annihilation by a miracle and presumably the Padre thought this justified administering the sacrament.

And now Major Bennett got to work. His first action was to condemn the battery position and rightly so for the guns should never have been placed in a lane that could be enfiladed by the enemy's guns. He surveyed the limited area at his disposal and decided to move the guns to an open field to the rear of the village. After considerable trouble he obtained a supply of timber and corrugated iron and set all hands to prepare platforms for the howitzers and shelters for themselves. By April 12 the new position was finished and the two sound guns moved across. Next evening the two damaged guns were returned from ordnance workshops as repaired and these were brought into position. All that remained was to shift the ammunition and a fatigue party under Bdr Perry completed the task in a few days. Incidentally the men nearly drove the unfortunate NCO to distraction and at night he would come to me for sympathy and advice as to how to control his riotous hands.

Major Bennett's judgment was sound for the new position was held until May 31 with comparatively few casualties although the village of Hannescamps itself was severely shelled, indeed it seemed to fall to pieces before our eyes and before we left it was nothing but a heap of ruins. Nevertheless the move was decidedly unpopular. Here were fifty men in an open field with a decidedly limited amount of building material at our disposal and only those who have experienced the construction of sleeping quarters, BC Post, telephone exchange, cookhouse etc all from the virgin soil can realise the amount of labour entailed and it is not to be wondered that many would have preferred living in the cellars of the rapidly disappearing village dangerous though it be. But this was strictly forbidden. But Major Bennett incurred the dislike of the men, particularly the regulars, because he had dared to criticise his predecessor's selection of the first position. The new CO expressed his opinion on this pretty freely in front of men and this greatly embittered many of them. Since his death Major Warren had worn a martyr's crown and who was this interloper to dispute the wisdom of the dead man's choice. I verily believe many would have preferred to have stayed in the sunken road until they had all been killed merely to vindicate the memory of the fallen hero. It was pointed out that Major Warren had met his death on horseback like a soldier whereas the new CO had arrived at the battery on foot looking like a bloody commercial traveller. The fact that he had in fact been a consulting engineer did not endear him to the troops.

Neither did Major Bennett's subsequent behaviour enhance his popularity. He visited the Horse Lines at Bienvillers and condemned them as insanitary and much too near the line thereby exposing man and beast to unnecessary risk. He found infinitely better accommodation at Souastre a village where a few civilians were still living, where billets in houses could be obtained for the men and where the animals could be sheltered in some measure from the elements. Here again his orders were met with grumblings. The old cry was raised that what was good enough for Major Warren ought to be good enough for his successor.

But the greatest surprise of all came when Major Bennett announced his intention of living at the battery position. This was disconcerting news to officers and men alike. Previously the Officers' Mess had always been located at rear billets and officers had a daily rota for battery duty the CO restricting himself to occasional visits. It was plain that the new CO intended taking charge of the firing himself. Capt Fletcher was sent to Souastre on the grounds that he could do with a rest and here in one of the village houses the second in command set up the Officers' Mess while his chief dined off Maconochies in the little dug out communicating with the BC Post. Naturally the subalterns objected to being left in the cold so Major Bennett allowed one in turn to stay with him at the battery while there was, of course, the Observation Post to be manned. Here the CO insisted on taking his turn with the other officers, a thing never dreamed of before. On such occasions Capt Fletcher would come up to take charge of the battery and would talk about old times; what a splendid man Major Bennett was, how efficient and so on but, whoever heard of a Battery Commander doing observation duty – there was something lost when Major Warren died.

The two CO's had one thing in common, their mutual dislike of Lt Page. Major Bennett's way with the unpopular officer was to keep him in perpetuity at the Horse Lines in fact he was designated officer i/c. This move had repercussions. The drivers were more than a match for Page but the thought that the CO regarded the Horse Lines as a dumping ground for unwanted officers resulted in a host of applications for transfer to the battery position. In particular Sgt Rolfe the senior NCO resented the lines being regarded as a scrounger's paradise as the CO was alleged to have said and was determined to take his place on the guns even if it meant losing his rank. Nothing so drastic happened but the sergeant took his place as No.1 on one of the guns and a Corporal whom Major Bennett had cause to censure over bad shooting was sent back to Souastre to replace him. Quite a number of NCO's, Gunners and even Signallers were sent to the Horse Lines at this stage. Major Bennett seemed to think that everyone should be as keen as himself at the post of honour and if anyone showed himself either incompetent or unwilling to do his damnest, well, the CO didn't want him near him – that was all. Never was such a chance of dodging the column yet such was the implication of disgrace that no one would willingly avail himself of the opportunity.

At the science of gunnery Major Bennett was without equal but one needed to work with him at the BC Post to appreciate his wonderful shooting. Particularly did he excel in aeroplane shoots.[6] Before a pre-arranged shoot Bush and I would calculate the line and range and also work out the combined factor (the relationship between the elevation and the line so that both could be corrected together). The CO would always check our figures (this was something new for us) and the guns would be laid ready for firing. The wireless operator would report that the aeroplane had called him up and was now flying towards the target. Once the airman had approached the vital spot he would swing due north and observe the target, then he would make his way westward and transmit his readings on a clock face arrangement and so circle back to the target to observe the next round. It was essential that the shells should burst on the target the precise moment that the aeroplane had arrived so the time of flight of the shells had to be taken into account. Aeroplane shoots always started with a salvo so that the airman should have no difficulty in identifying his battery. Then the guns would fire in turn, the corrections being applied immediately the observation had been received.

The order of firing would be thus: *"Battery stand by for a salvo – Salvo fire!"*. Major Bennett would always throw the salvo well over the target so that if things went according to plan the airman would be able to locate his shots. From the observation sent down the CO would then correct all the guns for line and throw the first single shot well short thus bracketing the target. The next round would be half way between the two points so if all went well the battery would be ranged in an incredibly short time. But it sometimes happened that one particular gun was obstinate. This might be due to the gun itself or to faulty work on the part of the crew. The Major seemed to have an uncanny knack of telling where the trouble lay. He would call to the duty officer *"Saville, go and check the lay on No. 3 gun,"* and sure enough he had diagnosed the fault. For bad gunnery he had no mercy and I have seen a sergeant removed from his post in the middle of a shoot and replaced by a junior NCO or even a Gunner. It was said that Major Bennett would forgive anything but bad shooting and that a man so long as he was efficient could do no wrong in his eyes.

His attempts to administer justice were ludicrous in the extreme for he invariably took the side of the prisoner and would cross examine the NCO bringing the charge with an energy worthy of defending counsel. When running a delinquent many NCO's are inclined to pomposity. With Major Bennett this was absolutely fatal and any mispronunciation or misapplication of an aspirate or the part of the accuser would provoke his ironic laughter. He would, however, never poke fun at the prisoner. He would usually conclude the case by awarding some trivial punishment such as one day's confinement to camp which meant precisely nothing or more likely an injunction to both parties not to be a pair of damned fools in future.

But such leniency brought no popularity to Major Bennett and those who benefited from it were the first to turn against him. After all the military crimes were relatively simple. A Corporal's order was disobeyed and the NCO placed the offender under arrest and ran him before the CO. Both parties expected the affair to be treated seriously and the fact that the CO gave no support to his subordinates in the maintenance of discipline while expecting his own orders to be obeyed implicitly brought no gratitude from the men and only contempt from the NCO's. The regular soldiers were particularly indignant at such behaviour which, accustomed as they were to army discipline they were quite unable to understand.

Beyond requiring certain calculations to be worked out in yards instead of the more rough and ready degrees and minutes and of amending the method of recording shoots Major Bennett made little alteration to the running of the BC Post. In due course Corpl Bush returned from the Horse Lines and was introduced to the new CO but by then my own position was well entrenched and I doubt whether the Major realised for some time that here was the senior BCA. Bush proved himself less adaptable than I over the changes that were introduced and was inclined to argue when he would be pulled up sharply by his superior officer. The new BC Post was very small so Bush and I spent the nights alternately at Souastre where comfortable billets in a cellar had been obtained for us. Soon the firing slackened down so much as to allow us to spend alternate days away from the battery. We had earned the CO's confidence and enjoyed it right to the end obtaining many privileges thereby.

With regards to the sergeants and Corporals in charge of the guns things were rather different. Major Bennett never quite trusted his Gun Captains and took as much responsibility away from them as he could. In night firing it had been the practice to give the targets to the Gun Captains with instructions to arrange the shoots among themselves. This practice was terminated. A night programme was arranged in the BC Post and it was the duty of Bush or myself to call out the detachments at the stipulated times and to see that the guns were properly fired. All gun corrections were performed by us and the final figures given to the guns. Thus we could no longer say *"drop 20 minutes"* but would give out the actual elevation on each occasion so that there would be no excuse for any wrong setting of the cyclonometers. Later on though not in this position, we fixed aiming points for the guns instead of allowing the sergeants to pick their own.

This encroachment into the preservers of the Gun Captains coupled as it was by the officers frequently checking the gun sights was very much resented and a good deal of the ill feeling was reflected on the two BCA's. I found that when at rest at Souastre I was no longer welcome in the men's company. On the other hand, although I might make a fourth hand at cards when at the BC Post, I was not one with the officers. Bush with his condescending ways was no real companion and so I developed a feeling of isolation which was retained right to the end.

Towards the end of April two more guns were supplied and again we became a six gun battery. The additional guns added to the CO's responsibility and Major Bennett informed the BCA's that we must be prepared to spend the whole of our time with the guns and forego our excursions to Souastre. This seemed no great hardship.

It was now felt that something ought to be done about the BC Post. The original building was very small and afforded but little protection. Matters were brought to a head when the Germans neatly bracketed the post, dropping a heavy shell five yards in front followed by another a similar distance in rear of the place. I was on duty at the time and agreed with Major Bennett that we ought to make ourselves more secure. A mound of earth some six feet high was discovered a little distance away but within hailing distance of the guns. The

CO thought that if we could construct a new post underneath the mound the additional weight of soil would afford some protection for us. Ignoring the claims of the junior NCO's to command a working party the CO enquired personally, if any of the Gunners had been a miner in civilian life and, one of them stepping forward, took him to the site and asked for his advice. Delighted with this opportunity of displaying his superior knowledge, the ex-miner demonstrated how a first-rate dug-out could be constructed and stated how much timber would be required. The necessary stores obtained the Gunner and three colleagues of his own choosing were given a free hand. Soon they had dug a trench and were burrowing under the mount. In a few days the new BC Post was ready for occupation.

It was in the latter stages that I discovered that Bush had stolen a march on me and in the absence of the CO at the Observation Post had arranged for one bunk only to be supplied for the use of the BCA's. As there were now supposed to be the two of us always on duty this meant that I as junior was to be crowded out of the BC Post at night. Bush and I had a very serious quarrel over this attempt to exclude me from the BC Post. To do him justice I do not think the idea of the extra security of the post ever entered into his head. It was merely that he never forgave me for the favourable impression I had created with the new CO during Bush's absence at Souastre and was determined to take very step to assert his superior rank.

But with all our petty jealousies we soon realised that we might have to join forces to meet other rivals. Reinforcements were now arriving in large numbers and all these were not trained as Gunners. The action of the base in sending up Signallers and Observers in lieu of Gunners caused many heart burnings both to the reinforcements themselves and to the old hands. The newcomers naturally enough expected employment at the jobs for which they were trained but no vacancies existed and they were perforce drafted to the guns, a job for which they had little aptitude and where their unskilful attempts met with the derision I knew only too well. Several new Signallers were now manning the guns and it was noticed that two of the reinforcements, a Corporal and a Gunner wore the laurel wreath and the 'O' of the Observer. The Gunner, I never knew his name, did not trouble us for long. Obviously unwell on arrival, he at once reported sick and in a short time was away again down the line.

Corporal Tebbs[7] was a more serious proposition. This NCO had been the regular BCA of another battery and had been casualtied. An elderly man, of good address but not particularly robust he was obviously better fitted for work in the BC Post than to take charge of a gun which was his first job in 81 Battery. His detachment was a tough lot and at first thought Tebbs a fair sport but he had not been a house agent for nothing and soon talked them round. While he acted as Gun Captain there was not a more popular NCO in the battery and his crew gladly taught him how to fight the gun.

So Bush and I were able to breathe again. Perry was making the most of his job on the ammunition and could no longer be regarded as a competitor, the unknown Gunner had left the battery, while Corpl Tebbs seemed to be thoroughly enjoying himself on the guns. Meanwhile we expected our acting ranks to be confirmed at any time, while for myself the main thing was that I was now in receipt of proficiency pay as an Observer. The cash benefit 4½d a day was trifling, what meant most to me was that my position as a BCA was acknowledged.

At the beginning of May it was decided to divide the battery. It was but rarely all six guns engaged the same target, the usual practice being for four guns to conduct a pre-arranged shoot leaving the other two to engage any odd targets that showed up. At this time some enemy batteries in the vicinity of Logest Wood were giving trouble. They could not be effectively countered from Hannescamps and accordingly it was decided to send a couple of guns forward to Essarts about a mile ahead for this purpose.

Work started at Essarts on May 2 and the position was ready for occupation two days later. Then came the question of allocating staff. Mr Morkill a most popular young officer was to take charge of the advanced section and I was delighted to learn that I was to accompany him as BCA. Bush was quite welcome to the new BC Post at Hannescamps. I should now have a BC Post of my own. The fact that the position at Essarts was almost in line with the support trenches worried me not in the least.

Now that we were to part company Bush and I discovered what excellent fellows we were. Bush gave me plenty of tips on running the BC Post all of which I took seriously determined nevertheless to follow my own inclination. The two guns were to be advanced on the late evening of May 5. Bush was off duty the previous night and he proffered to bring with him on his return sufficient to provide a little supper to celebrate the occasion. With this he left me full of confidence for the future.

Soon after he had gone (May 4) the dispatch rider arrived with the night programme. It transpired that a rather important shoot was timed to start at 5am and finish at 7am the following morning. Our business was to sweep a certain road which was believed to carry a lot of early morning traffic. It was ordered that section salvos (two guns at once) should be fired at two minute intervals but in no particular sequence so that the enemy should not be able to tell where the next round would fall. Major Bennett decided that the fire must be controlled by the BCA that is by myself. Accordingly I took up my stand behind the guns and started timing the shoot. This business of giving orders to the guns was known as "fighting the battery" but it did not seem particularly glorious that spring morning when, watch in hand I shouted directions *"Left Section, next – one minute to go – stand by left – salvo fire – Right Section now,"* and so on. It was a very cold morning and breakfast would not be ready until 7.30. The Gunners when not actually working were stamping their feet trying to keep warm. At last a wisp of smoke showed that the cook was about but breakfast was still a long way off.

At 6am Major Bennett appeared on the scene and, satisfied that the shoot was proceeding according to programme, left the position to take a spell of duty at the Observation Post.

Shortly afterwards there were signs of activity from the direction of the dug-out which the RAF wireless operator and his mate occupied in company with Reg Perry and about 6.30 Perry himself appeared with a dixie of boiling hot cocoa. *"I thought it might be a bit cold up there,"* he said handing me the drink. Good old Perry, always so considerate. I took a sip but it was too hot just now. I lay down the dixie while I went on giving orders. A few minutes later I took another drink. The cocoa was still hot and had a bitter unpleasant taste. Perhaps the cocoa-au-lait was a bit off but I had drunk worse things and I was chilled to the bone. Without more ado I drained the dixie.

By 7am the last salvo had been fired and the guns were being sponged out. I made my way to the BC Post but as I passed the wireless dug-out was rather surprised to find no one in sight. When breakfast came round I was in no mood to enjoy it, my throat and stomach seemed aflame and the hot tea seemed only to aggravate the pain. I felt now that I had been the victim of some particularly stupid practical joke particularly as there was no sign of Perry and his companions. At 10 am A/M Thomas put his head in the BC Post door and called out *"I say, Hall, did you find anything wrong with the cocoa this morning?"* but the moment I saw his face I saw that this was no practical joke.

Explanations followed. Walters the relief operator and Perry were writhing in agony in their bunks. Thomas was in little better plight. Perry had it seemed, obtained a large tin of Nestles Cocoa-au-lait, a great favourite of the troops at that time. Knowing that I had been on duty since 5 o'clock and that the wireless men were early risers he thought that a hot drink would be acceptable to us and had accordingly prepared the beverage of which all four of us had partaken. Nothing had been added to the mixture but tinned food had been known to be tainted. Then something prompted me to probe deeper into the matter. *"Where did you get the water?"* I asked. *"Out of the shell-hole at the back of the BC Post,"* came the astonishing reply. *"Not the big one?"* I exclaimed. *"Yes. It's all right isn't it?"* he answered between his groans. Thomas and I went to investigate but we knew what to expect. The shell hole was about six feet in diameter and half full of dark green water for it had been raining recently. To confirm our suspicion of the cause of the discolouration the lower portion of an exploded gas shell was visible through the scum its foul contents still contaminating the water. How anyone in their sane senses could have obtained drinking water from such a source is still beyond my comprehension but the fact remained that we four had between us imbibed a couple of pints of that liquid poison.

Strange enough neither Perry nor Walters had noticed anything wrong with the cocoa. Thomas had a faint suspicion at the time but thought the preparation might not have been up to standard. There was only one thing to do. Capt Fletcher must be informed and at once. I wished it had been any other officer for the Captain was of the old school and apt to be regimental. Had it not been Major Bennett's day for the OP things might have been easier.

Capt Fletcher had a long look at Perry and Walters who were certainly in a terrible state, tossing about in their bunks and groaning in agony. Nothing was concealed and before us all Reginald Perry told the officer where he had obtained the water and accepted full responsibility for the unfortunate affair. In view of what transpired later this proved to be of the utmost importance. Capt Fletcher then went with me to inspect the shell hole. When he saw the state of the water he exclaimed, *"The bloody fool"*. Then we went back to the BC Post.

The Captain was most upset. *"This is a damned serious business, you know Hall,"* he said, *"they'll be a hell of a row about."* But row or no row it was obvious that Perry and Walters must receive medical attention without delay and Capt Fletcher gave orders for them to be rushed to the First Aid Post. *"Tell them everything,"* he ordered, *"it's your only chance."* Thomas and I were given the option of accompanying them but we elected to remain at the battery to see if local treatment was of any avail. The Captain gave us each a stiff glass of whisky but that did nothing to ease the pain. Then he decided we must try to get rid of the poison. Hot water and salt were procured and so until 2pm we tried to vomit the wretched stuff but all in vain.

Dinner had at first no appeal but at length some instinct prompted me to go to the cook house in search of fat which I thought might ease the pain. The cook at that time was by no means a star artist and had produced a particularly revolting stew of which now only the dregs remained. In the ordinary way I should probably foregone the meal but on this occasion seized with alacrity the despised portions of fat pork and the bacon rind which the cook imagined improved the flavour of the stew. The awful stuff seemed to ease my throat considerably and I thought that after all I might be able to stay in the battery.

But by 3pm Thomas had completely collapsed and Capt Fletcher feeling that he could no longer accept the responsibility of having two poisoned men on his hands ordered us both to the Field Ambulance so in spite of our protests we were handed over to the RAMC.

---

1 84930 Dvr David Crankshaw from Blackburn. Previously served in 377 Siege Battery.

2 Air Mechanic.

3 The war diary (WO95/225 48 Brigade RGA) confirmed Hall's account and states that a large percentage of the German shells were gas. This bombardment occurred on 5 April between 5.30 and 11.30am.

4 Major W.D. Bennett took command on 6 April having been posted from 303 Siege Battery.

5 The church at Puisieux was used by 81 Siege Battery for registration.

6 One of the main functions of the Royal Flying Corps (later, the RAF) was to spot targets for the artillery.

7 119646 Cpl Arthur John Tebbs (known as John) from Southwick. Observer, aged 37. Went to France and Flanders 17 March 1917 with 278 Siege Battery and was transferred to 81 Siege Battery on 29 April 1918.

CHAPTER 22
THE GAS-POISONING AFFAIR

The gas poisoning incident was a very serious matter but we have no record of the outcome for Perry the perpetrator. Contrary to expectations when reading Gnr Hall's account, he came out of the affair with another wound stripe on his sleeve. On returning to his battery it was spending a quiet period at rest up to late June when 81 Siege Battery moved forward again.

At the Field Ambulance our arrival was not unexpected. *"There were two more of your chaps here this morning,"* we were told, *"and they were in a bad way too."* The Medical Officer took our temperature and decided that we were urgent cases. Red labels to that effect were tied on our stretchers. Even in our condition we were conscious of our priority over the ordinary wounded. More disconcerting was the close examination of our eyes and when the MO directed that they were to be bandaged we felt that we were in trouble indeed. So our eyes were bathed and a heavy bandage applied. Then at length we felt our stretchers lifted on to the motor ambulance and we were carried away to the Casualty Clearing Station. And then came a wonderful sense of peace. Of course I could see nothing but by the breeze on my face I could tell that the ambulance doors had been left open. No longer did I feel apprehension for the future and the fact that my eyesight might be affected troubled me not at all. Life had much in store for me.

The Casualty Clearing Station at Doullens was reached by 7pm (May 5). It had been a busy day for them and many gas cases had been admitted. It is possible that we might have gone through with the others for the Medical Officer in attendance queried *"Gas?"* We deemed it advisable however to make a statement for after all the poison was still in our system. On this the doctor segregated us from the rest.

It was while we were waiting allocation to a ward that the sickly stew did its work and I began to vomit copiously. Blankets and floor were in a terrible state. I ventured to apologise but the RAMC orderly put me at ease. *"Never mind, lad,"* he said, *"that'll do you a world of good,"* and he hurried off to tell the doctor. The MO returned with him. *"That's splendid, boy,"* he said examining the vomit. *"That's yellow cross stuff you've been drinking."* And so I realised that I had been poisoned by the dreaded mustard gas the most deadly used in the war.

After the sickness I felt a good deal better and presently Thomas and I were carried to the ward, undressed and put into bed alongside the very seedy looking Perry and Walters. I was the only one who had vomited and consequently cleared my system of the foreign matter comparatively early. The other three seemed to be in great pain. So much better did I feel that I asked if I might possibly be returned to my unit but the MO would not hear of it, possibly wishing to keep us together in case of further developments. He paid particular attention to our story and told us what we already knew, that drinking shell hole water was an offence. *"I'll make it as easy as I can for you,"* he said and promptly altered the diagnosis on our cards to read 'gastroenteritis'. This might have stood us in good stead had we been able to return to the battery.

Unfortunately Perry and Walters made but little progress and their temperature charts presented an alarming appearance. For myself my temperature remained well below normal and I was told I must remain in bed until it rose again. The nurses were very good to us although we were twitted a bit about being the *"boys who have been trying to poison themselves"*.

On May 7 the Medical Officer decided that we had not made sufficient progress to justify our retention at the CCS and that we must be transferred to a base hospital. We all begged to be allowed to remain a little longer so that we could re-join our unit. The MO though sympathetic was obdurate. We must be evacuated on the morrow. The ambulance train left at 1pm May 8 and this time we travelled as "first class passengers" as the saying went, that is we were carried on stretchers. An MO travelled on the train and soon after we started he examined all the serious cases to see who required attention en route. When our turn came he examined our cards and pressed for further details. Plainly he was not satisfied with the diagnosis.

Bdr Perry spoke up and again accepted full responsibility for the unfortunate business. Perry to do him credit was most distressed about the business and was insistent that nothing should be concealed. At every stage when he told his tale he insisted that his companions were quite blameless. On this occasion we were all closely questioned together. It appeared that Thomas had made the fire while Perry went in search of water. What made Perry's lapse more inexplicable was that there was plenty of pure water in the battery position, the water tanks having been filled up the night before and no restrictions placed on their use. The MO listened attentively and then gave his decision. We were all placed under open arrest and our cards amended to read *"Gas poisoning caused through drinking water from contaminated shell-holes"*. Perry completely broke down at this, not for himself but for the trouble he had caused to others. The MO though sympathetic explained that he had no alternative. It was his job to give the Base Hospital all the information possible in order to assist them in the treatment and once the origin of the poison was disclosed arrest must follow as a matter of course. He pointed out that the arrest would not take place until we had re-joined our unit when Perry's statement would exonerate the rest of us. With this he passed on.

The ambulance train arrived outside the 10 General Hospital at Rouen in the small hours of May 9 and we were promptly taken to a ward and put into bed. Later in the day we were examined. I was by far the best case; the others seemed to be making no progress while Perry, possibly on account of mental disturbance, had weakened considerably. For the next three days I was allowed out of bed for a couple of hours. At first I felt very weak and my temperature kept consistently low. By the 12 May however it had returned to normal and on the 13 May I was marked fit for Convalescent Camp. Thomas was now on the road to recovery but the others were still in bed when I left and I learnt afterwards that their recovery was so protracted that they were eventually evacuated to England.

It was 8pm May 13 that I parted from my comrades never to see them again. I was fitted out in khaki and with a large company made my way to the Convalescent Camp.

At No.2 CC Rouen we were under canvas. Here I began to wonder how I stood as regards my rank for my appointment had not been confirmed when I left the battery and perhaps I should have removed my stripe. However I did not do so. The little Bombardier sounded pleased and I thought the assumed rank might allow me to negotiate the difficult passage through the Base and possibly ensure my return to 81 Siege Battery. This proved correct. I was put in charge of a tent with eleven soldiers of different regiments as companions.

May 14 was spent on physical drill, fatigues and the like but the treatment was harsh and the food indifferent. At night the canteen resounded with complaints; one expected some consideration in a Convalescent Camp but here we were treated like soldiers fit for active service. One Corporal in particular had given his orders in a most brutal manner. Threats were freely used; men compared notes and the conduct of the higher command at the time of the retreat was freely commented on. Such incidents as the way the Staff scuttled from Doullens received particularly attention. Plainly trouble was in the air.

The next day May 15 it was found from my medical record that I had not been inoculated since leaving England and was accordingly due for a second dose. I was inoculated there and then and allowed twenty-four hours for recovery. I heard harrowing tales of the men's treatment on parade, how they had been kept standing an unreasonable time and marched about until some had collapsed from sheer exhaustion and none were fit men and some recovering from severe wounds.

On May 16 the storm broke. There had it appeared been a number of Canadian soldiers on parade and one of their number had collapsed. Our friend, the Corporal (on the camp staff of course) had made some caustic remark and immediately the rest of the Canadians rushed towards him. This affected the others and almost at once the parade of several hundred men broke loose. In a few minutes the whole camp was in a state of mutiny. At the first rush the Corporal fled and was out of camp on his way to the town. The mob then went to the guard room, explanations followed and the guard joined in the revolt. Soon a body of 50 men were on their way down the hill after the unfortunate man. They had secured a rope and expressed their intention of hanging the Corporal. The sight of these grim men going forward on their terrible mission was memorable. They patrolled the streets, searched the estaminets and would I am convinced have wrecked their vengeance on the man had they found him. He managed to elude the lynching party however and at midnight they returned still carrying the noose.

In the camp pandemonium raged. Tents were pulled down and some buildings set on fire. The Camp Commandant, a Colonel, appeared but was met with howls of execration and beat a hasty retreat. The situation was at length saved by a young Canadian Captain. It was a long time before he could get a hearing but at last he succeeded. *"Now, you chaps,"* he shouted.

"What do you really want?" What did we want? Not very much. *"No early morning parades,"* went up the cry, surely not unreasonable for men just discharged from hospital. *"Better food – better treatment – sack the NCOs"* were other demands. The young Captain retired and after a time returned with the commandant's reply. These were simply that we should return to our tents. But things had gone too far for that, indeed pickets had been posted to prevent faint hearts giving way to such threats.

Then came the message that unless we would disperse peacefully troops would be obtained to dislodge us. *"Let 'em all come,"* we shouted and struck up the popular cry "Are we downhearted? No." It was a good thing that an attempt was not made to quell the disturbance by force for it was pretty certain the disaffection would have spread to others also the use of British troops against Canadians might have led to very serious repercussions. So the young Captain returned to inform the commandant of our defiance while the demonstration outside the officers' quarters continued.

It was now dark and lights had been extinguished by the rebels. Time after time the Captain appeared. He was always granted an audience and it was plain that his sympathies we with us. *"It's no good, boys, the Colonel won't give way,"* he informed us. *"Tell him to cancel the early morning parade, sir – we won't go back until he does – sack the NCOs"* and similar rejoinders were made and back again the Captain went to plead our cause.

At last the commandant weakened and as might be expected first of all sacrificed his subordinates. *"The Colonel wants to know who you want to get rid of,"* came the message. The Corporal who had been the cause of the trouble and about half a dozen others were named all subordinate NCO's who had abused their positions. The response was even better than we expected. The offenders would be dismissed forthwith and we learnt afterwards that this indeed was the case. The commandant vented his spleen on those who had served him and at a moment's notice the whole lot were packed off up the line. A message was sent through somehow to the Corporal who had bolted and was hiding in town that on no account was he to return to camp but go direct to his base who would send him up the line. This action would probably seal the fate of the NCO's. At some stage they would be certain to be recognised and the vengeance would follow.

Cheer after cheer greeted the report of the dismissals and now we were not surprised when the commandant capitulated on the other points. The early morning parade was cancelled and the other matters in dispute soon dealt with. Food – *"The Colonel is sorry that you have had to complain about the food – he will see the cook tomorrow"*. Medical attention – *"The Colonel will see that the Medical Officers do their duty in future"*. These were the last messages, *"And now, boys, you've got all you want, it's getting late, so go back to your tents"*. A few voices called out *"No victimisation"*. *"You know me, boys,"* came the reply, *"I'll see that there is no victimisation and now don't forget the parade 9 o'clock on the square."* Three hearty cheers were given for the Captain and *"For he's a jolly good fellow"* lustily rendered. The self-appointed intermediary certainly deserved the praise for the situation was as ugly as I have ever seen and Heaven knows where the disaffection might have spread had it not been checked. As it was no more damage had been done than a few burnt huts and broken windows while a number of tents had been struck to prevent waverers occupying them at the crucial moment.

Much must have been done after the camp had quietened down for on the morrow a first rate breakfast was ready for us and when we paraded at the respectable hour of 9am new faces were observed, fresh NCO's to replace those summarily dismissed. The Colonel was on parade but no reference was made to events of the night before. The usual orders were given but somehow the sting had gone from the words of command and they were promptly obeyed. It was noticed that those men obviously unfit were segregated and no longer expected to keep up with the others; physical drill was light as befits convalescents and rests more frequent – plainly the commandant was keeping his promises. Dinner too was perfectly satisfactory.

The real test came with the medical inspection. As usual we passed before a Medical Officer for his decision as to whether we were fit for the line. Previously this had been a most perfunctory affair but this time we had no cause for complaint. Every man was closely questioned as to his health, his temperature was taken and his heart tested. Finally he was asked if we felt well enough for further service and those who replied in the negative were allowed a further spell in the camp. Nevertheless there was a record number evacuated that day (May 17) and I myself joined the great majority who considered the new dispensation too good to last and felt that we would be well away from Rouen.

Those of us marked fit for service were removed to the camp of the cyclists corps a most dreary place. It was 4pm when we arrived and we spent a rather miserable night under canvas. In the morning we were segregated according to our different bases and I joined a group of artillerymen both Field and Garrison who were bound for Harfleur. This group left the cyclists camp at 7.45am May 18 and marched to Rue Verte station, Rouen, where we hung until 1 in the afternoon, then we entrained for Harfleur which we reached at 6pm.

At Harfleur the Garrison men parted company from the contingent of Field Artillery whose base was nearer the station than our own. As we marched past the RFA camp we were surprised to see the large number of infantrymen in occupation. Here then was confirmation of the rumours that had been current that casualties from the Field Artillery were being drafted into other regiments. Did a similar state of affairs exist in the RGA base? On this point however our minds were set at rest for when we reached our destination and were dismissed to our tents we learned that no such transfers had taken place from the RGA nor, so far as was known, any contemplated.

I was still a bit uneasy about my rank but I expected the question to be settled at the Base. Meantime I wore my chevron, also my Observer's badge and a wound stripe. I was addressed as Bdr Hall and put in charge of a tent containing eleven Gunners.

The following day (May 19) was Sunday. As I expected there was the usual 5.30am parade with the interminable waiting while the names of drafts were called out and after this a second parade when equipment was issued. After dinner we were free but could not leave the camp.

I fell into conversation with a Gunner in my tent an old sweat who had been through the base on several occasions and from him I leant that it was possible for NCO's though not Gunners to wangle a return to their own batteries. The proper course was to approach one of the office staff – a gratuity would usually have the desired effect. Having had experience of a good battery as well as a bad one I decided to try and return if at all possible to 81 Siege. I chose a quiet time there was only one NCO present in the Orderly Room. *"Well, Bombardier what can I do for you?"* he said. *"I am particularly anxious to return to my old battery, 81 Siege,"* I replied. *"Can anything be done?"* As I said this I laid a twenty franc note on the table (this represented four weeks' pay at the time). The note was immediately pocketed. *"You don't mind stopping here for a time until there is a draft?"* *"No."* *"All right then I'll see what can be done, what did you say was your battery?"* and the particulars were duly noted.

I remained at the base until June 1 and, while I was there, I saw not a few changes all for the better. Perhaps the riots at Rouen had repercussions even at Harfleur. The third day after my arrival the early morning parade for calling out drafts was cancelled and a simpler procedure adopted. An account of every man in each tent was now kept and the NCO in charge was warned overnight which of his Gunners were for draft in the morning. He was required to produce the men concerned or explain their absence, the others were allowed to slumber in peace. The system worked well. There were comings and goings among my men but those warned for draft never failed to turn up for the first parade, they were only too glad to get away.

As at Rouen I had the satisfaction of seeing some of the regular staff who had been at the Base since the beginning of the war summarily dismissed and sent up the line. One I remember particularly, a Bombardier who had so grossly abused his power that he was perhaps the most hated NCO in the regiment. It was he who, on my previous stay, had marched a hundred men in the rain so that he could address them while he was under cover. When I saw him on this occasion he was endeavouring to converse affably with a group of Gunners on the same draft as himself. But they were sullen and would have none of him. I am afraid he was in for a very rough time.

My stay at the Base although certainly easier than on the last occasion was by no means pleasant. Food still left much to be desired and the canteens were shockingly inadequate. We were not allowed out of camp and all our leisure time seemed to be taken up by queuing up in the Salvation Army hut for cups of tea. If served after a couple of hours we considered ourselves lucky. The NCO's seemed to have a better time than the Gunners and my rank real or assumed certainly excused me from some of the more unpleasant tasks. On May 27 the NCO at the Orderly Room told me privately that I was to return to my old battery in a few days' time. The stratagem had been successful.

On May 31 I was officially notified that I was for draft on the morrow. The customary tedious procedure was followed. Parade at 5.30am for roll call after which we got into full marching order and drew our rations for the journey and so we remained until 5pm (June 1) when we marched to Le Havre Maritime Station to the rousing strains of a military band. We were certainly in good time for the train which did not leave until 10pm.

Then followed the long journey up the line. Doullens had now become the railhead and we alighted at 8pm the next day (June 2). It was too late to sort us out so we were put in a rest camp for the night. This we left at noon (June 3) but only to proceed to the reinforcement depot a few yards away and here another night was spent.

The morning of June 4 was occupied in finding our respective destinations. When my turn came I was told I must first report to corps headquarters at the village of Authie someway up the river valley of the same name. Some twenty of us were sent forward in a lorry at noon and by 4pm we arrived at Authie. Here I was told that 81 Siege had pulled out of Hannescamps and were on rest at Authieule a village still further up the valley. There was no one else going in that direction, so I had better stay with them overnight and find my way up the valley next morning. I was accommodated in a Nissen hut and in the morning (June 5) after a snack breakfast I put on my equipment and set off by myself to locate the battery.

The Authie valley was pleasant enough and its landmarks only too familiar. I took my time and rested frequently. At length I came to Authieule. In a field a number of GS wagons were drawn up bearing the familiar recognition mark – the elephant. I soon found the Orderly Room and reported to Sgt-Major Spratley. *"Well you've come back Hall,"* he said as I handed in my papers. *"Yes, Sergeant-Major I've come back." "Well get to the cook house and get your dinner, I expect you can do with it. Then come back and see me again."* I needed no second telling and after four days of scratch meals did justice to the dixie of thick stew that I received from the cook. Then I went back to the Sergeant-Major.

When I re-joined Sgt-Major Spratley he enquired after my health and the progress of the other men. I told him that I understood that Perry and Walters had been evacuated to England. Then he asked me for my own account of the affair at Hannescamps and after I had given him a frank narration for I saw no reason for any concealment he said, *"Now, I suppose you know you're under arrest"*. I concurred and told him that I was prepared to face the music the sooner the better. *"Well we won't make it too hard for you,"* he replied and told me how the papers with the report of the Medical Officer on the ambulance train giving particulars of my arrest had preceded my arrival. *"You'll have to take those down,"* he said pointing to my chevrons. I was upset at this. *"So I'm to be punished before I am tried,"* I rejoined. *"Nothing of the kind."* It seemed that Bdr Lowe, the battery clerk had been dilatory in sending forward for confirmation the names of those promoted after the German offensive and that I had actually left the battery when the lists had been made up. Consequently my appointment had never been confirmed. Then came another point. Was I to go back to the guns? *"No,"* said the BSM *"Corporal Tebbs, he's our senior BCA now is running an Observer's school report to him."* With that I left the Sgt-Major.

The rank and file occupied a large barn and in one corner I found Corp Tebbs with Bush and some others. *"So you've come back,"* said Bush ungraciously. *"Yes, I've come back,"* I replied as I cast off my kit and awaited the next move. It was not until Tebbs was out of the way that I learnt how matters stood. Then Bush turned on me like a fury. It appeared that on the afternoon of May 5 he was enjoying a siesta at the Horse Lines. Everything had been arranged, he was coming to relieve me that evening while I was to take the two forward guns to Essarts. Then a telephone message came through, he was to go to Hannescamps at once as all the BC staff had been gassed. Once he had taken over it was realised that there was no BCA available for the forward position. Capt Fletcher had noticed a Corporal in possession of an Observer's badge who was serving on one of the guns. He sent for Corpl Tebbs, for that was his name, and finding him qualified in all respects, invited him to go to Essarts in my place. Unfortunately for Bush Corpl Tebbs was the senior NCO Bush maintained right to the end that Tebbs was incompetent. I think this was an exaggeration but he was certainly slow and easy going, no match for the virile, quick witted schoolmaster. He always seemed content to let others do most of the work yet in his quiet way took good care to see that his position was fully recognised. In civilian life he was a house agent from Brighton, an elderly bachelor with an inexhaustible fund of witty stories and he became a general favourite with officers and men alike. This was the man whom Corporal (or rather Acting Corporal) Bush must in future recognise as his superior officer – and Bush did not like playing second fiddle.

The forward position at Essarts turned out to be fiery and five serious casualties occurred in the first few days. As a result it was thought that Cpl Tebbs could do with an assistant. A Signaller, Gunner Frost, was accordingly admitted to the forward BC Post and receive instructions from Tebbs. As soon as he heard of this Bush at Hannescamps also called for help and the CO let him take for training a Welsh schoolteacher, Gunner Evans, who had recently arrived as a reinforcement. Major Bennett would have preferred another Signaller but Bush had pressed the claims of his fellow schoolteacher and the CO eventually agreed. Then as firing slackened down the Major decided that after all a Signaller should also be trained. This gave Bush another trainee Bryceson a young Scotsman. So with two Corporals and three trainees the Battery Commander had now certainly no shortage of assistants and it was not to be wondered that when I turned up like a bad penny I was not received into the happy family with any degree of enthusiasm.

It did not take me long to realise how matters stood. It was extremely unlikely that at the next position 4 BCA's would be required let alone 6. Young Bryceson was of no consequence. He seemed quite unable to grasp the elements of gunnery and, to tell the truth, no one made any endeavour to teach him. Soon afterwards he became an officer's servant. Frost had always his signalling to fall back on. Corpl Tebbs was quite indifferent as to what position he held. *"I've had some jolly times on the guns,"* he said, *"and don't mind going back among the boys. In any case,"* he continued, *"they can't take these away,"* pointing to his Corporal's stripes, *"and the pay's the same so why worry?"*

Bush, on the other hand, made it quite clear that in no circumstances would he relinquish his position. He made no attempt to conceal his contempt of Corpl Tebbs' capabilities and bragged incessantly of the work he had done at Ypres and during the retreat. Never did he give me credit for anything I may have done while working with him.

But from my point of view, the principal source of trouble lay with the newcomer Gunner Evans. With us two it was an immediate dislike which was to develop into an intense hatred which became patent to the whole battery. Welshmen can have a pretty bitter tongue but Evans was absolutely venomous. I gave as good as I got with the result that we could not be left together for five minutes without assailing one another with the bitterest vituperation. The bone of contention was of course too many BCA's. Bush after ventilating his own grievance at being second to Tebbs was inclined to be sympathetic towards me, spoke of the times we had at the BC Post and hinted that we might draw together again. This did not suit friend Evans who saw himself being superseded. *"Why the Hell did you come back?"* he once said. *"You'll have to go back on the guns, the Sergeant-Major should never have let you come with the staff,"* and it was he who suggested that the poisoning was a put up job to avoid my being sent to the forward position at Essarts. Evans moreover would appeal to Bush and I was only too well aware that the Corporal was turning against his old colleague and the two schoolteachers were conspiring to oust me from the staff. I never forgave Bush for this desertion and later on found plenty of opportunities of reminding him of it.

While at first I might have been willing to go back on the guns this opposition made me all the more determined to fight for my post on the BC staff. Some particularly caustic remark to the effect that Major Bennett never had any use for me sent me in search of the CO and disregarding all military discipline I presented myself at the door of the Officers' Mess with a request that Major Bennett should be good enough to see me. I was disappointed, Major Bennett had taken the opportunity of having a jaunt down the line for a few days but Lieut Morkill, an officer with whom I had always been on the most friendly terms came out at once. After returning my salute he shook my hand warmly, asked how I was, and expressed his delight at seeing me again. I told him of my unfortunate experiences, how I had lost my stripe, and hinted that certain influences were planning my removal from the BC staff. Mr Morkill was most indignant. He expressed his entire confidence in me and stated he would use all his influence to have me reinstated. *"Leave it to me,"* he said, *"I'll have a good talk to Major Bennett as soon as he returns."* He was as good as his word and every day until my trial he came to see me personally much to the chagrin of Bush and Evans. Sometimes he was accompanied by other officers. I felt now that I was putting up a pretty good show and that the first round was plainly in my favour.

True to his word the Sergeant-Major had given instructions that I was to be treated with consideration and Corpl Tebbs was a gentle enough jailer in all conscience. He urged me to take my place with the other BCA's as if nothing had happened but I would have none of this. If I was a prisoner I insisted on being treated as one. This meant one of the others had to stand guard over me. It also meant that Evans had to fetch all my meals from the cook-house a thing that enraged him intensely. In short I am afraid I nursed my grievances and made a nuisance of myself to the battery in general and the BC staff in particular. This state of affairs continued until June 8 when it was ordained that we should change billets again. Stores were packed, the guns limbered up and at 9pm we took to the road. This time six BCA's followed the limbered wagon all very unsociable and jealous of one another.

Shortly after midnight June 8/9 we arrived at our new quarters, a village a little further down the valley called Vauchelles-les-Authie. Here we took possession of a number of Nissen huts and were soon asleep. At breakfast I learned that Major Bennett had returned — now surely my fate would be decided.

Events took the precise course I had anticipated. The CO sent word for Corporal Tebbs to bring me in. Corpl Tebbs said *"We had better do things according to the book,"* and marched me into the Orderly Room removing my cap as he did so. No one could take exception to the Corporal's action as he had a remarkably weak voice and a manner quite unlike that of the conventional guard. Once inside the room after some bungling over the words of command he eventually brought me to a halt before the CO *"All right, all right Corpl Tebbs,"* snapped the Major and turning to me he enquired, *"Now, Hall, how are you?"*. I replied that I was feeling pretty fit but had had rather a tough time and that I did not expect he would see the others again. *"Well Hall,"* he replied, *"you'd better tell me exactly what happened."* So I recounted the whole story, how I had been offered that fateful cup of cocoa and how I learnt later that the water had been obtained from a contaminated source. How I had immediately informed Capt Fletcher and how later we had been sent down the line where the MO on the ambulance train had placed us all under open arrest. Major Bennett listened attentively. *"Now, Hall,"* he said, *"the whole point is, who made the cocoa?"* I replied that Bdr Perry had over and over again accepted full responsibility and that for my own part I had been controlling the fire of the battery for over two hours during which I had been under observation of everyone on the guns. There must have been dozens who saw the cocoa passed to me and actually saw me drink it. *"Well that's straight enough Hall and should let you out,"* said the Major, *"but I'm afraid you will have to go before the Colonel. There's nothing to be afraid of and Fletcher will be there to see you're all right."* He then reverted to the question of my health which evidently concerned him more than any alleged breach of discipline. I left the CO's presence in a jubilant mood confident that I should soon be acquitted *"without a stain on my character"*.

But I was soon to realise that a trial before Colonel Wakefield was a very different matter than appearing before the easy going Major. At noon on June 9 I was marched to brigade headquarters a little way down the village and handed over to the Regimental Sergeant Major. To the RSM I was no privileged person but merely an ordinary prisoner sent down for trial. I was placed between an escort, my cap removed and in the approved barrack room manner I was marched before the great man himself. Sitting on his right was Capt Fletcher.

The Colonel opened the case. *"Gunner Hall,"* he commenced, *"you are charged with, on the 5 May, contrary to orders, having drunk a quantity of water from a shell hole. What have you to say?"* I was taken aback at the abruptness of the charge, I expected something more in the nature of a Court of Enquiry; perhaps I had been spoilt by my close association with Major Bennett. I was convinced that had I admitted the charge and started off with an explanation I should have been cut short and bundled out with a fairly stiff sentence. But the direct and brutal way with which the charge had been framed aroused my hostility. I drew myself up, looked him squarely in the face and replied, *"Not guilty"* purposely omitting the *"Sir"*. Col Wakefield was evidently surprised at my attitude for he continued, *"Gunner Hall, what excuse have you to offer?"* which I countered with *"I repeat, Sir, NOT guilty of the charge"*. Whereupon the Colonel desisted from any further attempt to draw me and turning to the Captain said, *"Capt. Fletcher – your case"*.

But if I was surprised at the opening of the case, I was more astonished at Capt Fletcher's attitude for here was one who was well aware of the whole circumstances and whom Major Bennett had told me only the day before to regard as a friend in court taking upon himself the role of prosecuting counsel. He started, *"On ------ (a date a fortnight prior to the affair) I paraded the whole battery and read the following order"*. Here followed a long rigmarole to the effect that drinking shell hole water was dangerous and that anyone disregarding the order would be severely punished. By this time I was fuming and asked where the parade took place. Capt Fletcher replied at the Horse Lines at Souastre and repeated the date. I thereupon retorted that I had certainly not attended the parade in question, in fact I had not been at Souastre at all anywhere about that time. This brought an awkward pause. Colonel Wakefield looked hard at Capt Fletcher who then started to explain that he did not realise that Gunner Hall had not been present at the parade. The Colonel then turned to me saying, *"So, I suppose you plead ignorance of the regulations"*. This was too much for me. *"If it will help matters,"* I replied, *"I am prepared to admit that I was perfectly well aware that it was an offence to drink shell-water."* The Colonel whispered to Captain Fletcher and in a few minutes the trial started all over again with the offensive clause omitted. With the reference to the parade deleted, the charge against me appeared much less formidable and certainly did not take the character of a deliberate contravention of orders. I now felt certain that Capt Fletcher was, if not framing up a case, was making it look as black as possible.

The Captain proceeded with his evidence. *"On May 5 the prisoner informed me that he and the others were ill. I found that they all seemed to be suffering from the effects of gas poisoning and on enquiring the cause they stated that they had been drinking cocoa prepared from shell hole water. I at once ordered their arrest and sent them to the Dressing Station."* I challenged this statement at once. *"I deny,"* I said, *"that any one of us was put under arrest by Capt Fletcher. I certainly would not have gone down the line, that is willingly, had that been the case. The charge was laid on May 8 by the RAMC Medical Officer on the ambulance train."* Capt Fletcher had no compunction in withdrawing his evidence, he apologised to the Colonel explaining that he *"must have been mistaken"*. Col Wakefield referred to the papers before him and found my statement to be correct. By this time I was furious. Capt Fletcher had twice made statements which I had forced him to retract. Sometime later when we were in the BC Post together he referred to *"the rise I had taken out of him before the Colonel"* . *"Of course,"* as he explained, he *"had to make out the best case for himself."* To me the fact remains that here was an officer and a gentleman prepared to perjure himself and incidentally do his best to damn a Gunner's reputation rather than any of his own conduct should have been called to account.

Col Wakefield now turned to me and demanded, *"The point is, Hall, do you admit having drunk the cocoa?"* . *"Yes, Sir."* *"Did you know that it had been made from shell water?"* *"No, Sir."* *"Who made it then?"* *"That is not for me to say,"* I burst out, *"I am here to clear myself, not to incriminate my friends."*

I was sorry for this outburst as soon as I had made it, but looking backwards, I don't think it did any harm. Colonel Wakefield immediately changed his tone and turning to the RSM observed, *"Regimental-Sergeant-Major, I think you might withdraw for the present"*. After the Warrant Officer had left the Colonel turned to me and said quietly, *"Hall, don't you think you had better tell me all about it?"*. I could not of course resist this appeal for really there was nothing to tell. I had been offered a drink of cocoa and later learnt that it was contaminated. I had made no attempt to conceal the knowledge and moreover Bdr Perry had, in front of witnesses admitted full responsibility for the affair. At this juncture Capt Fletcher interposed that since I had reminded him of it, he remembered that Perry had admitted the offence.

This I fully expected would close the trial and was not a little surprised when Col Wakefield observed, *"Am I to understand then that you will take no punishment from me?"*. *"Certainly not, sir,"* I said flaring up again. *"You are prepared to face a Court-Martial?"* *"Yes Sir."* *"And who will you call as witness?"* *"I am prepared to call the whole battery, at least all who were on duty on May 5. I was on duty from 5 in the morning until after 7 controlling the fire of the guns and I never moved from my post. The cocoa was brought to me and they all saw me drink it, some of them said 'Good health'."* The Colonel started at this; he evidently remembered the shoot. *"You controlled the fire, you said. What about the officer on duty?"* *"He was asleep in the BC Post."* I retired. The discomfiture of Capt Fletcher was complete.

"For the rest," I continued, *"I must call Perry, Thomas and Walters, the Medical Officers at the Dressing Station, the CC. and the train also the sister and several of the nurses."* *"But you can't call all these, as you say Perry and Walters are in England and you can't bring in the doctors."* *"But that's not my fault, surely,"* I retorted. *"Well Hall it's going to be most difficult to send the case forward. What do you want me to do?"* A strange admission for a senior officer to make. I played my trump card. *"I look to you, sir, to clear my character."* *"Well I'll tell you what I'll do, I will submit the case to the Adjutant General but you must understand that it may mean a court-martial for you."* I replied that I was prepared for anything to secure justice and that concluded the trial. I was to understand that I was still under arrest but I noticed that I was allowed to leave the Colonel's presence of my own accord and without escort. I walked straight past the RSM in the outer office and made my way to my own quarters. I refused to give any account of the trial but

it soon became known that I had refused the Colonel's punishment and was remanded for a court-martial.

I was not kept in suspense long for two days later that is June 11 my fate was decided and Major Bennett lost no time in acquainting me with the result, indeed he sent for me immediately after the 9 o'clock parade. The decision came in the form of a minute from the Adjutant General's Staff to the Colonel and the CO read out the relevant part of the contents. The ruling ran thus, *"Owing to the difficulty in obtaining material witnesses it is not desirable that a court-martial should be held. If you are satisfied that Gunner Hall took no active part in the affair he should be released from arrest forthwith. In such case Gunner Hall should be informed that he will be reported as a battle casualty and be entitled to wear the wound stripe"*. He then informed me that both he and the Colonel were quite satisfied that I was blameless in the matter and was free again.

Having the Major to myself I decided to strike while the iron was hot. Without giving specific details I stated that there had been a good deal of unpleasantness between myself and certain members of the BC staff and the feeling had been expressed that I should return to the guns. Major Bennett replied that he had not yet decided what to do with all the BCA's but whoever was dropped it would not be me. So far as he was concerned the whole unfortunate business of the poisoning was over and when we returned to action I should continue my job as before.

Taking my departure I sought Gunner Crankshaw the battery tailor and finding that he had a supply of gold stripes ready for eventualities had one sewed on my sleeve straight away. I then swaggered to the BCA's, told them of my release from arrest showing the gold stripe as evidence of complete vindication. I then told them in no uncertain voice of the Major's orders that here I was and here I intended to remain.

I reported the events to my parents the same day but before they received my letter they had already been notified that I had been wounded in action.

Altogether we stayed at Vauchelles-les-Authie for 14 days which, with the week at Authieule meant that the battery was three weeks out of action. On the whole we had nothing to grumble about. Parades were at 9am and 2pm and most of us had finished by 4 in the afternoon. There were the usual guards to be mounted and some ceremonial to be observed, somewhat irksome after the free and easy life up the line but infinitely easier than the strict discipline of the base. There were lectures, physical training and the like but the six BCA's were left to our own devices. This meant that we divided ourselves into two parties each with a director and moved about in a field where we were just visible to one another. One man stood on guard while the rest went to sleep. On the approach of anyone of importance the alarm would be given, both parties would spring to attention and the directors would fly about in fine style, angles being shouted from one party to the other until the alarm had subsided when we would resume our siesta.

But with it all I got quite a lot of useful tips from Corpl Tebbs about laying the Lines of

Fire and bringing the guns into action, trade secrets which Bush had kept from me. I had of course plenty of theory which I had learnt at school but was still in the dark as to which of the half-dozen methods was used in actual practice. Actually it was the method of individual angles. I learnt this from Tebbs and used it later throughout our advance.

Since my acquittal an unofficial truce had been arranged between Evans and myself and the BCA's tended to divide into two groups Bush, Evans and Bryceson on the one hand and Tebbs, Frost and myself on the other. The balance was destroyed when young Bryceson was taken from the school to become an officer's servant, just as well he would never have made an efficient BCA. Now it appeared that staff jobs would be found for any redundant BCA, tension somewhat relaxed.

But the main thing about Vauchelles was the advent of Dennis the cook. Up to this time cooking had never been a strong point with 81 Siege Battery. There had been cooks at the battery position and at rear billets but their capabilities never rose above a very indifferent stew. The two cooks joined forces at Vaulx-Vraucourt and were later casualtied. Then we had Cousins one of the men who came from the base with me. Cousins was no better and no worse than his predecessors. Nevertheless there was much dissatisfaction at Vauchelles regarding the quality of the food supplied. There was no doubt that the people at the ration dump had been putting the screw on, the submarine menace was at its height and food was by no means as plentiful as before. Often hard biscuits were substituted for bread and preserved meat for fresh. The practice at the dump was to send up say 50lbs of fresh meat, 35lbs of bully beef, 10lbs Maconochies and 5lbs veal loaf a mixture that would puzzle an experienced chef let alone a Gunner like Cousins. The problem was complicated by the fact that since we had been on rest the sergeants had set up their own mess. So it happened that the cook had to supply first the Officers' Mess which with their servants took a dozen rations then the sergeants and their satellites say another 8. These twenty took their rations in fresh meat which proportionately increased the percentage of bully for the rank and file, the result a most loathsome, sickly looking stew was served to the rest of the battery.

On about the 17 June matters came to a head. The percentage of fresh meat had fallen to an all time low level. The cook was well aware of the general discontent but continued to supply the privileged classes with their full ration of fresh meat. All that remained for us was dirty pieces of skin and fat and these had been flung into the cooking pots along with bacon rind and bones, a quantity of raisins, broken biscuits, rice and potatoes with of course the inevitable vast quantity of bully beef. The result was half a dozen cooking tins full of a greeny coloured mess on the surface of which were floating pieces of sickly looking fat.

This was too much for us and someone suggested that we should complain to the orderly officer. The word was sent round that no one should touch the food until it was inspected. One of the corporals who was on our side (for the corporals were not included in the sergeants' mess) went off for the officer of the day. After some trouble he was found and came out grumbling about some chaps never being satisfied but as soon as he saw the stew he exclaimed, *"Oh, my God! The CO must see this"*. He returned with Major Bennett who was even more indignant. *"Throw the filthy stuff away,"* he ordered and Gunner Cousins was sacked forthwith.

So far so good but what about our dinner? The impetuous Major had dismissed Cousins without a thought about his successor. Now he looked round and enquired, *"Is there anybody who knows how to cook?"*. From a section of the crowd up went the cry *"Gunner Dennis"*. The supporters of Dennis were the section who had come over with 356 Battery in February. Dennis had it appeared been their cook but when their battery was broken Dennis lost his job and eventually became aeroplane spotter. The newcomers had often extolled the virtues of their late cook to the disparagement of ours but no noticed had been taken of them. Now the post had become vacant it was natural that they should press the claims of their man. Major Bennett asked Dennis if he would take over and somewhat reluctantly he agreed. The first thing was to give the troops something to eat. The CO and Dennis went into the cook-house where they found a supply of bully beef and biscuits. This was distributed so our belated dinner if cold was at any rate wholesome.

Quite a conference was held that afternoon. The CO, Mr Morkill, the Sgt-Major and the newly appointed cook while later the Quartermaster and the officers' cook were brought in. It was some time before the culinary arrangements were re-organised but once Dennis got into his stride we had the best cook in France and our messing arrangements were second to none. The first principle that Major Bennett insisted on was that the proportion of fresh meat and preserved meat should be maintained for officers, sergeants and men alike. At first Cpl Bush was called in to calculate the exact quantity for each mess but later a rough and ready method was substituted but however messes were in operation the same principles held to the end that all should have the same proportion of fresh and preserved meat, bread and biscuits, jam and cheese etc.

The chief sufferer was the Officers' Mess and Proud the officers' cook complained bitterly at the new method which from his point of view were over meticulous as for instance when he drew five eighths of a tin of jam and three quarters of a loaf plus six biscuits. Since they received no preferential treatment and were having to cook their own food the sergeants soon dropped their separate mess and joined in with the rest. When later on we came into action and following his usual practice the CO lived at the battery position he and the officer on duty had their meals from the same source the only difference being that they dined from plates whereas we used mess tins. Capt Fletcher and the officers off duty maintained the Officers' Mess at the Horse Lines for which Proud was the cook but I was informed by the officers on more than one occasion that the food supplied by Dennis was infinitely superior to that prepared by their own cook.

From the first Dennis set his face against bully stew, refusing to cook the preserved meat along with the fresh. His method of achieving this was to cook fresh meat only meantime accumulating a reserve of the corned beef. Periodically there would be cold meat days when we had corned beef and pickles and eaten this way the bully was quite appetizing. There was trouble in getting the system into operation as after our first meal the cookhouse was bare. As we were receiving rations consisting of 66% fresh and 33% preserved meat this meant short commons for the first few days while corned beef was being accumulated and Dennis was not without detractors among the gross feeders. The bulk of us who in any case threw away the red stringy mess of stewed bully suffered no privations however. Other revolutionary changes were introduced. Potatoes were peeled and cooked separately instead of being thrown unwashed into the stew and the latter no longer contained such unwanted trifles as raisins and bacon rind.

During the retreat some of the Gunners had managed to scrounge a large copper which had been left behind by the infantry (we were officially allowed only six cooking pots for all purposes) and Dennis made a rule that this should be used only for brewing tea. Consequently our tea no longer tasted of onions.

It was Dennis too who introduced supper into the battery. Oatmeal had it appeared been drawn from the ration dump for months but it had been fed to the horses, flogged to French peasants or merely thrown away. It was never used because it would not mix with the stew and was too much trouble to cook separately. Dennis prepared suppers of oatmeal porridge every night and most acceptable it was. Unfortunately there was little milk to cook it in so there was quite a run on the canteen for evaporated milk. Small parties would club up to purchase tins between them while gluttons in corners had been known to scoff a dixie-full of porridge along with a large tin of milk.

The boiled rice which followed as a second course to the midday meal was also much appreciated. It was prepared under great difficulty and those who liked it sweet had to make their own arrangements. Sugar was difficult to obtain but even so Dennis managed to save a little sometimes and further it was he who decided that raisins could be more usefully served with rice than stewed with the meat and onions. Mustard and pickles too were a welcome addition to the cold meat days, while on occasions Maconochies would be heated up and handed out one tin for each man.

As regards the preparation of the food it is impossible to praise Dennis adequately. Working under difficulties that would have reduced an experienced chef to hysterics, inadequate cooking utensils, sometimes insufficient water, late arrival of rations, cooking in the open without any protection from the elements, wet wood and logs covered with ivy that wouldn't burn to say nothing, when in action of shellfire and gas, Dennis always managed to have a first rate meal properly cooked and ready to time. It is true that he suffered no lack of helpers; there were always volunteers to peel potatoes, chop wood and attend to the fire while in this connection I myself often arranged to shoot on third charge instead of the more usual fuel so that he would have plenty of spare pads of NCT to help the wood to burn.

The esteem with which I regarded him has grown with years. I see him at night when we were comfortably sheltering in our dug outs there out in the open preparing porridge for our suppers. When rain came pouring down most of us were under cover but there was no shelter for the cook. He obtained, it is true, a special waterproof overall but there he was over his cooking pots while the rain all but extinguished his fires necessitating constant feeding with NCT or cordite. And if there was no shelter from the elements neither was there any from the enemy and I have seen Dennis on more than one occasion in his gas mask seasoning the stew. Though admired by all what reward did he get? By accepting the position of battery cook he closed all avenues to promotion and he was a first rate Gunner who might have won stripes fighting the guns. But who ever heard of even a Bombardier cook? Signallers, Gun Layers and Observers might get proficiency pay but there was no provision for such a reward for the cook. Again, some might perform such deeds as would merit a decoration but no one heard of a cook being so recognised yet in many ways he proved himself the bravest of us all.

Dennis had however a strange fondness for field mice and wherever we went he was sure to produce two or three out of his pockets. Sometimes he would keep them in boxes. He would feed his pets on dainties and I have seen him hold a tiny mouse on the palm of his hand against half a cheese and watch with pleasure the tiny creature nibbling. If anyone expostulated he would fly into a rage, for he was pretty quick tempered and threaten to throw up his job. His stock arguments were firstly that his mice were cleaner than the Gunners, they weren't lousy which was more than could be said of most of us and secondly it would take a lot of field mice to eat as much cheese as certain fat sergeants he could name. There was really no answer to such arguments and none dare interfere with Dennis and his pets.

There was another aspect to the vexed question of rations. Were we, as a battery, getting our fair share from the ration dump? Cousins our late cook, as part of his defence, always maintained we were not. It was difficult to decide but the NCO who fetched the rations was a very easy going type and probably accepted what was offered without question. Major Bennett considered that there would be no harm in having a change. We had in the battery at the time a professional illusionist, in peacetime on the staff of Maskelyn and Devant a very useful man for entertainments now we were on rest. He gave a display of sleight of hand at which the CO was present. After the show the Major suggested that he might accompany the Quartermaster to the ration dump and eventually take over the job. Major Bennett further suggested that if he could use his talents to the battery's advantage it would be appreciated. Whatever happened our talented friend found favour with those in charge of the dump and I was told that he kept the ASC men in a state of hilarity and never failed to claim some reward for his exertions. So whether it was an extra jar of pickles, an issue of butter instead of margarine or a case of raisins it was rarely that the GS wagon arrived at the cookhouse without some little extra to add to Dennis' stock. He would say *"This by rights belongs to ----."* How the stuff was obtained was no business of ours so long as it was diverted to our supply.

Another of Major Bennett's reforms was to have the whole of the rations brought up to Dennis instead of first going to the Horse Lines so that the serving Gunners should have the first choice. This was bitterly resented by the drivers but they had no say in the matter. When we went into action a separate mess was set up at the Horse Lines serving the drivers and the Gunners off duty. Dennis was scrupulously fair in sharing the rations but the cooking at the Horse Lines was always decidedly inferior. Thus as Vauchelles one of the major problems was solved once and for all that there was no further complaints about the food.

Our stay at Vauchelles-les-Authie was marred by air raids. We were no great distance from the line and the village was packed with troops. Most nights we received attention from hostile aircraft and the presence of 80 odd horses made things particularly bad for the drivers who, at the first alarm, had to turn out and comfort their charges. The night of June 21 was memorable. The aeroplanes worked in relays of twenty or thirty at a time, dropping their bombs and returning for more. There was no sleep for anyone that night and we stood shivering in the Horse Lines ready to lead the frightened beasts away in case the bombs dropped too close, but where to go was another matter for any movement would be sure to attract attention and draw more fire upon us. Our aerial defences seemed on this occasion to be absolutely useless. One uttered prayers of thankfulness when the enemy planes passed over to drop their bombs at the other end of the village where some infantry were quartered. Their buildings caught fire and this attracted the enemy who circled round the blazing huts and dropped bomb after bomb into the flames. Some hundreds of casualties were inflicted that night but our feelings were those of relief that we had not been the sufferers.

In the morning it was thought that the enemy, having completely destroyed the Nissen huts on one side of the village might return at night to work on the other end, the one we were occupying. Our best plan therefore was to go while the going was good. We made haste to demolish the Horse Lines and removed the animals to a barn where we joined them later in the day. A risk certainly for the village was just as vulnerable as the surrounding huts if not more so. Whether we were attacked that night I do not recollect but at any rate we suffered no casualties.

Our rest had now come to an end and we were ordered back to the line. There was little to be done in the way of preparation and at 3pm on June 23 we limbered up. We moved off and three hours later were back in Souastre.[1]

1 81 SB relieved 219 SB at map reference (Sheet 57d) E.21.a.80.70.

CHAPTER 23
THE TURN OF THE TIDE

The targets recorded in the Brigade war diary tell us that Gnr Hall was now close to the 1916 Somme battlefield. Targets included Rossignol Wood[1] (27 June, 100 rounds fired) and Miraumont (29 June). July was spent engaging various enemy targets but the amount of detail Hall provides on other activities occupying their time indicates that the battery was not participating in any significant operations. In late July this was to change as they moved again, this time to support the Canadians as a major offensive in early August approached.

Desirable billets did not long remain untenanted and it was no surprise to find that another unit had taken possession of our old Horse Lines at Souastre. There was nothing for it but to establish new quarters. We found a suitable pitch, halted and had tea, then the detachments were told off and went forward with the guns to take over our new battery position at Fonquevillers. I was disappointed though not surprised that I was not to accompany the guns. Bush and Evans went forward to lay out the Lines of Fire leaving Tebbs, Frost and myself behind at Souastre.

Work preparing the Horse Lines was most arduous. We were in an open field without cover of any kind or means of preparing any. A heavy rain was falling, water and food had to be found for the eighty horses and they had to be tied up for the night. We fastened them as best we could to the wagons and awaited the return of the gun teams. Horses and men arrived wet through in the early hours of the morning. All lent a hand at unharnessing the horses after which we fed and watered them and brushed some of the mud off their coats. Then we tied them up with the others. After this we ran the limbers into some sort of order and at last wet and miserable crowded into the empty wagons for the night.

We were roused early in the morning, helped the drivers to feed and water and then the real work of the day began. Load after load of timber and corrugated iron arrived and all hands buckled to make the place more hospitable.

As always the horses were our first charge. Two long poles were driven into the ground 50 yards apart and connected with a thick rope some three feet from the ground. To this rope the horses were tethered equal numbers of either side, the idea being that the pull on one side would be counterbalanced by that on the other. The horses secure we set to work on our own quarters and by evening (June 24) a number of rough huts were ready for occupation. We crowded into them conscious of a good day's work that deserved a night's repose.

Alas for fond hopes. At three o'clock in the morning the picket gave the alarm that the horses had broken loose. There appeared to have been some faulty work in the erection of the main posts and, as sometimes happened, the horses on one side had been struggling to get loose while the others instead of pulling in the contrary direction had remained more or less passive with the result that the posts proved unequal to the strain and collapsed. Subsequently some of the horses had broken loose and were wandering about the camp. With much profanity the straying beasts were recaptured while the heavy posts were fixed more securely than on the first occasion. The fact that it was pitch dark and raining heavily did not help at all but at length the animals were tied up so securely that as one driver remarked, *"If they were bloody elephants they couldn't get away"*.

The next day (June 25) the gun detachments changed over and the returning Gunners gave such glowing accounts of the new position that Frost and I began to wonder when our turn would come to do some decent BCA work instead of messing about with the damned horses. We pestered Corpl Tebbs calling on him to assert his authority as senior BCA and stop the two school-teachers at the battery position from making a close corporation to the exclusion of all others. But the easy going Tebbs was not easily spurred into action and I began to see myself after all my struggles being supplanted by Evans. One concession however Tebbs did secure. He approached the Sgt-Major and obtained permission for the BCA's to parade separately to roll call instead of with the sub-sections as hitherto. This meant that after parade we were dismissed to our own duties and were free from general work in the Horse Lines.

We three used our newly found freedom to construct a new dug out for ourselves. We found a good site on the bank side and obtained plenty of sand bags and corrugated iron. The dugout was started on June 26 and finished the following day. It was quite roomy being five feet wide and ten long a very substantial construction indeed.

None of us was satisfied however at being excluded from the battery position for so long and at last Corpl Tebbs managed to get in communication with the CO. As a result Tebbs and I relieved the two school-teachers on the morning of the 28 (Frost was left behind). They had had a long innings at the battery and had missed some very unpleasant days at the Horse Lines. Moreover we had made a first rate shelter for them at Souastre. As soon as Evans and I saw one another the inevitable row broke out but the presence of the CO eventually calmed us down. We then were told that a few men with some experience in gunnery were required by the Royal Engineers in connection with some sound ranging work that was being set up. Both Evans and I sent in written applications for the job not that either of us wanted it but that Major Bennett, who was aware how matters stood, should decide between us.

Tebbs and I remained a couple of days at Fonquevillers returning to the Horse Lines on July 1. On July 2 Lt Page the officer in charge had a message from the CO; Major Bennett had decided that Evans was to be released for the engineers. In the circumstances would I withdraw my application? I agreed to do so. Evans, it appeared would be sent for in about a fortnight's time. Meantime Corpl Bush had a stroke of luck. There were at that time a few, very few, special leaves for Paris. Two had been allocated to 81 Siege Battery and Bush had secured one of them. I don't think the privilege could have gone to one who would make a better use of it although he amused some of us by his account of the activities of the YMCA. The driver accompanying him he lost immediately on arrival and wherever the latter stayed it was certainly not at the YMCA. The fact that Major Bennett had given this valuable privilege to one of his staff did not add to his popularity. There were no more Paris leaves, they had been much abused and were withdrawn and seaside holidays substituted.

During Bush's absence in Paris Frost and I alternated with Tebbs and Evans, two days at the battery and two at the Horse Lines. Tebbs and Frost had previously worked together but the change had been arranged because Evans point blank refused to work with me. When Bush returned another job was found for Evans after which he went to the Royal Engineers.

Fonquevillers was a splendid battery position. We took it over from 326 Siege whose turn it was to go out on rest. The guns lay barely a mile south of our previous Hannescamps position alongside the road stretching from that village to Fonquevillers. The road was lined with trees and a small copse alongside made a further screen for the guns. In this copse was the remains of an old trench and here the cook-house was situated. The previous occupants had erected half a dozen field ovens. These were made of empty oil drums set lengthwise in a wall of mud and clay. The drums sloped slightly backwards to prevent the gravy running out. When Dennis took the ovens over he cut the meat into large pieces, inserted a piece in each tin and started a fire going. A primitive arrangement but it enabled us to enjoy roast beef for the first time since we arrived in France. Dennis was delighted with his field ovens and almost wept when we had to leave them behind. Alas they were a fixture and in due course we had to hand them over to our successors 256 Siege. Dennis was of course a fixture at Fonquevillers. Another fixture was Gunner Wiley. Major Bennett decided that he had been at the Horse Lines long enough and he was ordered to advance his canteen to the battery position.

The BC Post lay next to the cook-house; this enabled the BCA's to be first at meal times. Like the village smithy it lay under a spreading chestnut tree. It was a small chamber ten feet long by three wide and in this simple apartment Major Bennett lived and slept in state and from here was controlled the fire of the battery. A photograph of Mrs Bennett, a remarkably beautiful woman, hung from a nail driven into the wall. Considering that a couple of Gunners slept in the passage the CO enjoyed but little privacy but a piece of sacking separated the inner sanctum. Another peculiar compartment was dug into the mound at the back of the BC Post and here the BCA off duty used to sleep. This room was so tiny that it was impossible to lay at full length and it was an idea of mine to drive a tunnel to connect with the main apartment.

The guns lay in a room behind the BC Post, a most unusual arrangement as it meant facing the muzzles of the guns when controlling fire, rather unnerving and as I was to discover later a distinctly dangerous practice. In addition the guns appeared to the controller to be in the reverse order No.1 to the left and No.6 to the right instead of the other way round. This took a bit of getting used to and several times did I turn to No.6 guns and give the orders intended for No.1 and vice versa. The guns were widely spread out. No.3 the pivot gun was 30 yards directly in rear of the post but No.1 was 120 yards to the left and No.6 180 yards in the opposite direction the other guns occupying intermediate positions. This distance caused a good deal of vocal strain when calling out corrections. Incidentally owing to the distance the voice had to travel it was impossible to fire a perfect salvo at Fonquevillers as the command *"fire"* would reach one gun before the other had received it.

The problem of fire control was so serious that when Frost and I took over on July 3 the CO was seriously considering setting up section posts. This meant telephoning orders from the BC Post to three points behind the guns a method very wasteful in manpower and liable to lead to misinterpretation of orders. I myself was experiencing great difficulty in reaching the extreme guns with the hand megaphone provided and I persuaded him to let me design a larger one. With the aid of the Sergeant-Artificer a megaphone was made from the metal lining of a cartridge box. This instrument was two feet long and certainly eased our task considerably. I was still not satisfied and I collected sufficient metal to make a giant megaphone no less than six feet long which gave splendid magnification. It was much too cumbersome to handle so it was pivoted in the middle and hung from a branch of the chestnut tree. After this there was no more trouble with the guns not hearing our orders.

An upturned cartridge box to stand on and later a stand for holding papers followed as a matter of course. This was always referred to as the lectern and was an infinite source of amusement to the troops. As soon as any BCA mounted the cartridge box someone or other would shout out *"The first lesson is taken from the Fifth Chapter of the Book of the Prophet Isaiah"* or something equally appropriate. Custom never seemed to stale this joke.

The problem of hearing the orders now seemed to have been transferred from the guns to the BCA fighting the battery, for having mounted the rostrum it was difficult for the outside man to hear what was going on in the BC Post. After some experimenting I overcame this by extending the earpiece from a field telephone and strapping it to my ear. Now I was able to hear not only everything that was said in the BC Post but in the Observation Post as well. The net result of these innovations was a considerable speeding up of the shooting. Sometimes it was almost too quick for informal conversation between Observation Officer and the Battery Commander as say *"I think that was pretty near the mark,"* I would interpret as *"No 4 repeat"* without the latter opening his mouth while the command *"fire"* was acted upon as soon as it came from the OP instead of as formerly been heard over the 'phone by the Major, repeated by him to the Signaller, transmitted by the latter to the BCA who in turn shouted the order to the guns.

Altogether Fonquevillers was noted for hard work and good shooting. We were on counter-battery work again and silenced enemy battery after battery. Most of the shooting was by aeroplane observation as owing to the lay of the land comparatively little could be seen from the Observation Post. Bucquoy the village directly in front of us where many hostile guns were in action was hidden by a hill and completely invisible from the ground while little of profit could be discerned of Puisieux and Ablainzevelle which villages were four miles apart so the zone covered by our six guns was very wide and represented switches 30 degrees left and right of zero line.

The work entailed in covering such a wide angle was considerable as it meant continual shifting the guns from one side to the other. Often when shells were stacked for quick loading on an extreme switch we were ordered to fire on the other extreme angle which meant the whole lot had to be shifted. Later we got wise to this and have separate dumps in readiness on either side. Occasionally we had all six guns firing on the same target but this was the exception rather than the rule it being advisable to concentrate four guns on aeroplane work and leave the left section for picking up odd targets. I can remember the Adjutant's high pitched voice on the 'phone, *"Hello, 81 Siege, can you let me have a couple of guns for ten minutes?"* . *"Sorry, Sir, we're all engaged, 4 guns on an aeroplane shoot and two on the cross roads at −."* *"Well let me speak to the CO please,"* then sure enough would come the CO's instructions, take one gun off the aeroplane shoot and another off the cross roads, which translated to the guns meant, 1, 2 and 3 carry on, 4 and 5 cease firing and stand by for a new target, No. 6 double the rate of fire to make up for No. 5.

When firing on such diverse targets the guns presented a very untidy appearance. The right section might be slewed round firing at the limit of their range, Nos.3 and 4 firing at low elevation on Bucquoy near the zero line, while the left section at right angles from 1 and 2 might be calibrating on Beuregard dovecote.

Beuregard dovecote[2] was the only visible calibration point in the sector and not a particularly satisfactory one at that. It lay to the rear of Puisieux at the extreme end of the right switch and at a range of 9,000 yards. This was everything a calibration point should not be, well away from the zero line and at long range when erratic shooting was only to be expected. Still it was the only one available and its use by the Siege Artillery strictly rationed. Destructive bombardment of the dovecote was expressly forbidden and there was great indignation when one battery went so far as to score an OK on the building so rendering it less visible to others following.

Such calibration as was carried out revealed a disconcerting loss of muzzle velocity of some of the guns. One had lost as much as 120 foot seconds and could barely reach the dovecote while another was nearly as bad. The guns had been changed about so much during the retreat that we did not have the history of them all and there is no doubt that any piece that would fire at all had been reconditioned and put back into action and we had on charge some guns that should rightly have been condemned. The matter was reported but it was some time before the worn out guns were withdrawn.

Other factors which tendered to reduce the range were the new type of driving bands and the extensive use of 106 fuzes.[3]

The new bands were introduced to save copper which was very scarce. They were barely half an inch wide and roughly pressed into the body of the shell without any pretence of machining. Such bands allowed a considerable amount of gas to escape from the explosion chamber of the gun and so reduce its effective range. Moreover the rotation of the shell in flight was not so good and they tended to wobble. As we advanced later on I encountered quite a number of shells where the bands had come detached. In this respect the ammunition supplied towards the end of the war was, though plentiful, inferior in quality. On full charge the new type of shell reduced our range by nearly 1,000 yards, in fact it was regarded as useless to attempt to fire at over 9,000 yards with them. On instructions we now hoarded the old type of shell for use in calibration and long range shoots. The use of two types of shell brought into use a fresh range table and meant considerably more work both for the BCA's and for the Gunners who had to segregate the two types of ammunition.

The direct action fuze (No.106) further reduced the range by a matter of 150 yards at full charge owing to the fact that they did not taper to a point as did the original type of fuze and thus offered more resistance to the wind. Also they slowed down the rate of firing somewhat as the Gun Captain had to move the safety cap before loading. Notwithstanding these disadvantages I regard the introduction of this type of fuze as one of the greatest inventions of the war. Indeed I doubt whether we could have won the war without them.

The 106 fuze was essentially a development of the 100 type which was introduced towards the end of 1916. The original 100 fuze was obsolescent when I went out in 1917 having been replaced by the 101 and 101E known by the Gunners as "brass knob" and "blue knob" respectively, the difference being that while "brass knob" was supposed to burst on impact, "blue knob" had a delay action and would bury itself before explosion, in fact it had something of the effect of an armour piercing shell and could be used against deep dugouts and pill-boxes. But both types made big holes in the ground and may well have been responsible for the impasses in 1916 and 1917. After bombardment the enemy's defence system might be destroyed but the ground would be so churned up that the attacking force was unable to advance. The shell holes filled with water and formed the quagmire I encountered on the slopes beyond Ypres. Moreover such soft ground often failed to explode the shells in subsequent bombardments. Thousands of shells fell into the marshes of the Ancre with no more effect than stones thrown into a bog. Clearly another type of fuze was called for.

The 106 fuze was introduced late in 1917 but at first its use was restricted. It was rumoured that those in authority were divided as to its efficacy and that the majority were still in favour of heavy preliminary bombardments with the resultant big shell holes. After the German advance in March 1918 without the use of such bombardments the direct action fuze came into its own and now in July 1918 it was rarely that we use the older kind. The new type fuze was made of aluminium and differed from the others in having a "gaine" or stalk. When fuzing with 106 we first removed the safety plug from the shell and then inserted a small bag of tortyl colloquially known as "candle" (it resembled the candles used on aiming points at night), and on top of this the fuze was screwed, this incidentally usually burst the bag and so made de-fuzing a matter of difficulty.

Before the shell was rammed home it was necessary for someone, usually the No. 1, to remove the small cast iron cap. This was done just before loading so that it was not until the very last moment that the sensitive nose of the fuze was exposed. Even at this stage the fuze was still protected by a brass tape but this was thrown off by centrifugal force when the spinning shell left the breech and dropped a few yards in front of the gun. The sensitive nose of the fuze was thus exposed as the shell flew through the air. The slightest obstruction in its path, a bird on the wing, the smallest twig or even a blade of corn would probably set it off and explode the shell. With 106 fuzes the shell seemed to spread along the ground without the least attempt to bury. Compared with the other fuzes, the 101E would make a hole about 6 feet deep and 10 in diameter, the 101 about that size whereas the 106 fuze would make an indentation about the size and shape of a large soup plate. After a heavy bombardment with shells fuzed 106 a metalled road looked no worse than one rather badly pot-holed and was quite passable for lorries and even motor-cycles. The only appreciable disadvantage of the new fuzes was as I have said the slight loss in range which had to be allowed for when calculating a target.

None the less the effective range of the guns had through one cause or another been so much reduced that it was no longer possible to engage with confidence a target at more than 9,000 yards, whereas some months before we were able to fire half a mile further. In an attempt to restore the range a supplementary charge in the shape of a small bag of NCT was introduced. This was to be inserted in the breech after the shell and before the main cartridge was loaded. The experiment was not a success. The full charge fitted just comfortably into the explosion chamber and the attempt to pack any more propellant caused difficulty in closing the breech-block besides throwing an extra strain on the gun. Very few supplementary charges were issued and they were afterwards withdrawn. After Fonquevillers long-range firing became a thing of the past and the 6 inch howitzer and 60 pounder gun were re-classified as mobile units taking our place with the Field Artillery.

The introduction of the Martini-Metford locks in place of Percussion Tee tubes, a long overdue reform, took place at this time. I have already described the method of firing the guns by pulling out the Tee tubes. The energy expended in this operation was so great that the job of firing the gun was the most exhausting in the battery. Only strong men could be so employed and on a long shoot they frequently had to be relieved. The Martini-Metford locks were fashioned from the firing mechanism of an obsolete type of service rifle (hence the name) and fired blank .303 ammunition, the spark from which ignited the charge. In place of the trigger a small catch was fixed and a very light lanyard was attached. The energy required to fire the Martini-Metford locks was negligible no more than pulling the trigger of a rifle. The change took some getting used to and I have seen firing numbers when first introduced to the new locks pull the lanyard and not meeting the accustomed resistance of the Tee tube fall head over heels beside the gun. Occasionally the lanyard if left attached to the lock would become entangled with some obstruction and the gun would go off accidentally. Accordingly the practice of leaving the lanyard attached, though comparatively safe with the Tee tubes was strictly forbidden with the MM locks.

The Martini-Metford locks were not brought into use without considerable trouble. The first locks were fitted by Army Ordnance Corps men and were supposed to be conditioned by our own Artificer but they often jammed and the old mechanism had to be replaced while they were overhauled. At length the difficulties were overcome and the laborious Tee tube firing became a thing of the past.

At Fonquevillers we fired gas shells for the first time. (They had previously been used by 18 pounder and sixty pounder guns). On July 20 we carried out a minor operation, the capture of Rossignol Wood entirely by gas. Gas shells were detested by everyone. In the first place they had to be stacked separately in small pits some distance from the guns never more than twenty together. They had to be brought up one at a time and could not be fuzed in advance. Gas masks had to be carried at the alert position when handling such ammunition for fear of leaking shells while at first masks had to be worn when firing. To make matters worse several kinds of gas shells were supplied. At first we received the KSK a lachrymatory shell painted plain grey and a lethal shell, the NC grey with a single red band. In a gas shoot a burst of the lachrymatory shells was first sent over – this was the tear gas, in theory to blind the enemy and prevent his donning his gas mask. Then while he was unprotected the lethal NC which followed was supposed to do its deadly work. After a time the NC became obsolescent and was replaced by the CG grey with two red bands. There were about 6 other types of gas shell but all of these did not reach the line or at any rate our battery did not get them for which relief much thanks.

When floundering about the battery position on a dark night carrying the shells from the isolated pits trying to distinguish red bands from plain with the cumbersome gas mask hampering one's movements, one thought little of such new-fangled devices. Further when responding to SOS calls we could with ordinary shells work up to three rounds a minute. With gas the best we could ever do was one round a minute and we did not keep this up for long. Gas shells by the way left the muzzle of the gun with a peculiar wobble quite distinct from the bark of the ordinary shell.

Personally I have but little regard to gassing and I have never known an operation that could not have been done equally well if not better with high explosive shells using direct action fuzes. In order to accommodate the gas cylinder inside, the walls of the gas shell were considerably thinner and the explosive force of the projectile subsequently lessened. The CG shell had thicker walls and was in fact a sort of cross between the HE and lethal gas, the HE element predominating. On one or two occasions we responded to SOS calls with gas but it was not particularly effective for this purpose and after a time HE was substituted. Incidentally gas shells had to be strictly accounted for while with HE three or four hundred each way was of no moment.

I have already referred to the wide angle covered by our guns. This was a new endeavour to co-ordinate the fire of all guns in the neighbourhood instead of leaving matters to individual batteries. Previously it had been the practice to allocate a portion of the enemy's front to each battery, now apparently the object was for a group of batteries to combine to cover a much larger area. Thus two of our guns a couple of sixty pounders and a twelve inch howitzer might engage a hostile battery together while the other four would be engaged on another task with another link. Especially did we co-operate with one of 60 pounder batteries in the brigade which fired shrapnel at the same time as we sent over HE, a happy combination as we were so close as to be able to synchronise our fire perfectly.

The amount of ammunition expended at Fonquevillers was prodigious and our own GS[4] wagons would have been hard put to keep us supplied. They were not called upon to do so for we were supplied by other means. Every night a couple of tanks would make their slow and ungainly way across the fields. I forget how many rounds they carried but it seemed to be enormous and it was rather difficult to unload the machines. The standard type of tank was at first used but later a special type of ammunition carrying tank was brought into use which carried even more shells and was easier to access.

In addition to the ammunition brought up this way we had an extra thousand rounds for which we were never properly able to account. These were found in one of the trenches and appeared to have been concealed from view. They were certainly not in the stock handed over by 326 Siege. The general opinion was they represented the night firing of the previous battery who had dumped their quota in the ditch instead of firing it and so enjoyed an uninterrupted night's rest. Although such a practice was not playing the game it was not an infrequent occurrence. Major Bennett certainly took the view that the shells had been planted and after some trouble they were brought into our stock as salved. This discovery made the CO exercise stricter control on the guns. All night firing had to be controlled and one BCA must always be awake and on duty. Since therefore now four of us this was no great hardship. Two BCA's spent a couple of days at the battery position followed by two at Souastre. At the position two of us would be on duty from 8am until 10pm the senior man working out the targets and the junior on the rostrum outside controlling the fire. At 10pm one man would retire to the outside dug-out until 3am when he would be relieved by his colleague until 8am; I preferred to work the first turn. The heavy work of the day usually finished about 8pm then there was the ammunition followed by supper at 9. The dispatch rider would usually turn up soon afterwards with the night programme which having been worked out and passed to the guns Frost (and later Bush) would retire leaving me to control the fire until 3 in the morning. As was usual with counter-battery work night firing was never particularly strenuous and consisted of occasional bursts of fire on sensitive points at intervals of an hour or so. As was usually possible to divide out the targets so that only a couple of guns were in action at the same time while the remaining Gunners were resting. The BCA on duty would call up the proper guns a few minutes before firing was due, see that the necessary rounds were fired and retire to the post until the next burst was due.

It was rather weary waiting in the BC Post in the early hours of the morning and more than anything to while away the time I would start making porridge about 2am I had no difficulty in getting the oatmeal from Dennis which I cooked over an NCT fire. By 3am the porridge was ready and I went for my relief. We were all accustomed to waking on the instant and the two of us would consume the meal after which I would turn in to the recently vacated bunk and sleep until breakfast which would be brought to me and eaten in bed. And so began another day.

When Bush returned from Paris the rota had to be rearranged. Corpl Tebbs took Frost as his junior while I paired up with Bush. As was expected Evans dropped from the team altogether.

It was while controlling the fire from the lectern that I had what was probably my narrowest escape. I had called the battery into action and for some reason or other had ordered full charge for the cartridges although the target being comparatively close could easily have been met on third. The guns were standing by for a salvo. I had actually given the order *"fire"* when I noticed Sgt McIlroy on No.1 gun stop his firing number and actually withdraw the lanyard from his hand. The remaining guns had fired before I heard my old Sergeant call out *"She won't clear – come and have a look"*. I went over to the gun and looking along the barrel found the Sergeant's words only too true. We reversed the dial sight and looked through it. There focused in the glass was the chestnut tree and the platform where I had been standing only a few minutes before. I recalculated the target on third charge and with the increased elevation the gun cleared the trees comfortably. Of course the matter was reported to the CO and as a result prominent notices were posted both in the BC Post and on the gun itself that on no account should it be fired on less than a certain elevation. With such precautions one felt fairly safe but it brought home the disadvantages of controlling fire from the front of the guns and I fully realised that but for Sgt McIlroy's promptitude the gun would have been fired directly at my own person and, as we were using 106 fuzes, would by my own orders have blown myself to fragments.

In many ways Fonquevillers was a remarkable position. We sustained not a single casualty and in fact met very little opposition. According to all accounts the line in this part of the front was unchanged since the end of the German advance in March but whereas at Hannescamps we had been blown out of one position and lived in constant fear in the other, here, at Fonquevillers we felt perfectly secure. Yet barely a mile separated us from the former village and we were certainly no further away from the enemy. Somehow his resistance seemed to have broken down. Day after day we harassed his batteries, silencing them and keeping them on the move. So far did we go that a special map was supplied on which the hostile batteries were indicated by numbers and day after day our aircraft would call for fire on these numbered positions. Periodically a report would be forwarded from counter-batteries headquarters on which the results would be summarised in the following manner:

"Hostile position No 26 reported active 10.30 July 10
Silenced by 81 and 157 batteries by 11am

Active again 2pm
Silenced by 59 battery 2.30pm
Engaged by 59, 81, 157, 55 & 63 batteries 9am July 11
Battery reported as finally destroyed 3pm".

59 and 81 were 6 inch howitzers, 157, 60 pounder guns while 55 and 63 were Field batteries 18 pounder and 4.5 inch howitzers respectively. The destructive shoot lasted 6 hours, between 24 and 30 guns being engaged. The report shows the value of different batteries working together.

Even after making allowance for optimism in such reports became self-evident that we had now obtained mastery of the situation. And now another word appeared on the scene "Counterstroke". The word spread like wildfire, reinforcements brought it from the base, drivers heard it mentioned in back areas, the first words spoken by an officer when reporting to the CO *"Anything about counterstroke, sir?"*. The word echoed from one end of the front to the other. There was still some doleful news coming through from other fronts but here we felt that we had overcome the German assault and it was only a matter of time when we should take the offensive and drive him out of France altogether. This was the beginning of the end.

Towards the end of July an order from headquarters confirmed that there was something in the wind. All blankets were called in; in future we were to depend on our greatcoats for covering at night. Major Bennett was at first inclined to give full effect to the order but this was received with such dismay that he hinted that if one blanket per head were handed in he would consider the order carried out. Moreover no enquiries would be made as to the condition of any blankets surrendered. Accordingly many large blankets were torn in half and counted as two, horse blankets were sent in, old pieces of sacking, impregnated blankets for gas proofing, in fact anything that by any stretch of imagination could be called a blanket.

I take a certain amount of credit for the way in which Major Bennett allowed the order to go by default. When the order was received I was in the BC Post with him and he remarked, *"You'll have to tip up your blankets, Hall"*. On ascertaining the reason I expressed my opinion of the measure in no uncertain manner, stating that if HQ wanted to increase the mobility of the batteries (the reason stated in the order) they might well start by recalling the hundreds of spanners that were carried about in the limbers to say nothing of the three twenty foot gins weighing several tons which were never used. I dwelt on the discomfort of trying to sleep at night with no other covering than a wet overcoat and pointed out that there were many in the battery who would be permanently injured if the order was carried out.

Major Bennett agreed that there was something in what I said but stated that the order must be obeyed and that he proposed to call in one blanket per head which was all we were entitled to at that period. That would leave us in possession of all the spares we had scrounged during the retreat. As I had seven I had no cause for complaint. Most of us were in a similar state and once the official blankets were returned to store the others were pooled and we heard no more of the ruling.

What with the changes in ammunition, the excitement of destroying battery after battery without any serious resistance from the enemy to say nothing of the impending "Counterstroke", I enjoyed every minute I was in the battery position. The only trouble was that every couple of days at Fonquevillers had to be followed by a similar period with the Horse Lines at Souastre. I grew to hate the Horse Lines, the indifferent stew after the roasts that Dennis prepared at the battery, the ceremonial parades in contrast with the easy going ways at Fonquevillers, the interminable fatigues and the coarseness of the drivers. I was not alone in this; every Gunner preferred being up the line to the so-called rest and if it were possible to wangle a day or so extra duty with the guns it was always done.

The natural rivalry between Gunners and drivers developed into an active hostility which Major Bennett's attitude did nothing to allay. Major Bennett never visited the Horse Lines if he could avoid it. He was essentially a Gunners' man and privately admitted that as a class he disliked the drivers and regarded them as a set of malingers and cowards. Worse still he made no attempt to conceal his dislike. He used the Horse Lines to get rid of incompetent NCO's and even allowed prejudice to affect his sense of judgement; offences which he overlooked in a Gunner would be punished if committed by a driver.

Hitherto the drivers had been regarded as something of a superior caste and naturally chafed under the new regime. Some asked for transfer to the guns and I saw my old friend Swan now at work as a Gun Layer. As a horse drawn Siege battery we held a unique position (at this time there were only four in existence) and the Base refused to acknowledge our reality. With the Heavy Batteries (the sixty pounders) drivers and Gunners were interchangeable, not so with us. Most of the Gunners, like myself, were profoundly ignorant of horses and the more we saw of them and their ways the more we wanted to keep our distance. Such few of the reinforcements as had any knowledge of horsemanship were eagerly absorbed into the ranks of the drivers. At the Horse Lines of course the drivers had the upper hand. Capt Fletcher was in charge and the presence of the Sergeant-Major insured that discipline was to the fore. With a shortage of drivers, Gunners off duty were roped in for grooming and watering horses which could be painful to the inexperienced as I learnt to my cost.

As I have said Corpl Tebbs had obtained from the Sgt-Major the privilege of being treated as employed men but one day in his absence Sgt Salter took the parade and ordered Frost and myself the BCA's off duty to fall in with our detachments declaring that there would be no favouritism while he was in charge. Later when a group of us were engaged on some fatigue he called on me to get a move on adding *"You're not at the BC Post now, Hall"*. Whatever I may have done or left undone this last insult was so uncalled for that I retorted, *"No, Sergeant but I shall be there tomorrow,"* my intent being that once I got back to Fonquevillers I should make an effort to stop there and avoid going to the Horse Lines at all. The remark was most unfortunate and Sgt Salter took up the challenge. *"Is that a threat, Hall?"* *"No Sergeant,"* I replied, *"merely a statement"*, and this closed the episode. Unfortunately the altercation was overheard by some of his men.

But if I had any intention of getting even with Sgt Salter which I strenuously deny, fate played into my hands. Next day came the change over and Frost and I accompanied the relief teams to the battery. There was plenty of shooting until nightfall and Salter's gun (No.6) took its fair share of the targets. At ten o'clock a target was telephoned which I supposed I might have refused as it lay at long range quite out of reach of three of the guns which were badly worn. In addition Nos.1 and 2 guns were covering an SOS line on the opposite switch and could not be disturbed. If the target were to be engaged it was No.6 or nothing. If I had refused the target I might have had to justify my action in the morning. Accordingly I called Sgt Salter and his detachment into action.

It was a brisk burst of fire and soon over but the target once accepted could not subsequently be refused. No sooner had the gun been sponged out and the ammunition replaced and the Gunners had retired to their shelter than I was obliged to call them into action again. Time after time the same target came through and when Frost took over at 3am he had to carry on the good work. Morning saw the unfortunate team struggling to replace their spent ammunition in readiness for a scheduled aeroplane shoot. To add to their chagrin although No.6 had endured such a heavy night the rest of the battery had enjoyed an uninterrupted night's repose, no other targets having been notified.

Here was a pretty kettle of fish. Sgt Salter and his men were cursing each other vowing that I had kept them up out of spite and if the sergeant had been disposed to let matters rest there his gun crew spurred him into action. At 9am he strode up to the BC Post to lay his complaint before Major Bennett. Full of confidence Sgt Salter approached the CO in a rather truculent manner complaining that Gunner Hall, the BCA, had kept him and his team out all night and let off the rest of the battery. But the sergeant got no change out of the CO who was in fact as near to losing his temper as I have ever seen him. From the outset Major Bennett accepted full responsibility for all orders emanating from the BC Post, the BCA's orders must be obeyed explicitly as if they were his own. If the guns were worked forty-eight hours out of the forty-eight that was no business of anyone outside the BC Post and any further attempt to question a BCA's orders would be treated as insubordination. When I attempted to state my reasons for engaging the target he stopped me saying, *"Don't tell him, Hall, it's no business of his"*.

Sgt Salter made himself scarce after this and as soon as he had gone the CO remarked, *"Well, that's settled him, you won't have any more trouble from Sergeant Salter."* Then he approved my decision to engage the target even though only one gun was available. But that left me in a quandary and I explained to the Major that I was left in the position of giving orders to the Gun Captains one day and working under their direct supervision the next. I stated, *"You may have heard the last of this episode, I doubt whether I shall"*. Major Bennett then enquired as to how I spent my time at Souastre and when I told him that I had been working with the rest of the men he stated that this had never been his intention and must be corrected at once. He telephoned the Sergeant-Major that BCA's on rest were in future to be treated as employed men and not to be used for fatigues without his direct orders. He confirmed this in writing.

So the BCA's obtained their charter a position maintained not without difficulty to the end. Sometimes my name would be marked for guard duty but I would tell the Battery Orderly to erase it which he did though not without some grumbling also, when the call went for all hands to turn out, I would quietly draw attention to the ruling. I was very sorry about the quarrel with Sgt Salter the more so because of the events of March 22 when I was the bearer of the message enabling him to evacuate Vaulx-Vraucourt a few minutes before it was over-run by the enemy. Sgt Salter was highly appreciative of this service and was heard to remark on more than one occasion that I had saved his life, possible an exaggeration but his party would certainly have been captured had the message not come through in time. There was a decided coolness between us for some time but eventually this disappeared and we got on very well together again.

It did not follow that the BCA's off duty were necessarily idle and in any case we took care not to parade our relative freedom before others less fortunate. Usually jobs were found for us otherwise we would make ourselves scarce. One of the odd jobs given us was running a canteen. Gunner Wiley had been ordered to bring his canteen to the battery position at Fonquevillers and the drivers and Gunners off duty were complaining at their loss of the facilities. The CO agreed that a subsidiary canteen might well be started at the Horse Lines. He lent Bush and me a hundred francs and told us to do our best. We got a few tips from Wiley and on the first day off duty harnessed up the "gharri" (an Indian term for the light horse drawn cart) and drove over to a neighbouring village where a divisional store was located. After a long wait we laid out the money buying cigarettes, chocolate and biscuits only. On our return we put up a notice 'Canteen' outside our dug-out and waited for business. Somewhat to our embarrassment we sold out almost at once and the first night saw us devoid of stock but with a capital of 120 francs not a bad return for one day's work. This necessitated another visit to the stores and so we carried on until we changed over and Tebbs and Frost took over the stock (if any) and the cash. In a very short time we were able to repay the hundred francs and were working on profit only.

Altogether the canteen was a great success, the only difficulty being in obtaining supplies. Often the divisional stores were sold out and then we journeyed from village to village trying to find another supplier. It was rarely that we returned empty handed. We specialised in quick selling lines like cigarettes and chocolates although there was a small demand for sardines, tinned milk and fruit but we were careful not to overstock for fear of these being left on our hands. When eventually Souastre was vacated the canteen closed down and we handed over to Capt Fletcher several hundred francs the profits on a few weeks' trading and some valuable stock to Wiley. The profits were supposed to go to the battery funds whatever that might mean. At all events Bush as treasurer received an acquittance from the Captain and that closed the matter as far as we were concerned. I believe a large portion of the money eventually became a contribution towards Jagger's Artillery Memorial at Hyde Park Corner, London.

So between Souastre and Fonquevillers the time passed pleasantly enough and I remember many a pleasant sleep in the cornfields between the two places when, our spell of duty over, Bush and I made our way back to the Horse Lines.

At the battery the pace became hotter and hotter surely the long expected "Counterstroke" could not long be delayed.

On July 24 Bush and I were on duty. Bush was in the BC Post while I was scrounging for corrugated iron. I had persisted in my attempt to cut a way through from my shelter to the BC Post. Excavation was proceeding rapidly for I had succeeded in arousing the interest of the others in the project, in fact Tebbs and Frost had almost broken through the day before. Corrugated iron was now needed to prevent the walls from caving in. Frost had located a couple of sheets in a neighbouring battery position, unfortunately the rightful owners had been on the alert and he had been unable to secure them. I had been more lucky for the owners' attention being relaxed it was the work of a moment to draw them into our own position whence they could be carried openly. I was staggering back to the BC Post carrying the sheet on my head when Bush called out *"We won't be needing those we're moving tomorrow"*. It appeared that we were moving out of the sector the following night handing the position over to 256 Siege Battery.[5]

Thursday July 25 was one of the busiest days I ever remember. We started firing in the morning and continued right up to tea time. After tea we started packing up for we expected being relieved at dusk but after a short interval firing was resumed, one NF called after another being sent down from the aeroplanes. Ammunition was running short for we had received none the night before and the relieving battery were to bring up their own supply. Shells had to be carried from one emplacement to another, NCT cartridges ran out and we had to fall back on odd lots of cordite. The few remaining gas shells were pushed through as a make weight, any old shell would do, new bands or old, perfect or damaged.

At 7pm the teams arrived from Souastre to pull us out and soon afterwards the lorries of 256 Battery could be heard in the grove for of course they were a mechanised unit. But it was impossible to change over with all the shooting going on. Meanwhile their officers and men inspected the position and approved the field ovens but poor old Dennis was almost in tears at having to part with them. They enquired if my megaphone went with the position. On being told that we were taking it with us their officer said that in any case he preferred control from section posts and would see that telephones were erected from the BC Post to the guns. The Gunners were as little complimentary about the dug-outs as the officers were to the BC Post. Meanwhile we continued to fire furiously.

At 8.30 the ammunition supply on two of the guns had given out and they were put out of action. At 9pm we received orders to withdraw. The guns were limbered up, the waiting teams harnessed and the equipment strapped on. The dug outs were handed over to the newcomers. Bush and I were packing up our limbered wagon and the megaphone was taken down and placed in safety. The officers' kit was removed and last but by no means least the latrine seats were removed. We had gone to great pains making these and they definitely did not go with the position.

Major Bennett now formally handed over the position in the traditional way, over a bottle of whisky. The teams were all ready. Gunner Wheeler waited outside the post with Bess the CO's charger. The CO mounted, placed himself at the head of the column and, giving the order, *"81 Siege Battery – Walk march"* led the way to Souastre.

The BCA's limbered wagon formed the tail of the column and as we moved away we could see 256 Battery pulling their guns into our old emplacements. As we moved away the sounds became fainter and fainter until everything was swallowed up in the darkness. At length we approached the Horse Lines and tied up the teams leaving the guns limbered up ready for moving in the morning. Then we turned in, Bush and I joined Tebbs and Frost. We were a tight fit in the dug-out but even so had to make room for a number of Signallers. Overcrowding was the rule that night but as Sgt Clarke used to say *"Ca ne fait rien"* (it doesn't matter). Tomorrow we should take the road again.

---

1   Rossignol Wood was known to the Germans as Copse 125. This was the title of Ernst Jünger's epic chronicle of his service on the Western Front.

2   The location can be seen today on the left side of the lane where a smaller lane branches to the right as you travel north from Miraumont to Puisieux. The area is surrounded by a hedge but the buildings have not been restored.

3   Number 106 Fuze was the first British instantaneous percussion artillery fuze, first tested in action in late 1916 and deployed extensively in early 1917. This fuze detonated a high-explosive shell instantaneously when the nose made physical contact with the slightest object like a strand of barbed wire or the ground surface. Hence it was a 'direct action' rather than a 'graze' fuze.

4   General Service wagon pulled by two horses.

5   The Brigade war diary records that they were to move out to a new position in support of the Canadian Corps which was being relieved by XVII Corps on 30 July.

CHAPTER 24
PREPARATIONS FOR "COUNTERSTROKE"

The counterstroke that the gunners were anticipating was the Battle of Amiens which commenced on 8 August. The effect was so significant that Ludendorff described it as "the black day of the German army". 81 Siege Battery had moved north east in readiness to join the Canadian Corps but it was not until 24 August that the Canadians relieved the British XVII Corps which was a formation in the First Army. On 26 August the Brigade was transferred to the command of the Commander Royal Artillery, 2 Canadian Division, with 59 and 81 Siege Batteries in positions at Wancourt six miles SE of Arras just north of the boundary between the First Army and Third Army.[1]

At 9am July 26 the battery was on the move again, this being one of the few occasions when the whole unit moved together. It was the usual practice on the line of march for the battery to be split, either to have an advance party, or, more usually, leaving the Quartermaster with his heavy stores to follow the main body later. But on this occasion we were all on the road together and a very long column we made too from the Major on his black charger at the head to where there half dozen or so sick horses under the Veterinary Sergeant's care were led with halters at the tail of the column. In such circumstances movement was slow and it was not until 5pm that we reached our destination.

Nevertheless the march was a delight from beginning to end and took more of the nature of the country ramble than a movement of troops. It was a glorious day and we marched in our shirt sleeves, the whole of our equipment being carried on the wagons. Rests were frequent and at mid-day we halted for nearly three hours at a beautiful spot where the road forded a stream. Here we unharnessed and watered the horses and let them graze by the roadside while Dennis and his assistants unloaded their cooking utensils and prepared dinner, a cold meal of bully beef and pickles with a dixie-full of strong sweet tea. Afterwards most of the troops went to sleep. Some of us discovered a peculiar berry the size of a blackberry but a pale blue colour. It proved excellent eating with an excellent though unusual flavour. I have never been able to discover the nature of the pale blue berries we ate with such gusto on that July afternoon.

At length the journey was resumed and at 5pm we reached the village of Fosseau where we found quite comfortable quarters in a barn. We were now on the Arras front. There was no secrecy about the move, everyone knew that we were going north and that sooner or later the offensive would be launched before Arras. The civilians knew it too and everyone was in good spirits. "Counterstroke" was only a matter of time. We remained at Fosseau until August 3 just killing time in fact the only thing I remember was lying in a willow patch close to the road. Here I could watch the traffic on its way up and down the line but the spot was so secluded that I might have been miles from the war.

On August 3 we again moved for no apparent reason to Grand Servins.[2] For some unknown reason the move was made by night and consequently was rather trying. Grand Servins differed little from Fosseau, just another rear village and more killing time. We were nearer the line however and we BCA's spent most of our time on a ridge about half an hour's walk from our billets. Here were some ruined windmills that had evidently been destroyed by German long range guns. From this ridge we could see the flashes of our artillery in the distance. We took our directors to the ridge and made some pretence at observation. So far as Major Bennett was concerned we were out of the way and that was all he cared about.

At night we would adjourn to the estaminets in the village and drink white wine or coffee. Sometimes as an extra treat we would be able to purchase one of the local flat brown loaves which for some reason we preferred to the white bread supplied to the troops. The resources of the estaminets did not run to egg and chips.

There were the usual gambling schools set up and on one occasion I was invited to join in a game run by Corpl Tebbs I was literally down on my last penny which I threw on the diamond where it came up trebles and I was paid fourpence plus all the dirty notes in the kitty. Now a capitalist I started plunging and at the end of the session I was thirty francs (then about 25/–) in pocket. Not a bad return.

Generally speaking I was rather lucky at Crown and Anchor unlike Bdr Daly who seemed to put a positive blight on the game so much so that some Signallers refused to play in his presence. Daly was a plunger and would back his fancy without rhyme or reason but whatever he did he never seemed to win. Poor Daly could not resist the temptation of the Crown and Anchor board. When his money ran out his watch would go on the board which he would have to redeem later. His watch was always in pawn to one Signaller or another. He had another weakness, shaving. In spare moments when most of us would search out canteens Bdr Daly would retire to some quiet corner and shave. It was a long job and he would eventually emerge bleeding profusely. He would beg others to do the job for him and while most of the Signallers regarded this as a particularly mean way of securing an advantage it certainly appeared that the best way to escape from an unpleasant task was to volunteer to shave the Bombardier. In all else he was a strict disciplinarian and would keep the Signallers in order which was more than Sgt Clarke could ever hope to do.

We had almost given up hope of being in "Counterstroke" in fact we thought the battery had been forgotten altogether when on August 14 we were ordered into action. At 10am we packed up and after much delay we arrived at 5pm at a bare field near the village of Simencourt where the new Horse Lines were to be established. There was a good deal of confusion in this place as no one seemed to know who was to go forward and who to stay behind. Major Bennett and some Officers had gone forward to reconnoitre a position and nothing could be done until their return. At 9am the CO returned and ordered the guns and ammunition wagons forward. Here again I noticed a good deal of confusion quite different from his usual orderly way of advancing the guns. We seemed to wander all round the countryside until at last we halted outside what seemed to be a private park. Then the CO called for the centre section, Nos.3 and 4 guns and led them away down the road to the left. Plainly the battery was going to be split. Tebbs and Frost took up a director and accompanied this detached portion of the battery. The rest of us waited under the trees for what seemed like hours.

Then Bush who had guessed that the rest of the guns were to be accommodated somehow in the chateau grounds wandered off to see how the land lay. Meanwhile Evans and I were dozing against the limbered wagon. Evans whose job had petered out had re-joined the BCA's at Grand Servins. I was awakened by my name being called having been passed down the column. *"Tell Gunner Hall to bring the director along."* Evans was more than half asleep as I set to work to uncover the sheeting and get to the instrument. *"What's up?"* he demanded. *"Come on,"* I re-joined, *"the CO wants the director."* *"Don't you attempt to give me orders,"* he retorted. *"You're not an NCO."* *"Don't be a damned fool,"* I replied. *"The CO has told me to bring up the director and I'm going to have it."* *"You can't have it,"* he said. I wasted no more words but turned round and knocked him into the ditch. Then I took out the director and went off with it into the chateau grounds. I fancy that Evans being asleep did not hear the CO's order and thought I was trying to steal a march on him. We had another flare up the following day after which his orders came through and he left for the sound ranging company. The few Gunners who witnessed the sight of the two BCA's fighting for the director at two o'clock in the morning said it was too funny for words.

I made my way with the director through the gates of the park, along the winding drive, past the chateau and into a small clearing beyond. Here the rest of the battery was to be placed and here trouble awaited the CO for there was room for only two of the guns. It was extremely good work on the part of the drivers to bring Nos.1 and 2 guns into position. Bush and I set out to lay the Lines of Fire, a tricky job at night with only the light of a torch. The remaining two guns were packed off somewhere, where I didn't know and was past caring. There was ample accommodation in the chateau cellars. Bush had bagged one of the best as a BC Post, the position was oriented and we sat to await the morning.

But there was no rest for the wicked. Sgt Clarke had fixed an involved system of wiring and we now learnt that the left section had progressed satisfactorily and their guns were laid on the line of fire. And now came a call from the CO which altered things for me. *"I'm sorry Hall, you'll have to go down to the rear section and lay out their lines of fire and you had better stop there until I have the section moved."* This was the first I had heard of the rear section and on making enquiries I learned the last two guns had been sent back to Wailly[3] a village two miles in rear. Two new officers, Renshaw and Williams were in charge but they had neither instruments nor maps and until their guns were laid on the line of fire the CO was unable to report his battery in action. I set off with my director.

Wailly took a bit of finding but by following a telephone wire I eventually reached a field where lay the two guns. It was four o'clock in the morning. The two young officers were fresh out of England and were of the "silly ass" type so much parodied at the time. *"So you're the BCA are you?"* said one. *"Splendid fellow, come in and have a drink."* I readily assented I felt I could do with one. *"Well, what about these damned guns?"* was the next question. I replied that I had brought the director with me and had been sent to lay out the Lines of Fire. *"But it's too dark,"* was the answer. *"Besides, it doesn't really matter, we're at least twenty miles behind the lines."* I responded that we had already laid out the lines for the four advanced guns and the Major wanted to report the battery in action. *"Well why can't he?"* was the bright suggestion whereupon I respectfully indicated that apart from anything else the guns were actually pointing away from the enemy. *"Well it wouldn't be a bad plan to turn them round would it, they would look better anyway, now you leave things to me, Hall,"* said Williams. Whereupon he called out the detachments who slewed the guns round. *"Now for the pickets,"* he continued, *"plant one about there, Sergeant, and you, Corporal, somewhere at the back it doesn't really matter where, it's only for show – that's right now the lamps one on each picket both burning brightly and that's that. You can turn in your men."* And with that the two merry lads (as they came to be called) returned to the BC Post and glibly reported their section in action.

They did not seem so confident in the morning and it was Williams who called me up at 9am and suggested that it was high time that we got the job done properly before the Old Man turned up. We were only just in time and had the director out of the way and the pickets planted, in their proper position this time, when Major Bennett put in an appearance and seemed well satisfied with all he saw.

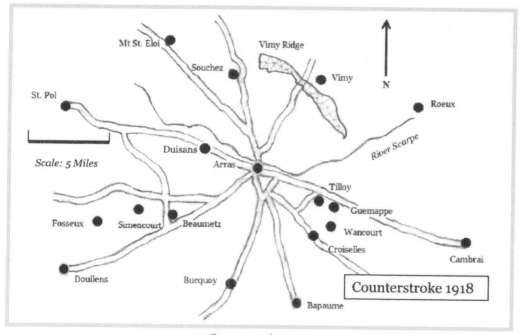

Counterstroke 1918

In contrast with the well ordered position at Fonquevillers the affairs of the battery seemed to have got in an extraordinary muddle. Two guns were in the grounds of Agny chateau, two in allotment gardens at Achicourt,[4] two rear guns in an old quarry at Wailly, the Horse Lines somewhere down at Simencourt[5] to say nothing of the Quartermaster and other odds and ends still awaiting orders at Grand Servins. We had it appeared taken over positions recently occupied by a six inch howitzer battery. The former occupants had previously held a position further forward but the German advance in March had driven them back. Arras like Ypres remained in British hands throughout the war and here the line had been practically static. Arras might be likened to the pivot from which the operations centred. The further south the greater the retreat. At Vaulx-Vraucourt we had retreated a matter of twenty miles, a mere fleabite compared to the hundred odd of the Fifth Army on our right but here at Arras the withdrawal had been a matter of only three or four miles. Nonetheless the shock to the defending troops had been considerable judging by the large number of Nissen huts which the enemy had destroyed by shell fire. Our predecessors seemed to have lost two guns and have been prepared for further withdrawals for the two guns at Agny chateau must have been firing and two others sent to the rear position when the attack petered out. They remained in this condition long after the German offensive was over. The object of replacing one battery by another of the same calibre is rather difficult to understand although it had happened to us before. Major Bennett for one did not appreciate the idea as he expressed it of being called in to straighten out the mess.

The position at Wailly was rather more than 9,000 yards from the German front line so the merry lads had exaggerated a little when they spoke of over twenty miles. It might well have been for all the good it was. We certainly had our SOS lines and at night the two guns were laid on the German front line but I doubt whether could effectively have responded to a call. The previous occupants had however plastered the BC Post with sheets of paper of which the line and range of presumptive targets had been calculated in case the enemy should resume the offensive. Agny chateau, Achiet crossroads and many other points were indicated down to a clump of trees less than 800 yards ahead. Rather morbid I called it.

True to his word Major Bennett at once set to work to vacate the rear position. There being no room in the chateau grounds he did the next best thing and started work on the Agny-Achiet road just outside. The guns from Wailly were brought up at 10pm on August 16 and so the rear section disappeared and the centre section came into existence. As a result of these manoeuvres Nos.3 and 4 guns had changed places with 5 and 6, a fact which was not realised until later when we paraded in the order 1, 2, 5, 6, 3, 4.

The abandoned Wailly position was handed over to the drivers who moved up from Simencourt where they were suffering great privations for they were without cover of any sort and had no building materials. The old quarry, although rather advanced, proved ideal for the Horse Lines owing to the concealment it gave to the animals. It was within easy reach of the guns and there was ample accommodation for man and beast.

At first Major Bennett tried to direct the fire of his divided battery from his headquarters at Agny Chateau. When I returned there on the night of August 16 I found Bush and Tebbs struggling with a couple of planchette boards one for the local guns and the other for the two guns at Achicourt and they were now preparing a third for the new centre section. Frost at the left section was in charge of the telephone there acting as BCA–cum–Telephonist transmitting the orders to the remote guns. But an aeroplane shoot conducted by guns a mile apart had proved far from successful. Clearly some other method must be tried.

The CO therefore conceived the plan of running the left section as a completely independent unit while controlling the right and centre sections from Agny. No.2 gun became the pivot gun for the double section No.1 being 20 yards to the right and 3 and 4 no less than 500 and 520 to its left. With such an enormous gun interval great care had to be used in concentrating all guns on their target but the system seemed to work all right. A section post was set up in rear of the centre guns and with its aid aeroplane shoots were successfully conducted. I was at Agny more or less spare for a couple of days and took the opportunity of exploring the grounds of the chateau which had suffered little from shell fire but the paths were overgrown, the lawns unkempt and the flower beds choked with weeds. Most of the damage to the building itself had been the British who had demolished the walls to afford additional protection to the spacious cellars.

On the morning of August 18 the change over took full effect and I was ordered to Achicourt to take over the BC Post there. I took with me the planchette board and a range rule I had made the day previously. I was rather surprised to find Lieutenants Randall and Williams in possession – evidently they had been changed over as well. After the picturesque surroundings of the other guns it was a little disappointing to come to the nondescript position of the left section. The two guns were in a small clearing made by some allotments, the shelters being little tin huts dug into a bank, perfectly dry but very small.

But I soon learnt that we had decided advantages over the main battery. In the first place the merry lads were not particularly fond of work particularly night firing. If it were possible to refuse a target they did so. We had our own zone and they were well aware of the limitations of our range. The actual working out of the targets was left to me as BCA but one or other of them always looked at the map to see if it were possible to shelve the shoot on to the main battery or disregard it altogether. So well did they succeed that it was rarely that our night's rest was disturbed.

The allotments were a surprise but more so an aged civilian who put in an appearance to tend them. He was apparently allowed to work there during certain hours at his own risk. Fresh vegetables proved too great a temptation to the troops and isolated cases of scrounging appeared. This brought a complaint from the peasant and the culprits were called to account. The merry lads stated that such a pilfering would be dealt with severely if found out. Cabbages pulled out promiscuously were bound to be noticed but if a row were systematically removed and the ground restored the thefts might not be detected. Besides the mean blighters who had pinched the cabbages the night before had not even left one for the Officers' Mess. Such a hint could not be disregarded. Every night a party of Gunners was warned for special duty and with the aid of electric torches remove a row of vegetables taking great care to obliterate all footmarks and leave the ground in an apparently undisturbed condition. The cultivated patch grew less and less and a share of the spoils was duly laid at the door of the Officers' Mess. The old Frenchman seemed to realise that something was going wrong with his allotment but so well had the scrounging been done that he made no further complaints though had we remained at Achicourt much longer the cabbage patch might have been reduced to microscopic proportions.

I enjoyed considerable freedom at this time and would wander off from the position as I wished. On one occasion I walked to Arras intending to look round the town but I was stopped by a Military Policeman who told me that the town had been closed to troops since the German advance. I had to content myself watching a fifteen inch howitzer on rail mountings in action outside the town.

I had a large number of hot baths, long overdue I am afraid. Somehow or other there was a regular epidemic of baths at Achicourt: the two young officers set the fashion I think. On one occasions I was in my bath tub (an empty cartridge case) when a target was telephoned from Agny. In the ordinary way one of the officers would have worked out the calculations for me but I suppose they thought the opportunity too good to be missed. At any rate I had to jump out of my bath, work out the target, then, throwing a blanket round me I rushed outside and shouted the directions to the guns much to the entertainment of the troops.

And so in light vein we carried on until August 25 the day before "Counterstroke".

---

1   The Brigade war diary gives a map reference of N.2a.1.9 at Tilloy and then N1.6c.8.2 near Wancourt (sheet 51b and 51c). They supported Canadian troop taking the Wancourt Tower Ridge as they advanced to the Drocourt-Quéant line, a strong German position.

2   According to the Brigade war diary (WO95/225 48 Brigade RGA) the Brigade was to be "in First Army reserve under VIII Corps administration'. On 13 August orders were received to move to XVII Corps by 15 August.

3   Wailly is 2 miles south west of Arras.

4   Agny chateau and Achicourt were mid-way to Arras, a mile north east of Wailly.

5   Simencourt is about two miles north west of Wailly.

CHAPTER 25
THE CAPTURE OF THE GERMAN FRONT

Although this chapter is short there are several signs that warfare on the Arras part of the British sector of the Western Front is changing. The battery is moving, not just from one part of the front to another but forwards. The German lines are also moving back and out of range of the guns hence further movement being ordered. Gnr Hall notes that they slept in dugouts occupied the previous night by enemy soldiers and the mood of the battery is rather different as, erroneously, they celebrate the capture of the Hindenburg Line and another step towards victory. This action was in fact part of the Battle of the Scarpe. An attack was ordered on a four mile front from the Scarpe in the north to Neuville Vitasse where the First and Third Army boundary was located. The British Official History records 48 Heavy Artillery Group (which included 81 Siege Battery) as being one of nine such groups participating in this action.[1]

Although we had been expecting "Counterstroke" for so long, the order when it arrived came with dramatic suddenness. The news was telephoned to us at the Left Section by Major Bennett at 7pm on August 25. In effect our orders were to put the guns out of action at once, pack up and prepare to join the main body on the road outside Agny chateau. The teams were already on their way. We dismantled the position and when the horses arrived were ready to limber up and proceed to the rendezvous.

At 9pm we were outside the chateau gates. The Centre Section was already lined up and we could hear the shouts of the drivers as they were guiding Nos.1 and 2 guns along the narrow winding carriage drive. The two officers and I made our way to the main BC Post to report our arrival to the CO.

The cellar which formed the BC Post and Battery Headquarters was well lit with candles stuck on the walls with pieces of clay. On an upturned cartridge box lay a bottle of whisky and two jars of service rum. Major Bennett helped the two Lieutenants to whisky and remarked that we might as well get the rum issue over. I made some fatuous remark about this but he rejoined *"There's no spirits for you or for you either Bush. You'll want all your brains tonight for this job".* I suppose I must have looked disconsolate at this for he promised us a double issue as soon as the business of the night was over. Then he read out the orders as he had received them. *"On the night of the 25/26 August at an hour to be notified later the Canadian Corps will advance and will capture the Hindenburg Line. After this they will proceed in the direction of Cambrai."*

Everybody gasped no less at the orders than the wording of them. So different were they from anything we had previously experienced. We knew when we moved to Arras that we were within the jurisdiction of the Canadian Corps but we had travelled about so much that a change of command meant nothing to us and we dismissed the exploits of the Dominion troops as so much newspaper talk. With the men themselves we had not yet come in contact although we knew they occupied the trenches in front of us. Now we realised that the Canadians were in reality shock troops to whom special tasks were entrusted and who in consequence enjoyed privileges denied to ordinary regiments. They possessed little or no artillery or indeed any of the specialised units. Consequently they had to rely on British batteries both Field and Garrison for their artillery support and this was the reason we had been sent to Arras to join them. When we came in contact with them we found them a magnificent body of men, far superior in physique and appearance to the British Tommy[2], in fact ideal troops to be entrusted with such a spectacular effort that was about to be staged.

The style of their orders which gave us such a shock at first later became our familiar pattern. Where the British would write *"An attack will be made on such and such a line,"* the Canadians always used the phrases *"The Canadian Corps will capture this defence and will advance beyond"*. Of course things did not always go according to plan but such direct orders certainly inspired confidence among the troops. If an order had said that the Canadian Corps will capture the moon they would have endeavoured to obey it.

The CO had no further orders except that he was to move his battery forward to Beaurains[3] where further instructions would be issued. And now the whole battery is lined up outside the chateau grounds, the men have had their tot of rum, a very big one and are in fine form sitting on the guns singing and spinning yarns, a sight that made Bush and I feel more miserable than ever. The Signallers have disconnected the telephone and reeled in the wire all except the single line connecting us with Brigade Headquarters. Half-past nine Major Bennett goes out to investigate. It is nearly dark enough to move. He speaks a few words to the Colonel. He will move forward at ten o'clock if that is all right. Yes, that satisfied the Colonel. *"Now, Sergeant Clarke, you can disconnect the phone."* A couple of Signallers go out, the reel between them, taking in the wire as they go. We are now cut off from Headquarters and will not be able to receive orders again until a new line has been laid.

Ten o'clock. *"Well, gentlemen, we might as well be moving,"* says Major Bennett. The officers leave the BC Post. Bush and I put out the lights and throw the candles into a sack with other oddments – candles always come in useful. As we walk down the drive the chateau is in total darkness. The CO quickly passes down the waiting column and warns the men not to smoke or talk loudly and to move very quietly. The officers take their posts in front of their respective guns. Major Bennett gives the order not in the ringing tones of the riding school but in a hoarse whisper which is passed down the line. *"Prepare to mount. Mount – walk march"*, and silently we follow our leader into the unknown.

As we go forward we realise that there are many other units on the road. A Field Battery approaches us, we can dimly see their guns, 4.5 inch howitzers but no words are spoken and they draw away somewhere to our left. We approach a village. At first it seems intact but later we dimly observe that it is nothing but a heap of ruins. At last a halt is called. A few minutes delay while the CO makes certain of the position. A whisper is heard *"No 1 gun"* and the team is urged forward over the uneven ground, the drivers making for a point of light where an officer holds his electric torch. On reaching this the drivers wheel right round leaving the gun pointing in the direction of the enemy and close where the officer is standing. The Gunners now gather round and on a whispered command lift the trail hook from its limber key. A final command *"Limber, drive on"* and the horses make off to the rear while No.2 gun is ordered forward. And so on until all six guns are drawn up in a line twenty yards apart alongside a ruined farm house. The ammunition wagons are now quickly unloaded and Sgt McIlroy who had succeeded Sgt Rolf at the Horse Lines is leading the teams back to Wailly.

Much remains to be done before the battery is in action. First the Lines of Fire. Bush and I set up the director in rear of No.3 gun and centralise the two bubbles. The CO gives us the zero line, due east, 90 degrees grid as we call it. Making allowance for magnetic variation, in this case 25° 40'. We set 115° 40' on the director and wait for the needle to settle. Then we clamp the telescope to the dial swing round to zero and the director is pointing in the required direction. Now to get the line to the guns. We release the telescope from the dial and call up the guns one by one. The Gun Captain shines his torch over his dial sight while Bush turns the instrument to the point of light. Meanwhile I shine my torch down a hole in the telescope lighting up the graticules. Soon he has located the light and I make a note of the reading on the dial. We take all guns in turn and to make doubly sure changeover I locating the guns while Bush takes the readings. We agree. Now we look at the readings. No 1 gun 56° 20' left deduct this from 180 and reverse the sign. So 123° 40' right is the angle for No.1 gun and so on with the rest. In the ordinary way we would sing out the angles to the guns but on this occasion we write the figures on slips of paper and pass them to the Gun Captains. These now go through a similar procedure. We shine a light on the director and with the angle we have given them set on their dial sights they order the trail to be moved left or right until they have centralised our light. Once this has been done and checked by the officer we can extinguish our torch and remove the director, but since this is their zero line the Gun Captains being careful not to move their guns reset their dial sights at '0'. All targets will be so many degrees right or left of this line.

There is now another action with which we as BCA's are not concerned. Now that the director has been removed the Gunners must find another aiming post. Since it is night no prominent objects can be seen so they must be content with an Auxiliary Aiming Post or Night Line. Still without moving the gun they set 180 degrees on their dial sight with the result that the Gun Layer is looking directly in rear of his gun. A couple of men run out one with a picket and the other with a maul and the inevitable torch. When about twenty yards in rear they move left or right until the Gun Layer located their picket right in the centre of his dial shift. Then with a few quick blows the picket is planted a lamp hung on the picket hook and the Sergeant reports his gun in action.

The BCA's have not finished however. The next job is to locate the exact position of the pivot gun (No.3) on the map. There are various ways of doing this and it is infinitely easier in daylight when various prominent objects can be picked out. In a pitch black night however it is a different matter so we enter into conference with Major Bennett who shows us on the map the path we have taken from Agny. According to him we should be somewhere near these cross roads. With a bit of luck we are able to identify the farm building on the map. We step out the distance from three points and then we have agreed the result we mark the exact place on the map with a cross. Here is No.3 gun. The others lay so many yards left or right.

It is a few minutes work to fix up the planchette board. The map is so arranged that the point marking the location of the battery comes in the centre of the left hand edge of the board. It is secured by drawing pins, the zero line is drawn in pencil, a glass headed pin acts as a pivot for the range rule and is fixed right on the pencilled cross. Then a celluloid scale marked in degrees is pinned on to the map with its centre point on the zero line. So with the rule we can find the range and with the scale the angle of any target that may be sent.

Meanwhile Sgt Clarke and his merry men have been busy running out a telephone line from the battery to the new Brigade Headquarters which have moved up somewhere near Agny chateau. They are now running out lines to the two adjoining batteries so that whatever happens we are unlikely to be cut off. Major Bennett takes up the instrument and reports his battery into action.

The work on the map is of course done in the BC Post such as it is. Major Bennett has bagged a cellar and a miserable place it is too for two of the walls and a good part of the roof has fallen in and the floor is covered with debris to a couple of feet. We have no time to straighten things out and if we did the place would probably cave in but squat on the fallen stones Bush and I in one corner and the Signallers in another. The officers are on the other side of the room. The shelter, bad as it is, is the only one in the neighbourhood. The Gunners their work over for the moment are for the most part asleep alongside their guns.

Midnight and the dispatch rider arrives with details of the barrage to be laid down. Almost simultaneously the CO receives a telephone message from Brigade HQ *"Zero hour 3am"*. With the instructions is a paper map of the sector marked with a series of parallel lines showing the course of the barrage. Each line represents three minutes of firing. They are numbered 0 to 208 which with the barrage starting at 3am it should be over by 6.28. The three minute intervals however are for the Field Artillery barrage which starts from no man's land. The Heavies keep 400 yards ahead of the Field pieces and take one jump for every three of the lighter guns thus remaining ten minutes on each point. Two red lines half an inch apart and representing a distance of two hundred yards on the map are drawn at right angles to the grid. This represents the 'Battery Lane' the path we have to follow in the creeping barrage.

The map is passed to Bush and me for action. First we draw the battery lane and our share of the barrage on the planchette board. We are not concerned with the rest of the map. Then we divide the lane into six parts one for each gun. We take the range and angle to each point and for the next hour or so squat in that miserable cellar over the flickering light of a candle, pencil and paper in hand, checking and counter checking target after target. Taking the range as shown on the rule, add so many yards for wear of the gun, deduct so many for the temperature of the air, and for the barometer, deduct for the temperature of the cartridge, add so much for the wind allow another 50 yards for using 106 fuzes, tot up and convert the result to degrees and minutes. Then for the angle take the reading on the protractor, add so many minutes left to allow for displacement of the guns, deduct so many right to allow for the wind. We plod on until we have covered every point of the barrage. Then we prepare on six sheets of foolscap the programme for each of the guns showing the elevation and the line and the time they are to remain on each point of the barrage.

Our task at length completed the programmes are passed to the CO for approval. Then and only then did we get our tot of rum. True to his word Major Bennett gives an enormous issue. We feel that we deserve but agree that the CO is wise in delaying the issue. It is bad enough performing such difficult calculations in such deplorable conditions when we are dog tired, it would have been impossible had we been intoxicated in the bargain. Bush and I unfold our blankets and first shifting some blocks of chalk in an attempt to find a more comfortable resting place try to doze off for an hour or so. Major Bennett has called in the Sergeants passed over the programme and is giving final directions for the attack.

We are aroused by the CO himself. *"Quarter to three – better be getting ready."* We rise, stretch ourselves and put our blankets out of the way. *"Now,"* directs the Major, *"you, Hall, come with me to fight the battery. Bush will remain in the BC Post to deal with any changes that may come through."* I follow the CO up the rotten stairs. The Gunners are already on their guns; the Sergeants' torches show that a final check is being made. Only a few minutes to zero hour. An officer reports that all guns are correctly laid. *"You've got a stronger voice than me Hall. Start them off,"* says the CO. *"Very good, sir,"* and turning to the guns I bellow out in my best voice, (there is no question of whispering now), *"All guns – load – report when ready"*. *"No 4 ready, sir,"* comes the reply, *"No 2 ready,"* numbers 1 and 3 report simultaneously with 5 and 6 seconds later. *"Battery ready, sir."* *"All right Hall, Salvo and Gun fire two minutes to go."* At this I shout *"Battery – stand by for a salvo."* And now I must follow the seconds on my watch for at ten seconds to the hour the order must be given so that precisely on the hour it will be acted upon. Like ages the seconds pass. At last the moment arrives. Slowly and deliberately I give the order *"Battery – salvo – fire,"* and on the last word the firing numbers jerk their lanyards and all six guns ring out. A perfect salvo. At last "Counterstroke" has begun. I now give the next order *"Gun fire"*. The guns are on their own now firing as quickly as possible until it is time for the first lift.

At three o'clock the whole front wakes up and we see our neighbours for the first time. A 4.5 inch howitzer battery to our left is firing a steady ten rounds a minute and very methodical they are about it too as they sit on their guns and pass the shells from hand to hand. In contract to the Field Artillery our own men are jumping about like monkeys, everyone shouting at the top of their voices *"Half way – Home"* they yell as they ram home the shells. *"On,"* shouts the Gun Layer as he locates the picket light on his dial sight. *"On,"* shouts the Sergeant as he centralises the bubble on his clinometer incidentally throwing the Gun Layer slightly off his line. *"On,"* again repeats the Layer as he picks up the point of light for a second time. *"Stand clear,"* now shouts the Sergeant giving the command *"Fire"* almost at once. And so we continue firing at two to three rounds a minute until at 3.10 precisely when I give an order which is new to many of the Gunners and which I have never used before for this is my first barrage as BCA *"Battery – lift"*. The guns engage the second target on the programmes and the barrage continues.

The barrage itself was surprisingly thin certainly nothing like those of 1917 before Bullecourt and Messines. Moreover there had been preliminary bombardment. The enemy replied at once but although he was searching and sweeping it was evident that he had not located the battery position and would be unable to do so until his aeroplanes were flying. From what we learned afterwards both Agny chateau and the allotments at Achicourt received some attention so we were well away from those positions. The first few minutes were the worst for we did not know what reply we should get once we started firing and we knew that whatever happened we should have to stick it. If the attack had failed the roads would be packed with batteries trying to find their way back to rear positions and the enemy well aware of this would play havoc with the retreating troops. As to how the infantry were faring we had but little news. The OP line had been severed but not before the Observation Officer had reported that they were out of their trenches. It was repaired but broke again and as little could be learnt at this time in the morning it was decided to let it go. The Adjutant rang up at 5am to say that he understood that the attack was going according to plan and we were to keep to our programme.

It was interesting to watch the effect of the ever lengthening range. When the barrage started we were firing second charge and looked practically level. As the barrage advanced elevation increased only to drop again when a change was made to third charge. Later full charge was use and in the final stages the guns were firing at 40 degrees and looked as if they were aiming into the sky. At this stage two guns could go no further and closed down but the remaining four continued firing at their maximum elevation of 45 degrees until 6.30 when they too ceased firing and were sponged out. Dennis had by now prepared breakfast and while waiting for orders we ate a hearty meal.

It was soon after breakfast that we learned the result of the action and Major Bennett at once communicated the news to the troops. Taking the megaphone he called out, *"The Battery is out of action – we have captured the Hindenburg Line"*.

Excitement was intense, tin hats and rammers were thrown into the air while cheer after cheer rang through the battery. Officers and men alike congratulated each other that the war would soon be over. For a short time the battery seemed to go mad. And now we must press forward with the attack. The enemy must not be allowed to escape this time. The CO telephoned to Wailly for the horses. *"Bring plenty of fodder,"* he ordered. *"We don't know when we're going to stop."* The battery packed up like magic and we awaited with impatience the arrival of the teams. What mattered it if the roads were blown up and trenches had to be filled in before we could go forward – somehow we would find a way.

At 9am we started off in fine style but not for long for the road we had to traverse had been fought over for three years and every imaginable obstruction lay in our path. Dead men and dead horses, ammunition limbers some that had been blown up years before, fallen trees, barbed wire, shell holes and yawning trenches. Already the Pioneers were at work and we were overtaken by lorries bringing up load after load of road metal. On several occasions we had to wait while trenches were filled in. There were about a dozen of them to negotiate to say nothing of craters in the roads and our progress was slow in the extreme. The reclaimed ground was spongy for any kind of debris had been flung into the cavities and threatened to engulf our heavy guns but at last we won through and mid-day saw us in what had been the day before an enemy outpost line.

Here then we were some little distance in front of Tilloy-les-Mofflaines while on our left lay a small copse shown on the map as Bois-des-Boeufs. Both village and wood had suffered severely from shell fire but much to our surprise a thick hedge was practically intact and behind this we drew our guns. It was evident that much work was necessary before we could come into action, the ground fell away behind the hedge and would have to be levelled and a good deal of the hedge itself would have to be lopped down if the guns were to be brought close to it. Trenches from which only that morning the enemy had been expelled honeycombed the neighbourhood and in these we found quite a number of passable dugouts. Clearly our bombardment had not reduced the trench system to ruins.

There was some uncertainty as to whether or not we were to come into action. According to the latest information the enemy was still in retreat and although Tilloy had been given as our new position it was doubtful whether in the changed circumstances it would be effective. Major Bennett sent for confirmation. Meanwhile Dennis eager as ever to do something for our comfort had unshipped the copper and prepared tea. A couple of guns were unlimbered in case they were needed in a hurry. Then it seemed that we were not required to come into action at Tilloy after all – the Germans had retreated right out of range.

We rested for some time enjoying the hot tea which with bully and biscuits formed our mid-day meal. Then at 4pm we limbered up again and moved forward over open country until we should resume contact with the enemy. The Major at this time had no idea when this would be and could get no definite information as to the whereabouts of the advancing infantry. A couple of officers were sent forward to reconnoitre while the battery slowly and painfully followed picked our way over the broken ground. On paper our progress seems very slow but when it is remembered that six teams of eight heavy draught horses apiece were hauling a five ton gun over ground that had been fought over for three years, where roads were practically indistinguishable and all kinds of obstacles encountered the magnitude of our task may be appreciated.

At last we entered a sinister looking valley and made our way up a narrow lane to where the outline of a village showed up dimly in the fading light. We did not enter Wancourt for the simple reason that the enemy were still in possession but halted about half a mile away quietly unlimbered and sent the teams back to Wailly. Then we stealthily trained the guns on Wancourt itself and looked for shelter for the night. We took possession of a number of dug-outs and in particular a sap that had been driven into the bank side. We did not feel particularly happy about our accommodation for the Germans had constructed these shelters and had been in possession until that morning. Many were the tales of booby traps that the enemy had laid for the unwary and it was a general principle that ex-enemy dug-outs should not be entered until declared safe by the Engineer experts. On this occasion we could not wait for the Engineers and there was no alternative but to occupy the shelters and hope they would not blow up. We entered the sap very gingerly tapping the floors and walls and cutting every wire that could be seen. Wires abounded for the sap had evidently been used by the Germans as a telephone exchange. There were a number of instruments lying around, all looked harmless enough but we took no chances and carefully put them into buckets of water before throwing them outside. Then we pitched out all the rubbish the previous tenants had left behind and settled for the night. So far as we could see there were no booby traps.

The night was very still. There was some rattle of machine guns and the bullets could be heard from time to time as the enemy enfiladed the valley but of artillery fire there was practically none save when some long range gun which had up to now been unable to join in the general advance fired an occasional round over our heads into the enemy lines.

I think we were all pretty scared that night and I must confess to fear such as I had not hitherto experienced. We would doze fitfully in the bunks that the Germans had occupied the night before and ever and anon go to the mouth of the sap and look down the valley at the silent village where lay the enemy. What would happen in the morning when he would see our guns? Perhaps he already suspected their presence in the valley.

Then came the dawn (August 27) and as soon as visibility was good enough Major Bennett decided to relay the Lines of Fire (really a check up on the night before) and pick up an aiming point. Then we could cover up until targets were notified. I took out the director and did the necessary work. As to the Aiming Point, I felt there could be only one, the village church which showed up plainly in the early morning sun. The church was just outside the village on the British side. I worked out individual angles for the guns and the Layers turned their dial sights until the weathercock showed up plainly in the cross lines. With such a splendid object I ignored the rule that the Aiming Point should wherever possible be well in rear of the guns. In the light of day Wancourt looked more peaceful than ever and it seemed that a short stroll up the valley would bring one past the church into the village itself. We could hardly realise that the place was occupied by German soldiers who sooner or later would have to be driven out. We moved about the position cautiously and fearful of attracting attention remaining under cover of the sap as much as possible. That is all except Dennis the lion-hearted who had lit his fire and was cheerfully frying bacon.

Breakfast over and still no orders. The delay to our anxiety for we knew that every minute enabled the enemy to improve his defences. At last the dispatch rider arrived. The attack was to be resumed at 10am our part being to lay down a creeping barrage behind which the Canadians were to advance.

We were soon to learn that launching an attack before dawn was one thing and to fire on a village half a mile away and in full view of the enemy was another. Immediately we opened fire he replied, and with gas shells too. Respirators were donned and with the Gunners stumbling about in their clumsy masks the rate of fire dropped considerably which was just what the enemy wanted. Everybody was in a state of tension and I don't think it would have take much to have set us all bolting along the valley away from the wretched place. A number of the old hands however had a calming influence on the troops notable among these being Sgt Marsden who treated the matter as a huge joke, the Sergeant received a Military Medal for this day's work and well he deserved it but there was another no less deserving who received no such award, Gunner Dennis the battery cook. Gas did not prevent his preparing a first rate dinner although he appreciated peeling potatoes in his gas mask as little as the Gunners did firing their guns.

The first we learned of the progress of our attack was when we noticed that the Germans were shelling Wancourt which meant that they had withdrawn from the village. One of their first rounds hit the church spire bringing down the weather cock. Soon after this the whole spire came crashing down. That meant that our Aiming Point was useless. It would have been better to have selected one in rear of the guns after all. We continued firing off our night pickets. By noon all was over. The Germans had ceased from troubling us and had stopped firing on Wancourt. Evidently he was withdrawing his artillery. Leaving us to continue firing until we were out of range Major Bennett went forward to reconnoitre a forward position. It was not long before he returned with the news that he had found a splendid place at Guemappe and that we had better be moving before another battery bagged the position.

---

1   *Military Operations. France and Belgium, 1918* (Volume IV), compiled by Brigadier-General Sir James E Edmonds, London, HMSO, 1947, Vol IV 8 Aug 26 Sept , page 306, f.n. 1.

2   Tommy was the nickname given to the British soldier just as Poilu ('hairy') was to the French and Digger to the Australian and New Zealand troops. The term derived from the name Tommy Atkins used on sample army forms to indicate a typical soldier.

3   Beaurains is a couple of miles south of Arras and now the French base for the Commonwealth War Graves Commission.

CHAPTER 26
THE CAPTURE OF THE DROCOURT-QUÉANT LINE

To block the advance of the British troops and to shorten their line the Germans had constructed the Hindenburg Line. Part of that system was the Drocourt-Quéant Line, a stretch of the defensive system running between two villages of those names. Known to the Germans as the Wotan Stellung, the Drocourt-Quéant Line (also known as the 'Drocourt-Quéant Switch' or, by the British Official Historian, the 'Drocourt-Quéant Position' - often shortened to the 'D-Q Position'), ran from a point in the Hindenburg Line about eleven miles west of Cambrai, passing about seven miles west of Douai.[1] It comprised 'a front system and a support system, each with two lines of trenches provided with concrete shelters and machine-gun posts, and very heavily wired. The front line was mainly on the crest, the support system on a reverse slope'.[2] 81 Siege Battery was attached to the Canadian Corps which formed part of the First Army and, when positioned at Guemappe, was in the 4 Canadian Division's part of the line. The operation that Gnr Hall records as being on 1 September was in fact the successful assault on Hendecourt Chateau and Crow's Nest, a strong point north of the chateau but, as he describes, the new British line was east of the Drocourt-Quéant Line by nightfall on 2 September. Further evidence of the advance was the inspection of German guns by British gunners and the sighting of undamaged villages ahead of them. Hall's notes on clearing the belts of barbed wire and filling sections of trench give a hint of the task facing French and Belgian civilians when they returned after the war to reclaim their land.

The new position was only a mile away to the east but presented a much more healthy appearance from the sinister valley we had just left. Here on high ground to the east of Guemappe Major Bennett had planted a picket bearing his visiting card on which he had written *"Reserved for 81 Siege Battery"*.

Guemappe was a second-hand position but in this case had been constructed by the enemy and it was with some satisfaction that we took possession of the dugouts he had erected and dragged our guns on to emplacements that had formerly held German howitzers. There was of course the danger in taking over ex-enemy positions in that their exact location was known to the enemy in advance but to us the fact of having adequate shelter for the night outweighed this drawback and when we looked at the bare fields where neighbouring units came into action we congratulated ourselves on the CO's wise choice.

From Guemappe we had an excellent view of the Route Nationale between Arras and Cambrai. We were in fact operating in what some of us called the ABC triangle. 'A' representing Arras, the most northerly town had always been in British hands. 'B' Bapaume twelve miles to the south had been in German hands until the great evacuation of March 1917 when it came into our possession only to be recovered by the enemy in the Spring Offensive of 1918 while 'C' Cambrai had always been in German hands although in the autumn of 1917 the British advancing from Bapaume and using tanks for the first time[3] had all but captured it. They were stopped at Bourlon Wood however and later driven back. The three towns were linked by Napoleonic roads straight as arrows lined with trees and metalled in the centre with wide verges for the passage of horses. Cambrai was roughly twenty two miles from the other towns. Having failed to reach it by the southern route from Bapaume would we now be more successful by the northern road from Arras? Cambrai represented the far horizon to the ordinary soldier and many felt that once Cambrai had been taken the war would be as good as won. It turned out that we were not far wrong. As the advance proceeded we saw *"To Cambrai"* chalked on quite a number of wagons. Following the fashion it was painted on the BCA's limber and on some of the guns.

There were of course many obstacles on the road to Cambrai. The first had been overcome but Major Bennett was at fault in saying on August 26 that we had captured the Hindenburg Line, perhaps he had taken the Canadians' order of the day too literally. As a result of their March offensive (1918) the Germans had advanced their front at this part nearly eight miles and it was these trenches that the troops had occupied. Still the enemy had been in possession five months and the new line was very strongly fortified. To capture the entire trench system and to drive the enemy into the open after little more than three hours and with no preliminary bombardment was a notable achievement. It was now fully expected that the Germans would fall back on their main line of defence from which they would have to be dislodged (hence the directive *"will capture the Hindenburg Line"*). The line was very strong at this point and known by us as the Drocourt-Quéant Switch. It embodied all that was known of military engineering, double deep trenches too wide to be crossed by tanks, heavily concreted with deep dug-outs and strong points at frequent intervals, the whole protected by triple lines of barbed wire entanglements each twenty feet deep. The wire used by the Germans was as thick as a pencil and the barbs over an inch long; it was crisscrossed in an amazing manner over stakes well driven into the ground. At the time in question both trenches and wire were intact and in perfect condition as they might well be as until our recent advance they were well out of range of all but the heaviest of our guns.

Instead of retreating direct to their stronghold, however, the Germans halted at an obsolete conglomeration of trenches stretching in a south-easterly direction a mile or so in front and known as the Vis-en-Artois Switch. We engaged him from Guemappe at 6pm August 27 and maintained a steady fire on the trenches all night in order to stop any renovation. Meantime our infantry rested all night in the open.

Our orders came about midnight. Couched in the flamboyant terms to which our sojourn with the Canadians had accustomed us they stated that on the morning of the 28 August the Canadian Corps would by *"a minor operation expel the enemy from the Vis-en-Artois Switch"*.

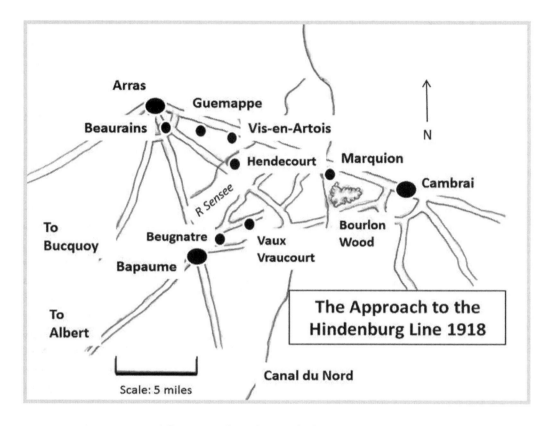

The approach to the Hindenburg Line 1918

The "minor operation" was launched early in the morning of August 28 and as was expected the village of Vis-en-Artois was easily captured. At this point however things appeared to go wrong, for the Germans instead of evacuating the whole of the switch as expected and retiring on the Drocourt-Quéant Line, persisted in retaining possession of certain strong points on the south of the switch, old trenches shown on the map as Opal, Onyx, Olive and Opera trenches together with two machine gun nests known as Smidhole and Oceanwerk. From these points he refused to be dislodged and inflicted such heavy losses on the attacking forces that they were obliged to withdraw leaving the Germans in possession of the southern portion of the switch.

With such magnificent defences to fall back on why did the Germans persist in holding on to the battered remains of the Vis-en-Artois Switch, shallow trenches for the most part that had been hurriedly thrown up some by the Germans but most by the British in the earliest days of the war, all obsolete and some caved in, stretching without rhyme or reason for purposes long since forgotten, all inadequately wired, some even (from the Germans' point of view) wired on the wrong side. It was this ramshackle conglomeration of ditches that Fritz was prepared to defend to the last man rather than retreat to their prepared concrete stronghold a mile or so in rear. Our higher command with rather unusual wisdom refused to be drawn and so for the next three days the opposing forces glowered at one another and so far as the infantry were concerned the advance was at a standstill.

It was during these three days that the artillery were called upon to force the Drocourt-Quéant Line for it was realised that sooner or later the enemy would be forced to evacuate their outposts and fall back on this, their main line of defence. We were handicapped in two ways, first because the state of the ground was such that the heavier guns (eight inch howitzers and above) could not be brought up and second because the short ranged Field guns could not be advanced near enough to engage the defences owing to the continued occupation of the Vis-en-Artois Switch by the enemy. The task of reducing the Drocourt-Quéant Line therefore fell entirely on the medium artillery the 6 inch howitzers and sixty pounder guns.

The greatest obstacle to be overcome was the barbed wire, sixty feet of it. Unless this were cut the infantry would be unable to advance and from what I saw of it later it was unthinkable that it could be cut by hand even if our men had been able to approach, which with the outposts in the possession of the enemy they were clearly unable to do. The only alternative was to blow it up by gunfire. To have cleared the whole lot would have taken months and it was decided that rather than attempt this the artillery should concentrate on cutting lanes through the wire down which at the crucial moment the Canadians would rush en masse and take the trenches, a reversal of the usual method of advancing in open order. The lanes were to be 50 yards apart the width being left for the zone of the guns to decide a matter of five yards or so. Six lanes were allocated to 81 Siege Battery one for each gun. The shoots were to be conducted entirely with 106 fuzes so as to disperse the maximum amount of wire yet damage the ground at little as possible. At all costs we were to avoid making big holes; the battlefield was not to be turned into another Ypres.[4]

With such narrow targets careful ranging was essential. Aeroplane ranging was always regarded with a certain amount of suspicion. Airmen were considered better at finding targets than ranging guns on them; they were inclined to be over-optimistic and signal OK's too readily. Ground observation was the ideal method and it was most disconcerting when our officers reported that they were unable to establish observation posts from which the barbed wire would be visible. A slight rise in the ground completely hid the Drocourt-Quéant Line from view and the only identifiable feature visible from our front line was an isolated building which stood on the highest part of the Arras-Cambrai road. This building which was known as Esperance Farm was destined to play a most important part in the attack for it was the only calibration point for all the artillery in the sector. Without Esperance Farm the guns could not have been properly ranged with the result that the barbed wire could not have been cut and the attack would probably have failed.

The farm lay well out of the line of barbed wire at a distance of 9,000 yards from the battery. As a calibration point for a target only 6,000 yards distant and a couple of miles to the right it was in the most unsatisfactory place possible. Still as there was nothing else it had to be used. Moreover its use was severely rationed and the Signallers brought amusing tales of Observation Officers waiting their turn to have a shoot at the farm. Our method of ranging was this. We opened fire on the barbed wire entanglements, calculating the target as closely as possible and making all allowances for ballistics. Then at a given moment we would switch the guns, one at a time, to the extreme right and fire a few rounds at Esperance. These were carefully observed and we were able to ascertain the difference between the calculated range and the actual range necessary to bracket the target. We applied these figures, suitably modified, for the shorter range and different line of the entanglements and continued the good work of bombarding the wire at a steady round a minute during the hours of daylight coupled with odd bursts at night to prevent any repairs being done.

The airmen went up to investigate periodically but for some time all they could report was that smoke was coming from the wire showing that our shells were bursting in the proper direction.

On the second day of the bombardment lulls in the fire were arranged during which our airmen photographed the line and when these were developed the lanes or gaps in the wire were clearly visible, some lanes obviously better than others. In our case it was evident that our No.5 gun was well off the mark. Everything possible was done to try and remedy this defect. The detachment was changed, the line of the gun checked and for some time Lt Saville himself acted as Gun Layer but it was all in vain and at the end it was found that the six guns had made only five lanes through the barbed wire. Four of these were perfect but in another case some wire was not completely destroyed. These were adequate for the infantry who at the moment of attack dashed down the lanes and opened out when they reached the trenches. The mystery of No.5 gun was never cleared up, the gun was new and the detachment experienced; it is possible the shells fell in another gun's lane.

By August 31 the wire was deemed to be sufficiently cut to enable the advance to be resumed and it was ordered that the enemy should be dislodged from the remainder of the Vis-en-Artois Switch so that an attack could be made on his main defences the Drocourt-Quéant Line.

The minor operation (as it was termed) of September 1 was, for the Canadians, one of the bloodiest encounters of the war. The trenches changed hands a dozen or more times and when other strong-points had fallen the Germans held Olive Trench and as often as they were dislodged did they return and expel our men. At 6pm the Canadian command withdrew all out troops leaving the Germans in possession of the outposts. Then they ordered all guns that could bear on to Olive Trench, howitzers to fire high explosive into the trench itself and 60 pounder guns to fire shrapnel to catch the men as they came out. The battle was short and decisive. An hour later the Canadians advanced and found the entire garrison killed or wounded. I spoke to some Canadians later who informed me that they had never seen a more ghastly sight than that presented by Olive Trench after the bombardment. The rotten earthworks were in ruins and such of the Germans who at the end tried to fly to the comparatively safety of the Drocourt Line had been mowed down by shrapnel and lay bleeding on the ground. The Canadians who were always gallant and chivalrous fighters turned into a rescue party and started digging out any Germans who were still alive and escorted them to the Dressing Station and I am told they preferred to remain in the open all night rather than occupy the ill-omened trenches. Both sides suffered grievously during the operation and a Canadian officer received the Victoria Cross for directing the attack though grievously wounded in both legs.[5] As for the battery we encountered some hostile fire but no casualties were suffered but if our part was not particularly glorious it can be said that we responded immediately to every call for assistance and took part in the bombardment that finished off Vis-en-Artois Switch.

After the switch had fallen we continued to maintain harassing fire on the Drocourt–Quéant Line to prevent the Germans from repairing the breaches in the barbed wire and it was not until midnight of September 1/2 that we were able to move forward to take our position for the Major Offensive.

Negotiation of the three miles between Guemappe and Cherisy our next battery position was a veritable nightmare. The secondary road between the two villages would in peacetime have been regarded as impracticable yet here we were at midnight urging our horses and the five ton guns along the narrow track. The Germans were shelling heavily and unlike ourselves had no scruples about making shell-holes, the bigger the hole the more it suited their purpose. It was pitch dark and we had to shine our torches on the ground before the advancing teams while the drivers guided by these feeble lights tried to pick their way ahead. I do not think there was a hundred yards where the teams could go straight forward. At other times it was a case of twisting and turning, manhandling wheels to avoid craters, laying down planks and using every expedient to get the guns forward. The smaller shell-holes, say a couple of feet across and almost as deep we took in our stride the guns and limbers lurching and swaying like ships in a storm. But there were larger craters some as much as twenty feet in diameter which blocked up the whole road forcing us through the ditches into the fields beyond. It was in executing such a manoeuvre that the off side wheel of No. 6 gun sank in the soft ground and despite the desperate endeavours of the drivers to save her the gun turned right over while men and beasts fell in an entangled heap. Luckily no one was hurt but after they had extricated themselves it was found that nothing could be done with the wretched gun until daybreak. Accordingly the team was sent back to Horse Lines while the gun lay grotesquely in the ditch, her muzzle buried in the earth. Meanwhile the rest of us went forward through the village of Cherisy until we came to an open plot of land where the country lane crossed the little river Sensee by a stone bridge shown on the map as Cherry Bridge.

The battery position at Cherisy was the most desolate I have ever encountered. Bad as had been the road the ground here was in infinitely worse condition, in fact it was reminiscent of Ypres which is saying a good deal. The enemy had, it appeared, been trying to destroy Cherry Bridge and during the past three days had been shelling the area with his heaviest artillery. Fortunately for us he had been unable to secure a direct hit on such a narrow target and the little bridge still remained intact. The River Sensee at this point was the merest trickle and the bridge itself only a few feet high, nevertheless had the Germans succeeded in its destruction, its loss would have put much of the artillery out of action until a new bridge had been built.

Getting the guns into position proved a most difficult job. Major Bennett had planted pickets showing the position of each gun, a very necessary precaution for in the darkness it was practically impossible to discover where the level patches of ground existed. Moreover the CO had indicated a path by which the emplacements might be reached, a serpentine way between the shell-holes and had taken pains to drive pegs into the ground to show the drivers their way. Lt Page who had accompanied the teams from the Horse Lines at first attempted to lead the guns into action on horseback in the approved parade ground style but was soon told by the Major not to be such a damned fool but dismount and point the way by torch light. Either by accident or design the horses, swinging round to avoid an obstacle knocked the unfortunate officer into a large shell-hole. The shock rendered him hors–de–combat for the rest of the business and after he had recovered he remounted his charger and returned to Wancourt.

Major Bennett now took over the job himself and seeing me at a loose end gave me his torch and told me to stand by one of the pickets shining the light so that the drivers could see it. The Gunners stood round the wheels helping the horses over the most difficult portion of the way. Then the Major shouted *"Now, Drivers make straight for Gunner Hall's light"*, which they did with so much effect that before I realised what was happening I had the leading horses on top of me and followed Lt. Page's way into a shell-hole. After I had emerged and the Drivers and I had indulged in a mutual slanging match the gun was drawn into a clearing and the teams departed. Now we BCA's preceded about our respective tasks, Frost and I taking the field work, that is laying out the Lines of Fire while the two Corporals retired to the BC Post to work out the targets. This allocation of duties was followed almost without exception to the end of the war.

After the guns had been laid Frost and I went off to find what Bush had bagged in the way of BC Posts. Bush had secured the best accommodation Cherisy had to offer, the largest shell-hole. Tebbs and he had scooped out a place for a seat and were sitting with the planchette board between them working out the targets for tomorrow's battle. They had almost finished and suggested that we might turn in until the attack; most of the officers had already retired and there was a nice little shell-hole next door. Well it was no use arguing and even a couple of hour's rest was acceptable. We two curled ourselves up in our blankets at the bottom of the hole and promptly fell asleep.

According to plan we were called a few minutes before 5am (September 2) and stretching our weary limbs which ached infernally owing the cramped position, rose from our narrow quarters. Already the Gunners had been roused and it was amusing to see them as they rose as it were from the ground cursing heartily as they did so. Apart from the five guns which showed up monstrous in the dim light of dawn the scene was as peaceful as one could wish. Just a country lane leading from the village across the brook whence turning to the right it mounted a little hill and so disappeared from view. Except for the battery personnel not a soul was visible.

In accordance with the now familiar practice the silence was suddenly broken at zero hour this time 5am September 2 when the artillery opened fire on the Drocourt-Quéant Line. Firing was even lighter than on the German front line a week previously for this time the heavier guns (8 inch and above) had not been able to advance and were unable to take part in the barrage. Ten minutes standing barrage on the first line was all that was allowed after which the infantry were supported to rush en masse down the gaps in the barbed wire and then fan out and attack the enemy. After 5.10 the barrage was timed to creep forward rapidly the troops following closely to the bursting shells. Some batteries, 81 Siege among them, actually fired on the Arras-Cambrai road using 106 fuzes in order to inflict the maximum damage to personnel and yet destroy the road surface as little as possible.

A few minutes past zero hour these particular guns suddenly ceased firing and at this moment a mobile force consisting of armoured cars and motor-cycle combinations armed with machine guns drove full tilt to get on its way and then the barrage closed in behind them. The mobile force was now unable to communicate with the main body, retreat was impossible owing to our own barrage while should they fail in their task the Germans would certainly exterminate them before they could re-join their own men. Their job was to make for a certain bridge and to prevent the Germans from destroying it during their retreat. The main force was timed to reach them three hours later. The force won through and in spite of heavy casualties were able to hand over the bridge intact.

The main attack was a great and glorious success. The Canadians advancing down the gaps in the barbed wire stormed the trenches and put the enemy to flight. So were the mighty fallen. This magnificent trench, the greatest defence system the world has ever known was unable to resist a ten minute bombardment and fell to the first attack of determined men. The work of eighteen months of the finest engineers had housed the Germans for exactly six hours and now they were flying for their lives leaving much booty in our hands. Best of all they were now in the open country. Trench warfare as we had known it was at an end.

There was much activity at Cherry Bridge. Soon after the attack had started a small convoy advanced down the road from Cherisy, crossed the bridge but instead of following the road up the hill, they turned sharply to the left across an open field and passed out of view. They were followed by other wagons and infantry moving up in support until the road became as congested as a fair. All did not cross the bridge safely for the enemy turned his heavy artillery on the spot and many gruesome sights came into view. Wounded horses were shot there and then and thrown into the brook while broken ammunition wagons followed suit. Human casualties were treated more gently and carried back to the dressing station and still the trek went on until the newly made path across the field was as worn as the road itself.

As the day wore on another procession met our gaze; wounded men and prisoners by the thousand came over the hill, across Cherry Bridge and so the villages in rear. All seemed to be in excellent spirits and strange to say walked together in a most friendly fashion. I saw a German officer and a Canadian Captain both badly wounded, their arms round each other's neck carrying on an animated conversation as they made their way slowly and painfully to the Dressing Station and this instance was typical of many. There were evidently insufficient stretchers and many improvisations were used. A couple of Canadians and the same number of Germans were carrying between them a blanket which dripped blood as they went on, their burden might have been of either nationality. The understanding between the Germans and the Canadians was truly remarkable. Neither side seemed to bear the least resentment to the other, and, although they had attacked one another with the utmost ferocity, once the actual fighting was over they joined forces with the closest harmony to clear up the mess and did everything possible for each other's comfort.

As for 81 Siege Battery, the fact that we had suffered no casualties during our short stay at Cherisy was more good luck than management. Whether the enemy was aware of our location or not, the bridge itself was too good a target to be missed and was being shelled the whole time. So seriously did he regard this strategic point that when his howitzers ceased firing he continued his bombardment with long range guns.

When at last our turn came to move forward we had to wait our opportunity to dash across the bridge in one of the quieter intervals. As we followed the path of so many troops we noticed that the parapets had been destroyed and a large hole made in one of the arches but Cherry Bridge must have been substantially built for though battered it easily bore the weight of our guns. On either side of the bridge a mound of dead horses and mules together with GS wagons marked the day's casualties.

A good many shells had landed between our guns but here we had remarkable luck. A deep hole like a shaft about 15 inches in diameter and many feet deep showed that an enemy battery of the largest calibre had secured a bull's eye but fortunately for us with a dud shell while in the vacant slot reserved for No.6 gun (now rescued from the ditch but too late to take part in the attack) was an enormous shell hole. But for these two remarkable coincidences it is certain that we should have suffered heavy casualties for there was no cover in the position except shell holes and some of the shells that fell in the vicinity were the largest I have ever encountered. I think we were really too excited to appreciate our danger.

Unlike our experience of the night before the road from Cherisy was easy of negotiation and we pressed forward with a couple of guns at a good pace until we came to the village of Hendecourt some two miles away. Here we halted brought the two guns into action at once and sent for the others to join us. By noon all five guns were blazing away at the enemy. But we could advance no further for to the right and left as far as the eye could reach stretched the tangled mass of barbed wire that marked the Drocourt-Quéant Line. It might well be said that the Drocourt-Quéant Line was more use to the Germans once they had lost it than it was in their possession. Here we were with all the heavy artillery and transport of the sector firmly anchored down behind the trenches and the barbed wire while the enemy was steadily retreating beyond the range of our guns. The infantry might be able to dash down the lanes in the barbed wire but no power on earth could get the guns across the trenches until they had been filled in.

Once we were in action at Hendecourt Major Bennett went forward to reconnoitre. He returned in a short time in a jubilant frame of mind. The roads east of Hendecourt were in excellent condition, the enemy was in full retreat and our infantry still in active pursuit although they were now feeling the lack of artillery support. Once the obstructions were removed there was nothing to stop us pushing forward to Cambrai and beyond. But even now the guns were firing at high elevation and by tea time all were out of range and we were still behind the barbed wire. The Engineers had not made a way for us; coiling up the barbed wire was a bigger job than anticipated. Then many loads of stone were needed to fill in the double line of trenches which stretched across the road.

Major Bennett, fretting and fuming went to right and to left in an attempt to find a way across the trenches but everywhere he was baffled. Only one road was open, the main Arras-Cambrai road and this was full of infantry and light transport. Even so the Major would have forced his way forward on the high road but permission was refused and there was nothing for it but to wait until the Engineers had cleared a way for us to the other side of Hendecourt.

It became obvious that the road would not be open that night so there was nothing for it but to make ourselves comfortable until next day. With such rapid movements means had perforce been somewhat neglected but now with a little time to himself Gunner Dennis prepared an enormous meal after which parties for want of something better to do started exploring the village and more particularly the famous Wotan[6] line in the hope of picking up some souvenirs.

The Drocourt-Quéant Line ran right through Hendecourt. Compared with some other places we had passed through the village did not appear to have suffered greatly although it had long since been evacuated by the civilians and subsequently there was nothing of value to be found. We toured the double line of trenches for a considerable distance and were duly impressed by their great strength and by the triple lines of barbed wire. The lanes the artillery had cut in the wire were naturally of considerable interest to us. Over half the lanes were excellent and the result resembled something like a path through a cornfield. In the other cases the results were not so good and it must be remembered that a single strand of uncut wire would present a formidable obstacle to men rushing headlong in the grey morning light. There were plenty of lanes however and the Canadians only used the best.

Out of morbid curiosity we examined the dead. Considering the magnitude of the operations there were remarkably few, far more Germans than Canadians although it is possible that the Dominion troops having a much higher regard for the dead than their British counterparts had already removed them to the cemeteries. As it was we encountered parties of Canadians who were clearing up the mess. Altogether we counted I suppose fifty or sixty corpses of whom probably half a dozen were Canadians. Most had been killed by rifle or machine gun fire and did not present such a ghastly picture as those who met their fate from high explosive, some indeed looked quite peaceful.

In their hasty retreat the Germans had left enormous quantities of materials behind, in fact the trenches looked in places like a huge rubbish dump. Souvenir hunters started to work with a will at the thousands of abandoned haversacks but little of value was found. Generally speaking German underwear was inferior to our own but a clean shirt even of enemy origin was better than a dirty British one and many took this opportunity of replacing their soiled underwear. Officers' kit was thoroughly ransacked as presenting more possibilities than that of the rank and file and I myself secured a very fine shirt from this source. Sufficient blankets were recovered to replace those called in at Fonquevillers but of more value was the large number of German ground-sheets. Although by no means as thoroughly waterproofed as ours they were a much better design being square in shape with buttons on two sides and button-holes on the other. The Germans were able to fasten any number of these ground-sheets together and with a number of short sticks which they carried could make tolerable bivouacs, which was more than we could do. After the discomfort of nights in the open this find proved a Godsend. We collected a great number of ground-sheets and sticks and they stood us in good stead on many occasions later on.

In addition to the useful material we collected an immense amount of rubbish, German helmets, gas masks and the like while some men accumulated about their persons such a variety of explosives that it was a wonder they did not go off with a bang. There had developed about this time a perfect mania for collecting fuzes and if ever dud shell was found some souvenir hunter would sally forth with hammer and cold chisel to secure the nose cap. Gunners who would moan to high Heaven about carrying their legitimate kit would cheerfully burden themselves with twenty or thirty fuzes of all shapes and sizes. When collectors got together they would bring out their treasures and compare them as if they had been pieces of valuable china.

When it grew too dark for scrounging we retired for the night occupying the little shelters that the enemy had so carefully prepared at intervals along the trenches. The Germans had left a good deal of equipment behind but this was soon thrown out to join the rest of the junk. Then realising that this was the end of a very long day but that there was no likelihood of further interruptions that night we turned in and slept like logs. Nor did we rise early in the morning. The barrier was still there. Most of the barbed wire had now been rolled up but the wide trenches across the road were still there and until they were filled in they were immovable.

All morning however lorries full of stone came rolling. The Royal Engineers were working with a will. Then a light motor roller appeared on the scene. By dinner time the road was clear, the teams were sent for and we advanced without further event to Cagnicourt some three miles ahead.

Once there we opened fire on the enemy but we were exactly twenty-four hours too late. Disaster had overtaken the infantry. After the capture of the Drocourt-Quéant Line the Canadians had pressed forward far beyond the range of our artillery and although all our guns were held up behind the barbed wire they continued to drive him back. But just when the Germans appeared to have been completely routed they reached the Canal du Nord and here the tables were turned.

The Canal du Nord was a major piece of engineering which the French had put in hand before the war. It was now half completed a huge ditch like a railway cutting stretching from north to south. Certain parts of the canal were flooded but for the most part it appeared like a huge chasm and here the Germans rallied and having first destroyed all the bridges were waiting for the Canadians with machine guns. Our men having no artillery support were unable to proceed further. Later they had to retire with heavy loss. The Canal du Nord lost us a valuable three weeks and might well have extended the war over the next year. Just as the extent of our victories had not been realised by those at home neither did our people appreciate how grievously the Canadians suffered on that day of September 3.

Cagnicourt was practically intact when we arrived. It is probable that civilians were in occupation up to a few weeks ago but these had been evacuated when the Germans retreated to the Drocourt-Quéant Line. There was still a little heavy furniture in the houses but most personal property had been removed. As we approached the village the first thing we saw was the communal cemetery. This had certainly suffered somewhat from shell-fire as a result of which a number of graves had been disturbed and the long buried dead brought to light, a most revolting sight. Beyond the cemetery on the right hand side of the road stood the usual collection of farms which appeared to have suffered little if at all. On the left hand side lay an open field and here we pulled in our guns.

Once again we occupied an old German position. There could be no doubt about this for on our arrival the guns were still there. The captured guns naturally caused considerable interest. There were four of them, 5.9 inch howitzers our opposite number, the ordnance from which our own guns had been designed. The fact of their capture added proof of the irresistible force of the attack, for of all positions there was none from which guns could more easily have been withdrawn, the flat field and the open country beyond – all that was needed was to bring up the teams, limber up and away. Did the enemy delay his withdrawal until the victorious Canadians appeared on the crest of the hill? If so they must have been firing point blank at 500 yards range before they were captured. A thousand pities that such a victorious advance had been checked at the Canal du Nord.

There was however something strange about the guns which we failed to appreciate for some time. Once our own guns were in position we realised that the captured pieces were facing in the same direction. So the Canadians in despair of obtaining artillery support from us had actually reversed the captured guns and had endeavoured to engage the enemy themselves. If so, their fire could have had but little effect. The dial sights had been removed presumably by the retreating foe so once the Germans were out of vision the guns would be useless. Moreover the most elementary rules of gunnery had been disregarded. Pickets had not been planted and no attempts had been made to adjust the charge to the range. I fancy that turning the guns on the flying foe was more of a moral gesture than of practicable use.

After our own howitzers the captured guns seemed roughly finished and crude in design and like all German machinery had suffered from lack of oil. There were however seats for two of the gun crew and a thin plate of armour which must have afforded the men a welcome protection. By contrast our own guns seemed very exposed and had this armour been adopted many lives would have been saved. The sliding breech seemed an improvement on our own divided screw mechanism and I should imagine the German weapon would fire more rapidly than its British counterpart. The ammunition seemed decidedly inferior, the shells being stocky affairs with no attempt at streamlining and had the narrowest of copper driving bands. Direct action fuzes like our famous 106 seemed to be unknown. The cartridges were packed in small boxes and consisted of silk bags filled with a black propellant for all the world like square bits of black cardboard. How they compared with our own NCT I have no idea but they proved excellent burning even after being soaked in water and Dennis commandeered the lot for his cook-house fire. The captured guns remained in our position for about a fortnight after which a salvage party arrived with a mule team and drew them ignominiously away.

On arrival at Cagnicourt I laid out the Lines of Fire as usual and then went in search of Corpl Bush. I found him in an altercation with an RAMC Captain. Bush had it appeared bagged a place for the BC Post and the Captain had laid claim to it for the wounded. We would have probably been disposed had not his subordinate arrived with the news that there was a more suitable place at the other end of the village. Once the RAMC men had gone, Bush led me to what he called the *"finest BC Post since Frezenberg"*.

Adjoining the cemetery was the family vault of the local aristocracy, a familiar enough figure in this part of the world. A small plot of enclosed ground lined with poplars in which stood a small chapel containing images and a few artificial flowers. In rear of this chapel a dozen steps led to the vault where slept the illustrious family of the Tailandiers. The gates had been thrown off their hinges and the way to the death chamber unbarred. *"Here,"* he exclaimed Bush proudly leading the way down the stone steps. *"Here is our BC Post."* I did not share his enthusiasm. The vault had a most unpleasant smell, a mixture of decay, blood, disinfectant and explosives and the floor was like a shambles. The Germans it appeared had broken into the vault and used it as a First Aid Post. It was in operation when the Canadians captured the village and for some time the German doctors tended friend and foe alike before being taken prisoner.

Our first job was to clear up the mess. We managed to secure a couple of buckets of water and with a brush borrowed from one of the guns swilled away the blood. Then a liberal dosing of creosote[7] gave the vault a more healthy aspect. The vault was a large one and built to hold twelve corpses but of the stone slabs which had been arranged three deep on either side of the compartment only four were occupied and I read on the marble facings that in one compartment reposed the mortal remains of Jean Pierre Tailandier, seemingly the founder of the family who died in 1876. On the slab below was enclosed the body of his wife who followed him eight years later while their married daughter and her husband occupied two more of the spaces. The last interment was in 1906 so the family had enjoyed quite a long rest before being so rudely disturbed.

Bush now started to allocate the remaining slabs among the living. One for the CO another for the officer in charge, three for the BCA's, two for the wireless operators and one for the Signaller on duty, anyone else would have to sleep on the floor. We fetched Major Bennett's valise and gave him the best position the middle slab on the end. Bush had the slab above the CO while I being the junior had to be content with the bottom compartment underneath old Tailandier and his spouse. We brought in a few boxes as chairs, fixed up the planchette board at the end of the vault and in a short time made the place look like home. Major Bennett had gone up the line to obtain first hand information as to the present situation but the officer left in charge professed himself quite pleased with the accommodation. It was in fact a choice between the family vault and a bivouac in the field, there were few cellars in the village and the barns seemed too exposed besides being some distance from the guns. Most of the Gunners had returned to Hendecourt with the wagons but the detachments on duty had erected little shelters behind their respective guns. The Signallers found another burial place even larger than ours though of a different design for the dead had been buried under the floor and a couple of telephonists occupied each slab chalking their names on the tombstones in order to reserve places for themselves.

It must be admitted that when Major Bennett returned he did not appreciate the BC Post that had been set up in his absence. One of the marble slabs had been broken probably by a fragment of shell and the cavity had been stopped up with a piece of sacking. The CO saying he did not like the look of the sacking pulled it out. Such a smell of corruption permeated the place that he quickly replaced it and called for more creosote.

For a little over a week the vault was used as a BC Post contact with the guns being maintained by means of a short telephone line to one of the shelters in rear. During the day Gnr Frost took up his position and shouted the orders to the guns as they were transmitted from the vault while at night the senior Sergeant on duty took any messages that came through.

Major Bennett was never in favour of remote control of the firing; he liked to be behind the guns the closer the better. Also there was no doubt he was prejudiced against the family vault. One evening one of the subalterns remarked *"I don't think our respected CO likes living down here,"* to which Major Bennett at once replied, *"No I don't. I strongly object to living in a graveyard and what's more, I'm going to build a BC Post in the good clean earth behind the guns. If you chaps won't help me I'll build it myself".*

Seeing that his mind was made up we staked a plot of ground in rear of No.3 gun dug down a foot or so and covered the hole with tarpaulin. The CO removed his kit to this rude shelter and never entered the vault again. The new BC Post was a tiny place to hold four of us, two officers, a BCA and a telephonist. This meant the BCA's working reliefs. I did a good deal of night work from 8pm until the morning, a rather miserable job as it meant sitting in a very cramped position in a corner of the shelter. Every day the officers' kit would be thrown out and we would deepen the dug out a little more until it became about eight feet deep. True to his word Major Bennett did the bulk of the work himself.

The BCA's remained faithful to our macabre quarters. After the officers had vacated it the telephone exchange was transferred to the vault and with the Signallers and wireless operators we made quite a merry party. It is true that with the hot weather the condition of the place did not improve and the late Jean Pierre Tailandier made his presence felt despite many pints of creosote poured into his tomb. So bad did things become that it was seriously considered that the old gentleman should be removed but there were no volunteers for the job and the proposal was dropped. For myself I slept more soundly in the vault than I had done for weeks if only because I knew that I was off duty and not likely to be disturbed with a mass of involved calculations.

We had several thunderstorms at this time and one night the telephonists on duty discovered water rushing down the steps threatening to flood the vault. There was nothing for it but to construct a sump so picks and crowbars were obtained and the heavy flagstones raised. Then a little spade work made a hole from which water could be baled. The remarkable thing was that I was asleep during the whole of the work which was done within a foot of my head, my considerate companions making a wall of clay to prevent the water reaching my blankets. When I awoke in the morning and saw the hole made in the stone floor and the picks and shovels leaning against the wall I was astonished and on being asked if I had had a disturbed night could only confess that I had not heard a sound.

The unwholesomeness of the vault did not strike us as much as it might owing to the prevalence of bad smells in the village. There were perhaps a dozen farms down the main street and in the courtyard of each the Germans had left a dead horse. I often wondered how the animals had got there and can only conclude that they had been killed elsewhere and brought to their present position for our especial benefit. Both French and Germans ate horseflesh and had flayed the hindquarters and cut away large quantities of meat. This action hastened decomposition and in the hot and thundery weather the stench was appalling. The worst case of all was in a farm yard where we used to go for water and it is impossible to describe the shocking putrescence of the carcases. The surprising thing is that no attempt was made to bury the carcases or even to throw chloride of lime over them. Large numbers of troops were quartered in the village and the Canadian YMCA opened a splendid canteen in one of the farm houses which had its own dead horse a particularly odoriferous specimen.

It is a great pity that the Canadians excellent soldiers as they were should have so little regard for camp sanitation. Their latrines were a disgrace, mere shallow holes devoid of seats and left exposed at all times. We had a sanitary orderly whose task it was to dig a trench six feet deep, improvise some sort of seat (we carried ours with us) and throw earth into the pit daily. Our latrines even in the most exposed positions were quite clean and emitted no smell whereas at Cagnicourt the Canadians in comparatively short time made the village vile, stinking and incredibly foul. One of our men fell into one of their open latrines one dark night and the subsequent task of cleansing himself was no joke either for himself or his comrades.

A somewhat similar though more amusing episode occurred at this time. One of our guns had been giving trouble, the usual thing lack of pressure. The front of the recuperator had been removed and men were pumping vigorously on the air compressor without apparent results. Lt Morkill went towards the muzzle to investigate and three Gunners gathered round. The officer had no sooner bent down to examine the pressure gauge than something gave way and he received twenty gallons of evil smelling mineral oil full in the face, blown out of the buffers with the force of 630lbs of compressed air. The force knocked him clean off his feet and in a moment Mr Morkill and the three Gunners were in a heap on the ground with oil spouting on all four. After they had extricated themselves Mr Morkill came tearing down to the BC Post calling frantically for hot water. Major Bennett attracted by the commotion directed all four to strip and have a hot bath at once. Water was quickly forthcoming and while the other Gunners ministered to their comrades in distress the CO helped his brother officer to get rid of the oil. Once clear of the filthy stuff it was found that all their uniform and underwear was ruined. The subaltern was rigged up in spare togs belonging to the Major pending the arrival of his second uniform from the Horse Lines. Incidentally it cost him twenty pounds to replace his ruined clothes. I rang up the Quartermaster-Sergeant to send up three sets of clothing for the men. He hummed and hawed. Clothing could not be replaced just like that. Meanwhile the three heroes were shivering in borrowed shirts and pants. Eventually I asked the Quartermaster to speak to the CO who quite lost his temper with the man but at any rate three brand new uniforms were sent up by special messenger.

It did not take us long to realise how complete was the hold-up before the Canal du Nord. No further attempts were made to follow up the attack and we merely fired at strategic points. Then after a few days the heavier guns moved up. A 9.2 inch howitzer made its slow and ponderous way to the shelter of a sunken road a little to our right and as we saw the men at work filling their cumbersome earth boxes (to hold the guns down when firing) we thanked our lucky stars that we were in a mobile unit. Eight inch howitzers and six inch long range guns that we had left behind at Arras were now moving forward until the whole front fairly bristled with guns.

There were in fact more guns than targets and it was these new comers that caused considerable trouble with the French authorities. To the east of the Canal du Nord lay a rich and fertile valley in which nestled a number of small but picturesque villages, Sauchy-Cauchy, Sauchy-Lestree, Oisy-le-Verger, Sains-le-Marquion and Marquion itself. All these villages were plainly visible from our observation posts and were practically undamaged by gun-fire. The Germans no doubt found the proximity of such villages a considerable benefit and so long as he held the Canal du Nord he would not have harmed them. It was the British immobile Siege Batteries who for want of something better to do started shelling the villages. Knowledge of this work of destruction somehow reached the French higher command and orders were received that such "joy shooting" must cease forthwith. Like so many orders a blind eye was turned to this and one of our officers on observation duty was able to tell us how he had seen Sauchy-Cauchy church spire crumble up and collapse under the bombardment of an eight inch howitzer battery. Some of our younger officers were eager to join in the good work but were restrained by Major Bennett. It was just as well. The destruction of Sauchy-Cauchy and Oisy-le-Verger churches led to such a storm of protest that we realised how completely the British Army was now subject to French command. (Since spring all the forces had been under the control of Marchel Foch and many directives were received in the original French with English translations appended.) There were telephone enquiries galore and Colonel Wakefield came down to conduct an enquiry. He inspected out log book, all the officers were questioned and we four BCA's came in for interrogation. *"What targets have you been using for calibration?"* *"Maison Isolate and a tree West of Oisy."* *"Have you ever fired on Sauchy-Cauchy church?"* We were all able to reply in the negative. Then came the turn of the Observation Officer. He plainly did not wish to give another unit away but had to admit that he had seen the church destroyed and suspected the eight inch battery to our right. His evidence was confirmed from other sources and there can be no doubt who was responsible for the destruction of the churches.

The outcome of the business was a special order forbidding the firing on villages in any circumstances. These instructions were received with dismay by the officers and Major Bennett level headed as a rule was heard to say that we *"might as well pack up and go home"*. In practice the order was not so drastic as it appeared. Very few enemy batteries were located in the villages themselves and there was no limit to the bombardment of cross roads and strategic points. It meant however sanctuary for enemy troops of which they were quick to take advantage for they were able to mass in front line villages with far more security than their concrete defences ever gave them. Incidentally the order reduced bombardment to a minimum and resulted in many batteries 81 Siege among them being transferred to counter-battery work. It is only fair to add that now the end was in sight the enemy was "playing the game". The Red Cross was meticulously respected by both sides and First Aid Posts were no longer located in dug-outs but were in tents in the open.

About this time we were favoured with a visit from no less a person than the General himself. The CO had been given twenty-four hours' notice of the great man's arrival and immediately called in the Sergeant-Major for consultation. BSM Spratley at first horrified at the CO's levity at describing our distinguished visitor as a *"full blown General, red tabs, little flag and all"* soon entered into the spirit of the thing. A guard must be provided. *"Leave that to me, sir,"* he said. *"I'll give you the smartest guard outside India."* Somewhat curious Major Bennett asked the Warrant Officer whom he had in mind. Well, first of all there was the Sanitary Orderly, the man who looked after the horses forage and the cook's mate from the Horse Lines with a Bombardier who was always in trouble for bad gun laying in charge. A more disreputable crowd it was difficult to find. But BSM Spratley knew his men. They had all served with him in India and dressed in new uniforms specially borrowed for the occasion they certainly did him credit. The General was due at eleven so a short time before the hour the selected four were enjoying a quiet game of cards in the improvised Guard Room while a well trusted scout was scanning the main road with the CO's binoculars. This Observer eventually spotted Red Tab's approach and gave the alarm. The guard packed up their cards and put on their bandoliers, the sentry marched smartly up and down his post. All the Gunners tucked their soft caps out of sight, put on steel helmets and fixed gas masks at the ready. An officer took charge of the firing while we BCA's made ourselves scarce. When the great man approached the guard turned out and presented arms with alacrity while the officer fighting the guns pulled the battery to attention. Then Major Bennett approached, saluted the General smartly and awaited his orders. The two then disappeared into the BC Post. Eventually the great man took his departure and as he disappeared from view Major Bennett, to the delight of the troops shouted, *"All clear,"* and replaced his steel helmet with his soft cap. The Gunners followed suit, gas masks were tossed aside, the guard disbanded itself, the officer on duty handed the control of the guns to the BCA and helped himself to a glass of whisky while the CO exclaimed, *"Thank God, that's over"*. In the afternoon Gunner Moody might be seen in his old uniform disinfecting the latrines the glamour of the *"smartest guard outside India"* had departed.

Notwithstanding its lighter side, our stay at Cagnicourt was causing grave anxiety. With the fall of the German front on August 25 followed by the still more formidable Drocourt-Quéant Line on September 1 hopes had risen for a speedy end of the war but now as the days lengthened into weeks with the enemy still in occupation of the Canal du Nord we were more apprehensive for the future. The days were shortening, there were violent thunderstorms and much bad weather while the falling of the leaves heralded the approach of winter. More serious for us the German resistance had stiffened considerably. Cagnicourt showed signs of wear and tear and it was no longer safe to walk about the village. Casualties from which we had been remarkably free for some months now put in an unwelcomed reappearance, nor were they confined to one area. The battery position, the Observation Post and even the Horse Lines all paid toll.

One of the first to suffer was the dearly loved officer 2/Lt Morkill. He with a couple of Signallers were at the Observation Post one afternoon when a shell burst among them. I actually heard the explosion in the BC Post for I was on the telephone to them at the time.

After a moment's pause I heard Gunner Jones say, *"Mr Morkill has been hit, what are we to do?"*. The CO ascertaining that the officer would be able to walk ordered the others to bring him in and evacuate the post. The two Signallers appeared an hour later helping a very pale and unsteady Morkill, his tunic thrown loosely over him and a shell dressing on his shoulder. He had it appeared received a large splinter in the back which knocked him out for a time. He soon recovered consciousness and the two men gave him a liberal dosage of iodine and bound up the wound with a shell dressing that one of them fortunately carried. Meticulous to the last Lt Morkill had insisted on plenty of iodine and no less than four ampoules were poured into an open wound six inches long. *"How he stood it without flinching Heaven only knows,"* Jones said to me later. After a short rest he was escorted to the Field Dressing Station and so passed from our ken, a grievous loss to the battery and to Major Bennett in particular for he was the CO's right hand man, a most conscientious and hard working officer.

Grave of 154454 Gnr W. Gray, Bac du Sud British Cemetery

The death of Gunner Gray[8] on September 6 was particularly affecting to me. Gray was a policeman in civilian life, a man of mighty strength. Like the rest of us he was very anxious to know how the war was progressing and what would be the outcome. A few days previously he stopped me and started, a protracted discussion as to the probable termination of hostilities.

The fact that he was carrying a hundred pound shell on his shoulder at the time seemed to me a rather inopportune moment to engage in such a debate. Still if he wanted my views he should have them. I ventured my opinion that the war would be over by Xmas and the discussion waged loud and long so that Gray strong though he was began to feel the weight of the shell and kept shifting it round on his shoulder. A group of Gunners gathered round and it was not until one of them burst out laughing that he grasped the situation, angrily threw down the shell and walked away. Poor Gray. The end of the war did not interest him after all. He was grievously wounded a few days later and died on his stretcher before reaching the First Aid Post.

Most of the other casualties were of a less serious nature but on September 16 no less than eight Gunners were wounded at once completely disorganising the working of the battery for there were only thirty on duty at the time.

Bac du Sud British Cemetery

There were repercussions to these casualties. The CO decided that he must have more men on the guns to allow for possible losses. He therefore ordered the detachments on duty to be brought up from five to six men per gun. This meant that one man in turn must be retained at the battery position to work an extra 24 hour shift although the individual selected should whenever possible be allowed an undisturbed night's rest. Mild though the Major's orders were, they were received with the utmost indignation and matters went so far that a deputation of Gunners waited on the CO to lay their grievances before him. It was really remarkable that Major Bennett consented to receive the deputation at all and his attempt to argue with the ring-leaders only added to his growing unpopularity. The Gunners' point of view was that being detained at the battery position exposed them to increased danger. Major Bennett's reply was that the regulations provided for ten men per gun let alone six (as I knew to my cost at 242 battery) and that while he was opposed to having men hanging about the position when not actually needed he would not imperil the working of the guns by under manning. With this the deputation had to withdraw.

The drive to avoid unnecessary risks call it "safety first", "caution" or even "cowardice" showed a marked change in the tone of the battery. Fatalism had passed away; it was no longer a case of "My turn sooner or later" but "with the end in sight can I win through?" This feeling was very marked in the last stages of the war and was common to all ranks and units. It is possible that in an attempt to counter this attitude awards for individual acts of bravery were much more freely given than hitherto. Several Military Medals were distributed among the battery between now and the Armistice but I am unaware of any really outstanding acts of gallantry to justify them and the awards only cause discontent among the old hands who, looking backwards, remembered Ypres.

It must be recognised however that there was no security at Cagnicourt, no dug outs and no means of making them, no sand bags, no corrugated iron, no expanded metal and no timber. Only canvas bivouacs made from German groundsheets scrounged at Hendecourt. These at first were on ground level but, following the CO's example, the troops gradually sunk them into the ground. Even so there was but little protection as one or two direct hits showed only too well. The vault was really the only safe place at Cagnicourt and even that received a direct hit which destroyed the steps. Of course we had expected our stay to be of short duration but at the end of September everything pointed to our being located there for the winter.

So far did things go that Major Bennett held a consultation with the Sergeants as to the best means of protecting the position and arrangements were made to move the guns forward a matter of a hundred yards or so to the shelter of a bank-side and to drive deep saps into the ground between the guns, work to begin as soon as the necessary iron and timber could be obtained. No sooner had preparations begun than it was learned that renewal of the attack was imminent. Major Bennett called another conference with the Sergeants when it was agreed that in the circumstances no good purpose would be served by proceeding with the work and it was best to remain in bivouacs until the position was evacuated.

1   *History of the Corps of Royal Engineers'* (Volume V), Chatham, The Institution of Royal Engineers, 1952, p.416, f.n.1.

2   *Military Operations. France and Belgium, 1918* (Volume IV), compiled by Brigadier-General Sir James E Edmonds, London, HMSO, 1947, p.396

3   Tanks had first been used at Flers on the Somme in September 1916.

4   A battlefield heavily marked with deep shell holes also impeded the movement of tanks and, now that warfare was being more mobile, the guns.

5   The most likely soldier to fit this description is Lt Col C. W. Peck VC DSO and Bar.

6   The Wotan Line i.e. Wotan Stellung or the Drocourt-Quéant Line.

7   This was probably Creosol, a disinfectant.

8   154454 Gnr W. Gray, 81 Siege Battery, Royal Garrison Artillery, died of wounds 8 September 1918. Buried at Bac du Sud British Cemetery, Bailleulval, plot 5, row A, grave 14. Gnr Hall's account is erroneous as it would appear that Gray was evacuated well to the rear where he died.

CHAPTER 27
THE CAPTURE OF THE CANAL DU NORD

Construction of the Canal du Nord commenced in 1908 but was halted by the outbreak of the Great War.[1] Nevertheless it presented a significant obstacle to the Allies. 81 Siege Battery was in support of the attack, to the south of the Arras-Cambrai Roman road, which was part of a scheme to take the higher ground from Sailly-Haynecourt-Epinoy north-west of Cambrai. This would be part of the overall Canadian Corps' operation "to force the passage of the Canal du Nord on a narrow frontage of about 2,500 yards where the canal was dry or had very little water in it, and then spread out to 9,700 yards and secure a line between the Schelde and Sensee canals".[2] Overall, the operation was great success for the Corps but 27 September was also a day of personal triumph for Gnr Hall.

Unlike the previous attacks we had several days' warning of the renewal of the offensive leading to the capture of the Canal du Nord.

On September 24 Major Bennett rose early in the morning and set off alone in an easterly direction in search of an advanced position. He returned about mid-day successful in his quest and set out preparing orders for the advance. This was one of the very few occasions when the CO committed himself to paper for he disliked written orders as a rule. This time however he set forth his orders for the advance in the utmost detail; seeking assistance from none he directed every man to his post, deciding who should go forward and who should stay behind and against his orders there was no appeal.

His task was to get the six guns to Baralle a village two miles ahead and only half a mile from the enemy. Here the CO had found a villa of a superior type with a well-built brick wall enclosing a large orchard. Under cover of this wall we should be safe from prying eyes. The road to Baralle was in pretty sound condition and once we could get up the guns we were fairly safe. The trouble was that the whole route was under open observation and the Germans were continuously sending up star shells which gave a most brilliant light. If with the aid of these illuminations they located the advancing guns there was bound to be trouble. Nevertheless the job had to be done.

Late on the evening of September 24 a couple of teams arrived at Cagnicourt, limbered up Nos. 1 and 2 guns and made their way eastwards, the Gunners following in rear. The strictest silence was enjoined no smoking allowed and the horses' hooves were wrapped in sacking to deaden the sound. Whether by extra caution or good luck the teams arrived at Baralle safely, the guns were drawn up under the shelter of the ivy clad wall and the party conducting the operation went straight back to the Horse Lines at Hendecourt leaving four of their number on guard. Instructions for the guard were merely to keep out of sight; there were excellent cellars at the villa and here the four men whiled away the time playing cards and eating cold

Maconochies for no fires were permitted. Meanwhile the four remaining guns at Cagnicourt kept up a lively bombardment of hostile positions.

On the night of the 25 it was the turn of the centre section. They too were successful in advancing their guns, the guard was relieved and the others returned to Hendecourt. The left section now had a very busy time for the two guns had to do the work of six in order to deceive the enemy as to the preparations for the attack.

My particular job came on the morning of September 26 when in accordance with the CO's programme I was to go to Baralle and lay out the Lines of Fire for the four forward guns. Major Bennett showed he had considerable confidence in entrusting me with such a task for there would be no opportunity in checking the lines before the attack and upon that morning's work the success of the subsequent firing depended. One of the Signallers went with me to make some preparations for the new telephone exchange, the instruments having been sent up the night before an together we set off in fine style at ten o'clock in the morning.

We noticed that the road to Baralle seemed singularly deserted but in due course we reached the villa and found the four guns under net camouflages against the wall. The four men in charge seemed a bit surprised to see us and more so when our mission was explained. It was pretty hefty work getting the four guns into position for no attempt had been made previously even to point them in the right direction. Planks had to be laid and the guns run back on to them, then they had to be pulled round to zero line and re-camouflaged. The Signaller lent a hand and I too when not occupied with the director. At length we had the four guns laid at zero line 110 degrees grid as usual parallel to the Arras-Cambrai road. We had a look round the villa and fixed on the kitchen as the best place for the BC Post. There was comparatively little activity and the guard told us that they had been troubled little with shelling except for a few "whiz bangs" (field gun shells). There was a good deal of machine gun fire about but most had been stopped by the orchard wall. I certainly should not have liked to have laid the Lines of Fire without its protection.

My companion having finished his work on the new telephone exchange we took our leave of the guard and made our way back to Cagnicourt. Soon we found ourselves on an unfamiliar road and discovered that somehow we must have taken a wrong turning. There was no one to ask so we set across country in what we thought was the right direction. After a time we saw an officer and a couple of Signallers, that is to say we saw the top of their steel helmets for they were in a slit trench on the parapet of which the officer was resting his binoculars. We enquired our way and were directed to a road in the distance. Then I am afraid I put a "silly ass" question, *"What are you chaps doing in that hole?"*. The answer came as a shock, *"This is the Forward Observation of --- Field Battery"*. The officer who had hitherto kept silent now joined in. *"Do you chaps realise that you are under open observation?" "No, sir, where is the enemy?" "Where isn't he? — he's all round, he's in possession of all those hills and has been potting at us all morning — now be good chaps and clear off, and by the way, that road over there, he's got a machine gun trained on it so do be careful."*

We took our leave. The way seemed interminable, everywhere we could see the hills in possession of the Germans; there seemed to be no way of getting out of his view. Once we reached the road we realised that what the officer had said was correct; there was a machine gun waiting for us. Being chased down a road by machine gun fire is not pleasant but there was nothing for it but to take to our heels and trust to luck. And luck was certainly with us for we kept on running until looking back we could no longer see the hills and knew that at any rate we were out of observation. A little shrapnel encouraged us on our way but this did not trouble us over much and at length we reached Cagnicourt our missions performed. Dinner had been served hot but the cook knowing of our absence had placed on one side an excellent portion to which we did full justice observing that there is nothing like machine gun fire to sharpen the appetite.

I was off duty the rest of the day and at 10pm the remaining two guns were advanced to Baralle without incident. These guns picked up their Lines of Fire from No. 4 gun without the aid of the Director. We had brought a lot of ammunition with us and when this was unloaded everyone adjourned to the farmhouse until morning.

The attack[3] was timed for 5.30am but most of us were astir an hour previously. There was but little preparation to be done for now that we were on counter-battery work we should have to pick up our targets as the battle developed, in fact that only orders we received were *"At 5.30am September 27 the Canadian Corps will advance and will capture the Canal du Nord. Counter-batteries will co-operate in neutralising the fire of hostile batteries as notified by aerial observers. In the intervals fire on certain suspected enemy positions will be maintained"*. Then followed a list of strong points eight of which were allocated to 81 Siege Battery. Dividing eight targets between six guns presented a rather tricky problem which we solved by making two of the guns do double duty engaging two targets alternately at five minute intervals.

All was in readiness and at the appointed hour Major Bennett himself gave the order to fire. Frankly we expected trouble. To advance to within a thousand yards of the enemy and to open fire on points calculated to cause him most irritation was simply asking for it. But it was still in grey light of dawn, too dark for the aeroplanes to be about and we were in new positions presumably unknown to the enemy. In a few minutes we heard the scream of shells passing over our heads and bursting well to our rear. The very audacity of the move had been our salvation and the fields of Cagnicourt were well pasted before the Germans realised that the birds had flown. As in all offensives the first few minutes were the worst and when the CO that for the moment the enemy had not located us he returned to the BC Post; the anxiety that had burdened him for the past few days disappeared and he became his genial self again.

For the first hour there was but little doing, we poured shell after shell on the "suspected positions" the left section changing over every five minutes to engage its double quota of targets. The Germans were doing some searching and sweeping but without much effect. The soundly built wall proved to be a Godsend concealing our gun flashes and being an effective shield against machine gun bullets which could be plainly heard over the general hubbub. Moreover shells which burst on the far side of the wall (and they were not a few) were rendered harmless by this effective barricade.

At half-past six the real business started. It was now light enough for our aeroplanes to be about and they seemed to pass over the enemy lines in hundreds. Then came the targets, so many that the two wireless operators had difficulty in noting them all down as the signal to some extent jammed one another. Except for the SOS every kind of signal was received, the plain "NF" call followed by co-ordinates which showed the airman had spotted guns firing from a specified position, the "GF" call indicating the movement of troops, the "MGF" call "many guns firing" from such a locality and many more.

When the targets started coming through I was sitting at a table left by the former occupants in front of the planchette board. The others were at breakfast and I was holding the fort until relieved. I at once stopped the guns firing on "suspected positions" in favour of "positions known to be active" and from the dozen or more targets that had been sent up selected three of the most favourable and switched a couple of guns on each.

From 6.30 to 10.30 was the busiest time I ever remember. Targets continued to pour in, the wireless operators noted them on pieces of paper with the time received and placed them in a growing pile by my side. I drew from the top of the pile, working out the ranges and line and passed them over to Bush who this time acted as runner and passed them to the guns. Many targets I had to reject as being out of range or line or being too vaguely described as to merit changing a gun already occupied.

At first we gave every target ten minutes rapid fire from a couple of guns but later in order to cope with the extraordinary number of calls we found it necessary to respond with one gun only and the battery presented an extraordinary appearance, the guns pointing in all directions and firing at different elevations. It was quite impossible to avoid a certain amount of cross firing always regarded as a dangerous practice the axiom being that when engaging different targets the battery should open out like a fan No.1 engaging the extreme right and No.6 the extreme left respectively. Any spare moments were taken were occupied in swapping targets and straightening out the guns.

The telephone was buzzing the whole of the time. The other batteries in the brigade were inundated with targets the same as us. Major Bennett took all the calls himself and would ask for instance *"Are we engaging 28 C 7.5?"*. *"Yes sir No. 5 gun."* *"Well I'm going to give that to 59 Battery."* *"Very good, sir,"* then I would order *"Stop No. 5"*. Major Smith would telephone our CO *"You can have that target now and we'll take on 27 D 3.2"*. In a few minutes No. 5 gun would be firing on a new target.

Naturally the guns would not stand such treatment indefinitely and the Sergeant-Artificer and his mate were occupied testing the pressure and watching the recoil of the guns. Occasionally a gun would run hot and the muzzle even glow to redness. Tiffy would then ask for the piece to be put out of action and for a time the place would be permeated with the offensive smell of burning mineral oil with which the barrels were beings sponged to cool them down. Altogether the guns behaved magnificently and although they lost a certain amount of pressure it was not found necessary to pump them up during the action.

There was a certain amount of visual shooting but only enough to verify the line. One gun at a time was taken off the aeroplane work and handed over to Cpl Bush who in conjunction with Mr Rimer at the Observation Post fired a few rounds on a fixed object. In all cases it was found that the guns were firing true to line and range and that no corrections were necessary.

With the exception of this calibration work I had the honour of controlling the fire for the whole of the attack for the simple reason that it was not deemed expedient to change over BCA's during a shoot. At seven o'clock Major Bennett asked me if I could carry on and on my own assurance that I was all right ordered me not to be disturbed. Both Tebbs and Bush to their credit showed no resentment at the junior positions to which they had been delegated. They ran between the BC Post and the guns carrying the orders and entered the targets in the log book.

September 27 was for me a red letter day. Up to 10.30[4] I must have calculated hundreds of targets and switched the guns about scores of times for when we came to total up it was found that 985 rounds had been expended all in what we called ha'porths and pen'orths that is 5 and 10 rounds of rapid fire or at the utmost a ten minute concentration. And the effect. As we engaged the enemy batteries we silenced them temporarily at any rate, although some were very obstinate and our airmen called for gun fire on them time after time. One battery that we fired on tried to pull out and was captured intact by the advancing Canadians.

And the result was that the Canadians had at last captured the last stronghold of the enemy. The Canal du Nord had fallen and the Germans were in headlong retreat – the issue was no longer in doubt. Victory, victory thrice glorious victory was ours, the German front, the Drocourt-Quéant Line and now the Canal du Nord the crowing triumph of all!

By 10.30 the main offensive was over. There was still a little long range firing to be done on the roads near Epinoy and I was glad to hand over the planchette board to Corpl Bush. It was then I realised that I had become famous. Major Bennett absolutely radiant shook me by the hand calling *"Magnificent, Hall, magnificent"*. Other officers followed suit. Somehow the news go round to the guns and when I emerged from the BC Post the Gunners crowded round offering congratulations. My old friend Sgt McIlroy was one of the first. *"You old ----,"* he said, *"you haven't half kept us at it these last four hours,"* and he showed me a list of targets he had engaged. Truly it was a day to be remembered and looking back after all these years I can still recall the glory of that hour. It was some time later when the Gunners were still crowding round eager to know what had happened in the BC Post that morning that Major Bennett approached me and remarked, *"Well Hall, you see what it's like being a hero"*. I made some fatuous reply but followed this up with *"Seriously, sir, what do you make of it all?"*. He paused for a few minutes and then speaking slowly answered, *"We have today won a decisive victory, the greatest the British have ever fought, one that will go down in history as greater than Agincourt, greater than Crecy and greater than Waterloo"*. I think that he was right and it was a great disappointment to me when on my return to civil life I found that the battle was not appreciated indeed hardly recognised.

Soon after dinner Major Bennett sent for the gun teams and they arrived before the order to advance had been received. The CO sent an Officer to reconnoitre, meantime I wandered off until I found the canal itself. There it stretched like a huge railway cutting, no wonder it formed such a formidable obstacle. What interested me most was a trestle bridge which the Royal Engineers were erecting. The Engineers started work as soon as the Germans had been expelled from the canal bank that is about 10am. It was now 2pm and the bridge was rapidly approaching completion. Only those who had seen it could appreciate the magnitude of the work. Hundreds of loads of timber must have been used and the bulk of this had been brought up previous to the attack. When I saw it the bridge was a spidery looking contraption but the Sergeant in charge told me it would hold ten tons and it would be ready in a couple of hours time.

I informed Major Bennett who went to have a look at the bridge for himself but he told me that while he appreciated the work of the Engineers he did not feel like risking the passage. One of the officers had reported that the bridge at Inchy-en-Artois was still standing and he preferred to take the longer journey south along the canal bank to this village and then northwards along the eastern side.

At 4.30pm we were on the move again.

The trek from Baralle was comparatively easy. Nevertheless the march was the most horrible I remember. The road south to the crossing at Inchy-en-Artois had been no man's land since the failure of the attack of September 2 and we encountered the bodies of hundreds of Canadians who had perished in that ill-fated offensive. The past three weeks had been intensively hot with frequent thunderstorms and the effect on the corpses was appalling. Droves of flies rose angrily as we approached nor was that the worst of the horrors. We could not fail to observe that open wounds were alive with maggots nor that much of the flesh had been devoured by rats and other vermin. The stench from the decaying bodies was indescribable and though I have seen death in many forms never did it present a more ghastly spectacle than on that September afternoon.[5]

At length we made our way out of that valley of corruption and crossed the canal by the bridge at Inchy-en-Artois. The bridge at Inchy Mill had stood for three weeks in no man's land and the Germans had been unable to reach it and complete its destruction. It bore the weight of our guns nobly and well and soon we were on the eastern bank or as we called it Jerry's side of the canal. Here we turned sharply northwards on a track parallel to the one we had taken from Baralle.

We encountered little trouble until we approached the village of Sains-les-Marquion a point opposite the trestle bridge the erection of which I had seen in the morning. Here was a bottle neck for traffic was pouring across the bridge and joining transport which like us had made the passage lower down the valley. All was congested in the narrow village streets and to add to the confusion the Germans were concentrating their fire on this point. It speaks well for the enemy that even at this moment of defeat he could direct his artillery so as to cover our most vulnerable point. There was nothing for it but to gallop through the village and this was the last time I beheld the poor heavy draft horses being urged forward at full speed. It always seemed to me a most pitiable sight that these magnificent animals whose speed should never have exceeded walking pace being whipped and spurred until they galloped through the inferno of bursting shells. But the desperate remedy worked and we emerged through Sains-les-Marquion without a casualty.

Once clear of the village we halted, gathered round the terrified horses, petted and made much of them, gave them some corn and rubbed the sweat from their shiny coats. It was some time before we were able to proceed further. Then we moved from Sains-les-Marquion to Marquion a larger village.

The road approaching Marquion had been the scene of much of the morning's activities and here I located the position of many of the batteries we had engaged. It was here too that saw at first hand the effect of one of our shoots. On receipt of an "NF" call we had engaged and according to the airmen secured a direct hit on an enemy battery caught pulling out. We usually discounted aerial reports of "OK's" as being over optimistic but there was no doubt its accuracy on this occasion. By the roadside lay a broken limber and such a tangled humanity and horseflesh that it was impossible to tell how many had perished. On looking at that horrible mass of death I did not feel so proud of my achievement of a few hours earlier when I myself had prepared that target for the guns.

But if we had rendered a good account of ourselves that morning this did not hold good in all cases for a short distance away I noticed laying on the ground many hundred of eight inch shells which had failed to explode and there were a lot of deep holes where the projectiles had buried themselves without effect. Investigation soon revealed the cause of this phenomenon. One battery at any rate had been bombarding an important cross roads without even bothering to fuze their shells. It is not difficult to realise why some offensives failed if practices like this were carried out and it is no wonder that ill feeling existed when the infantry saw how badly they were being supported.

We now reached the village of Marquion and changed our course to an easterly direction. Clear of the village a gaunt wooden sign across the road bore the words in letters a foot high – "Achtung! Eisenbahn".

The meaning of this sign puzzled us for some time until we realised that this was the German way of warning traffic of approaching a level crossing for we soon came to a railway depot on the branch line which threaded its serpentine course between Arras and Cambrai, a place known to the French as the Garage de Malakoff and here we pulled in.

The Garage de Malakoff was another ex-enemy position and was unique in that we ourselves that fired in the morning on what was to be our quarters for the night. Other batteries had also paid attention to the place with such good effect that although the enemy had succeeded in getting his guns away the emplacements had literally been obliterated and it was only excavation that brought the gun platforms to light. The gun position was sheltered by a high bank in which a number of small dugouts had been constructed their entrances in most cases blocked by our gun fire.

On our arrival Malakoff simply reeked of a mixture of gas and acetylene the presence of the latter being accounted for by the fact that the enemy had been destroying the railway depot. In the siding were a fair number of railway wagons which the Germans were unable to remove containing some sinister looking objects which proved to be bombs. There were also a number of food containers like large vacuum flasks which contained Jerry's dinner. When broken open we found the contents steaming hot, a thick white stew, quite appetising in appearance but seemingly devoid of meat The flasks showed how concerned the enemy was about the welfare of his troops but the contents indicated only too clearly the privations he was suffering. In similar circumstances our men would have been supplied with an abundance of lukewarm and unappetising stew.

We stayed at the Garage de Malakoff until the 30 September three days of irritation and anxiety for we fully expected that with the capture of the Canal du Nord we had overcome every obstacle in the way of Cambrai. All the Canadians we met at the canteens were chafing at the delay and bitter words were spoken about the troops on our left flank who were alleged to be holding up the advance. The adjoining Corps (22 Corps) had in fact been lagging behind ever since the start of the Counterstroke and the Canadians were blaming them for their disaster before the Canal du Nord. The feeling between the British and the Canadian forces at this stage had developed into definite antagonism. We escaped this once the Canadians realised that we were part of their artillery but on more than one occasion we would have been turned out of their canteens had not our identity been established.

The Canadian canteens were particularly good and kept remarkably close to the line, moving forward in many cases the same day as the first troops. The stock was strange to us being mainly of trans-Atlantic origin. There was no shortage of sugar and really delightful biscuits were obtainable at very low cost. Once they realised that we were actually attached to the Corps and not mere interlopers from the 22 Corps the Canadians proved delightful hosts and would often stand treat to our men refusing to let them pay on the grounds that they received about six times as much money as ourselves. A remarkably large proportion normally spoke French and it was something of a revelation when these six-foot giants, these magnificent specimens of British manhood stumbled over English pronunciation and fell back on French idiom.

The men of the 22 Corps were of much inferior physique to the Canadians – the difference being so obvious as to be pitiful. The reason for this was plain. The Canadians had limited their contribution of troops to one Army Corps. They replaced their casualties but not their strength whereas we in Britain in order to meet our ever increasing obligations lowered every standard until many of our divisions seemed to consist solely of undersized and weedy looking youths. It was futile to expect such material to keep pace with the magnificent shock troops such as the Canadians.

There was another reason for the delay. The boundary between the Canadian and the 22 Corps was marked by the sluggish river Sensee which here flowed west to east and just north of the Arras-Cambrai road. The river formed a mass of shallow lagoons and marshes stretching for miles along its bank, country over which neither British nor Canadians had any wish to operate. It was thought therefore that if the British to the north and the Dominion troops to the south of this inhospitable territory and Germans would be forced to withdraw. To prevent reinforcement by the enemy all the bridges over the Sensee were well bombarded. Most of our work at Malakoff consisted in the bombardment to destruction of the bridges over the Sensee and it was felt that with the destruction of the bridges the Germans would withdraw to the east.

Unfortunately things did not work out that way. Large bodies of Germans remained in the marshes when their comrades on the high ground on either side of the river had been driven back. Such stragglers had to be searched for and dislodged a painful and laborious task which fell entirely on the 22 Corps, very different from the gallant headlong dashes of the Canadians on the Arras-Cambrai road. But the rounding up took time which was exactly what the enemy wanted. Retreat was now inevitable but it was his policy to withdraw in an orderly manner as possible inflicting the maximum damage as he did so.

Our first night at the Garage de Malakoff gave ample proof of this. In every direction the sky blazed with light while dull explosions rent the air. Most of the fires were accompanied with pyrotechnic displays indicating that ammunition dumps were being destroyed but in other cases they burned steadily with much smoke. Obviously villages were being put to the flames. What caused us the most anxiety was the huge mass of black smoke to the south east. I oriented the spot and confirmed our worst suspicions. The prize for which we had been fighting all these weeks was lost. Cambrai was in flames.

All those three days the pall of smoke rose from the doomed city and the smell of burning was wafted across the valley on the wind. It is impossible to describe our disappointment as we looked towards the south east. The Canadians were furious and privately at any rate threw all the blame on the unfortunate 22 Corps.

This third rate manufacturing town that no-one had heard of before the war and which since has sunk back into oblivion meant at that time so much to us. For weeks we had dreamed of nothing else but liberating Cambrai, complete with its inhabitants, from the hands of the invader and now the townspeople had fled and the town burning itself away. Whether the Germans set fire to Cambrai or whether it caught fire by accident is not clear but once started there was no way of extinguishing the flames and we could only look on helplessly at that pillar of smoke by day and the ruddy glow by night that marked the ruin of that once prosperous town.

On September 30 we resumed the offensive and the Germans started retreating almost as soon as the first shell was fired. The teams were sent for and by dinner time the guns had reached the limit of their range and were put out of action.

We expected moving forward as before but at the last moment plans were changed and we learned to our dismay that we were not to advance with our friends the Canadians but were transferred to the 22 Corps and so the entire battery, guns, transport, spare horses and all were drawn up near the marshalling yard while Major Bennett rode forward to select a position north of the Arras–Cambrai road.

Cagnicourt British Cemetery

While we were assembled there tragedy descended on us. From the east came a single shell. As Gunners we knew what that meant. This was no ranged shot but merely a case of the Germans emptying a gun at extreme elevation before moving off. We had done the same thing scores of times. The shell made its unsteady way wobbling as it came. In those seconds we knew it was going to burst among us but exactly where we could not tell. And so it dropped at the feet of Gunner Cox[6] and blew him to fragments. Cox of all people, the Major's batman. I was not particularly fond of officers' servants as a rule, they were usually a disagreeable, supercilious lot but Cox was different, a most friendly chap. He and I had a heart to heart talk only a few days previously in which he confided that while he disliked the idea of "service" he had his wife and children to think of and that now the end of the war was in sight he might as well have what he called a "comparatively safe job". And he was the one man to be picked out. We sent for the Padre, gathering up what we could find of the unfortunate man and buried the remains near the spot where he had fallen. When Major Bennett returned he was told of the fate of his batman and was much affected. Major Bennett had now lost his best friend (Mr Morkill) and his batman who would be the next to go?

---

1   The canal remained derelict after the war and construction was not restarted until 1960. The canal opened for traffic in 1965.

2   *Military Operations. France and Belgium, 1918* (Volume V), 26th September–11th November The Advance to Victory compiled by Brigadier-General Sir James E Edmonds and Lieut-Colonel R. Maxwell-Hyslop, London, HMSO, 1947 p17.

3   For a detailed account of the Canadian Corps on 27 September 1918 see *Military Operations. France and Belgium, 1918* (Volume V), *26th September–11th November The Advance to Victory* compiled by Brigadier-General Sir James E Edmonds and Lieut-Colonel R. Maxwell-Hyslop, London, HMSO, 1947 p19-25.

4   The fighting went on much later in the day but at this stage either German targets were out of range of the battery or advancing troops made further shelling unnecessary.

5   Just over 300 Canadians killed on 2 September are buried nearby at Dury Mill British Cemetery.

6   35025 Gnr Alfred Aaron Cox, killed in action 30 September 1918, buried in Cagnicourt British Cemetery, plot 1, row C, grave 2.

CHAPTER 28
A CHANGE OF DIRECTION

*A*rtillery batteries such as Gnr Hall's were used where they were needed and so in late September *it moved northwards to join the adjacent XXII Corps (operating on the First Army's right wing).[1] This period was spent shelling the enemy as they fell back leaving rearguards behind but finally Cambrai was taken. Within the battery a change of command occurs when Major Bennett is wounded and the impact of that change is made clear by Gnr Hall. However, the war had to be fought and the alarming emergence from the fog of a large group of German POWs was yet another sign of the gradual breakdown of enemy resistance.*

With our transfer to 22 Corps our troubles began. We were delayed a considerable time at the Garage de Malakoff waiting for Major Bennett to return. When at last he put in an appearance the horses were due for feed and water and it was decided that we might as well have tea before starting for the road. This meant unpacking the cook's wagon and making a fire for the cooking pots. When all was packed up again and the battery actually started to move it was 7.30pm (September 30).

We struck out in a northerly direction and soon reached the Arras–Cambrai road. As we expected the road was congested with traffic and our progress was slow but after a mile or so we left the Route Nationale and took a faint track leading north. The lane was in vile condition and in the absence of fences could hardly be distinguished from the surrounding countryside. We followed the twisting and turnings of the track in the rapidly falling light when things became more difficult than ever. At every road junction the Major called a halt; it was obvious that he was uncertain of the way. Many of us had fears that we were heading in the wrong direction and these were confirmed when we saw in the distance a long line of poplars marking the main road. There was nothing for it but to continue and in due course we re-joined the Arras–Cambrai road at the same spot that we had left it.

As we reached the familiar spot the troops took advantage of the darkness to give ironical cheers which would undoubtedly have reached the Major's ears but he paid no attention and called on the column to halt while he and his orderly went forth in search of the missing lane. They returned after a short time and we resumed our journey down the main Cambrai road. Then he led us down a branch so similar to the first that it was no wonder that he had mistaken the track in the darkness.

Even now we seemed to travel for miles in the most desolate country. There were no villages or even houses on that serpentine way, nothing but rough cart tracks across fields along which our patient teams drew the lumbering guns. It was past midnight when the CO called a halt but he had done so so often before that we thought he was merely verifying his position and did not realise then at long last we had reached our destination. There was indeed nothing to indicate that this was to be our next battery position. It was merely a sunken farm track leading across an open field quite indistinguishable from the miles we had already traversed and without protection of any kind. To add to our discomfort it was now raining heavily.

We unlimbered the guns at intervals alongside the sunken track secured our personal belongings and stood in groups awaiting orders. I had already seen the Major about the Lines of Fire but he told me not to bother as we should not go into action before morning. Then we untethered the horses, locked a number of wagons and gun limbers together so as to be immovable, strung a stout drag rope between them and tied up the horses to this for the night. Then everyone turned in under the wagons stretching the (German) ground sheets from the wheels to keep out the rain. I was honoured for I lay under the same wagon as the CO himself along with Bush and half a dozen Signallers.

At 6am October 1 Major Bennett stretched himself and called us from our repose. There was much to be done; the guns to be laid on the Line of Fire and brought into action, telephone lines to be laid, Horse Lines to be set up some distance in rear ammunition to be unloaded and prepared for firing. Once these tasks were done we could look to our own comfort. It was surprising how quickly the various tasks were performed and events fully justified the CO's rather irregular action in leaving the jobs until morning.

In the grey morning light a slight elevation was seen behind which permanent Horse Lines were established and while the drivers were sinking poles and fixing cables the Gunners were unloading the wagons of ammunition behind the guns and stores in the sunken road.

Laying out Lines of Fire presented no difficulty. Zero line was at 45 degrees grid i.e. north east by the compass but the actual site of the pivot gun had to be located by orientation from three distant points as it was quite impossible to fix the location on the map by any other means. Three churches were taken for this purpose and the fact that at least one of them was in enemy hands only added zest to the game. Following our usual practice we called this position Epinoy after the nearest village although this was a considerable distance away and we never went in it.

The Epinoy position was certainly under partial observation from the enemy as indeed were all our battery positions north of the Arras-Cambrai road and we had the unique experience of seeing our own shells bursting in enemy lines for the Germans held all the high ground to the right of the River Sensee.

The battery once in action we set about making ourselves as comfortable as possible. Here the German ground sheets came in useful. We buttoned them together and made bivouacs in the sunken road. We also had our own canvas covering about twelve feet square and between the two soon had cover for all the battery personnel. As for the BC Post Major Bennett had a bright idea. We had exchanged our limber for a GS wagon some time ago. We had pushed this wagon down the sunken road as it contained delicate instruments and could not be unloaded until we had some place to put them. The Major's idea was to convert the wagon into a caravan and use it as a travelling BC Post so that in similar circumstances the battery could be controlled if not in comfort at any rate in the dry.

Converting an open wagon into a caravan was a more difficult task than appeared at first sight but we managed to scrounge a few pieces of wood which we nailed to the sides and we stretched canvas over this framework, the result being a grotesque looking structure so top heavy that it threatened to fall over at any moment. But it served its purpose. Officer, BCA and telephonists were duly installed. There was no room for the wireless operators so they had to make their quarters underneath. From this contraption we controlled the battery and when we came to move we simply filled it with stores and were ready for the road again when the caravan caused not a little amusement. The caravan served only for those actually on duty. A canvas bivouac at one end of the sunken road became at once the CO's quarters and the Officers' Mess while the BCA's off duty had their own little shelter a short distance away.

We remained at Epinoy until October 9 firing northwards the whole time at bridges across the River Sensee to prevent movement of enemy troops and in all the circumstances it is surprising that we had only one casualty. But this was the most serious of all, Major Bennett himself. It happened on October 2. An enemy aeroplane was seen firing at our observation balloons. A good resistance was put up however by our anti-aircraft guns and the intruder was forced to withdraw. On his way back he flew over our battery position and seeing our conglomeration of shelters decided to have a pot at us with his machine gun. All the bullets went wide except one which went through the CO's bivouac and penetrated the fleshy part of the arm. Colonel Wakefield had paid a visit that morning and was actually in conversation with the Major at the time. I was, I think, the first in the battery to hear of the casualty for I was passing by when the Colonel called out *"Your CO has been wounded"*. Then I saw Major Bennett with his tunic removed and the Colonel applying iodine to the injured limb. Asked what I should do the CO called out *"Tell Fletcher to come"*. I found the Captain at the Horse Lines only a few yards away and he at once accompanied me to the bivouac.

Col. Wakefield had by now bound up the Major's arm and the two officers were engaged in earnest conversation. *"It's no good,"* I heard the Colonel say. *"You'll have to go down the line."* Then resigned to his fate the CO replied, *"Very good, sir, I'll go down,"* and turning to Capt Fletcher and I who were standing at the entrance said, *"Tell Proud to pack up my things"*. *"Get the gharry ready as well,"* said the Colonel. *"You can't walk you know."* *"Very well,"* assented the CO and I set about my assignments.

It was not long before the light cart disappeared at the end of the sunken road and Pride and I hoisted the CO's belongings aboard. Then we helped Major Bennett to his seat, the driver started up the horse and the CO departed as quietly as he had arrived six months earlier.

Apart from Colonel Wakefield and Capt Fletcher, Pride and I were the only ones to see him off, indeed the whole business happened so quickly that no one else realised that he had been wounded. I must have looked pretty dispirited at his departure for he said to me, *"Cheer up, Hall, we'll meet again sometime,"* but, of course, we never did. As that splendid and much misunderstood man passed out of sight I felt that the bottom had dropped out of my life.

Capt Fletcher once more took over control of the battery as he had done before when we lost Major Warren. His first move was to order the construction of a new BC Post well dug into the ground in rear of the guns. Needless to say the Captain did not follow the example of his predecessor and lend a hand in its construction, neither for that matter did the BCA's. The senior Sergeant was told to detail a party for the job and that was that. In a short time a hole appeared which was covered with railway sleepers scrounged from a nearby dump and the result was a chamber, small and dark, but at any rate secure from splinters and machine gun fire.

The post was manned day and night by a BCA in turn. The Captain used the post in the day time but did not sleep there; the Signallers had their own quarters. Somehow it fell to my lot to be on duty one night from 8pm until 4am when I was relieved by Frost. As there was no night firing to relieve the monotony and the post was rather remote from the guns night duty at Epinoy was something like solitary confinement and I can remember sitting alone in that dank and miserable hole in the earth with a single candle for illumination gazing at my watch at the interminable hours when my relief would arrive. Which at last he put in an appearance I made my way to our shack, pulled off my boots and tunic, took a good swig of rum and turned into the blankets Frost had just vacated.

We BCA's had managed to accumulate a fair share of rum at this time as there were quite a number of teetotallers in the battery who did not take their issue and Major Bennett allowed a few of us to share the residue. My actions must have been observed for before I fell asleep a ghostly hand appeared under a flap in the canvas. I admit to being scared at the moment but when the man withdrew taking with it my water bottle (which was full of rum) I rushed outside in search of the intruder but he was nowhere to be seen. When I awoke in the morning my water bottle had been restored but it was empty.

A few days after the departure of Major Bennett the lust for scrounging became too much for a couple of the Signallers who regardless of security set off in full view of the enemy for a village on the banks of the Sensee. They returned some hours later tired but extremely happy and bowed down beneath the weight of their plunder, to wit, bottles of soda water. After disgorging an immense number of bottles they told their story. After many exciting adventures they had advanced within a short distance of the enemy lines and heedless of snipers' bullets, which came so close that they had to crawl part of the way, they reached the village and discovered of all things an abandoned soda-water factory so they helped themselves to as many bottles as they could carry and returned to the battery. The return journey was even more difficult for they had to dodge bullets with every pocket full of bottles but with a persistence worthy of a better cause got back in triumph their precious burden intact. A couple of bottles reached Capt Fletcher who though he pronounced it excellent with whisky let it be known that such expeditions did not meet with his approval. The soda water factory was to figure in later exploits.

It was not until October 9 that any considerable amount of firing was done.[2] Then an attack was launched that once and for all was to capture Cambrai. The offensive started at the unusual hour of 1.30am and at 8am all was over. This time we were in for a shock. The morning was very misty at first and just as we were getting ready for breakfast we saw coming at us through the gloom hundreds of grey clad figures. *"Good God, they've got us,"* came the cry from all quarters. The officers doubled back to their quarters and emerged carrying their revolvers. Men looked round for rifles but where were they? There were supposed to be six somewhere but they could not be found. They had been dumped weeks before along with the battery machine gun. Even if they had been found six rifles would not go far among a hundred odd men. But there were other weapons available, heavy spanners, ram rods, handspikes, picks and shovels. Yes we were determined to sell our lives dearly and what could be said of Sgt Clarke, our own Nobby who, brandishing a flag pole, the only weapon he could lay his hand on, shouted *"After me boys, give 'em Hell"*.

An instant later we realised our mistake. Commands to the advancing troops were barked out in a foreign tongue and every one of the invaders held his hands smartly above his head while the leader in perfect English addressed us saying, *"We are Prisoners of War – would you mind directing us to the nearest cage?"*. The absurdity of the situation burst upon us. Our improvised weapons were cast aside. While we rocked with hilarious laughter which, scared as they were, even spread to the Germans, one of our party found tongue and replied civilly that being strangers to these parts we didn't rightly know but if they continued straight down the lane they would come to a village where they would no doubt find someone to direct them. The German officer thanked us kindly for this information and the procession moved on, so many of that that we did not see how there could be any Germans left to fight. Later we learned the full story. It appeared that when our infantry advanced large numbers of Germans surrendered. Rather than be burdened with them they were told to find their own way to the rear without escort. This they did with such effect as to give us the shock of a lifetime. Later in the day more German prisoners appeared but these were under escort even if the escort consisted of an undersized youth carefully shepherding a hundred or more hefty Germans.

By noon the battery was definitely out of action and Capt Fletcher went to headquarters for orders. Large numbers of us paid a visit to the soda water factory and during the afternoon the success of our enterprise was toasted in this not particularly exciting beverage.

At tea time Capt Fletcher stated that a new position had been found and that we should be moving forward by nightfall. At 8pm we moved forward and a few hours later pulled in to field outside Cuvillers.

Cuvillers was a position very similar to the one we had left, on high ground remote from the village and utterly devoid of shelter. We were not particularly worried however for we felt that the enemy's resistance had been completely overcome and that in a few hours we should again be in pursuit of the flying foe.

On the morning of the 10 October therefore we proceeded in a leisurely and confident manner to man the guns. We had our instructions comparatively simple this time, more bombardment of bridges and crossroads and the fact that the high ground to our left, which showed up so prominently at day break, was still in enemy hands worried us not at all. We were soon to be undeceived. No sooner had our first shot been fired than the Germans replied with such a fusillade of shells that we were forced to forsake our guns. When we withdrew the bombardment stopped but, as soon as we returned, the concentration was resumed heavier than ever. In half an hour two of our guns had suffered so much damage as to render them unusable.

What had happened was obvious to us all. Here we were on the top of a hill under direct view of the enemy who was determined to make the most of his advantage. Capt Fletcher had certainly not been very successful in his first choice of battery position. To make matters worse an important battle was raging for this day was to see the capture of Cambrai. After more unsuccessful attempts to man the guns the Captain was driven to the humiliating expedient of explaining the state of affairs to the Colonel and asking for the battery to be put out of action. Fortunately for us his petition was granted and the three other batteries in the brigade were able to take over our targets. All that remained for us was to sit disconsolately in a ditch watching the other batteries merrily at work and feeling very much in the cold. The defection of one battery did not affect the progress of the battle and that same afternoon (October 10) the Canadians entered the blackened ruins of Cambrai.

There was one of us however who did not avail himself of the shelter of the ditch. When the battery arrived the night before Dennis selected the site for his cookhouse, a little to the left of No 6 gun. He was first to rise in the morning and had prepared an excellent breakfast for us. When we were shelled out for the first time he was in the middle of washing up. He retired with the rest of us but was soon back at his post. Between our abortive attempts to fight the guns he had managed to get the copper boiling for dinner though most cooks would have let the meal take care of itself. But Dennis was made of sterner stuff. The smoke from his cookhouse certainly attracted enemy fire and the Germans now well aware that the position was still in occupation continued their bombardment. But nothing would deter Dennis. He took cover in a large shell hole a little distance away and to see his dash from his sanctuary to give the stew a stir and throw a piece of wood on the fire was a sight to remember. I can still see him, pepper pot in one hand and a ladle in the other covering the short distance to his cooking pots with remarkable alacrity for he was a heavy man. Never was a meal prepared under such difficulty and stranger still it was ready on time and of excellent quality.

Punctually at one o'clock our worthy cook took up his stand by the copper shouting, *"Dinner up – don't all come at once"*. The latter injunction, however, was hardly necessary for faint hearts showed no inclination to go to the cookhouse at all for when some of us lined up the enemy redoubled his shelling and there were others who preferred to forego their meal than run the gauntlet of shell fire. Dennis was not of Irish extraction for nothing and the vituperation he poured on those who hesitated was sufficient to scorch them. This encouragement brought others up to scratch but there were still thirty or forty whom abuse and even the cook's drastic threat to give the food away to all who would fetch it, would not move. Then Dennis proceeded to carry out his threat. He called out for volunteers and enjoining us not to give any food to the *"White livered curs who would let good grub waste rather than risk a bit of shelling,"* gave all who responded a second helping. Whether greed in my case overcame fear, it must be recorded that not only did I consume two dinners that day but I collected a dixie-full for supper thereby making a friend for life of our dauntless cook.

As soon as it was dark we pulled out and by the irony of fate found a place only five hundred yards away which met all the requirements of a good battery position. We were in a slight defile down which passed a good metalled road affording easy access for the ammunition wagons; a rise in the ground protected us from enemy observation while in the vicinity were a number of dug-outs affording ample shelter for the troops. This we called Cuvillers No.2 position.

The two damaged guns were sent to the workshops for repair while the remaining four were drawn up two on either side of the road. I had cause to remember their exact location as I had considerable difficulty in laying out the Lines of Fire before light failed altogether. Nos.1 and 2 guns were on the right hand side of the road ten yards apart while a space of 180 yards separated them from the left section. This was an unusual layout but the idea was to have the guns as near as possible to the dug-outs and also to leave room for a centre section should the two guns be returned from Ordnance while we were still there.

The BC Post had been established in a small dug-out 100 yards in rear of No. 1 gun. After I had laid the Lines of Fire I reported the exact position of the guns to Bush who meantime had prepared the planchette board. There was no night firing anticipated and the guns once on their SOS lines, the troops were only too glad to turn in for it had been a very tiring and exciting day. My luck was out this time and it fell to my lot to take night duty while my colleagues retired to their shelter leaving me alone in the BC Post. Nothing of moment occurred until 1am when a change of SOS lines was telephoned from headquarters. This was a switch from the previous line and I considered it advisable that the guns should be relaid on their fresh targets. Accordingly I worked out the lines for the four guns wrote out slips and went out just as I was to find the Sergeants. The Gun Captain of No.1 gun was easily roused and on being told of the alteration called up a couple of his men leaving the rest in peace. The four of us soon had the trail swung round and in a few minutes the men were resuming their interrupted repose. No.2 gun was re-laid with as little ceremony and while the men were returning to their shelter I set off towards the left section.

One hundred and eighty yards I well knew separated the left section from No.2 gun and I set off counting my steps as I went for it was pitch dark under my feet but when I reached the end of the 180 steps I looked for the gun but it was nowhere to be found. I realised my error. I had certainly taken 180 steps from No.2 gun but in what direction? Well I had crossed the road so I thought that if I looked round a bit I must surely find the missing guns. But I was wrong again and in my desperation I did the worst thing possible I took 180 steps back thinking I should find the right section. But again I was mistaken. I was now hopelessly lost on a pitch black night without cap or tunic or what was more important a gas mask.

I confess I was in a hopeless panic. I called out but my cries were unheard. To make matters worse the enemy started searching and sweeping and my nostrils detected the acrid smell of gas for the Germans had developed the unpleasant habit of mixing gas shells with their HE so that a man never knew when his respirator would be needed. Then I walked down the road hoping to locate some telephone line which might lead me back to civilisation. So far as I was concerned the left section could go hang all I wanted was to get back to my BC Post. But confusion became more confounded. The road forked and in my dilemma I must have taken the wrong direction, at any rate I wandered far out of the valley. I stumbled over an obstruction and discovered it was a dead horse. Some distance away was a Field battery with two guns in action. I enquired of the Gunners but they had never heard of 81 Siege Battery nor indeed had they any knowledge of any heavy artillery in the vicinity. It was evident I was getting dangerously close to the front line. I retraced my steps and eventually found the bifurcation of the roads but again I was no more successful for after following the road for what seemed to be miles I found myself back with the deceased animal. Four times altogether did I come back to that infernal dead horse and it was not until I was in a state of desperation that I tripped over what was to me a lifeline a yellow telephone cable lying by the road side. I took the line in my hand determined to follow it wherever it might lead and imagine my joy when at last I heard voices. They were not belonging to 81 Battery but near enough. I stumbled over the line linking one of our sixty pounder batteries with their Observation Post and this had led me to their telephone exchange. The two Signallers on duty were astonished to see me as I stumbled upon them, without cap or tunic and in a state of collapse. I explained my difficulty and they were able to help. As I expected the batteries were connected together and they placed my hand on a telephone cable which led to 81. In quarter of an hour I had arrived at our own exchange and from there had no difficulty in locating the BC Post.

The place was in darkness the candles having long since burnt out. When I looked at my watch it was 4am so I had been wandering about in the darkness for three hours. Bush should have relieved me at three but I was too overcome even to venture the small distance between the post and his dugout. He came upon me at 6am lying trembling and exhausted across the planchette board. When I explained what had happened he put me into his bed and later brought my breakfast. In the light of morning my adventure seemed incredible for there lay the guns two on either side of the road. Later in the day I tried to retrace my steps but although I found the road fork where I had gone astray I was unable to locate either the Field Battery or the dead horse that had figured so largely in the night's adventures.

Although the second position at Cuvillers was so much safer than the first that we were able to fight our guns without interruption our short sojourn did not pass without casualties. One of the cook's unofficial helpers was killed[3] and two others wounded while assisting Dennis to prepare the mid-day meal. Dennis was extremely popular and the men were helping him by chopping wood when a 4.2 shell burst among them. Dennis himself was uninjured and carried on his work even while the Sanitary Orderly was cleansing the spot where his late helpers fell.

On the morning of the 12 October enemy resistance suddenly collapsed and it was necessary to follow up the attack. Two guns were on the road by 5am and the rest of the battery followed two hours later.

We reached Eswars which was as far as we could advance owing to the River Escaut which lay directly across our path but so rapid had been the German retreat that the first section was out of range as soon as it arrived.

We remained at Eswars the whole of the day pending orders as to the passage of the Escaut. The village presented little opportunity for plunder and our minds turned on the soda-water factory we had found while at Epinoy. The factory was now of course well behind our lines and we thought that we should be able to secure sufficient soda-water to last us for a very long time. Capt Fletcher entered into the spirit of the raid and ordered a GS wagon to accompany the party so that the Officers' Mess might also be supplied. When we arrived however it was discovered that a guard was in possession and on enquiry were told that by orders of some headquarter officers no more soda-water was to be taken. We were rather taken aback at this and wandered disconsolately about the building. Meanwhile our numbers were reinforced by other units who were endeavouring to draw supplies. Indignation meetings were held and at last some of us found a trap door in the rear of the factory. We managed to squeeze a way through and once inside opened a larger rear door and the rest of the troops surged inside the building.

Removal of the soda-water presented no difficulties. Wagon after wagon was loaded up and sent away. Meanwhile at the front of the place the guard kept watch, solemnly marching to and fro heedless of the depredations taking place in their rear. We were still not satisfied the fact that the hated Staff Officers had endeavoured to corner the stuff moved us to such indignation that when someone suggested that we should destroy the damned place the idea caught on like wildfire. Bottle after bottle of soda-water was flung in all directions and finding this not quick enough whole cases were thrown to the ground until the whole building was flowing with the liquid. Such timber as might be of any use was removed bodily and eventually the whole place collapsed. It is noteworthy that the whole of the work of destruction was done from the back of the factory while at the front the guard continued pacing to and fro. At last we withdrew leaving behind us a wreck of fallen timber and broken bottles.

Eswars might be said to mark the end of "Counterstroke", that great and glorious attack which commenced before Arras at 3am on August 26. We had advanced the 22 miles between

Arras and Cambrai breaking down German resistance at every point. The German Front, the Vis-en-Artois Switch and the Drocourt-Quéant Line had in turn fallen, then the Canal du Nord which had so opportunely falling into his hands and which had turned into the greatest defence system of all and finally we had dislodged his reluctant hold from the Sensee marshes.

Now he was playing his last cards, orderly retreat whenever possible wrecking as much damage as he could. The first evidence of this policy lay in front of us for one the Escaut a deep canalised river the bridges were down for miles. East of the river however the Germans were retreating fast with our infantry in full pursuit.

The passage of the Escaut was an epic in itself of which too little was heard. The river was about 8 feet deep by 12 wide. Such of the infantry as could swim did so the rest ferried themselves across on rafts made from house doors. Practically every door from the surrounding villages had been requisitioned for the purpose.

---

1   *Military Operations. France and Belgium, 1918* (Volume V), *26th September-11th November The Advance to Victory* compiled by Brigadier-General Sir James E Edmonds and Lieut-Colonel R. Maxwell-Hyslop, London, HMSO, 1947 sketch 18.

2   *Military Operations France and Belgium 1918* Vol 5 p227 states that "for XXII Corps, except for taking over part of the Canadian Corps frontage, the 9th October was a quiet day".

3   109897 Cpl Walter Frederick Martin, aged 41, son of the late Charles and Sarah Martin of Twerton-on-Avon, Bath; husband of the late Maud Caroline Martin, killed in action 11 October 1918, buried in Cagnicourt British Cemetery, plot 1, row D, grave 13.

At noon on the 20 October came an imperative call from Brigade headquarters to send a groom with the CO's charger to escort Major Gale to his new command. Gunner Wheeler dressed in his best went on his brown horse leading the black mare Bess and later in the afternoon the new CO arrived on horseback, the groom following the regulation distance in rear. A guard had been mounted in readiness and they turned out smartly and presented arms. The Major dismounted, handed his charger to Wheeler and inspected the guard. Captain Fletcher appeared, pulled up the battery to attention and saluted. The salute was gravely returned; our new master has assumed control.

Capt Fletcher left the battery almost at once, glad to be relieved of his responsibility. After the debacle at Cuvillers No. 1 his nerves were in a shocking state and it seemed strange that an officer who had endured all the rigours of eighteen months on the Ypres Salient should crack up so suddenly and at such a trivial occurrence a few hours resistance by a defeated enemy. He returned to England and spent the next few months in hospital. First Lt Morkill, then Major Bennett and now Capt Fletcher casualties. Nor was that all. Lt Saville had received a long overdue promotion some weeks ago and had been transferred to another battery while Lt Brown had been evacuated with some internal complaint. Of the old school of officers only Mr. Lakin remained and he was soon to be transferred to the Horse Lines bringing the unlovable Page back to the battery.

Major Gale was every inch a soldier there was no doubt about that and for a unit with a history such as 81 Siege Battery centred round a nucleus of time serving soldiers he was the ideal commander. Where Major Bennett had been despised, Major Gale was worshipped. From all sides he was acclaimed as a leader worthy of the battery and I often heard the remark *"At last we've got rid of that blasted commercial traveller"* for the notion that Major Bennett followed this occupation persisted – in fact he was a practical man, an engineer. Yet Major Gale was a strict disciplinarian, tyrannical, inconsistent and unjust, a heavy drinker so much so that before many days all the battery had seen him the worse for liquor and, to cap all, a remarkably ignorant man. He had one virtue, his love of horses. With Major Bennett the transport was a necessary evil and he never concealed his dislike for drivers as a class. Before Major Gale had been in control 24 hours the position was reversed. He had shown himself to be a drivers' man. No longer were the Horse Lines to be used as a dumping ground for incompetent Gunners and NCO's for whom the CO had no use. To be seconded to the Horse Lines was a privilege. During the next few days a complete change took place; Sgt Rolfe went back to the Horse Lines as senior Sergeant, Driver Swan changed from laying No.1 gun to become leader of No.1 team while of course Mr Lakin now senior officer under the Major abandoned his Signallers and took charge of the drivers.

We four BCA's were apprehensive as to our fate under the new dispensation and the new CO's attitude did little to relieve our anxiety. I happened to be on duty in the BC Post when Major Gale arrived and his first words were *"What's that man doing here"*. Capt Fletcher explained that I was the BCA on duty and from the conversation that followed it appeared that the CO was dissatisfied that anyone not of commissioned rank should be in the BC Post at all. When Bush and later Tebbs put in an appearance he was more disgruntled than ever, declaring that there were too many BCA's altogether and that he would see to it that some of us did a bit of work on the guns before long. Somewhat to my surprise Bush took up the challenge at once. He stated that he had not asked for the job, it had been thrust upon him at Ypres eighteen months ago and that if the CO wished him to return to the guns he was prepared to do so here and now. Both Tebbs and I echoed his words and this called the Major's bluff. In a more consolatory tone he explained that we had better leave things as they were for the present. He enquired about our duties and when told that in addition to calculating targets and laying out the Lines of Fire we were in charge of all the ammunition, which with the constant shifting of the battery was a hefty job in itself, he became considerably mollified so much so that we were able to introduce Frost as the battery commander's confidential telephonist particularly valuable because of his knowledge of BCA work. One thing however became evident. Major Gale from the first set his face against the practice that had developed of all and sundry popping in to the BC Post for a cosy chat and our relations under the new regime were to be of a strictly formal nature.

The new CO did not have much time to take stock of the battery position for the same night as he arrived orders were received to prepare for an advance and the next morning (October 21) Major Gale led us forward to an open position close to Haspres.

Bush, still sore from the rebuff we had received, made no attempt to lay out the Lines of Fire and the job devolved on Frost and myself. The Major seemed surprised at seeing two Gunners engaged on such important work without any form of supervision but, beyond enquiring if this were the usual battery practice, made no further comment.

The final test between Major Gale and the BCA's occurred in this position and it was Corpl Bush who discovered the Achilles heel of the new CO. A target had been notified and Bush was preparing to work out the range when the Major came forward and questioned some of the calculations. But Bush was more than a match for him and it did not take long for the ex-school teacher to discover that whatever qualifications his superior officer possessed he had no head for figures. This was Bush's opportunity and he made the most of it. Never omitting to treat the Major with all the respect due to his rank he nevertheless contrived to treat the CO as if he were a particularly backward child, explaining in a detached voice that five and eight made thirteen and not fourteen as shown by Major Gale and so on through the whole calculation. Even when the CO on being detected in a glaring error ejaculated *"Have it your own way then"*. Bush could not resist a final jibe, *"Not my way, sir, Euclid's way"*. The stratagem was successful. Never again did Major Gale attempt with the theoretical side of gunnery nor suggest that we BCA's might be better employed on manual work. Indeed we enjoyed in many ways considerably more liberty than we had known under Major Bennett. Our targets were never checked nor our decisions questioned. Even aeroplane shoots which the late CO always conducted himself were handed over to the BCA's.

Nevertheless we deemed it advisable to sub-divide our duties so that there should not be too many of us in sight at once. The two Corporals divided the day's work in the BC Post between them while to my lot fell all the night duty plus control of the ammunition. Frost ostensibly returned to signalling it being understood however that he should always man the telephone in the post. The CO approved the scheme and rather surprised me by saying that he saw no reason why I should keep awake at night. If I would take any targets that came in and would send off the situation report at 3am he would be satisfied.

I won his approbation over this report a few days later. A fairly substantial BC Post had been erected for in the matter of shelters Major Gale would stand no nonsense. As soon as we arrived at a position we were ordered to dig in and take advantage of whatever cover was afforded. The orders were obeyed without question and at Haspres a pit ten feet square by six deep gave cover for the BC's staff and the Signaller on duty. The officers slept elsewhere none being detailed for night duty. There was no guard so that, when the guns were not in action the only man actually awake at night was the telephonist. The arrangement was that, in the event of any targets being notified or of any untoward incidents the telephonist was to rouse me at once, the subsequent responsibility for engaging the target or any other action falling on my shoulders. There was comparatively little night firing but I slept very lightly and was soon able to distinguish what batteries, friend or foe were firing without leaving my bunk. At 3am I never failed to wake and dictated to the telephonist my report of the previous six hours operations. On one of these reports we were complimented by Corps Headquarters for it contained more details than those of the neighbouring batteries. Major Gale was extremely gratified on being informed that 81 Battery report was being used as a model and was quick to congratulate me. I did not think it advisable to inform him that the whole of the information had been tabulated without my setting foot outside the BC Post.

Meanwhile the encircling of Valenciennes[4] was proceeding on the same lines as that of Denain. It proved a much harder nut to crack however owing to the tenacity with which the enemy held to the surrounding villages (and which of course we were not allowed to shell). The high ground overlooking the town was captured on October 21. After this all exits were closed by the destruction of the bridges one of our chief targets being Ponte Rade to the west of the town. At Valenciennes the Escaut divides and the effect of our bombardment was to render the town an island completely cut off from the mainland on either side. Within this island several thousand civilians awaited with more or less patience the hour of deliverance.

An attack[5] was launched at 7am October 24 which was an unqualified success. The enemy retreated so quickly that within two hours he was out of range. At 10.30 we were officially put out of action and transferred to reserve. At this point our activity seemed to come to an end it being the original intention of the higher command that heavy artillery should take no further part in the campaign.

The respite did not last long, however. Cleaning up operations on October 25 revealed that the forces on both sides were in a terrible tangle. Our infantry had advanced too far in some places, not far enough in others. It was impossible to tell which villages were held by the Germans and which by our own forces. Units on both sides were cut off from the main body and in some places the artillery was in advance of the infantry. To add to the confusion all the bridges over the Escaut and its tributary the Escallion were down some destroyed by accident, some by intent. The enemy was known to be evacuating Valenciennes but to what extent no one knew. The whole day was occupied not so much in fighting but in straightening out the line. By a sort of tacit understanding large tracts of territory were exchanged. In some places our men retired leaving whole villages to the enemy while as if in exchange the Germans abandoned miles of land to our troops.

By night the brief respite was over and it was decided after all the heavy artillery should continue to advance with the infantry.

Early in the morning of October 26 we advanced and at 8am were in action in the village of Monchaux-sur-Ecaillon. We were able to fire only 100 rounds when we were pulled up suddenly with the news that the enemy had retired out of range.

The rest of the day we hung about the farm where we had placed our guns. The main building had collapsed under direct hit and some of us searched the debris to see if there was anything of worth taking. All I found was an enormous vegetable marrow quite undamaged although several tons of masonry had fallen upon it. I bore it off in triumph to Proud the officers' cook who promised to let me have a share when he prepared it for dinner. Alas the officers pronounced it excellent and ate the lot.

That night I was to see Major Gale in another light. I reported for duty at 8pm to the BC Post the one undamaged room in the building. Bush left on my arrival and I found myself alone with the CO who was sitting on a chair puffing away at his pipe with a bottle of whisky at his elbow. He grunted something on my arrival and relapsed into silence while for my part I looked over the various documents that Bush had left for me. For two hours we sat thus, when we were disturbed by a buzz on the telephone, a call for the CO from Colonel Wakefield.

I passed over the instrument. The conversation that ensued, one sided though it was, surprised me. *"What, at this time of night,"* exclaimed Major Gale. It was evident that we were being ordered to advance and it was equally obvious that the CO had no intention of being disturbed. I heard him remonstrating, tomorrow would be early enough; he blamed the weather, the state of the roads, the condition of the horses any excuse rather than move. As the conversation proceeded his words became more violent and it was evident that the Major did not intend giving to his superior officer that blind obedience he expected from his subordinates. I remember his last words, *"Look here, the horses are tired, the men are tired and I'm bloody well tired and I'm not moving tonight and you can do what the Hell you like about it"*. With this he banged down the receiver, drank up his whisky and took another stiff peg.

Suddenly he turned on me and said, *"Hall, you heard that conversation?"*. *"Sir,"* I replied for I could think of no better rejoinder. *"Can you forget it?"* he continued. *"I have already done so,"*

I replied. *"Good man,"* he said and no further words passed but it was easy to tell the trend of his thoughts. He knew that he had committed the unpardonable offence of refusing to obey the lawful orders of his superior officer. There he sat for hours it seemed, his head between his hands, the empty glass and the cold pipe alongside. I saw before me what might well be a ruined man. It was past midnight when he rose and with an abrupt *"Good night"* retired to his own quarters. I heard no more of this episode and of course kept my own counsel of the conversation. Somehow or other Major Gale's defiance must have been hushed up and little incidents afterwards showed that my silence was appreciated.

Shortly after the Major retired I had a visitor, a dispatch rider bearing a message for some headquarters north of Valenciennes. His route was to take him over a certain bridge and through the town and he called to verify the present position. I told him that according to my latest information the bridge was down and the town still in enemy hands. I telephoned Brigade who confirmed this. My visitor stated that he had been told that the route was quite safe, however he decided to avoid Valenciennes. This episode typifies the confusion that existed regarding the enemy's whereabouts.

---

1   *Military Operations. France and Belgium, 1918* (Volume V), *26th September–11th November The Advance to Victory* compiled by Brigadier-General Sir James E. Edmonds and Lieut-Colonel R. Maxwell-Hyslop, London, HMSO, 1947 p384.

2   Brigadier Henry John Gordon Gale DSO & Bar (3 July 1883 – 12 August 1944) was the son of a Colonel in the Royal Engineers. He was educated at Malvern College and the Royal Military Academy, Woolwich and was commissioned Second Lieutenant in the Royal Garrison Artillery (later Royal Artillery) in December 1902. He was promoted Lieutenant in December 1905. In 1908 he was posted to the Hong Kong-Singapore Battalion and between November 1912 and 1916 he served with the Indian Mountain Artillery in the North-West Frontier. He was promoted Captain in 1914. From 1916 to 1918 he served on the Western Front, where he was promoted Major in June 1917, was wounded twice, mentioned in despatches twice and was awarded the Distinguished Service Order (DSO) in June 1918. He took command of 81 Siege Battery on 20 October 1918 (unit history p24 refers). Gale then served in the Russian Civil War in 1919, for which he was awarded a bar to his DSO in January 1920. In 1920 he returned to the North-West Frontier and the Indian Army Mountain Artillery, where he commanded a battery and then a brigade. He was promoted Lieutenant-Colonel in May 1932. In April 1936 he was promoted Colonel and returned to England as Commander Royal Artillery (CRA) of the 43rd (Wessex) Division of the Territorial Army. He was promoted Brigadier in November 1937 and retired in October 1939. In 1940 he returned to the Army but retired again in October 1942.

3   Distinguished Service Order.

4   See *Military Operations France and Belgium 1918* Vol 5 Sketch 28.

5   The correct date is 25 October 1918.

CHAPTER 30
LIBERATION OF THE CIVILIANS

With the final weeks of the war approaching Major Gale continued to stamp his own mark on the battery and just a few days before the Armistice certain Gunners were appointed to Acting Lance Bombardier but not Gnr Hall. This was to be the final occasion when his ambition was blunted and his pride hurt. However, further advances plus difficulties in the supply of ammunition and periods of inactivity were typical of those final days of the campaign. It would also be the final occasion that Gnr Hall called 'Battery Action'. He also comments on the civilians returning to their pillaged homes and how the machinery of a lace making factory, a source of employment, was damaged; it would not just be the civilians in the former front line areas that face an onerous task rebuilding their homes and lives. The battery remained in XXII Corps (First Army) area until the Armistice.

As if eager to redeem his fault of the previous night Major Gale had us up early in the morning and we were on the road in record time. There was some trouble in crossing the river Escaut the bridge being still under repair. It was probably impassable the previous night and this night might have saved the Major from the consequences of his reckless conduct in refusing to advance previously.

Eventually we arrived at an open position south west of Maing where we put up bivouacs against the hillside and here we remained until November 1.

Even now the enemy's resistance was by no means broken. The Germans still held some high ground to the north of the Escaut known as Mount Houy and the attack and ultimate capture of this stronghold loomed large at the time.

Maing was for me an unfortunate position. When I came to lay out the Lines of Fire the director I had been accustomed to use was not available and I had to make shift with another instrument received from Ordnance some time previously. The afternoon of our arrival was marked by an aeroplane shoot young Mr Rimer being the officer in charge. We opened up with a salvo but were astonished when the airmen reported no shots visible. A second salvo gave similar results while a third on a different target gave totally unexpected results. Lt Rimer had never conducted an aeroplane shoot before and lost his head trying to range the guns singly before the grouping of the salvos had been fully established. We were in a pretty hopeless tangle when Lt Page arrived. Page now senior officer on the guns was more arrogant than ever. It was he who took control out of the young subaltern's hands and finding it still impossible to range the guns calls off the shoot. After this, Page enquired who had laid out the Lines of Fire and finding that I was responsible vented his wrath upon my head. I brought out the director set it up in a different place and verified my figures. As these were correct the only possible explanation was that the director was faulty. We checked the director needle against a prismatic compass and found the former three degrees out of true.

The trouble was now put right and the guns re-laid on the corrected lines. The airman called shortly afterwards to find out what went wrong with the shoot and on being assured that the trouble had been rectified went his way. As we had promised we were able to repeat the shoot with excellent results. It was very unfortunate that the error should have occurred and doubly so that it should have been detected by Lt Page. He did not fail to make capital out of the business reporting the whole matter to the CO and stressing the part he had played in correcting the error. As a result the officer whom Major Warren had publicly reprimanded and Major Bennett disgraced now ranked high in the esteem of Major Gale and took a very active part in the running of the battery.

I was destined to have a brush with the CO before long. Major Gale had discovered that all the BCA's and most of the Signallers had been continuously with the guns since the beginning of the offensive. This did not meet with his approval and I was sent down to the Horse Lines for a short rest. On arrival I was promptly bagged for some particularly disagreeable fatigue and on protesting was told by the Sergeant in charge that Major Bennett's veto on the employment of BCA's was no longer operative. When I returned to the battery Major Gale asked how I had enjoyed my rest. This was too much. I told him plainly that from this experience of the Horse Lines I infinitely preferred being with the battery. That settled it. The CO furious at my "ingratitude" exclaimed, *"If you want to stop at the battery you bloody well shall – only if it gets too hot for you don't ask to be taken away – that's all"*. And so I remained with the guns until the end of hostilities.

As if we had not enough unpleasantness at this time the unwelcomed figure of Gunner Evans appeared on the scene. Now that open warfare had been resumed the sound-ranging[1] job to which he had been seconded had petered out and the volunteers had been returned to their units. Evans made straight for the BC Post where I am afraid I was sufficiently malicious to greet him with his own words used to me six months previously *"What the Hell have you come back for?"* Corpl Bush still alarmed at Major Gale's treatment of the BCA's told his friend in no uncertain voice that there was no room for him in the BC Post and advised him to report for duty to the Sergeant-Major. Evans, nothing if not persistent, managed to find the CO. He might well have saved himself the trouble for after Major Gale had asked him what the Hell he meant in addressing an officer he was bluntly informed that four BCA's were quite enough, in fact, a damned sight too many and on no account would their number be increased. Evans had a positive dread of any kind of manual work but had to obey orders and the next time I saw him he was serving on a gun crew.

On November 1 Mount Houy[2] fell and I for one was not sorry when we were able to resume the advance. The march was a long one and we started early in the morning it was not until 3pm that we reached our destination and at the village of Famars were able to come into action. Scenes of destruction met our gaze throughout the march. I remember a long viaduct across a valley; every arch had been destroyed. Most of the crossroads had been dynamited and our progress seemed to be from one crater to another.

At each crossroad we halted while the CO decided on the course to be followed. On one occasion the explosion had not been complete and we made our way round the crater with six inches to spare. A slip would have precipitated guns and teams into a hole thirty feet deep. In another case we avoided the cross roads by unharnessing the teams, turning the guns round in the road, re-harnessing and taking the column through the farm yard and across a ploughed field where the guns threatened to sink up to their axles in the soft ground. The worst obstruction was a crater where a secondary road left the highway we were traversing. Engineers were hard at work when we arrived and the CO decided to make use of the enforced rest by calling a halt for lunch. Ever resourceful, Dennis soon had a fire going and brewed tea by the roadside while bully beef and biscuits were distributed to the troops. Meanwhile we witnessed a novel display of road mending. A substantial house stood by the crater and when we arrived this seemed to have suffered little from the explosion except for broken windows. After the Engineers had been at work however little was left of the property. The whole of the furniture was tipped into the crater and it was a memorable sight to see piano, tables, chairs, mattresses and household goods tossed ruthlessly into the yawning abyss. Farm implements followed. Meanwhile others had been at work on the foundations of the house. One side of the building came down with a rush and fell into the crater. Barrow loads of manure, earth and stone followed until a way spongy and treacherous it is true, was made, over which we piloted our guns to safety.

Soon after this we met our first civilian. A peasant woman some forty years of age lay dead by the roadside horribly mangled by shell fire. I have, I suppose, seen thousands of corpses in France but never have I met such a terrible sight. Somehow death in uniform does not seem so bad but the fact that we should be met by the dead body of one whom we set out to save and one who had met her fate at the hands of the British artillery, not improbably our own battery, for we had been firing on the road, seemed macabre in the extreme.

It was not long after passing the dead woman that we came to our most formidable obstacle. In the village of Famars the railway crossed the main street by a high viaduct. This had been dynamited and the debris, hundreds of tons of bricks, stone and crumpled rails lay in a gigantic heap almost up to the house tops completely blocking the road. The village was quite deserted and so far as we could ascertain no other unit had essayed the way before us. We fully expected Major Gale to halt and try to find another way forward when, to our astonishment, he shouted *"Drag ropes out"* and boldly led the way over the obstacle. It was magnificent. Every man pulling on the ropes on either side of the gun wheels, the drivers lashing away at the sweating horses as one after another guns and wagons cleared the obstruction. The descent too was difficult. Once over the crest, brakes were firmly applied and the drag ropes reversed while we hung on like grim death to prevent the heavy load running away with the horses. At last the column was all safely over from the leading gun right down to Chinnery and his white horses and water cart who brought up the rear. The selected position as not far distant and soon we were in action.

A few days previously we had been transferred back to counter battery work and now our first job was to harass and silence the German guns. But the task proved more difficult that was anticipated. Although the enemy was retreating fast it did not follow that he was beaten. Since Epinoy very few prisoners had been taken and no material of any consequence. We were only too well aware that their guns were intact and ready for action if and when they determined to make a stand. On the other hand our position was perilous in the extreme. The heavy guns (8 inch and over) had dropped out of the fight since the capture of the Canal du Nord and now many of the 6 inch mechanised batteries seemed unable to advance. Much is to be said of mechanisation but the process must be something more scientific than the mere tying of a gun to the back of a motor lorry which was all that was done in the war. Practically all the 6 inch howitzer batteries had been so adapted and it followed that such units had been unable to negotiate the craters, ploughed fields and masses of debris which had formed our path from Maing. So far as we could see 59 and 81 Siege were the only medium howitzers in action. The 60 pounder guns still faithful to horse transport had been able to get through and of course most of the Field Artillery.

Ammunition too was now a problem. By ruthlessly jettisoning all unnecessary stores and utilising every available wagon we had managed to bring up 300 rounds of high explosive but there was no immediate possibility of further supplies. The lorries on which we depended were unable to advance and the horses too tired to make the journey to the far off ammunition dumps. My job in looking after ammunition was proving no sinecure and from now until the Armistice I kept up our meagre supplies by scrounging from other batteries. Fuzes were our greatest trouble as the invaluable 106 type were simply not available and I well remember stealing (there is no other word for it) a couple of boxes from a neighbouring sixty-pounder battery.

Such was the state of affairs when we pitted our strength against the German artillery. We were out-ranged, out-gunned and out-numbered by as many as ten to one. We were obliged to spread the guns to cover as wide an area as possible and even when, as on several occasions, we located an active enemy position we were allowed to expend only ten or twenty rounds on the target.

There were casualties at Famars and several times the position had to be evacuated. On one particularly hot strafe Lt Randall who was in charge gave the order *"Suave que peur"*. When at last it entered our thick heads that this was a classic way of saying, *"Every man for himself"* we made a bolt for the flank to return some time later to carry on the good work. Mr Randall gave his famous *"Suave que peur"* which now became known as *"soaky poo"* later in the day but on this occasion was wounded himself as was Gunner Britt[3] who came to his aid. Both received awards for gallantry. Two more cases of wounding on November 2 brought our long line of casualties to an end.

The BC Post at Famars was in a farmhouse and this time there was no thought of security. As one of the upper rooms seemed comfortable we promptly bagged it and set up the planchette board. As usual I was on night duty and so had to keep watch while my companions with the officer and half a dozen telephonists were comfortably asleep on a bed of dried bracken. I had only one candle for it was advisable not to show too much light while the room beneath which communicated with ours by a steep stairway was in total darkness. At two o'clock in the morning I was conscious of movement in the room below. I would of course have roused my companions who would have been more than a match for any German straggler who had chanced to find his way to the farm house but I realised to my horror that no human being could move so stealthily. Inaction proved my undoing. Frozen with terror I heard the thing move about in the room below and then mount the stairs. I could do nothing but glue my eyes to the aperture watching for the horror to make its appearance. And after what seemed hours the apparition approached, a large grey tom cat, another inhabitant had returned home. I must have been pretty far gone for even when I realised how homely was the intruder, I felt no sense of relief and could only follow its movements with my eyes. It was only when it behaved in an offensive manner and on the planchette board itself that I roused myself. Then the animal fled and I applied myself to cleaning up. My experience with the "supernatural" was treated as a huge joke in the morning but never have I felt such utter terror as on that night.

On November 2 and 3 the pressure on the battery position was considerably relaxed. First the German heavy guns ceased to trouble then the fire from the Field pieces became weaker. It became evident that the withdrawal was being resumed. After some trouble we were able to secure some more ammunition. As a matter of fact the Horse Lines people, now stationed at Monchaux, had been collecting shells from our former positions and had brought up supplies by the wagon load for it was still impossible for motor lorries to traverse the roads. Rations too were frequently late of arrival and the quantity reduced. It was difficult enough to secure stores for the guns while non-essential clothing and equipment was quite impossible to obtain. Most of our men possessed merely the clothes they stood up in plus a few blankets; spare underwear and odd items of equipment had been dumped soon after the advance had started.

On the morning of November 4 it was evident that a further advance was necessary although according to our latest information we were not yet out of range. Intelligence as to the enemy's exact movements was very meagre and the CO took the unusual course of taking two guns forward to an, as yet, unknown destination, leaving the others till in action at Famars but with instructions to follow if and when required.

A very small party left with the two guns at 6.30am I accompanied them in case my services as BCA were required. We traversed a considerable distance over the countryside without meeting a soul, friend or enemy. It was rather eerie as the guns rumbled through the deserted villages. In one case white flags were flying at every window, sheets and tablecloths being used for the purpose. Here I suppose the German defenders of the village must have surrendered to our men but conqueror and vanquished alike had departed before we arrived. What puzzled us most was the complete absence of civilians especially as we knew that some thousands had been liberated at Denain and Valenciennes and even now the inhabitants of the former town were celebrating their deliverance before the Prince of Wales. Yet we had advanced considerably further eastwards and the villages were completely deserted. The answer to this paradox was that on our advance the peasants flocked to the towns, whether on their own initiative or under German direction I have never been quite able to ascertain. Those who had chosen Denain and Valenciennes were able to return to their homes as soon as the British Military Authority certified them safe for habitation but those who had chosen Douai were to remain under German yoke a few more days.

When the civilians returned they found in most cases that their homes had been pillaged. Our battery did its share although most of the damage had been done before our arrival. Still the incentive to ransack the personal belongings of other people proved too much for many of us. The looting was futile in the extreme. Nothing that was taken could have been the slightest use to the troops. I remember entering a house where the bedrooms presented a scene of indescribable confusion, drawers and cupboards having been wrenched open and their contents strewn on the floor. The culprits in this case were the infantry who had captured the village. We were second on the scene and by the time others had passed through the place there would be little left for the unfortunate owners. The charge for this damage was laid to the Germans but I am afraid that in these later days the responsibility must rest with the liberators. The cause for most of the destruction was, I think, merely souvenir hunting gone mad. It was now or never, the war had not long to go and the most absurd articles were taken from a child's plate to an old pair of corsets while I must plead guilty to scrounging a pre-war railway guide and a small exercise book.

By eleven o'clock we had advanced a good way into what was still regarded as "territory still in enemy occupation". At the village of Curgies a halt was called while the CO went forward to reconnoitre. Needless to say scroungers made full use of the respite to explore the deserted buildings. In a short time Major Gale returned in a violent hurry. The enemy had been located and was making a stand further east. Gunfire was urgently needed to dislodge him.

As was expected a mine crater of considerable magnitude lay right in the centre of the village. This needed careful negotiation and so little of the road was left that we had to un-harness the teams and manhandle the guns over what little ground was left at the side of the crater. Then the horses were led forward, not without difficulty, re-harnessed and the column advanced again. Once clear of Curgies we went a short distance down the Sebourg road when Major Gale led the way into a field, gave me a target and told me to get the two guns into action.

This was the smartest piece of work we ever performed and the guns were actually firing within ten minutes of receiving the order. The time for bringing a battery into action varies considerably. With six inch howitzers we usually took two to three hours but I remember the twenty-four hours or more of damnably hard work that seemed necessary before we could get the 8 inch howitzers into action. I have always entertained some doubts as to the incredibly short time taken by the RFA on displays. The calculations simply could not have been done in the time and I think that the pieces were merely firing blind.

Altogether I regard the work at Curgies to be highly creditable especially as the guns were on the road and loaded with stores when the order was received and platforms, rough it is true, had to be laid to prevent their sinking in the soft ground. Moreover the Lines of Fire were correctly laid and the targets properly calculated. Two stages were perforce omitted, picking up aiming posts and planning pickets. In order to save time I laid the director on the target and switching round to the guns gave the Gun Captains the converted angles telling them to use the Director as an aiming post.

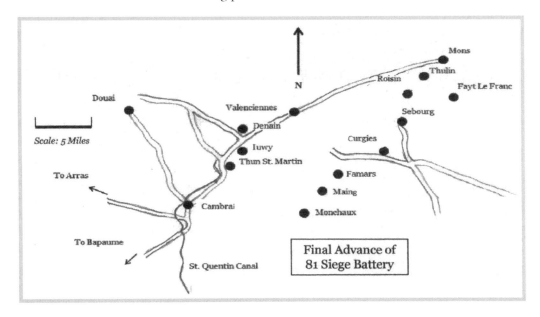

Final Advance of 81st Siege Battery

After fifty or sixty rounds had been fired we were stopped from firing by the news that the enemy were again in full retreat. In a short time we received information that no more firing was to be done west of a certain line which meant that the battery was virtually out of action. Major Gale thereupon ordered the platforms to be removed and the stores replaced on the gun trails. Meanwhile the other two guns (we had now reverted to a four gun battery – the two damaged at Cuvillers were never replaced) had arrived from Famars and on seeking instructions I was told to lay these parallel to the right section but not to bother planting pickets.

The CO accompanied by Mr Lakin now started off down the road to Sebourg in search of an advanced battery position leaving the four guns laid on their zero lines but resting on soft ground and with all their stores strapped to their carriages ready to resume the advance on his return. There were only about 24 of us in the position and no cover except for a small tent that had been run up for Mr Rimer who became officer in charge. The rest of the men were either helping to advance the Horse Lines from Monchaux or were resting at Curgies.

Major Gale and his brother officers, were away some considerable time and I was beginning to wonder if after all it would not be better to plant pickets and pack up the director on which dew was beginning to fall. I was eating a piece of bread and cheese when heard my name being called from the tent. I ran there to hear that an SOS call had just come through, a target well to our right but within the red line. I confirmed the target with Brigade Headquarters and shouted, for the last time as it transpired *"Battery, action!"*.

But there was not the usual response, no mad rush to the guns, throwing off the breech and muzzle covers and the members standing round handspikes in hand ready to throw over the trail. Instead a few men put in a dilatory appearance. There were cries *"What's the joke, Hall, you know we're out of action"*. *"No joke at all,"* I exclaimed. *"This is an SOS call."* *"Tell that to your Grandmother"*. Nevertheless the troops went to their guns and sullenly began to unload the stores and prepare for action while I retired to the tent and started working out the target. Lt Rimer was enjoying an afternoon nap and when I succeeded in waking him he was as incredulous as the Gunners. Still there was a target to be engaged and at pretty short range too less than 6,000 yards. When I shouted out the elevation and particularly when the troops saw that it was third charge they began to see that something had gone wrong and to take notice.

Still we were not yet out of the wood. The target necessitated a wide switch to the right and without platforms it was a hefty job pulling the guns over. After the first round two of the guns ran back and their spades dug into the soft ground rendering them immovable and well off their line. The other two did not even get as far as that but began to sink before coming into action. Here was a pretty kettle of fish, all four guns out of action. I called to Mr Rimer but all the young officer could say was *"What can I do?"*. The troops standing round the guns were inclined to treat the matter as a joke. In desperation I turned to my old Sergeant McIlroy. *"Mac,"* I said. *"We must get those guns into action somehow, there'll be a Hell of a row if we don't."* *"It's serious then?"* asked McIlroy. *"Dead serious,"* I rejoined. *"I don't know what the trouble is but the target has been confirmed by HQ."* Then Sgt McIlroy got to work. He cursed the Gunners up hill and down dale. Starting with No.1 gun a couple of men laid down planks while everyone else in the battery position hung on to the drag ropes and hauled her on to the improvised platform. Five men were left to fire the gun whilst the rest repeated the performance with the next gun. Mr Rimer had now taken heart and was laying on the rope with a will as were the rest of us Signallers, cooks and all. At last all the four guns were firing although No.4 managed to get off only five rounds when the order to cease fire came through.

Later in the afternoon Major Gale returned and seeing the guns back on their platforms enquired how we came to be back in action again. He appeared to be pretty excited and no wonder when we heard of his experiences. He directed us to pack up again and said he would lead us forward as soon as we had lunch. By four o'clock we were on the move.

Major Gale led his battery straight forward to Sebourg some three miles distant. There was no mistaking the village for its name had been painted on the first house in letters three feet high. It was a long straggling place built round the junction of two roads the one on which we had advanced from Curgies running from east to west and the other at right angles to it. We were now in an industrial area; the farm houses had given way to long rows of workmen's cottages and a large brick built factory was a prominent object in the centre of the village. The peace time industry was lace making for Sebourg was an offshoot of Valenciennes, the Nottingham of France. It was at Sebourg that we encountered our first civilians; the Major and Mr Lakin had met them first when reconnoitring for a position. The CO had fully believed Sebourg to be clear of the enemy and the two officers had gone forward in expectation of establishing a position somewhere east of the village. According to Mr Lakin's account they were riding gaily down the Curgies road when they became aware of fierce hand to hand fighting going on all around them. To make matters worse the Germans seeing mounted men thought our cavalry were upon them, some were for surrender while others were prepared to sell their lives dearly. As the two officers had no better arms than a pair of prismatic compasses the attitude of either party caused them some considerable embarrassment. One of our infantry officers then put in an appearance and informed Major Gale that the village was full of Germans who were actively resisting eviction from the houses. It was then that the two officers observed a few frightened faces pressed against the window panes, the first of the liberated civilians.

Major Gale and his companion quickly dismounted and for some time watched the fighting from a safer place. Then when they deemed the combing up to be so far advanced that the most of the Curgies road was free of Germans they went back for the guns.

We were in position soon after 5pm (November 5) firing at suspected strong points far ahead. When we arrived fighting was still in progress around the cross roads and the CO advised us to give the village a wide berth unless we wanted to be drawn into the scrap. Actually our battery was planted on an open space west of the first house of the village, the one on which the enemy had painted its name. The shouting and the rifle fire continued well into the night and it was not until the following morning (November 6) that Sebourg could be added to the growing list of liberated villages.

The most pressing need after the guns had been brought into action was, of course, to find quarters for the night. The CO lined us up under the shadow of a wall and delivered a short address. He was now going to billet us in the adjoining houses but on no account must we break open any doors nor must the property be disturbed more than necessary. Nothing must be pillaged for the rightful owners might return at any time.

With these words Major Gale tried the door of the first cottage. It opened. The CO entered and after a brief inspection claimed it as a BC Post and Signallers' quarters. So he went down the terrace of houses, allocating one to each section, Officers' Mess, cook's quarters, stores and so on. In most cases the doors were unfastened, it being an offence for civilians to bar the doors against German troops but in one or two cases they were locked. These presented no difficulty; one of our men obtained entry through a back window and removed the locks.

These simple homes represented the height of luxury to us at the time. For myself I occupied the sitting room as BC Post. I pinned the map to the dining table, raked out the ashes from the grate and soon had a good fire roaring. Then I set to work to give the apartments a spring clean. With some cotton waste I dusted the ornaments, re-arranged the furniture and changed most of the pictures. The latter leaning forward as they did was a source of annoyance so I simply re-hung them flat against the wall. Some I disliked so I removed them to the bedrooms. A jar of flowers made the place look more like home. But matters did not rest there. If looting was prohibited nothing was said about swapping furniture. It was really so simple. You entered No.8 house in the terrace and if our preferred their dining room suite to your own you simply secured the assistance of two or three pals and effected the exchange. I think I did No.1 a good turn. Their taste in pictures was simply appalling so next day I was able to change them for some really neat prints from No.10. Some more ambitious moved pianos. I can well imagine some trouble when the civilians returned and tried to straighten out their belongings.

The attitude of the civilians at Sebourg was rather peculiar. As I have said we found the first terraces of houses evacuated by their occupants yet civilians were still living in the east end of the town. We learnt the reason for this some days later from one of our Signallers. This man, though London born, had lived in France for many years before the war and could speak the language fluently. He became very useful in dealing with the French civilians. The day after our arrival he penetrated to the east end of Sebourg, now clear of the enemy and introduced himself to an old French lady who welcomed him like a long lost son. He left the billets at No.1 The Terrace and boasted that he slept between sheets at the other end of the town. On occasions he invited selected parties to lunch when he introduced his hostess. Contributions such as Maconochies and Bully Beef were always acceptable to the old lady who had not fed so well for many a long year.

From this French lady we learnt much about the German occupation. When the English were approaching the commandant advised inhabitants to clear to Douai informing them that if they stayed behind they did so at their own risk. Incidentally he gave the British soldiers a very bad name. Most of the "westenders" decided to evacuate the town hence the deserted houses but the "eastenders" in general followed the old lady's example and spent a couple of miserable days in their cellars while fighting was in progress. At last deliverance came and they ventured out again. The first man seen by our hostess was a Scotsman who heedless of her presence entered her house and proceeded to ransack her cupboards. He relieved her of a cherished tin of cocoa a great deal to one who had been in a state of semi-starvation for four years. Naturally we did our best to atone for the soldier's dereliction but it was regrettable that the first of the liberators should have behaved in such a manner.

The old lady was not particularly vindictive towards the Germans although she hated the system that had brought her such privations. Her only son had joined up in the first days of the war but whether alive or dead she had no idea having completely lost touch with all her relations during the past four years.

According to our informant the German rule though just was very strict and the many prohibitions weighed heavily on the civilians. The eight o'clock curfew was severe on young people. Food was very scarce and of poor quality although she must in justice admit that the conquerors fared no better than the victims. Then came the inevitable question *"What about German atrocities?"* We were disappointed when the old lady was unable to give us any first hand information. The Germans kept a pretty tight hand over their own men. There were of course petty thefts, similar as the old lady said with a sly wink, to that of the Scotsman who stole her cocoa but is established these were punished with such severity that in most cases the civilians preferred not to lay the charges.

Sebourg had suffered great privations owing to the complete dislocation of its lace trade. The town was centred round a lace factory which in normal times gave employment to the whole population. The Germans had commandeered the building for use as a hospital and had removed the machinery to an adjoining warehouse. Later I had an opportunity of seeing the large mass of complicated machines stacked on top of each other. It had been alleged that the Germans in their retreat wilfully destroyed much valuable machinery in this manufacturing area in northern France but I certainly found no evidence of this in Sebourg. Nonetheless the plant had suffered considerably from exposure and inexpert packing and I fear that most of it was little better than scrap. The factory itself was quite undamaged. The enemy had removed all traces of his hospital weeks before and it was difficult to connect the empty buildings first with the noise and bustle of lace making and later with the quiet and orderly hospital wards.

Their only occupation gone the inhabitants must have suffered considerably. There was of course work for all in the munition factories but naturally it was repugnant for them to help in the manufacture of arms to be used against their own kindred. Most of the young people had left the village but our informant was not aware that any form of compulsion had been used. In these occupied areas however the inhabitants were completely dependent on their German masters for support and if the conqueror ordained that, in order to eat, the vanquished must work for them there was no alternative but to offer their services.

The old lady explained this state of affairs clearly enough but many of us were disappointed that she had nothing concrete to give us about "German atrocities". The troops had heard so much about these in the press that it seemed a pity if we were to return home without having encountered at least one of these horrors. At length sensationalism seemed to be satisfied. Like wildfire the news spread round that in one of the houses opposite a Scots soldier had been found foully done to death, his wrists tied together, while he had been stabbed in the back. Some of our own men had spoken to troops who had actually seen the corpse and could testify to the truth of the statement. When I suggested that we should investigate the matter for ourselves I was called a "Doubting Thomas" and it was indicated pretty clearly that I was possessed of a morbid mind. The fact was that the troops did not wish to see their illusion shattered.

Finding no one willing to accompany me I determined to view the body myself. I had no difficulty in finding the house which was almost opposite our own billet. True enough the unfortunate man lay dead in the entrance hall, an unpleasant enough sight but the rest of the tale was apocryphal. I examined the dead man's wrists and ankles but found no signs of tying up while so far from having been stabbed in the back had been shot through the heart. The cause of death was obvious. While searching the house the Scot had come face to face with a German soldier and the latter had been quicker on the draw. I reported my findings to my comrades but they were not appreciated and many an acrimonious dispute followed and many persisted to the end of their belief in a "German atrocity".

During our short stay in Sebourg we saw quite a lot of the civilians. After the Germans had evacuated the east side of the town many came round to see our guns in action and we never lacked an appreciative audience of children. For the most part the civilians looked dispirited, worn and very emaciated. Old people and children predominated and able bodied males rarely encountered. Unwanted food was eagerly cherished and the child lucky enough to secure a tin of bully beef bore it off in triumph to its mother. Some high feeling however occurred at the Horse Lines which had been brought up to Sebourg soon after our arrival. A horse had broken a limb and the Veterinary Sergeant decided that it had better be shot. As this happened late in the evening it was decided to leave the body where it was and bury it in the morning but the civilians in some mysterious way became cognizant of the slaughter and when the burial party arrived it was discovered that the hind quarters had been flayed and large chunks of horse meat taken away. The horse had been a general favourite and great indignation was expressed against the ghouls who had desecrated the corpse. Semi-starvation and the fact that the lower class French had no prejudice against eating horse flesh was deemed no excuse. The remains were quickly interred with plenty of chloride of lime to prevent further mutilation.

Hostile artillery was now but little in evidence and our tasks consisted mainly in the destruction of machine gun nests which were proving a positive curse to the infantry. Trenches had by now disappeared but the enemy made full use of the sunken roads which abounded in the vicinity. These roads were in places up to twenty feet deep and afforded splendid protection in this kind of warfare; when things got too hot for the machine gunners they simply moved to another spot. We were still very short of ammunition and were unable to deliver the prolonged bombardments which were the only way of dealing with the menace. Many of these machine gun nests therefore had to be carried by the infantry at the point of the bayonet and accordingly their losses even at this late stage of the war were considerable.

Ranging the guns from the Observation Post was always an unsatisfactory job and Major Bennett, an expert in gunnery if there ever was one, would never essay the task. The duty of an Observation Officer he would say was to observe and to report to the Battery Commander. The latter knowing how his guns were firing and being informed where the shells were falling was in a better position to apply the necessary corrections to bring them on the target. At Sebourg however Major Gale determined to range from the OP. When he arrived at the post he called us up and told Bush to repeat to the guns the corrections he would send down. It soon became evident that Major Gale was getting in a tangle and forgetting to apply the necessary factors when giving his orders. As the shoot proceeded and the guns were still giving contrary results Major Gale became more and more irritable. He vowed that the guns were being laid incorrectly and ordered an officer to check the dial sights. Never would he admit that his own corrections might be at fault. Suddenly and without any warning a German aeroplane appeared from behind a cloud and swooped low over the battery position. The aeroplane spotter blew the alarm, three short blasts on his whistle and in accordance with accepted practice the guns stopped firing and covered up. At this moment the CO unaware of what was happening at the battery gave the order *"Fire!"*. Bush replied somewhat abruptly *"Can't fire, aeroplane up."* At this Major Gale seemed to lose his head and said *"Who the Hell do you think you are giving orders? I'm CO here and you'll do as I tell you. Fire No 1"*. The aeroplane was by now dangerously low but being unable to see any signs of activity would probably have turned away. The Gunners looked astonished when the order was repeated to them. Never before, except in most urgent cases had we fired when hostile aircraft was overhead. They made no great hurry to obey so much so that the angry voice on the phone asked what the Hell we were waiting for and had we given the order. Bush replied that the order had been given. The gun was fired in full view of the hostile plane. The machine deliberately circled round the position evidently taking photographs. The CO sent down his corrections and presently enquired if the intruder had gone. *"No, Sir,"* replied Bush. *"He has returned and is photographing us."* *"All right, you can cover up, but remember to ask my permission in future,"* and this order we passed to the guns.

Both NCO's and Gunners were furious at what had happened and Bush and I came in for quite a lot of criticism. In self defence we had to tell them that Major Gale had committed the cardinal sin of deliberately giving away the battery position. He lost a great deal of prestige over the business which might well have caused our complete annihilation. Only a few days ago, the result of such an action would have been to bring down on our heads such a bombardment that severe casualties would have been inevitable. As luck had it we escaped scot free; possibly the Germans had no artillery available even for such a promising target as a six inch howitzer battery.

Major Gale's love of discipline showed itself in another way. Whenever he visited headquarters, which was frequently, he rode on horseback accompanied by his groom Gunner Wheeler. On one such occasion he sent for his charger and Wheeler appeared immaculately attired and with the two horses perfectly groomed. There was, alas, one blot on the landscape, Gunner Wheeler was in possession of a beautiful black eye. After much persuasion and some threats the CO learned the origin of the decoration. The two grooms had been fighting and Riley the diminutive second groom had punched the tall and dignified looking Wheeler in the eye with disastrous results. The two grooms made up their quarrel immediately but the mischief had been done and what we called the "Sebourg Bombardiers" was the result.

The appointment of half a dozen men to the post of supernumery Acting Lance Bombardier brought no distinction to the holders but dealt a mortal blow to the familiarity which had hitherto distinguished the battery. It brought everyone directly under some form of discipline. Wheeler as senior groom now sported a stripe. If challenged by Driver Riley again he would have no alternative but to put the fiery little Irishman under arrest. Similar appointments were Proud the senior officer's servant and Dennis[4] as senior cook. Even Wiley of the canteen was honoured in this way. The last promotion was particularly resented. He had carried on in his easy going way stocking goods that nobody wanted and offering tinned sausages to those who came in for cigarettes. Wiley frankly did not want the stripe; he said it was bad for trade and he was right. There was no sport in slanging a Bombardier however junior who might order one to the guard room and the result of his elevation was a virtual boycott of the canteen.

I must confess, however, that I was bitterly disappointed when I discovered that my name was not among the list of NCO's and I went so far as to complain to Mr Lakin. After all I pointed out there was more responsibility in running the BC Post than a canteen. Mr Lakin confirmed what I already knew that the appointments were merely the Major's way of introducing more discipline into the battery and that with Tebbs and Bush he considered that the BCA's had a fair proportion of NCO's. This afforded me no consolation. I was aware that the end of the war was imminent and was apprehensive as to my future. Once the guns ceased to fire my job must come to an end, my contact with those in high places would cease and I would be indistinguishable from any other Gunner. Even a protection stripe would have picked me out from the common herd. But it was not to be.[5]

So life passed at Sebourg until November 7. On the whole we had a quiet time and whenever we opened up we could be sure of an admiring audience of boys and girls. They would stand open mouthed watching us fire the guns and some bolder than the rest would even attempt to lift the shells, a task far beyond their capabilities. Sometime, who knows, I may revisit Sebourg and speak to someone who as a child remembers the coming of the great battery.

1 Sound ranging is a good example of a technique that developed faster in wartime as a result of the army striving for improvements. The method uses several pairs of microphones to enable a bearing to be taken (using the differences in the time of arrival of the sound at the microphones) to the source of a sound such as an enemy gun shooting. The point at which these bearings intersect is the location of that enemy gun.

2 So far as First Army was concerned, the period 1-3 November was the Battle of Valenciennes. See *Military Operations. France and Belgium, 1918 (Volume V), 26th September–11th November The Advance to Victory* compiled by Brigadier-General Sir James E. Edmonds and Lieut-Colonel R. Maxwell-Hyslop, London, HMSO, 1947 ch 29 p455.

3   32601 Gnr John Britt, Supplement to the London Gazette 23 July 1919, page 9357 lists him a being awarded the Military Medal. His medal index card confirms the MM and shows his first theatre of war as France and Flanders from 1 July 1915. His brother 38084 Gnr William Edward Britt also served in the battery but, as recorded in the unit history (p13), he had died of wounds before Hall joined the battery. Gnr W.E. Britt died on 16 July 1917 and is buried in Lijssenthoek Military Cemetery plot XVI, row F, grave 13.

4   Supplement to The London Gazette, 3 June, 1919. 6871 162849 Gnr. (L./Bomdr.) Dennis, E., 81st Siege By. (Reading). Awarded the MSM. (Meritorious Service Medal).

5   Some members of the battery also received awards which appeared in The London Gazette including:

Supplement to The London Gazette, 23 December, 1918, page 15036 2nd Lt. E. Page, attd. 81st Siege By. Mention in Despatches. (Sir Douglas Haig's despatch dated 8 November 1918.)

Supplement to The London Gazette, 1 January, 1919, page 41 34492 Sjt. E. J. Lee, 81st Sge. By., R.G.A.(Fulham). Awarded the DCM.

Supplement to The London Gazette, 8 March, 1919, Lt. John Harry Fisher-Evans, R.G.A. (Spec. Res.), attd. 81st Sge By, page 3239 awarded MC.

Supplement to The London Gazette, 17 June, 1919, 48379 Gnr. Jones, H., 81st Siege By. (Rawtenstall), page 7654 - Military Medal.

CHAPTER 31
THE ARMISTICE AND AFTERWARDS

Although the Armistice was about to be declared some formations would be required to continue to Germany as part of an Allied Army of Occupation. As Gnr Hall notes, this was a very unpopular course of action but First Army was spared this period of extended service. Major Gale's idea that the battery wanted to be part of that army was a serious miscalculation and was vehemently opposed by his men. This, along with their resistance to spit and polish, was commonplace as the troops were keen to get home and secure jobs and keeping them occupied was a challenge for the officers. In the next chapter we discover how Gnr Hall influenced his own demobilisation.

There was no night firing on November 6 but orders were received that we were to move the following morning. We had a farewell supper with the old lady and as a parting gift left her sufficient bully beef and flour to last her many a long day. We retired early for we had a long day in front of us and the town offered few inducements to keep us from our quarters. For one thing it was "bone dry" and the canteens were miles behind.

Our triumphal march from Sebourg will ever be remembered by all who took part in it. There was no particular hurry to get away. We breakfasted, packed up, took our places in the column and at 10am November 7 Major Gale, mounted, gave the order *"Walk march"* and we started our journey eastward.

All the civilians turned out to see us off. As we passed the cottage of our late hostess the old lady came forward and recognising Bush and myself following the BCA's wagon came forward and gave us a hearty kiss. The poor half-starved creatures certainly gave a good send off. Old men pulled themselves to attention and saluted as we passed and Major Gale gravely returned the compliment. Many of the women were weeping tears of joy at their deliverance. Everyone was shouting and cheering us on while for our part we did our best to reply to their greeting with cries of *"La guerre est fini"*, *"Vive la France"*, *"à Berlin"* and similar slogans. There was no desire to sing our marching songs; it was just a question of exchanging repartee in vile French accompanied with a wealth of gesture *"A bas les Boches"* *"Boche no bonne"* from our part while from the civilians came *"Les braves Soldats Anglais"* and *"Vive l'Angleterre"* while one or two cracked voices made a valiant attempt to sing the National Anthem. And so we left Sebourg feeling for the first time what great heroes we were!

We passed through other villages on our march forward and here again all the civilians turned out to greet us. As at Sebourg old people predominated but there were a number of girls who given sufficient food and adequate clothing might have been considered pretty. But they like the rest had a faded and prematurely aged appearance due to prolonged underfeeding and although they had donned their best clothes there were incongruities about their attire that under less tragic circumstances would have been considered comical.

But who could laugh when some poor pale faced girl in tattered clothes, her eyes streaming with tears and unable to contain herself longer would dash to the column fling herself on the neck of one of the Gunners and pour a torrent of kisses upon him. In these circumstances there was nothing to do but to lead the girl gently to her place by the roadside where her elder relatives would take care of her. In the line of march I was kissed many times by persons of both sexes and took it as an act of devotion and gratitude for their deliverance. Then they threw flowers in our path and if the flowers, like themselves, were often faded and sometimes were even weeds, the spirit was there. Many of us were too full for words and we too wept copiously as we marched.

As we passed through those French villages we must have presented a strange appearance and I could not help thinking that our own people never saw the British soldier as he really was, so different from the troops on their route marches in England. Up to now Major Gale had not bothered with march discipline; so long as we kept up with the column he was satisfied – our dress and bearing he left to our personal inclination.

As regards cleanliness had we undergone the closest inspection little fault would have been found. Every man had washed and shaved. Shaving in fact had become a ritual. The winning side always shaved; the losers were so dispirited that they neglected to do so and when we saw German prisoners with several days' growth of beard we knew that their morale was broken. That made us all the more determined to show up at our best. Boots too were brightly polished and buttons shone like gold. This was of course in flat disobedience to the instructions that, on Active Service all buttons were to be blacked to avoid being conspicuous. It was a difficult job removing the paint and cleaning up the brass as there were few tins of metal polish available. Still it was considered worth the trouble.

The rest of our attire would have sent a drill sergeant into hysterics. We all wore the soft forage cap, not in the approved service way well down over the forehead, but tilted at an angle of 45 degrees right at the back of the head; one of those strange army fashions which kept cropping up from time to time until a scandalised headquarters ordered their instant suppression. Although it was chilly we wore no great-coats and our tunics were open at the top to impress the civilians and show how hardy we were. Bandoliers were worn and in most cases were well polished. An artilleryman never felt quite dressed without this useless ornamentation which served to distinguish us from the infantry who wore the more serviceable web equipment. The belt was in a totally different category. No one wore a belt unless forced and whenever they were reissued they were dumped at the first opportunity. I suppose I must have dumped a dozen belts in my time. The true Gunner would sooner have his equipment flying all over the place than have it kept in position by the wretched belt.

For the rest we carried the steel helmet on the right shoulder and the gas mask on the back. We hated wearing the steel helmet which we considered made us look "windy". The box respirator too should not be too accessible. It was considered "bad form" to have the buttons unfastened and we loathed having to wear it at the alert or even in the ready position.

All who had them wore breeches instead of trousers although it was ordained that only drivers were really entitled to the former. The average Gunner would have sold his soul for a pair of riding breeches. They were very difficult to come by however and I never succeeded in obtaining a pair by fair means or foul although I had promised the man in charge of the stores fifty francs (about £2 the equivalent of eight weeks pay) for a pair no matter in what condition. Higher sums than this had been paid and the lucky owners considered them worth every penny.

But if "pukka" breeches were not available, Gunner Crankshaw the battery tailor made quite a nice income in producing a counterfeit article from a pair of slacks and a large number of us wore these imitation breeches. Regimentally of course they were all wrong and the process involved the complete destruction of the trousers for Crankshaw cut about a foot from the bottom of each leg and tightened up the remainder into a kind of knickerbocker. Still they were comfortable in use and they enabled us to wear our puttees upside down, another unauthorised fashion. Some of the old hands sneered at Crankshaw's converted slacks but personally I found them infinitely preferable to the ridiculous army practice of wrapping the puttees over the trousers and turning down the latter till they looked like singularly ill-fitting plus fours.

All our old kit was carried on the wagons or strapped to the gun trails so that we did not feel like walking Xmas trees. A few men wore their haversacks and where a man was seen carrying his water bottle it was certain that it contained something more valuable than drinking water. And so we marched on feeling like crusaders of old. It would not have taken much to have started us singing hymns. The ribald marching songs would have been unthinkable on such an occasion.

Sometimes however our triumphal progress was marred by the presence of other and more mobile units who claimed the right of the road. I remember one peppery old General who ordered our CO to draw his *"bloody old cart horses"* to the side of the road to let the cavalry get through. On this occasion there was nothing to do but obey but other times when some officer or equal or lower rank than Major Gale claimed the privilege a wordy altercation ensued which started by the respective commanding officers was continued the whole length of the column. On such occasions London cabmen could not have equalled the opposing teams in vituperation and it was a wonder that the contest did not develop into a free fight. In the case of a Field Artillery battery trying to force their way past us in a narrow lane whips were freely used by the opposing drivers against one another. The Field team, cursing and swearing, eventually forced their way ahead but not before several of their men (and ours) had received some nasty cuts.

And so we passed from village to village until we reached Roisin where Major Gale called a halt.

It was five o'clock in the afternoon and our movements were still uncertain. The enemy was reported to be holding a small town called Fayt-le-Franc and it was uncertain whether he would withdraw on his own accord or whether our services would be required to hasten his retirement. Meanwhile our horses were tired and needed food and water while on our own part we were distinctly hungry. Major Gale had noticed a stream of clear water running through the village and he ordered the teams to be unharnessed and led away leaving the guns in the village street.

Roisin was a very small place but as usual all the inhabitants turned out to greet us. One old man on seeing our approach dashed back to the house only to reappear a few minutes later in a very old and dilapidated uniform, military or civilian we were unable to ascertain. He lived in the largest house in the village which is not saying much for all were small cottages. He was certainly the post-master possibly this accounted for his ceremonial attire. He also ran the communal bakery and seemed to do some farming in a small way. But he might have been the bourgmaster of the largest city by the way he conducted himself. When he saw the CO after gravely saluting he offered the hospitality of his house and the village. Major Gale knew very little French but enough to satisfy the old man's vanity. He returned the salute then, leaping from his charger warmly shook the old man's hand. Thereupon, Madame, hurriedly dressed in her best came forward to greet the English officer and then it was the turn of their grandson a little boy of seven to greet the deliverer.

Introductions over, Major Gale explained his mission through the medium of our Signaller-interpreter who was discreetly hovering in the background and the three went out to view the old man's orchard. The Postmaster evidently knew something about artillery methods for he explained to Major Gale with a wealth of gesture how the guns might be placed to the best advantage. From our distance we could follow the Frenchman's pantomime. He indicated spaces between the fruit trees through which we could fire, he pointed to the sky and made a noise as of dropping bombs and evidently explaining how the orchard would screen us from aerial attack, he pointed out his house for the use of the officers and indicated an outbuilding we could use as a BC Post. If the old chap had been trying to sell the property he could not have been more helpful.

Major Gale, evidently took him at his word. The teams were sent for and the guns pulled into the exact positions in the orchard indicated by our host, the Postmaster viewing with approval the execution of his directions. Then he led the way to a building in the yard upon reaching which the CO called Bush and I forward. The first thing that met us was the delightful odour of baking bread and we saw in one corner a large oven. The day's baking had evidently been completed before our arrival but the smell of the process still hung about the place, the embers of the fire were still alight and the chamber insufferably hot. The side opposite the oven was packed with fuel for the fire largely a kind of dried bracken and branches of trees. Of coal there was none; the baker evidently carried on his trade with difficulty.

Leaving Bush and I in possession of the bakehouse-cum-BC Post the CO followed his guide into the house, the dining-room of which was evidently to become the Officers' Mess for later we saw all the officers sitting round the dining table enjoying their evening meal. The rest of the troops were accommodated in a couple of barns belonging to our host and to one of his neighbours while the horses were tied up in another orchard some little distance away. So about 150 men and 60 horses were accommodated for the night.

It was growing dark before we saw Major Gale again. He seemed to enjoy his hospitality so much that he had neglected to give information as to the line of fire or the night's work. He now brought up the directions he had received from Brigade Headquarters. The enemy were still in possession of Fayt-le-Franc and our job was to carry out a desultory bombardment of the approaches to the village in preparation for an attack in the morning. As usual great care was to be taken to avoid shelling the village itself which was known to be sheltering a large number of civilians. It was now dark. I brought out the director and proceeded to lay out the Lines of Fire, the pickets were planted in rear of the guns and the night lamps showed their narrow points of light. Bush meanwhile had worked out the targets and handed the slips to the Sergeants who detailed men necessary to carry out the programmes, the rest of the detachments retiring for the night.

As usual I was on night duty and I went out once or twice to confirm that the guns were firing to programme. I could not help thinking how few guns appeared to be in action, the continuity of flashes by which the front line used to be traced had completely gone. Occasional booms rang out as some battery fired a few rounds but other than this was total silence. As for the heavies 81 and 59 battery a short distance away seemed to be the only guns in action.

I suppose we fired in all 100 rounds in bursts of fire at irregular intervals the last burst being at 4.30am November 9. Then the guns were sponged out and the men retired pending further instructions.

The dispatch rider arrived at 5.30am and in the absence of any commissioned officer I examined the papers he had delivered. The most important dispatch notified the resumption of the offensive timed for 6am with the object of driving the enemy from Fay-le-Franc. There was little time to be lost; I sent a Signaller to rouse Major Gale and called the detachments out for duty.

As the men came tumbling out I had a feeling that something was not right with one of the guns. A closer examination confirmed that No.3 gun was not lying parallel to the others although the error might have passed unnoticed to the casual observer. With action imminent it would be well to put the matter right at once. I set up my director again and found that while the other guns were correctly laid No.3 gun was 3 degrees out of true. The cause was apparent. The night picket had been planted about a yard to the right. It was the work of a few minutes to adjust the error and once the picket had been re-planted I set out to find what damage, if any, had been caused by the error. It was as I feared, the error of a single yard in the auxiliary aiming point was multiplied many times in the range of 6,000 yards at which we were firing with the result that No.3 gun instead of firing on the outside roads had been dropping shells all night right in the centre of Fayt-le-Franc.

The cause of the error and its effects alike remained a mystery. I had fortunately kept a note of my director readings the night before and they corresponded in all cases. The fact that the other three guns had been correctly laid should serve to exonerate me and I was quite satisfied in my own mind that the error lay in the planting of the picket. Sgt Driscoll was notoriously careless in such matters and had on more than one occasion been called to account for bad gunnery. It was quite dark when the pickets were planted and this made his task much more difficult. Perhaps if Major Gale had given us the zero line earlier the mistake would not have arisen.

Altogether the whole business was most unsatisfactory but whatever mischief had been done could not be rectified and we could only hope that the civilians at Fayt-le-Franc had escaped casualties but what actually happened at the village we never knew. After its capture I thought of investigating for myself but on reconsideration decided to let sleeping dogs lie.

At 6am Bush came to relieve me and the CO appeared on the scene. I saw the opening of the shoot and went in search of breakfast and a few hours sleep. I awoke at eleven. The shoot had finished at nine; Fayt-le-Franc had been captured and the Germans were in full retreat. Bush had drawn a red line on the map. After 10am no guns must be fired west of this, the effect of this edict being to put the battery out of action.

This as it transpired was our last shoot. I had calculated the last target and Bush had issued the last commands. We packed up in readiness for moving but the order never came and by nightfall the infantry had advanced far ahead. The familiar rumble of the guns had now ceased and all that could be seen were the flashes of the few Field batteries that had managed to keep up.

On November 10 the remainder of the Horse Line personnel was brought up from Sebourg and the whole of the battery came under the eye of the CO. Additional billets were taken. No other unit seemed to have any claim on Roisin and accordingly we were able to spread into the village. The Officers' Mess moved into a house with a bay window, a rather unusual feature, some way down the street and no longer enjoyed the Postman's hospitality.

The Postman spent a considerable time in the bakehouse-cum-BC Post and became very friendly disposed to Bush and myself while his little grandson became great friends with Dennis the cook. Dennis who had established his cookhouse in front of the main building would send a couple of platefuls of food to the old people a gift that was much appreciated but the little boy preferred to dine with the troops. Someone had given him an old mess-tin and whenever Dennis shouted *"Dinner up"* he would take his place in the line. It was very amusing to see the little chap line up at the head of the queue and pass his dixie for the various helpings. He ate as much as a man and seemed to fatten out visibly. After a time he became rather cheeky and some of the older men resented his appearance in the queue but Dennis took him under his wing and as the cook was not a man to be offended with impunity the boy stayed and enjoyed army rations all the time we were there.

Among the last to arrive at Roisin was Crankshaw the battery tailor. He and some others were billeted at a house some way down the village the occupants of which were a young man of about twenty and his sister a year or so younger the two obviously devoted to each other. Like everyone else in the liberated regions they had suffered very much from malnutrition but with the spare rations we were able to supply (the whole village was in receipt of gifts of food from the battery) they improved rapidly, particularly the girl, who from being a gaunt haggard looking woman, blossomed into a comely peasant girl before our eyes. Crankshaw got on exceedingly well with the couple particularly the girl. Although the worst linguist I have ever met he managed to convey the information that he was the battery tailor and as such he made himself responsible for her attire. Nothing daunted by lack of material, Crankshaw scrounged a couple of army blankets, took the girl's measurements and in the best West End fashion proceeded to cut out a coat and skirt. Then mounted on the kitchen table and sitting cross legged he started stitching away, happy as a sandboy. After several fittings the garments were completed to his satisfaction. His model certainly did him credit and with that extraordinary chic inborn in every French woman paraded round the village proudly displaying her new tailor-made.

During the first days at Roisin we saw a good deal of French family life. In one of the homes where some Signallers were billeted a happy event was imminent. The baby was born on Armistice night and when the husband informed the Signallers, some of them, still clinging to their ideas of German atrocities, foolishly attempted to sympathise with him thereby implying that the youngster was of Teutonic parentage. The Frenchman was most indignant at these aspersions on the legitimacy of his offspring.

The night of November 10 was quieter than ever. The front had advanced beyond sight or hearing and for the first time we seemed to be enveloped in a deadly silence. Accounts of the fighting reached us from various sources; how the German resistance had been completely broken; Mons had fallen and the end of the war might be expected at any moment.

We learnt of the Armistice on the morning of November 11. The news brought in a sealed letter from Brigade. Such correspondence marked "confidential" was passed over to be opened by the CO himself. I remember how he broke the seals and said quietly *"Armistice at eleven o'clock"*. Then he told everyone in the post not to say anything to the troops; he would tell the men himself.

He ordered a parade of every officer and man in the battery without exception such an unusual command that all knew that something of the utmost moment was to be announced.

As soon as we were all paraded he began his oration. *"Battery, attention! I have just received the following dispatch from Headquarters. 'An armistice has been signed and will take effect from eleven o'clock today when all firing will cease'."* He then folded the paper and replaced it in his pocket. But if any of us were disposed to cheer this information we were forestalled for he continued, *"And now, go to your guns and wagons, clean them well and polish them up – Battery dismiss"*. We might well have been let free for this one day. It was a pity that we were not even allowed to cheer. Major Bennett would have behaved differently. But we were commanded by one of the old school one of the "spit and polish brigade" – the war was over but discipline must be maintained. As for myself I realised "Othello's occupation's gone" I went to the bakehouse and finding myself alone burst into a flood of uncontrolled weeping.

Round the guns groups of men assembled discussing the news. What exactly did an armistice mean? We had not heard any details of the terms and it was not until several days later that we heard of the enormous surrender of war material by the Germans that made a resumption of hostilities impossible. At the time we thought that an Armistice was simply a case of ceasing fire during which peace terms would be discussed and that fighting might be resumed at any moment.

We were not long kept in ignorance of the CO's intentions regarding the "cleaning and polishing up". Major Gale called for the Sergeants and explained what he required. First of all the guns and wagons to be thoroughly scrubbed and cleaned, all mud removed from the wheels, spokes to be rubbed with mineral oil, all chains to be polished all paint to be scraped from the grease boxes, all brass work to be made to shine and so on.

147623 Gnr W. Usher (on leading Clydesdale) 81st SB, Belgium 1918

The orders went far beyond the reasonable requirements of putting the column into decent fettle. All except the actual working parts of the guns and vehicles were of "war finish" that is rough cast and painted a serviceable green. For the task of polishing these parts so that they "glittered in the sun" we had four large files for the whole battery and of course no emery paper or metal polish. We were told to finish off with crushed bricks and water, a party being told off to scrounge bricks and crush them into powder for use on the chains. A more heart-breaking task it was impossible to conceive. Pieces of chain were allocated to each man and he was to set to work polishing, polishing, polishing hour after hour and it transpired day after day. Work on the brass caps of the axle boxes was equally as bad. When the paint was removed it was found that the surface was pitted with innumerable small holes for they had been supplied rough cast and not machined. To attain a really smooth surface meant in some cases removing quarter of an inch of metal. There were over 100 such caps on the various guns and wagons and the job of reducing them with brick dust can be imagined. The days immediately following the Armistice saw the battery groaning at its work and seething with discontent. Truly it was said that the reward for our efforts in the war was that we were treated worse than convicts.

The only celebration of the Armistice was that on the evening of November 11 a few of us dined with the village postman. What the meal lacked in quality it made up in ceremonial. The Postmaster donned his uniform in honour of the occasion while Madame had put on her best gown. Our hosts were unable to provide anything but a green salad and cups of substitute coffee but the salad was good and there was some remarkably good dressing. For our part we provided the meat, a seven pound tin of bully beef which Corpl Tebbs as senior NCO carved. A tot of rum helped the coffee go down. The Frenchman seized upon the opportunity to make a long and fervent speech which as it was in his own language was little understood but warmly applauded. Bush who could speak a little French suitably replied and many toasts were drunk. Altogether a most successful evening.

It was over a fortnight before the accessories were polished up well enough to meet Major Gale's approval and I must admit that I dodged the greater part of the work. There were always a large number of returns to be rendered from the BC Post. The situation report, the casualty returns, the report on hostile shelling, ammunition return and so on were duly forwarded on November 11 and 12 but on the 13 we judged them meaningless and neglected to send them. Brigade Headquarters however telephoned for the returns and the Adjutant was most annoyed that we had stopped sending them without his instructions. Bush who was now becoming very irritable and moody was so disgusted with this tomfoolery that he suggested that I might do the job as he had no intention of completing the "nil" returns. I seized the opportunity on the understanding that this was to be a whole time job and so returned to the BC Post where I ruled out the necessary forms and writing "nil" across them took them at the stipulated time to the CO for signature. This solemn farce was enacted until the end of November and at 9pm I could be seen marching across to the CO whom I saluted and held out my "nil" returns for his signature. For a change of occupation I would take stock of shells replacing the 106 fuzes by plugs and steadfastly refused offers of assistance from the disgruntled and "fed up" Gunners.

I was now the sole survivor of the band of BCA's. Frost had returned to the Signallers while the two Corporals took charge of various fatigue parties. Tebbs as always was cheerful enough and did his best to keep up the spirits of the men under him but Bush on the other hand might be seen, hand in pockets, sullenly supervising a squad of men polishing chains, never lending a hand himself and continuously cursing the Army, "red tape", "spit and polish" and above all Major Gale himself. Altogether a most unpleasant overseer.

Corpl Bush had in fact taken up a most unreasonable attitude. He refused to be associated with the tomfoolery of sending up the "nil" returns while on the other hand he loathed the cleaning up regime initiated by the CO If ever a soldier had been devoted to duty it was Corpl Bush. Conceited and selfish he may have been but a more conscientious, efficient and heroic man I have never seen. "Bullshine" and "spit and polish" had changed him into a cynic, a mischief maker, a rebel and a thorn in the flesh of Major Gale. Within four days of the Armistice Corpl Bush had nearly formented a riot. The trouble arose at morning parade. The terms of the Armistice were now common knowledge and the question in everyone's mind was what British troops were to follow up the Germans to the Rhine. Major Gale appeared singularly affable and before dismissing the troops to their respective duties went on to say that *"You will be pleased to know that on behalf of the Battery I have volunteered for service with the Army of Occupation"*. Unlike his speech on Armistice Day he paused for applause but the Major met with a very different response. Then throwing discretion aside Corpl Bush shouted out at the top of his voice *"We don't want to go"*. The cry was taken up on all sides *"We don't want to go, We don't want to go"*. The effect on Major Gale was electrical; all self-confidence and affability disappeared in an instant and had he ordered some drastic punishment then and there I should not have been surprised. Instead he controlled himself and said *"I have always had your interests at heart and I thought I had interpreted the wishes of my men. However, it seems I am mistaken. I shall withdraw the application"*. We were then dismissed. But Bush was still not satisfied. He went round the battery speaking to men singly and in groups urging resistance to the "bullshine". Bush the agitator gloried in his self-appointed task, no communist could have been more active. He made many converts all pledged to resistance an event went so far as to compose a revolutionary marching song the chorus of which ran *"We don't want this spit and polish, we won't march up to the Rhine"* for some days the streets of Roisin rang with these words.

So the revolution began and in other circumstances Bush might have gone far. He might even have been another Lenin. Major Gale must have been cognisant of what was happening for at night the troops led by Corpl Bush marched outside the Officers' Mess singing their hymn with all the fervour of revolutionaries. The restraint of the CO was however admirable. He ignored the proceedings and always greeted Bush with the utmost cordiality which rather spoilt the effect for the school teacher was ripe for martyrdom. On parade a few days later the CO was to say with the suggestion of a sneer that *"You will be pleased to learn that we are not joining the Army of Occupation. The Second Army has been selected for this task"* (we were in the Third[1] Army).

From what I heard later the disturbance was by no means an isolated occurrence. Similar incidents took place over the whole front and it would have taken little to have broken out into open mutiny. And the cause? It has been stated that the troops were war-weary and pressing for demobilisation. I do not think that the soldiers were so unreasonable as to expect returning to civilian life within a couple of weeks of the Armistice. Rather would I blame the military mind who seized upon the opportunity of putting on the screw and forcing severer discipline upon us. As the victorious advance progressed we had become I suppose more and more out of hand, a free and easy spirit prevailed and rank had to all intents and purposes disappeared. But the various ordinances after the Armistice were designed to pull us up with a jerk and to make us remember that we were soldiers and not merely "Civilians in khaki" (a favourite expression at the time) and as such were amenable to the spirit and letter of Military Law.

Sometimes authority as if feeling that it had overstepped the mark would sense the pressure and some concessions were secured as witness the relaxation of the censorship a most sensible move by Higher Command. Henceforth we could tell those at home where we were stationed and I headed my next letter home "Rue de la Calvari No.1, Roisin, Department du Nord, France", information which meant precisely nothing. Another fit of generosity abolished the left hand salute. All ranks now saluted with the right hand a privilege hitherto reserved for officers. A tiny concession but it meant a lot to us at the time.

On the other hand the increase of the number of rifles on November 20 from six to sixty per battery was regarded as a calamity of the first magnitude. Every true Gunner and Driver detested rifles although looking backwards there is no doubt that we should have carried some means of personal defence, if not rifles at any rate revolvers. The picture is not pleasant of men during the retreat having to fall back on sticks and spanners for their defence nor of Signallers going forward to the Observation Post with no better protection than a pick handle. It is ironical that the military mind which denied us reasonable protection when it was needed, should on the return of peace burden us with small arms.

The rifles were a constant source of irritation, the more so because distribution meant something like two rifles between every five men. The man unfortunate enough to be selected for the honour of carrying a rifle was responsible for the cleanliness of the weapon and had to appear with it on parade. Most of the NCO's avoided taking rifles but somehow I was not smart enough and was duly issued with one although it is only fair to say that I succeeded in palming it off to another Gunner a couple of days later.

There was no instructions in musketry but rifles meant plenty of rifle drill and it soon appeared that when after prodigious efforts for metal parts of the guns and wagons began to "Glister in the sun" other means were found to keep the troops fully employed. A fortnight after Armistice life for the bulk of us meant a continuous round of physical drill, gun drill, rifle drill, squad drill and now above all ceremonial parades.

Ceremonial drill was the most difficult. Marching in line may look fine to the spectators but it involved a considerable strain to the participants. One man a fraction ahead of his neighbour would throw the whole line out of straight and we had to go through the manoeuvres time after time until we were perfect. To make matters more difficult we were given the order "Eyes right" which meant marching one way and looking another with the added danger of getting out of line. Presenting arms added another complication. In addition to the quick march we did the far more difficult slow march and learnt how to conduct ourselves at a military funeral. We "rested on our arms reversed" with befitting solemnity. But what of the headless corpses of Brazier and his companions so quickly buried at Sapignies or of the men left to die in the barn at Vaulx-Vraucourt.

I frankly admit that I dodged every parade I could and I blessed the Adjutant on his daily reports. Useless though they were at any rate they kept me off the parade ground.

On November 11 we relinquished the BC post. Our presence interfered with the baking arrangements and I was billeted in a house nearby. I was sorry to leave the old place; it seemed that my job was slipping away.

I still kept on sending my nil returns however and now good food and lack of exercise were beginning to tell on my figure. One day Major Gale remarked *"Hall, you're getting as fat as a pig, why don't you turn up for physical jerks in a morning?"*. I explained that I still had the situation report which was due at 3.30 in the morning. Of course it was now prepared in advance but the Major allowed the fiction to pass. I promised however that I would turn out for the early morning parade. Next morning I duly appeared but the parade was unfortunately taken by Lt Page who was in a foul temper at being selected and determined to make the drill as unpleasant as possible. I would have enjoyed a spot of Swedish drill but doubling round and doing rifle drill was another matter and I determined that unless the CO supplemented his request by a definite order I should find my multifarious duties prevented my appearance at the early parade.

As the days grew darker the early morning parades were discontinued and by the end of November we reverted to more normal times 9am and 2pm At the same time Headquarters at one swoop cancelled the whole of the war returns and with the cessation of these my job as Battery Commander's Assistant came to an abrupt termination. Like Mr Micawber I had confident hopes of something turning up but in the meantime there was nothing for it but to rejoin my sub-section with as good a grace as I could muster.

News now began to circulate much more freely. We got the Continental Daily Mail every day and read with interest the appalling terms inflicted on the defeated Germans. Generally speaking the peace terms were not popular with the troops and the feeling was expressed that no good would come of applying such pressure. Jerry as we knew him had put up a good fight and the last prisoners to pass through Roisin were quite cordially treated, an amount of good natured banter passing between ourselves and the Germans. At this time too the French civilians seemed to bear no resentment against the late occupiers. The few days preceding the Armistice were marked with a remarkable toleration between the three nationalities.

This phase passed quickly. The Germans were of course the villains of the piece but before the month had elapsed it was plain that the French and the British were getting on each other's nerves. The fault I think lay largely with the British Higher Command. The French are a practical race and were anxious to get back to normal conditions as soon as possible. The war had left their country in a terrible state and they were very shorthanded, women and children doing men's work. Peasants were returning to their property and making heroic efforts to patch up their ruined homes and working against time to cultivate their land before winter rendered any further attempts abortive. It is not to be wondered that such people viewed with irritation the presence of thousands of idlers in their midst. Here we were strong healthy men doing nothing but polish chains and doing monkey tricks with rifles. The horses too were eating their heads off in the lines and the wagons would have been a Godsend but they dare not be moved for fear of dirtying them.

Throughout the whole war zone the same thing applied. There was nothing the troops would have liked better than to have helped the civilians to clear up the mess but they were not allowed to do anything and instead kept on "bullshine" and silly ceremonial. For our own part 81 Siege Battery had left ammunition laying about in a dozen abandoned positions between Arras and Roisin. It would have been an easy job to have cleared them all and removed the material to dumps for disposal. But nothing so sensible was done, instead it seemed that the authorities were forcing us to be as regimental as the Guards.

The unfortunate Second Army who advanced to the Rhine suffered terribly. All the glowing accounts that appeared in the press could not conceal that while the defeated Germans rode home in trains and lorries our victorious troops marched in full pack and often to attention, day after day, often on short rations until they arrived at their destination in an exhausted condition. The tales that reached us of these men's sufferings were appalling. It is strange that while we were advancing over hostile ground we suffered no privations and food was always plentiful and good but once the dangers of war were over the whole commissariat seemed to go to pieces.

It was at this time that Major Gale acting on instructions from higher authority endeavoured to obtain volunteers for further service in the forces. He interviewed every man separately and explained that the regular army was not so black as it was painted. We were having a rough time now but once things had settled down it was a really fine life and the pay was good. What about signing on for another two years? Most of the time serving men agreed but otherwise there was little response to the appeal. Nor did the increase in pay from 1/- to 1/6 a day attract us. The increased scale was not so good as it seemed for it absorbed the specialists' award of 3d a day. This allowance was enjoyed by the Signallers and by myself as BCA and an additional 1/9 a week did not seem an extravagant sum to pay for the added responsibilities. The new award put us back to the same level as the most ignorant and lazy Gunner. Moreover it seemed to emphasise how transient had been my occupation as Battery Commander's Assistant.

It appeared then that the battery personnel with few exceptions were all out for rapid demobilisation and return to civilian life at the earliest possible moment. The demand for early release seemed to pervade the forces and were probably the cause of the special instructions read out to us by Major Gale. This was called the War Office scheme for returning men to civilian life.

The project was most disappointing and the memorandum opened with the words that demobilisation must necessarily be a lengthy process. The first men to be released were to form a Corps of Demobilisers whose job it would be to operate the machinery that would liberate the rest of the troops. These men would have to give an undertaking that they would remain on duty until all the rest of the troops had passed through their hands when they themselves would be allowed to return to civilian employment.

The selection of this Corps of Demobilisers was a heavy task in itself and it would be *"a considerable time before they would be ready to deal with the men"*. Then came the selection of the men to be released. The first to go would be the "key men" whose return to civilian life would give employment to others. After these all other cases would be considered on their merits, length of service overseas, age, whether married or single, locality of civilian employment and many other factors would all be taken into account. Illustrative examples were given whereby it was possible to deduce how an ex-plumber living at Preston, aged 35 who had served two years in France compared with a single joiner aged 25 from Sidmouth who had joined up in 1914. Then there was the special case of Dominion troops and those serving on other fronts to be considered but we may rest assured that the work would be done as expeditiously as possible. Meanwhile home leave would be greatly accelerated.

The last words were the only comfort that could be drawn from the memorandum. Leave had always been regarded as a privilege and not a right. Although the authorities aimed at an interval of twelve months between each period, it had been impossible to maintain this during the advance with the result that many of our men had been eighteen months or more without seeing home. The authorities were as good as their word and the most deserving cases in the battery were sent home a dozen at a time. At this rate the interval was soon narrowed down and by mid-December it had been reduced to thirteen months. It was this more than anything else that reconciled us to our fate. It was plain that the powers that be would not be hurried and as the days went by there was no sign of the scheme being put into operation. Application for the thousands of "demobiliser" posts had not been solicited let alone considered. It was best to take our home leave.

---

1   81 Siege Battery was in fact still attached to XXII Corps in First Army – see *Military Operations France and Belgium 1918* Vol 5 Sketch 37.

CHAPTER 32
I RETURN HOME

The initial resistance to cleaning and polishing the guns dissipated but a more revealing observation is made on the gunners' attitude to British POWs making their way home from Germany having endured a dreadful time in German hands. Apart from his own diary Gnr Hall made a further contribution to the battery by drafting a history of the unit which was published after the war and a few copies remain. His own copy is liberally annotated with corrections and he notes here his disappointment that the manuscript was not checked before publication. A period of leave proved to be his advancement to demobilisation and by mid-February 1919 he was again a civilian.

We left Roisin on the 28 November. Incidentally we departed from France for our next location was Thulin a small town over the Belgian frontier and here we took possession of very handsome residence in one of the main streets. The main rooms of the house were of truly magnificent proportions and I remember the painted ceilings in the main rooms downstairs. Adjoining was a large conservatory now devoid of plants. The bedrooms were by no means so imposing and I noted with some surprise that the approach to the only bathroom was through a panel door in the conservatory and thence up an iron spiral staircase.

When we arrived, the sole occupant of the place was a very old lady, the housekeeper, whom we understood had been there since the invasion. A few days after our arrival, however, the proprietress returned and was greeted by the retainer. After a good deal of kissing and weeping the two women carefully went through every room in the house and from what we could gather the mistress was quite pleased with the condition of her property. Madame, it appeared, had fled into France on the invasion in 1914 and had no idea as to whether her house was even standing. What had happened to the furniture we didn't know. Except for a couple of rooms in the basement which were occupied by the housekeeper the place was completely empty.

There was no promiscuous billeting at Thulin. Parties were allocated to the different rooms and parades took place in the courtyard in fair weather and in the conservatory when it was wet. So large was the latter that a hundred men could muster therein. The horses were accommodated in the adjoining stables and for the first time in many months the poor beasts enjoyed shelter against the elements. As for the guns we parked them in the village square alongside those of our sister batteries. There were twenty pieces of ordnance so parked and they seemed to be a source of wonder at first although doubtless they became a decided inconvenience to the returning natives.

The resentment that was felt immediately after the Armistice seemed to have died a natural death. For one thing most of the donkey work was over; hours of elbow grease had had its effect on the rough castings of the limbers and they shone sufficiently to satisfy the critical eye of Major Gale. Of course the journey from Roisin had soiled the wheels but they were soon cleaned and brought into excellent fettle again.

Relations between officers and men improved considerably. This was I think largely due to Major Gale. Regimental and autocratic though he was he had a happy knack of unbending at times which won the heart of the troops. When he had over indulged in liquor, which was not infrequent, he became particularly jovial and would seek out the company of rank and file and exchange yarns. On one such occasion he appeared in the conservatory wearing his steel helmet and before we realised what was happening he flung his ungainly headgear on the tiled floor with a resounding bang exclaiming at the same time *"Now, boys, we've done with these bloody things"*. The temptation was irresistible and with one accord we dashed into our apartments and, returning with the detested tin hats, threw on the conservatory floor until the place range with the clash of steel. Meantime our tipsy CO was rocking with laughter and calling out *"Pile 'em up boys"*. The unholy din brought out the Quartermaster-Sergeant from his stores nearby who, unaware of the Major's presence demanded what the Hell we were up to. When he noticed the CO he saluted and apologised for his language but was still upset and, pointing to the ever increasingly pile to which the drivers were now adding their quota, respectfully enquired what he should do with them. The CO promptly told him, a joke which set everyone except the unfortunate NCO into roars of uncontrollable laughter. In a moment or two Major Gale checked us and directed that the steel helmets should be neatly stacked in a corner of the conservatory until they were called in.

The tin hats however were never called in. They were subsequently reissued and as everyone knows became part of the dress of the British soldier. I have always felt very strongly on this subject, I should be the last one to disparage the use of the steel helmet. It afforded the best protection against shrapnel and flying splinters and as such must have saved many thousands of lives but against this must be set the terribly depressing effect of wearing such heavy and unprepossessing headgear. There had grown, in the artillery at any rate, quite an etiquette governing the wearing of the tin hat to offend against which was considered bad form. At the Horse Lines for instance tin hats were never worn and it was considered the height of bad taste to wear steel helmets once the battery had been put out of action. Even when in action it was best to err on the safe side and wear the forage cap unless there was a positive danger of being shelled and I have seen more than one man pulled up with a sneer by both officers and NCO's *"Hello, have you got the wind up?"* for wearing the steel helmet unnecessarily. It was therefore with surprise and disgust that I read of resurrecting the steel helmet for use in peacetime.

It is worth recording that the box respirator was used for ceremonial purposes before the steel helmet and it was laid down that we were not to appear in Mons and similar towns (this was after the Armistice) unless correctly attired wearing forage cap, puttees (riding boots and spurs for mounted troops) belt or bandolier (not both) and gas helmet in the ordinary position no reference being made to the tin hat.

Major Gale, by the way, encouraged us to visit Mons while we had the chance, a town which he prophesised would take a prominent place in English history. We did not realise at the time that this town marked both the beginning and the end of the war. It seemed a typical Flemish town with the usual Grand Place and picturesque houses. It did not appear to have suffered from shellfire or bombing. It is impossible to get anything to eat in the town. Every shop was completely empty and although we were freely admitted into the cafés the proprietors regretfully informed us that they had neither beer, wine nor coffee to offer us so there was nothing to do but sit to the empty tables, smoke our own cigarettes and resume our journey. In one café however we were fortunate in securing a cup of substitute coffee with a little cognac added. For this we were charged one franc (9d) per head and the proprietor rationed us to one cup each. We looked in vain for a canteen but none had penetrated as far as Mons and we returned hungry to Thulin.

Altogether canteens were conspicuous by their absence about this time and we would have fared ill had it been necessary to supplement our rations as we had to on some previous occasions.

The improvement both in quality and amount of the rations however was remarkable and I can truly say I have never eaten so much food in my life as I did at Thulin. No longer subject to the inconvenience of cooking in the open, Dennis proceeded to show what a chef he could make. Now he was master cook with a vengeance for he had at least half a dozen full time assistants to say nothing of the hangers-on. For breakfast we had porridge and bacon. After that while his underlings were washing the utensils Dennis started cutting up the meat into huge steaks at least an inch thick. Later the cook and his mates could be seen at work frying the steaks while dixies of onions and potatoes were boiling merrily.

Serving dinner was quite a ceremony. First Dennis would hand out a steak to each man, then the first assistant would serve a couple of Spanish onions, the second assistant would add two or three potatoes while a third would bring from the pot tins of Maconochies to server as gravy, one tin between two men. This little extra alone amounted to six ounces of meat and vegetables per head and every man went away with not only his dixie but also the lid filled to overflowing. Nor was that all. There was always rice pudding and raisins to follow.

Tea was the usual bread and cheese while porridge and cocoa figured for supper. In addition there were always tins of bully beef to be had for the asking but few took advantage of this generosity and box after box was handed over to the civilians while the children who thronged round the cook-house never went empty away. I am convinced that we were over-issued with rations and can only imagine that someone must be going short, probably the unfortunate troops on their way to the Rhine.

Situated as we were in a backwater away from the line of march we did not encounter the stream of traffic on its way to Germany. From time to time, however, strange bodies of troops passed through Thulin in the opposite direction, the returning prisoners of war. The treatment of these men was one of the scandals of the war and unfortunately their unhappy position was largely the fault of the British. The Armistice terms specifically stated that all Allied prisoners of war were to be released "forthwith" and the Germans obeyed these instructions literally simply by opening the cages and letting the captives free[1] without food or adequate clothing and anything up to two hundred miles away from their compatriots. The men who passed through Thulin were in a terrible condition, filthy, in rags and practically starving. They had to find their own way through Germany and Belgium hoping that someone would take them in charge but no one had any instructions about them and every unit referred them further down the line. We were no better than the rest and resented these hordes of filthy tramps who descended upon us. Incredible as it may seem we had no sympathy for them as they hung about our cookhouse. We gave them tins of bully and some broken bread which they wolfed like wild beasts and then we returned to our duties while they resumed their weary trek where we did not know or care. But this buffeting about from pillar to post must stop sometime and perhaps they would find a depot somewhere where they could rest, draw proper rations and become decent men again.

The day following our arrival at Thulin, Major Gale who loved scrounging as well as any of us discovered in a disused brewery a number of wooden vats and an iron boiler. He sent a GS wagon to collect them and had them set up near the parade ground. There was wood and water in abundance and no lack of volunteers. The boiler was filled and while the water was getting hot the CO called a parade. *"I expected to find baths at Thulin,"* he said, *"but, seeing as there are none, we have had to provide our own. Now let's do our best to get clean and rid ourselves of those filthy things, lice."* It was a good speech and went down well.

Half a dozen men were detailed for the job and were at work from morning to night, boiling water and replenishing the tubs two of which were used for washing underwear while four men in each of the others tubs were wallowing in the unwonted luxury of a bath. The attendants did their work well throwing buckets of nearly boiling water over them. For a consideration they would scrub our backs and some made quite a good thing out of washing underwear.

Washing underwear consisted more in boiling than scrubbing and everything went in together, shirts, pants, socks and all, the object being to kill the lice rather than actual cleaning. Some garments were considered too filthy for boiling and were ruthlessly burnt and underclothes were donned while still steaming wet. There was no limit to the number of baths and attendance at the wash-house excused all parades.

Cleansing the battery proved as big a job as polishing the brass-work but it was the only way of getting rid of the lice. Whenever the vermin were discovered we stripped threw our clothes into the boiling water and had another bath. I myself had three baths in one day and felt half boiled in consequence. Some lice lingered in blankets and escaped for a time the vigorous shaking we gave them but at last we overcame the enemy and for the first time since we landed in France we became bodily clean. Major Gale took a personal interest in these operations and would often climb into one of the tubs calling vigorously for the attendants to throw on more hot water but the junior officers preferred to take their ablutions in private.

One of the bath attendants was Cousins one of the thirteen who joined 81 Siege Battery with me in January. We compared notes and found that we two were the only survivors. Four had been killed and the rest wounded.

The Army Educational Scheme was launched on December 2. This was a makeshift way of passing the time and afforded some change from the interminable drills. The scheme was initiated by Headquarters and all who had any knowledge of teaching were called upon to give their services. We had three ex-teachers in the battery, Bush, Evans and a young subaltern whose name I have forgotten. In addition there were a number of men with a specialized knowledge who could be roped in. Frost for instance was a first rate accountant. Of all these Bush was the most qualified and the CO gave him a free hand to organise the scheme.

The first thing Bush did was to demand a secretary and so rescued me from oblivion. Together we drew up a most elaborate plan which included advanced mathematics, French and Latin. Then we went canvassing for scholars with surprising success but I am afraid the desire to dodge parades rather than a thirst for knowledge actuated the volunteers. When more detailed instructions came to hand it was found that the authorities required a much more elementary course to be taken and mathematics and Latin had to be scrapped. As for the rest Bush went straight ahead. He sent home for his books and was soon drilling the three R's into classes of 30 to 40 men. When my secretarial duties permitted I attended the classes. Bush to give him credit was a first rate teacher but the young officer who had left college to enlist was very nervous at taking the classes.

Then Major Gale gave one or two of his breezy talks and what with the baths, route marches and looking after the horses we found life not so unpleasant after all. We even got used to ceremonial drill and found that once we had mastered the fundamentals the rest was easy. We ceased to regret the past and with the prospect of any early leave in the offing were quite content with our present life.

I was not long with Bush however when I was called for another task, the preparation of a History of the Battery.

The idea of a souvenir handbook giving the movements of the battery with a list of casualties and awards was one of Major Gale's pet projects. It was intended to be published in an attractive form at a reasonable price and it was hoped that all members of the battery would take up one or more copies and so be in possession of an authentic account of the part they played in the Great War. I was selected for the task mainly I suppose because I was a BCA out of a job. Also I was known to have kept a diary and was qualified to collect the information. The original idea was that I was to record the details leaving the actual compilation for other hands but as more data came to hand I was able to set up the work in narrative form, the first part of which Major Gale read and approved and allowed work to continue.

The work was interesting but more difficult than I imagined. The framework from the beginning of 1918 was that part of my diary from the time I joined 81 Siege Battery. Before then I had to rely on the memory of "old timers" and such battery records as were intact.

THE GUNNER.

280

R.A. GAMES FUND.

1. At a meeting of the Committee held in the R.A. Institution on October 3rd, 1919, the following were elected to the Committee: Brig.-General H. E. Stockdale, C.B., C.M.G., D.S.O., R.A. (re-elected).

Lt.-Colonel C. A. Lyon, D.S.O., R.G.A.

Lt.-Colonel C. R. Gillett, D.S.O., R.G.A.

Major R. L. Palmer, D.S.O., M.C., R.A.

Major E. B. Maxwell, M.C., R.A.

A member to be nominated by the Inspector General, Royal Artillery.

2. It was decided to draw the attention of all members to the value of assistance to be derived from the Army Sports Control Board in general and the Ground Committee in particular, especially in those cases where the claims were submitted for the object of reconstruction or rehabilitation of grounds, tennis courts, pavilions, etc. which have deteriorated owing to the war. Claims for such assistance should be made primarily to the Command Secretary of the Ground Committee in the particular Command in which the Unit is stationed, and the result of such application should be made known to the Secretary of the R.A. Games' Committee in the event of failure.

Oct. 10th, 1919.   Wilfred Jelf, Lt.-Col.,
                            Hon. Sec., R.A. Games' Fund.

RUBY FOOTBALL. Woolwich v. Sandhurst.

The R.M.A. play the R.M.C. at Queen's Club on November 8th.

FOR SALE.

A brake, in good condition, property of the 24th Brigade, R.F.A. on account of Brigade proceeding to India.   Apply:— Secretary, Brake Fund, 24th Brigade, R.F.A., Winchester.

The History of 81 Siege Battery, R.G.A.

"The History of 81 Siege Battery, R.G.A.—From August 4th, 1914 to December 31st 1918." By Major H. J. G. Gale, D.S.O., R.G.A. has now been published. Copies can be obtained direct from the publishers:—Messrs. J. & E. Bumpus, Ltd., 350, Oxford Street, London, W. Price 1/8 post free.

---

303 Siege Battery's Souvenir Picture.

Copies of 303 Siege Battery's Souvenir Picture can be obtained by those interested, if they will forward a Postal Order for 2/- to The Secretary, Canteen Committee, 303 Siege Battery, R.G.A., British Army of the Rhine.

Advertisement in Gunner magazine 1919

The fighting records which were kept at the BC Post went back only six months, I myself had burnt many records and a large number of valuable maps during the March retreat. The more personal records, lists of casualties and awards were in better condition having been retained in the Orderly Room under the control of Bdr Lowe. From these much valuable information was extracted but the main difficulty in tracing the movements of the battery remained. On parade, Major Gale asked all ranks who, like myself, had kept diaries (actually an offence at the time) to divulge the contents to me, any confidential matter being kept secret of course. About half a dozen men responded but most were comparatively newcomers and their diaries were largely copies of my own. Nevertheless I was able to trace the movements back to the beginning of 1917.

The next stage was that of interviewing the old sweats. I had now established my office and interviewing room in an estaminet across the square. Brewing had been resumed the product being a very thin and flat type of beer. Had it not been for the beer the earlier history of the battery would never have been compiled. The CO readily agreed to my request to interview all the old hands and released from parade all whom I wished to interview. The Sergeant-Major came first and was a mine of information all the more remarkable because he had not been in half the positions himself. I took the others in turn. I found it advisable to have a glass of beer ready for my clients and to have it replenished at frequent intervals. Fortunately liquor was cheap otherwise the compilation of the records would have involved me in considerable expense for I cannot remember any of my clients ever paying. Altogether I saw some twenty men most of whom had been with the unit since 1915 and from them I fixed up the semblance of a story.

From these old timers I picked up much irrelevant matter regarding their sojourn in India. The regular soldiers appeared to be genuinely fond of the army or at any rate of its peacetime aspect and the main concern of many of them was that now their period of service was drawing to a close they would be thrown on the labour market. Even the Sergeant-Major so far unbent as to enquire what I considered the prospects to be of a job in the steel works. He had it seemed married a wife much younger than himself and they had a young baby. The end of the war evidently meant great changes for some of us.

The veterans would discuss their dead comrades and how they met their ends and here I made a remarkable discovery. The survivors in every case owed their immunity to prolonged spells at the Horse Lines or absence from the battery either by sickness or minor casualty. There was not a single man of whom it could be said that he had served the guns continuously from 1915 to the Armistice. The casualties among the Gunners were twelve times those of the drivers and a spell at the Horse Lines meant a period of comparative safety. The officer casualties too were much less than those of the "other ranks" notwithstanding the Observation Post duty which they did in turn. Here again the cause was more frequent spells in the rear.

Battle casualties totalled 244 almost double the authorised personnel. In 1915 and 1916 they were trivial but in 1917 one position alone (Dead End Ypres July to September) claimed 100 victims. Dead End was regarded as a nightmare by all I interviewed for in addition to losses caused by gunfire, two guns had blown up killing their detachments. The cause was uncertain but faulty ammunition was suspected. This was the time of the Zenith Fuze scare. Altogether the artillery suffered more severely in the autumn of 1917 than at any other period.

I had collected all the information by December 11 and I reckoned that drafting would take another week when I was informed that my home leave was imminent. The news was brought me by Major Gale who urged me to complete the narrative so that he could arrange for publication. I promised that the manuscript would be in his hands the same night and he agreed saying that he was in touch with a firm of printers and all being well the proofs would be ready for me to correct on my return from leave. I worked steadily throughout the day and at 8pm I called at the Officers' Mess with my manuscript apologising for my writing and for any errors that might have crept in. The CO scanned the papers and appeared quite satisfied. Then he wished me a pleasant leave and I withdrew.

My leave pass was ready for me to collect and I drew all the pay to which I was entitled. I had hopes of securing some new clothing from the Quartermaster as on my previous leave but here I was disappointed. New uniforms had been indented for but had not yet arrived. I managed to secure for 5 francs a pair of second hand field boots, a size too large but in good condition and better than my frayed puttees and down at heel boots. I had no spare underwear and wore a civilian shirt which I had scrounged. Even my greatcoat was an old Royal Air Force type.

On December 12 I breakfasted, the last meal I was to have with the battery or for that matter with the army at all. Then on parade the leave men were called out. There were only two of us this time, a driver and myself. We were told we were free to leave the battery at any time we wished but would have to make our own way to Valenciennes station from whence a leave train departed between six and ten in the evening.

My companion had not been on leave before and was all for starting at once. I would have preferred to wait until after dinner but he fretted and fumed so much that eventually I gave in and at 10am we two started on our journey. My friends were all at their various tasks and as we gathered up our kit and left the battery there was none to whom we might say good bye, so we left Thulin making for Valenciennes my companion vowing that we should miss the train and urging me to hurry along. For my part I declined to be hustled and by dint of part walking and part lorry jumping we reached Valenciennes by mid-day.

Valenciennes itself had suffered little from shelling but the station was in a terrible state. The town was an important junction and the station with its half-dozen platforms had been covered by a single span of glass while the main road had been carried over the lines by a very fine bridge. The retreating Germans had dynamited both bridge and station. Our engineers had fixed up a level crossing of sorts and had cleared a single line to the goods shed. This was the only approach to one of the most important rail-heads on the front.

There was of course no sign of a train and the Railway Operating Department men had no idea when one was expected. My companion however would not leave the shed in case one might arrive. For myself I was beginning to feel hungry and went in search of refreshment. I might have saved myself the trouble. Like Mons, the town was completely empty, the cafés were open but merely as a rendezvous for groups of civilians and a few soldiers; of food there was not a trace.

Before returning to the station I rid myself of what I regarded as surplus kit. My steel helmet I threw over a wall, my box respirator I left in a public convenience. When I returned I would be able to think of some excuse for their absence, at any rate I was not going to lug these cumbersome relics of the war over France and half of England.

I found my comrade stretched out asleep on the floor of the goods depot and did not disturb him. I was still sore at being brought into a draughty goods shed so much ahead of time. Soon afterwards we drifted apart and I did not see him again.

Towards evening the shed began to fill up. Both civilians and soldiers arrived the former carrying enormous quantities of luggage. At 8pm (December 12) some of us went to make enquiries. We were told that there would be no train that evening. One was due to leave at 3am (December 13) but where bound for the railway official had no idea. The goods shed represented a strange appearance that night. An oil lamp was hanging here and there and some candles were stuck on the wooden supports. With this feeble illumination the depot was a vast cavern of gloom and shadows and here some hundreds of people, soldiers and civilians, men, women and children were congregated, some lying on the floor others propped against the walls and pillars. With total disregard to the company a French girl laid down a couple of blankets, removed most of her clothes and composed herself for sleep. Another girl was asleep with her head on a soldier's knees while the latter was philosophically smoking a pipe and stroking her dark hair. There were many children, some crying and clinging to their parents while others sought comfort from the soldiers.

At 3.30am with many a groan and squeal a train drew into the gloomy shed. Its stock consisted of carriages of antiquated design and when some of our men tried to board her I was not surprised at their being warned off. This train carried off most of the civilians and we soldiers felt more at home when at 9am another train consisting solely of the familiar six wheeled box wagons (40 hommes 8 chevaux) pulled in. This then was the leave train at last. We scrambled aboard and were soon bound for Boulogne and England.

The journey was long and trying. The track had not yet been entirely relaid and we travelled at a snail's pace. Then we approached Arras and crossed what had been no man's land, the track was laid round enormous craters and the train slowly wound its way round the serpentine path. After Arras speed increased slightly but it could not have been very speedy for it was not until 6am the following morning (December 14) that we arrived at Boulogne.

Having had nothing to eat since breakfast two days previously I anticipated a breakfast at Rest Billets on arrival. We lined up but the column was halted in the courtyard. News had been received that there might possibly be room for a few more troops on the morning boat. I happened to be at the head of the column and the first hundred or so of us were told that if we cared we could be marched down to the docks. It would be at our own risk and those that could not be accommodated would have to return and await the afternoon boat.

Even though it meant missing breakfast there could be no two ways about this. The lucky hundred were marched to the docks where we joined the tail end of an enormous queue gathered on the quay. After an interminable length of time we reached the boat side and the troops could be seen packed like sardines until it seemed that impossible to take any more and it seemed more than likely that our long wait had been in vain. As it was a transport officer made his way down the line and stretching out his hand divided the queue a very short distance from where I was standing. Only eight men succeeded in boarding the vessel after me the rest being marched back to camp. A few minutes after we fortunates had mounted the gangway and literally forced our way into the seething mass the vessel cast off and we set sail for Folkestone, this time without the destroyer escort.

At 11am we arrived at Folkestone and without much delay we boarded the waiting train. Two o'clock saw us in Victoria Station and I was free to find my own way home. I had no idea what time a train left for the north and there was no one to ask. The voluntary guides who had displayed such concern as to my welfare on previous occasions were no longer in evidence. Perhaps they had disbanded themselves. I hung about the station for some little time debating with myself how I should get across London to St. Pancras when I became conscious for the first time of my own shabbiness. I had been without food since breakfast at Thulin 60 hours previously and had no proper sleep. I felt very weary and anxious to get home. There was still a long journey in front of me and I didn't want to miss the train.

I stumbled down the steps to the Underground, sank into the first Inner Circle train and waited for St. Pancras to come round. When I got there I found that the next train for Sheffield left at 5.30pm so I had still a little time to spare. I made my way to King's Cross where a war time canteen had been established. But scarcity ruled here like everywhere else and all I succeeded in obtaining was a cup of weak tea and a few biscuits. A wash and shave at Faulkner's and I felt a little better and now there was nothing to do but wait for the train. It came well to time and at 8.30pm we reached Sheffield.

I made a sprint for a tramcar where I remember I was the sole passenger for I sat in the saloon and chatted to the conductor the whole time. It was 9pm (December 14) when I arrived home where I was expected although my actual time of arrival was unknown for I had omitted to send a telegram. Then I sat down to a hearty meal, had the comfort of a hot bath and best of all a good night's rest in bed.

Although I did not realise it at the time my life in the forces came to an abrupt end when the troop train pulled into Victoria Station and I stood hungry and bewildered on the platform. I was now starting my second leave from France and I fully expected a considerable delay before I was finally released from the army. It had been the aim of the authorities to grant leave from the Western Front every twelve months but this was not always possible; during the offensives leave had a habit of being suspended, all leave was cancelled for instance during the German Spring Offensives and during the greater part of Counterstroke. I think I was fortunate regarding my leaves; I went home in January 1918 after just twelve months' service and here I was again in little over eleven. Then I expected back to France, perhaps another leave and final demobilisation in 1920.

But while the British troops accepted the War Office plan as inevitable the Dominion contingents were not so easily satisfied. It had been impracticable to go back home on leave and they usually spent their time in London, naturally they were very homesick. They accepted the accelerated leave with rather ill grace but when they were due to return overseas and realised how vast were their numbers they demonstrated at Dover and refused to embark on the Channel steamer which eventually left without them. Their numbers were swollen the following day and it became evident that the position at the Channel Ports was getting out of hand.

So serious a view was taken by the Government that the Dominion troops were allowed to remain at the ports while their case was being considered. The War Office plan was scrapped and Sir Eric Geddes the super-organiser under Lloyd George was entrusted in drawing up a completely new plan for demobilisation. Sir Eric certainly enhanced his reputation for the new scheme was ready in a couple of days and it represented a considerable acceleration over the original scheme. Troops were to be released on the basis of "first in-first out", leave was to be drastically reduced but instead every boat available was to be used in bringing soldiers home for demobilisation. The demonstrators at the ports were to be sent home as soon as transport could be arranged. Of importance to me was the ruling that any soldier irrespective of age or category who happened to be on leave at the moment should be allowed to remain in England pending demobilisation provided there was work for him. The only formality required was a written statement from his former employers that they were prepared to re-engage him, the signature to be attested by the manager of the local Labour Exchange.

This information was given to the press on December 24 only four days before I was due to return to my battery. With Christmas intervening prompt action was required if I were to take advantage of the offer. My old friend Mr H. Roberts was delighted to issue the certificate on behalf of my previous employers Messrs John Brown & Co. Ltd. and further obtained the signature of Mr Stanley, manager of the Sheffield Labour Exchange. My formal application for "Demobilisation without returning overseas" was forwarded with the certificate attached to the Officer in Charge, RGA Records, Dover by registered post the same afternoon.

No reply could be expected on Christmas Day but I became more apprehensive on Boxing Day for under the terms of my leave warrant I should have to leave home not later than 8 o'clock in the evening. I had indeed gone so far as to don my uniform when a telegram arrived with the words *"Seven days leave granted await orders"*. Demobilisation of course did not follow at the end of that time and I collected quite a sheaf of telegrams extending my leave first in spells of seven days, then fortnightly and at last indefinitely pending completion of formalities.

Then at last I received a memorandum asking me to *"Return my Leave Warrant to France"*. The wording of this note was so ambiguous that I consulted several authorities for a ruling and on the advice of the Police I returned the warrant to the Issuing Officer that is the OC 81 Siege Battery British Expeditionary Force, France. I received an acknowledgement and the result of my action resulted in my case being completely lost and all communications with Dover stopped. Eventually I saw the Commandant of Hillsbro' Barracks in his capacity of OC Troops, Sheffield and on his advice wrote to Records stating exactly what had happened. The letter had good effects and in a few days my case was re-opened.

On February 14 I received my final instructions. I was to proceed to Clipstone Camp, Mansfield,[2] and present my credentials to the authorities there who would demobilise me forthwith. Accordingly I donned khaki gathered up what little kit I possessed and departed for the camp.

Clipstone Camp

Clipstone Camp was a very busy place at that time and a large body of men had arrived from France for demobilisation. I felt very much at home as I joined the party. We passed from one hut to another, depositing equipment in one place, spare kit in another, drawing back pay in a third until at last our Certificates of Demobilisation were prepared and handed to us. A train was waiting in the special siding and after we had all filed in now civilians again it started off taking us to Sheffield and beyond.

We soon reached Victoria Station, Sheffield, where I alighted. There was one more formality. We were allowed to keep our greatcoats but were given the alternative of handing it in to a local railway official who would give £1 for it. I had no use for my coat, which in any case was Royal Air Force old pattern with cross buttoning and looked mighty incongruous with my driver's knee boots. It was thrown on a pile with others and I received my pound note in exchange.

It was not long before I was home removing my old worn uniform. I never wore it again and in due course it was thrown away.

Some months afterwards I wrote to the CO of 81 Siege Battery asking him what had happened to the Battery History on which I was engaged before I went on leave. I got quite a friendly letter from Major Gale wishing me success in civilian life and stating that my history had been published and how many copies would I like.

I sent for a couple of copies but was most disappointed when they arrived. It seemed that the proofs had never been corrected and consequently there were quite a lot of mis-spellings particularly of the French names.

Sydney Hall with his son Dennis

A year later I tried to get in touch with my fellow BCA Gunner Frost. Frost also came from Sheffield (the only other Sheffielder in the battery) and I understood he worked in one of the largest cutlery works. I rang up the firm and asked if they could put me in touch with him and was surprised to learn that not only had he been demobilised but had been appointed secretary of the company and would I care to speak to him? He seemed very pleased to hear from me and invited me to tea the same evening; his wife was out of town and we could have a good talk about old times. I readily agreed and at first we had quite a pleasant time during which he told me about the conversation he overheard at Sapignies on March 24 when it seemed that the battery would be sacrificed to the enemy. He also told me that soon after I had gone on leave he had a severe heart attack. He had completely recovered however and had said nothing about this to his wife or his employers.

As the night wore on he seemed to become very excited and then without any warning he suddenly collapsed. I laid him on the settee, unloosened his clothes and managing to find some brandy gave him a stiff dose. This seemed to be having some effect and while I was what help I should obtain, the door opened and his wife walked in to see her husband whom she always thought in the best of health, lying semi-conscious on the settee with a total stranger bending over him. Fortunately she quickly grasped the situation as I explained who I was and what had happened. I gave her my address but explained that as I may have been responsible for her husband's distressing condition, perhaps it would be better if I did not see him again. I never did.

After this unfortunate episode I made no further attempt to contact any of my former comrades. I had one or two addresses in my diary but I never followed them up. There were no reunions, that was hardly likely in a unit of such mixed origins as a Siege Battery.

As well as my "History" I have a few maps, my tattered diaries and some manuscript range and wind correction tables I made out for my personal use. This is all I have to remind me of those terrible yet glorious days.

Twenty years later Sydney Hall again was called upon to serve his country. His son Dennis adds this postscript:

> "*After about four years we moved to Sheffield and were still there when WWII broke out. Determined to do his duty he joined the Auxiliary Fire Service.*
>
> *He later moved to Newcastle upon Tyne followed by Edinburgh. On retiring Mum and he moved to Southport, living happily until he suffered a stroke followed by 10 years of total blindness before he died*".

Sydney Hall with the Auxiliary Fire Service in the Second World War

Postscript (Brian Hall, grandson of Sydney Hall)

Reading about my grandfather's experiences during the Great War was a revelation when I came across his manuscript many years after he died. I now think it is appropriate that I provide a final few words about his post-war life.

My sons are now several years older than he was when he enlisted in 1916. This gives me a perspective. It is unimaginable that they would ever experience what he and millions of others did. These days we are aware of post-traumatic stress syndrome. But in his time it would seem that most of the men returning home at the end of the war simply took off their uniforms and got on with life.

And get on with life is what he did. He married my grandmother, Florrie, and had one son, my father, Dennis. He joined the civil service, moved around the country and worked his way up to a relatively senior role in the Customs and Excise in Edinburgh, before retiring to a sunny bungalow in Southport in Lancashire (now Merseyside).

My earliest memories are of my family spending summer holidays there, visiting the funfairs, amusement arcades, boating lake, miniature railway and model village. When I was a little older my grandfather took me to London to visit the galleries and museums. Later still, as a teenager, I lived with my grandparents for a year, when I was working locally, and got to know them well.

I am pleased to say that my grandfather found a profound happiness with my grandmother. I remember him as an energetic, engaging and gentlemanly character who loved reading and sharing his knowledge and experiences.

Those experiences included his time as a volunteer fireman in Sheffield during World War II, with hair raising adventures such as fighting a fire in a paint factory during an air raid. The owner of the factory had to give the fireman a barrel of turpentine to get their uniforms clean. It is typical of my grandfather to find humour in what must have been a very frightening and potentially explosive experience.

I understand that ordinary soldiers were prohibited from keeping diaries, one regulation my grandfather clearly ignored. Otherwise this book could not have been written. And there is an honesty to its contents, even when this doesn't reflect well on the author. He must have known this but in my view he probably concluded that authenticity was the most important thing. I respect him for this.

I am sorry I never read his book while he was alive. But seeing his words in print now makes me proud. I believe writing it must have helped him deal with what he experienced. It makes me wonder how others returning home managed.

---

1   This was not so. Many POW remained confined to their camps for several weeks before being repatriated.

2   Clipstone Camp was first occupied in May 1915 and at its height could hold 30,000 troops.

BIBLIOGRAPHY

Cole, Lt Col Howard. (1951). *The Story of Aldershot*. Gale & Polden: Aldershot.

Edmonds, Brigadier-General Sir James E. (1939). *Military Operations. France and Belgium, 1918 (Volume III) May-July: The German Offensives and the First Allied Counter-Offensive.* London, Macmillan and Co Limited: London.

Edmonds, Brigadier-General Sir James E. (1947). *Military Operations. France and Belgium, 1918 (Volume IV), 8th August-26th September The Franco-British Offensive.* HMSO: London.

Edmonds, Brigadier-General Sir James E. and Maxwell-Hyslop, Lieut-Colonel R. (1947). *Military Operations. France and Belgium, 1918 (Volume V), 26th September-11th November The Advance to Victory.* HMSO. London.

Falls, Capt. Cyril. (1940). *Military Operations – France and Belgium 1917 – The German Retreat to the Hindenburg Line and the Battles of Arras.* Imperial War Museum: London.

Gale, Major H.J.G. RGA, CO 81st Siege Battery. *History of 81st Siege Battery RGA – From August 4th 1914 to December 31st 1918.* J & E Bumpas Ltd, 350, Oxford Street, London W.

Hart, Peter. (2008). *1918 A Very British Victory*. Phoenix: London.

Hurst, Sidney C. (1929). *The Silent Cities*. Methuen & Co Ltd: London.

James, Brig E.A. (1978). *British Regiments 1914-18*. Samson Books: London.

Junger, Ernst. *Copse 125*. (2003). Howard Fertig Inc: New York.

McCarthy, Chris. (1995). *The Third Ypres Passchendaele The Day by Day Account*. Arms & Armour Press: London.

Middlebrook, Martin. (1971) *The First Day on the Somme 1st July 1916*. Allen Lane.

Middlebrook, Martin. (1978). *The Kaiser's Battle 21 March 1918: the First Day of the German Spring Offensive.* Penguin. Harmondsworth: 1978

Ministry of Pensions. (1923). *Location of Hospitals and Casualty Clearing Stations, British Expeditionary Force 1914-1919.*

Moore, William. (1975). *See How They Ran – The British Retreat of 1918*. Sphere Books Limited: London.

Steel, Nigel and Hart, Peter. (2000). *Passchendaele The Sacrificial Ground*. Cassell & Co: London.

The Institution of Royal Engineers. (1952). *History of the Corps of Royal Engineers'* (Volume V), Chatham.

Young, Michael. (2000). *Army Service Corps 1902-1918*. Leo Cooper. Barnsley: 2000

War Diaries (The National Archives)

WO 95/225 48 Brigade, Royal Garrison Artillery

WO 95/335 221 Siege Battery, Royal Garrison Artillery

WO 95/467 242 Siege Battery, Royal Garrison Artillery

INDEX